WITHDRAWN

Bernd Jähne

Digital Image Processing

Concepts, Algorithms,
and Scientific Applications

Third Edition
with 168 Figures and 16 Color Plates

Springer-Verlag
Berlin Heidelberg NewYork
London Paris Tokyo
Hong Kong Barcelona Budapest

Dr. Bernd Jähne

Scripps Institution of Oceanography
University of California, San Diego
La Jolla, CA 92093-0230, USA
E-mail: bjaehne @ucsd.edu

ISBN 3-540-59298-9 3rd ed. Springer-Verlag Berlin Heidelberg New York
ISBN 3-540-56941-3 2nd ed. Springer-Verlag Berlin Heidelberg New York

Library of Congress Cataloging-in-Publication Data
Jähne, Bernd
Digital image processing: concepts, algorithms, and scientific applications /
Bernd Jähne. -- 3rd ed.
  Includes bibliographical references and index.
  1. Image processing -- Digital techniques.   I. Title.
TA 1637.J34   1995
621.36'7--dc20

Typesetting: Camera ready by author
Printing: Mercedes-Druck, Berlin; Binding: Lüderitz & Bauer, Berlin
SPIN: 10498784   61/3020-5 4 3 2 1 0 - Printed on acid -free paper

Preface to the Third Edition

Digital image processing is a fascinating subject in several aspects. Human beings perceive most of the information about their environment through their visual sense. While for a long time images could only be captured by photography, we are now at the edge of another technological revolution which allows image data to be captured, manipulated, and evaluated electronically with computers.

With breathtaking pace, computers are becoming more powerful and at the same time less expensive, so that widespread applications for digital image processing emerge. In this way, image processing is becoming a tremendous tool to analyze image data in all areas of natural science. For more and more scientists digital image processing will be the key to study complex scientific problems they could not have dreamed to tackle only a few years ago. A door is opening for new interdisciplinary cooperations merging computer science with the corresponding research areas.

Many students, engineers, and researchers in all natural sciences are faced with the problem of needing to know more about digital image processing. This book is written to meet this need. The author — himself educated in physics — describes digital image processing as a new tool for scientific research. The book starts with the essentials of image processing and leads — in selected areas — to the state-of-the art. This approach gives an insight as to how image processing really works. The selection of the material is guided by the needs of a researcher who wants to apply image processing techniques in his or her field. In this sense, this book tries to offer an integral view of image processing from image acquisition to the extraction of the data of interest. Many concepts and mathematical tools which find widespread application in natural sciences are also applied in digital image processing. Such analogies are pointed out, since they provide an easy access to many complex problems in digital image processing for readers with a general background in natural sciences. The discussion of the general concepts is supplemented with examples from applications on PC-based image processing systems and ready-to-use implementations of important algorithms. Part of these examples are demonstrated with BioScan OPTIMAS, a high-quality image processing software package for PC-based image processing systems (BioScan, Inc., Edmonds, WA). A special feature of this book is the extensive treatment of three-dimensional images and image sequences. The synthetic images used for illustration were designed and computed with Caligari Broadcast (Octree Software, N.Y.) on a Commodore Amiga by AEON Verlag, Hanau, FRG.

After studying this book, the reader should be able to apply even quite complex digital image processing techniques in his or her research area. This book is based on courses given by the author since 1986 in the Physics Department and the Interdisciplinary Center for Scientific Computing at the University of Heidelberg. It is assumed that the reader is familiar with elementary matrix algebra as well as the Fourier transform. Wherever possible, mathematical topics are described intuitively making use of the fact that image processing is an ideal subject to illustrate even complex mathematical relations.

I am deeply indebted to the many individuals who helped me to write this book. I do this by tracing its history. In the early 1980s, when I worked on the physics of small-scale air-sea interaction at the Institute of Environmental Physics at Heidelberg University, it became obvious that these complex phenomena could not be adequately treated with point measuring probes. Consequently, a number of area extended measuring techniques were developed. Then I searched for techniques to extract the physically relevant data from the images and sought for colleagues with experience in digital image processing. The first contacts were established with the Institute for Applied Physics at Heidelberg University and the German Cancer Research Center in Heidelberg. I would like to thank Prof. Dr. J. Bille, Dr. J. Dengler and Dr. M. Schmidt cordially for many eye-opening conversations and their cooperation.

Then I contacted the faculty for computer science at Karlsruhe University and the Fraunhofer Institute for Information and Data Processing in Karlsruhe. I learnt a great deal from the course of Prof. Dr. H.-H. Nagel and Dr. R. Kories on "Algorithmic Interpretation of Image Sequences" that I attended in the summer term 1986.

In April 1989, a German edition of this book was published by Springer-Verlag. This is not a straightforward translation, but a completely revised edition with many augmentations, notably with many more practical examples, listings of important algorithms, a new chapter on shape, updated information on the latest image processing hardware, a new set of color tables, and countless small improvements.

I would like to express my sincere thanks to Dr. Klaus Riemer. He drafted several chapters of the lecture notes for my courses at Heidelberg University. He also designed a number of drawings for this book. Many individuals have reviewed various drafts of the manuscript. I would like to thank Robert I. Birenbaum, Thomas Fendrich, Karl-Heinz Grosser, Jochen Klinke, Dr. Dietmar Wierzimok and many others for valuable comments and suggestions on different parts of the manuscript. I am mostly grateful for the help of my friends at AEON Verlag. They sacrificed many night hours for proofreading, designing computer graphics, and providing general editorial assistance.

Many researchers and companies provided me with material from their research. The following list shows the many applications of digital image processing:

- Dr. K. S. Baker, Scripps Institution of Oceanography, La Jolla, California; R. C. Smith, University of California at Santa Barbara, California; O. B. Brown, Rosenstiel School of Marine and Atmospheric Science, University of Miami, Florida
- Dr. J. P. Burt, David Sarnoff Research Center, Princeton, New Jersey
- Dr. P. de Loor and Drs. D. van Halsema, Physics and Electronics Laboratory, TNO, Den Haag
- Dr. J. Dengler, Department of Medical and Biological Computer Science, German

Cancer Research Center, Heidelberg, and Dr. M. Schmidt, Alfred Wegener Institute, Bremerhaven
- Dr. W. Enkelmann, Fraunhofer-Institute for Information and Data Processing, Karlsruhe
- Prof. Dr. G. Granlund, Computer Vision Laboratory, University of Linköping
- Dr. R. Kories, Fraunhofer-Institute for Information and Data Processing, Karlsruhe
- Prof. Dr. E. C. Hildreth, Center for Biological Information Processing, Massachusetts Institute of Technology, Cambridge, Massachusetts
- Prof. Dr. A. C. Kak, School of Electrical Engineering, Purdue University, West Lafayette, Indiana
- Dr. K. Riemer and Dr. D. Wierzimok, Institute for Environmental Physics, University of Heidelberg
- Dr. B. Schmitt and Prof. Dr. D. Komitowski, Department for Histodiagnostics and Pathomorphological Documentation, German Cancer Research Center, Heidelberg
- J. Steurer, Institute for Communications Technology, Technical University of Munich
- Prof. Dr. J. Wolfrum and Dr. H. Becker, Institute for Physical Chemistry, University of Heidelberg
- Imaging Technology Inc., Woburn, Massachusetts, and Stemmer PC-Systeme GmbH, Munich
- Matrox Electronic Systems Limited, Dorval, Quebec, and Rauscher GmbH, Munich
- Techex Computer + Grafik Vertriebs GmbH, Munich

I would also like to thank Prof. Dr. K. O. Münnich, director of the Institute for Environmental Physics. From the beginning, he was open-minded about new ideas to apply digital image processing techniques in environmental physics. It is due to his farsightedness and substantial support that the research group "Digital Image Processing in Environmental Physics" could develop so fruitfully at his institute. Many of the examples shown in this book are taken from my research at Heidelberg University and the Scripps Institution of Oceanography. I gratefully acknowledge financial support for this research from the German Science Foundation, the European Community, the National Science Foundation (OCE89 11224), and the Office of Naval Research (N00014-89-J-3222). Most of this book has been written while I was guest professor at the Interdisciplinary Research Center for Scientific Computing at Heidelberg University. I would like to thank Prof. Dr. Jäger for his hospitality. I would also like to express my sincere thanks to the staff of Springer-Verlag for their constant interest in this book and their professional advice.

For the third edition, the proven and well-received concept of the first and second editions has been maintained and only some errors have been corrected. However, Appendix B (PC-Based Image Processing Systems) has been completely rewritten to accomodate to the considerable progress in hardware during the last two years. Again, I would like to thank all readers in advance for their comments on further improvements or additions. I am also grateful for hints on errors, omissions or typing errors which, despite all the care taken, may still have slipped attention.

La Jolla, California and Heidelberg, February 1995 Bernd Jähne

Contents

1 Introduction

1.1 Digital Image Processing — A New Research Tool

From the beginning of science, visual observation has played a major role. At that time, the only way to document the results of an experiment was by verbal description and manual drawings. The next major step was the invention of photography which enabled results to be documented objectively. Three prominent examples of scientific applications of photography are astronomy, photogrammetry, and particle physics. Astronomers were able to measure positions and magnitudes of stars accurately. Aerial images were used to produce topographic maps. Searching through countless images from hydrogen bubble chambers led to the discovery of many elementary particles in physics. These manual evaluation procedures, however, were time consuming. Some semi- or even fully automated optomechanical devices were designed. However, they were adapted to a single specific purpose. This is why quantitative evaluation of images never found widespread application at that time. Generally, images were only used for documentation, qualitative description and illustration of the phenomena observed.

Nowadays, we are in the middle of a second revolution sparked by the rapid progress in video and computer technology. Personal computers and workstations have become powerful enough to process image data. They have also become cheap enough to be widely used. In consequence, image processing is turning from a specialized science in areas such as astronomy, remote sensing, electrical engineering, and computer science into a standard scientific tool. Applications in image processing have now been applied to virtually all the natural sciences.

A simple example clearly demonstrates the power of visual information. Imagine you had the task to write an article about a new technical system, for example, a new type of a solar power plant. It would take an enormous effort to describe the system if you could not include images and technical drawings. The reader of your imageless article would also have a frustrating experience. He would spend a lot of time trying to figure out how the new solar power plant worked and he might end up with only a poor picture of what it looked like.

Technical drawings and photographs of the solar power plant would be of enormous help for the reader of your article. First, he would immediately have an idea of the plant. Secondly, he could study details in the drawings and photographs which were not described in the text, but which caught his attention. Pictorial information provides much more details, a fact which can be precisely summarized by the saying that "a picture is worth a thousand words".

Another observation is of interest. If the reader later heard of the new solar plant, he could easily recall what it looked like, the object "solar plant" being instantaneously associated with an image.

1.2   Components of an Image Processing System

In this section, the technical innovations that enabled the widespread application of image processing in science are briefly reviewed. It will outline the capabilities of modern image processing systems and the progress in image sensors, image storage, and image processing.

1.2.1   Image Sensors

Digital processing requires images to be obtained in the form of electrical signals. These signals can be digitized into sequences of numbers which then can be processed by a computer. There are many ways to convert images into digital numbers. Here, we will focus on video technology, since it is the most common and affordable approach.

The milestone in image sensing technology was the invention of semiconductor photodetector arrays. There are many types of such sensors, the most common being the *charge coupled device* or CCD. Such a sensor consists of a large number of photosensitive elements. A typical high resolution CCD sensor (RS 170 norm) has 486 lines of 768 elements on a $10.5 \times 11 \, \mu$m grid. During the accumulation phase, each element collects electrical charges, which are generated by absorbed photons. Thus the collected charge is proportional to the illumination. In the read-out phase, these charges are sequentially transported across the chip from sensor to sensor and finally converted to an electric voltage.

Semiconductor imaging sensors have a number of significant advantages:

- *Precise and stable geometry.* This feature simply results from the manufacturing procedure. Geometric distortion is virtually absent. More important, the sensor is stable in position, showing only a minor temperature dependence due to the low linear thermal expansion coefficient of silicon ($2 \cdot 10^{-6}$/K). These features allow precise size and position measurements. A new measuring technology named *videometry* is emerging. We might think that because of the limited number of sensor elements only quite coarse measurements are possible in comparison with other physical measurements. We will learn later, in section 17.4.5, that the positions of objects can be determined with accuracies well below a tenth of the distance between two sensor elements. This degree of accuracy can, of course, only be gained if the other components in the camera system do not introduce any significant error. Also, the geometric distortion caused by the camera lens has to be taken into consideration (section 2.2.4).

- *High sensitivity.* The quantum efficiency, i.e., the fraction of elementary charges generated per photon, is close to one. However, commercial CCDs cannot be used at low light levels because of the thermally generated electrons. But if CCD devices are cooled down to low temperatures, they are among the most sensitive imagers. Such devices are commonly used in astronomy and are about one hundred times more sensitive than photographic material.
- *Small and rugged.* A final advantage is the small size of the sensor and its insensitivity to external influences such as magnetic fields and vibrations.

Images are not restricted to visible light. Nowadays, imaging sensor systems are available for the whole range of the electromagnetic spectrum from *gamma radiation* to *radio waves*. In this way, the application range of digital image processing techniques has broadened enormously. To a large extent, this development has been initiated by astronomy. Astronomers have no other way to obtain knowledge about the distant objects they are studying than by measuring the faint emitted radiation. Thus it was natural that they developed and continue to develop sensors for the widest possible range.

These considerations lead us to the conclusion that a scientist using an image processing technique is not interested in the image brightness itself, but in specific physical, chemical, or biological characteristics of the objects he or she is studying. The electromagnetic radiation collected on the image plane is only used as a medium to learn about the features of interest.

The following example is taken from satellite oceanography. Plate 1a shows an image of the coastal Pacific in Southern California taken with the Coastal Zone Color Scanner (CZCS) in the visible green/blue range. The light emitted from the ocean surface water in this spectral region is basically determined by the chlorophyll concentration. Thus plate 1a directly shows the chlorophyll concentration in a pseudo color code as indicated in the color plate.

The same area was also observed by the NOA6 satellite at the same time in the far infrared. The radiation in this wavelength region is related to the ocean surface temperature (plate 1b). The temperature and chlorophyll concentration show similar spatial patterns which allow different water masses to be distinguished and ocean mixing and biological activities to be studied. Provided that the parameters can be determined accurately enough and without bias, the area extended measurements from satellites yield a much more detailed view of these processes than profiles taken from ships. Satellite images taken simultaneously in many different spectral regions, so-called *multichannel images*, have become a very valuable tool in *remote sensing*.

Microwaves and *radio waves* allow active remote sensing. These waves with wavelengths from meters to millimeters can be sent via an antenna onto the ocean surface. Because of the roughness of the sea surface, i.e., small-scale water surface waves, part of the emitted radiation is scattered back in all directions. Thus the power received by the satellite antenna contains a world of information about processes influencing the small-scale waves on the ocean surface [*de Loor and Brunsveld van Hulten*, 1978].

In the right margin of figure 1.1 in the mud-flats between the two islands, strong variations in the radar backscatter can be observed which first puzzled scientists considerably. Then it turned out that they were caused by a complex chain of interactions.

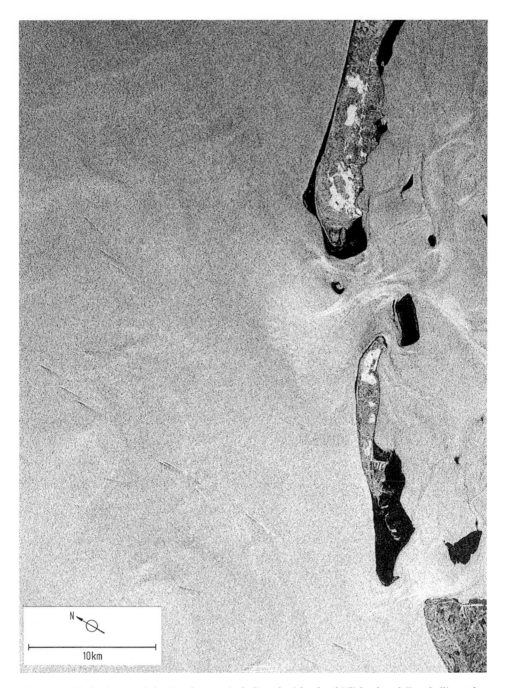

Figure 1.1: Radar image of the Dutch coast including the islands of Vlieland and Terschelling taken with the synthetic aperture radar of the SEASAT satellite on October 9, 1978 and evaluated by FVLR/GSOC. The resolution of the image is about 25 m. Image kindly provided by D. van Halsema, TNO, the Netherlands.

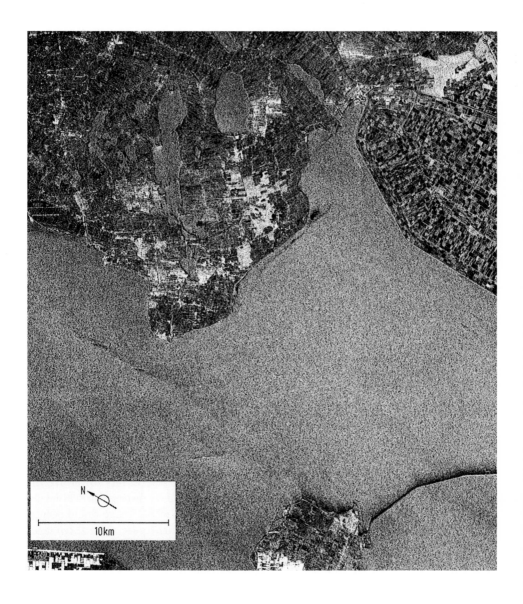

Figure 1.2: Another SAR-SEASAT image taken at the same day as figure 1.1 showing a sector of the Dutch Ijsselmeer. Image kindly provided by D. van Halsema, TNO.

Because of the low water depth, there are strong tidal currents in this region which are modulated by the varying water depth. The changing currents, in turn, influence the small-scale water surface waves. In this complex way, measurements on the ocean surface with radiation which does not penetrate the water, still provide clues about the bottom topography. This is an extreme example illustrating the common fact that features observed in satellite imagery may have very complex causes.

On the open ocean (figure 1.1 left side) and in the isolated Ijsselmeer (figure 1.2), surface currents are much lower. Consequently, the radar backscatter is quite homogeneous. In both images, several ship tracks one to three kilometers long are visible.

In the eastern part of figure 1.2 (top right), different agricultural areas can be recognized as small rectangles with considerably different brightnesses. Thus radar images are also useful to distinguish different types of surface areas on continents. Since radio- and microwaves penetrate clouds, remote sensing of the earth's surface is possible despite of weather conditions.

Carver et al. [1985] give a review of microwave remote sensing, and *Goetz et al.* [1985] survey optical remote sensing. *Stewart* [1985] describes all aspects of satellite oceanography.

Image sensors draw attention to the relationship between the image intensity and the features of the observed object; this is the first task for a scientist applying any digital image processing. This aspect is often not adequately considered in computer science literature.

So far, image sensors and images have been considered as data sets with two spatial coordinates. A higher level of abstraction is possible. Actually all data with two coordinates can be treated in the same manner as spatial images. In this wider context, image sensors may be any kind of instrument which registers data as a function of two variables.

1.2.2   Image Storage

Images contain huge amounts of data. As an example take a standard image from a 35 mm camera which measures 24 mm × 36 mm. If we assume a resolution of 0.01 mm, it consists of more than 10^7 data points. Each point needs several bits to resolve the different gray values of the image. It is a common standard to distinguish 256 levels. One image point can be stored in eight bits or one *byte*. The whole image would occupy 10 Mbytes. A color image would require three times as much space since three color channels, red, green, and blue, must be stored.

Most images which are now processed are captured by video cameras which provide a much lower resolution. A widespread standard contains 512 × 512 image points. One gray value image with 8 bits/point contains 256 kbytes of data.

However, applications which analyze time varying processes cannot be studied with single frames, but require the analysis of *image sequences*. The storage requirements then increase tremendously. A single second of video images with 30 frames/s needs 7.5 Mbytes of storage. Three-dimensional imagery, which can really adequately picture the three-dimensional world, also needs huge storage space. A single 512 × 512 × 512 image occupies 128 Mbytes.

These examples emphasize the enormous storage requirements involved in the handling of image data. The storage densities of semiconductor memory are increasing exponentially with time since their invention. When my research group used one of the first microcomputer based image processing boards in the early 1980s, an IP-512 from Imaging Technology, a board packed with memory chips could just hold a single 512×512 image. Less then ten years later, several image processing boards are available, e. g., the VISTA board from Truevision, which offers a frame buffer 16 times larger (4 Mbytes) on a board half the size (see also appendix B).

Thus even personal computers can handle single images without any problems. It is still difficult to store digitized image sequences at video rate. One rather expensive solution is a large one Gbyte or more in capacity fast peripheral storage device, a so-called *real-time magnetic disk*. This device has a read/write bandwidth larger than 10 Mbytes/s so that digitized video images can be read or written in real time. With this device video image sequences with up to several thousand images can be digitized in real time.

Video recording is also making tremendous progress. New recording standards such as S-VHS offer a much higher resolution and better recording quality than the old Umatic standard which is widely used in scientific applications. Videotapes are a cheap recording medium for enormous amounts of image data. One hour of gray value images corresponds to 21.6 Gbytes of data if digitized with a resolution of 512×512 and 8 bits per image point. However, a serious deficit remains: it is still tedious and expensive to get random access to specific images on the tape. A special controller is necessary and the operation involves significant tape wear, since images can only be digitized from a running videotape.

A real breakthrough has been the new generation of video recording equipment. These devices, which appeared on the market in 1989, record analog video images on an optical disk with a high quality. Each side of the disk holds about 40,000 images equivalent to half an hour of continuous videotape recording. Both recording of continuous image sequences and of single frames are possible. Fast random access to any image on the disk is possible within less than 0.5 s. Extremely useful for image sequence processing is the high-quality forward and backward playback with variable speed from 1/255 to 3 times the normal speed. The near future will certainly bring both further enhancements and cheaper systems. Digital storage of images on standard optical disks is a cheaper alternative, but access to the images is considerably slower. Another significant development are CD-ROM players. These cheap devices allow the wide distribution of image material, e. g., satellite images.

The newest technology are VLSI chips such as the CL550A from C-Cube Microsystems which allow gray value and color video images to be compressed and decompressed in real-time, i. e., at a rate of 30 frames/s. Compression is not error free, but degradation of the images is not visible with typical compression rates of 10:1 to 30:1. With such rates, the data is reduced to such an extent that video image sequences can be stored on a fast hard disk in real time. If the slight degradation of the images is acceptable, this is a much cheaper and more flexible solution than a real-time magnetic disk.

1.2.3   Image Processing Speed

Because of the immense amount of data in images, successful image processing requires large computing power. A current personal computer is about as powerful as a main frame ten years ago and sufficiently fast to perform not too complex image operations. We will discuss many examples in this book in detail.

Complex operations, image sequence analysis, and reconstruction from projections, however, need more processing power. These demands can also be met with current PC-based systems, which are equipped with image processing hardware for specific operations.

Another promising possibility is the use of modern RISC (reduced instruction set computing) processors as, e. g., the Intel i860 chip [*Margulis*, 1990]. In contrast to special image processing hardware, which is much more difficult to program, these general purpose processors can be programmed with standard development tools. This advantage should not be underestimated.

Finally, parallel processing has a bright future in digital image processing. Many image processing operations can easily be implemented for parallel computers. Often used are *transputers*. These are RISC processors with the feature of special hardware for fast serial links. Systems with many transputers (so-called superclusters) are being more commonly used for image processing. At the Interdisciplinary Center for Scientific Computing at Heidelberg University, a supercluster with 128 transputers has been installed in 1990 and is now extensively used for image sequence processing.

1.3   Human and Computer Vision

We cannot think of image processing without considering the human visual system. This seems to be a trivial statement, but it has far-reaching consequences. We observe and evaluate the images which we are processing with our visual system. Without taking this elementary fact into consideration, we may be much misled in the interpretation of images.

The first simple questions we should ask are:
- What intensity differences can we distinguish?
- What is the spatial resolution of our eye?
- How accurately can we estimate and compare distances and areas?
- What role do colors play in human vision?

It is obvious that a deeper knowledge would be of immense help for computer vision. Here is not the place to give an overview of the human visual system. The intention is rather to make us aware of the connection between human and computer vision, and to pick out some elementary facts we are confronted with when we perform digital image processing. A detailed comparison of human and computer vision can be found in *Levine* [1985].

The reader can perform some experiments by himself. Figure 1.3 shows several test images concerning the question of estimation of distance and area. He will have no

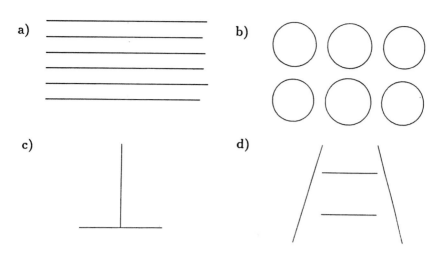

Figure 1.3: Test images for distance and area estimation: a) parallel lines with up to 5 % difference in length; b) circles with up to 10 % difference in radius; c) the vertical line appears longer, though it has the same length as the horizontal line; d) deception by perspective: the upper line (in the background) appears longer than the lower line (in the foreground), though both are equally long.

problem in seeing even small changes in the length of the parallel lines in figure 1.3a. A similar area comparison with circles is considerably more difficult (figure 1.3b). The other examples show how the estimate is biased by the context in the image. Such phenomena are known as *optical deception*. Two examples of estimates for length are shown in figure 1.3c, d. These examples point out that the human visual system interprets the context in its estimate of length. Consequently, we should be very careful in our visual estimates of lengths and areas in images.

We can draw similar conclusions for the estimate of *absolute* gray values. Figure 1.4a shows that the small rectangular area with a medium brightness appears brighter in the dark background than in the light background, though its absolute brightness is the same. This deception only disappears when the two areas merge. The step case-like increase in the brightness in figure 1.4b shows a similar effect. The brightness of one step appears to increase towards the next darker step.

Because of the low brightness resolution of printed images, we cannot perform similar experiments regarding the brightness resolution of our visual sense. It shows a logarithmic rather than a linear response. This means that we can distinguish relative but not absolute brightness differences. In a wide range of brightnesses, we can resolve relative differences of about 2 %.

These characteristics of the human visual system are quite different from those of a machine vision system. Typically only 256 gray values are resolved. Thus a digitized image has much lower dynamics than the human visual system. This is the reason why the quality of a digitized image, especially of a scene with high contrast in brightness, appears inferior to us compared to what we see directly. Although the *relative* brightness resolution is far better than 2 % in the bright parts of the image, it is poor in the dark

Figure 1.4: Distinction of gray values: a) small rectangular areas of constant gray value are placed in different arrangements in a darker and brighter background; b) a linear stepwise increase in brightness.

parts of the images. At a gray value of 10, the brightness resolution is only 10 %.

In order to cope with this problem, video cameras generally convert the light intensity I not linearly, but with an exponential law into the gray value g:

$$G = I^\gamma. \tag{1.1}$$

The exponent γ is denoted the *gamma value*. Typically, γ has a value of 0.4. With this exponential conversion, the logarithmic characteristic of the human visual system may be approximated. Here the contrast range is significantly enhanced. If we presume a minimum relative brightness resolution of 10 %, we get useable contrast ranges of 25 and 316 with $\gamma = 1$ and $\gamma = 0.4$, respectively. For many scientific applications, however, it is essential that a linear relation exists between the light intensity and the gray value ($\gamma = 1$). Many CCD cameras provide a jumper or a trimmer to switch or adjust the gamma value.

Now we turn to the question of the recognition of objects in images. Although figure 1.5 contains only a few lines and is a planar image not containing any direct information on the depth, we immediately recognize a cube in the right and left image and its orientation in space. The only clues from which we can draw this conclusion are the hidden lines and our knowledge about the shape of a cube. The medium image, which also shows the hidden lines, is ambivalent. With some training, we can switch between the two possible orientations in space.

Figure 1.6 shows another remarkable feature of the human visual system. With ease we see sharp boundaries between the different textures in figure 1.6a and immediately recognize the figure 5. In figure 1.6b we identify a white equally sided triangle, although part of the boundaries do not exist.

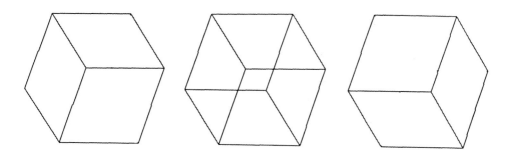

Figure 1.5: Recognition of three-dimensional objects: three different representations of a cube with identical edges in the image plane.

From these few observations, we can conclude that the human visual system is extremely powerful in recognizing objects, but has some deficiencies in the absolute estimation of gray values, distances, and areas. Of course, the performance of the visual system is related to how the visual information is processed. We might be tempted to measure the power of a vision system with a few figures as the number of sensor elements and the number of operations it can perform per time. The retina contains approximately 130 millions photo receptors. These are many more sensor elements than on a CCD chip. Compared to computers with clock times of several 10 MHz, the switching time of neural processor elements is about 10^4 times slower. Despite this slower timing and the huge number of receptors, the human visual system is much more powerful than any computer vision system. We constantly rely on the fact that it can analyze even complex scenes in *real time* so that we can react correspondingly.

In comparison, the power of computer vision systems is marginal and should make us feel humble. A digital image processing system can only perform some elementary or well defined fixed image processing tasks such as quality control in industry production in real time. More complex tasks such as the analysis of motion or the reconstruction of an observed three-dimensional scene from two-dimensional image data require tremendous processing time. We are still worlds away from a universal digital image processing which is capable of "understanding" images as human beings do.

There is another connection between human and computer vision which is worth noting. Important developments in computer vision have been made through progress in understanding the human visual system. We will encounter several examples in this book: the *pyramid* as an efficient data structure for image processing (chapter 8), the concept of local orientation (chapter 7), and motion determination by filter techniques (chapter 17).

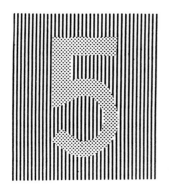 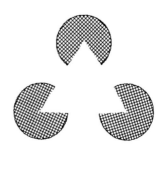

Figure 1.6: a) Recognition of boundaries between textures; b) "interpolation" of object boundaries.

1.4   Examples of Scientific Applications

In this section the considerable progress which evolved with the usage of image measuring techniques is described. The following examples are typical for scientific applications of digital image processing in the sense that image processing enables complex phenomena to be evaluated, which could not be adequately accessed with conventional measuring techniques.

The first examples are the exchange processes between the atmosphere and the oceans which play a major role in global climate and distribution of pollutants on the planet earth [Dahlem Workshop *The Changing Atmosphere*, 1987]. One of these processes is the exchange of gases. Carbon dioxide, methane, and other trace gases are climate active gases, since they absorb infrared radiation. The observed concentration increase of these gases has a significant influence on the global climate. Although there are still considerable uncertainties, all evidence so far indicates that we face serious climate changes, particularly *global warming*. Thus it is of great importance to know how these gases are exchanged between the atmosphere and the ocean.

The physics of gas exchange is only poorly understood, since it is a complex problem. The critical processes take place in a very thin layer at the ocean surface, which is only several $10\,\mu$m thick. In this layer, the gases penetrate from the atmosphere into the ocean surface by molecular diffusion and are then swept into deeper layers by irregular, turbulent velocity fluctuations.

Processes that take place in such a thin layer at the ocean surface undulated by surface waves are very difficult to investigate experimentally. Conventional measuring technique determines the mean flux density of a gas tracer across the interface. If this information is represented in an image, it would just show an area of a constant gray value. The brightness would be proportional to the flux density and we would not learn anything about how the gas exchange process works.

A new method now allows the penetration of the gas tracer into the water surface to be made visible. The technique uses reactive gases and fluorescent dyes [*Jähne*, 1990]. The intensity of the fluorescent light is proportional to the penetration depth

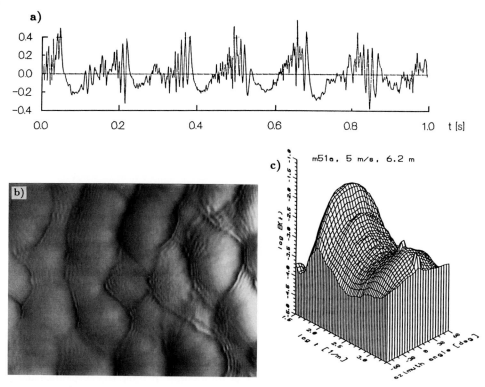

Figure 1.7: a) Time series of the slope of water surface waves; b) image of the wave slope; c) wave number power spectrum computed from about 200 images; from measurements of the author performed in the wind/wave facility at the Institut de Mécanique Statistique de la Turbulence, University of Marseille; wind speed: 5 m/s, fetch: 6.2 m.

of the gas tracer. We can now obtain an image which gives a detailed insight into the processes taking place at the water surface (plate 2a and b). At first glance, we see that the gas exchange process changes significantly when waves occur at the water surface. Evaluation of single images and image sequences yields a new world of information about the gas exchange process. First, we can determine the mean penetration depth of the gas tracer which directly yields the exchange rate as with conventional techniques. Then we can estimate size, velocity and lifetime of the eddies which transport the gas across the boundary layer and thus understand how the exchange process works.

A similar technique allows vertical profiles to be measured in laboratory wind/water facilities [*Jähne*, 1990]. This time, the intensity of the fluorescent light is directly proportional to the gas tracer concentration. Fluorescence is stimulated by an argon-ion laser piercing the water surface perpendicularly from above. A CCD camera is placed just below the water level outside the water channel and observes the laser beam from aside. Time series of the vertical profile are shown in plate 2c as an image with one space and one time coordinate, known as a *space-time image*.

Another example is the measurement of small-scale waves on the ocean surface [*Jähne and Waas*, 1989; *Jähne and Riemer*, 1990]. Point measurements with a laser

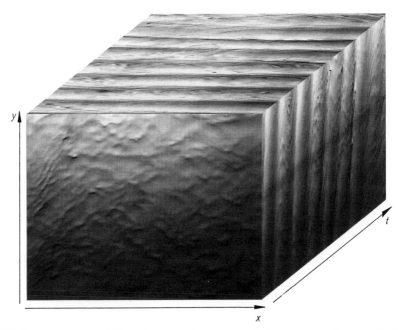

Figure 1.8: Image sequence of the water wave slope represented as a wave cube; unpublished data taken by the author in the Marseille wind/wave facility.

probe result in time series from which it is impossible to infer the two-dimensional structure of the waves on the water surface. In figure 1.7a, we recognize that small waves are predominantly located on just one side of the larger waves, but we do not know from which direction these waves are coming. A video image of the water surface showing the slope coded in gray values contains all this information (figure 1.7b). From many of such images 2-D wave number spectra can be calculated (figure 1.7c, plate 5). Finally, an image sequence of the wave slope contains both the temporal and spatial characteristics of the waves (figure 1.8).

The last example is taken from physical chemistry. It illustrates how complex chemical processes can be made visible and the effort required to image such processes. The research group of Prof. Dr. Wolfrum at the Institute for Physical Chemistry at Heidelberg University has studied the mechanisms of technical combustion. *Suntz et al.* [1988] have measured the OH-radical concentration in an experimental combustion engine. They used a XeCl eximer laser with a wavelength of 308 nm to stimulate an excited electron state of the OH-radical in a small planar light sheet which is 25 mm wide and 75 μm thick (figure 1.9). The resulting fluorescent light is measured by a light-intensified CCD camera and an illumination time of 25 ns. This short illumination time is necessary to suppress the light generation by combustion.

Results with a lean combustion mixture are shown in plate 2d. High OH-Radical concentrations are yielded at the flame front. The concentrations correlate with the shape of the front. They are significantly higher with concave rather than convex lines.

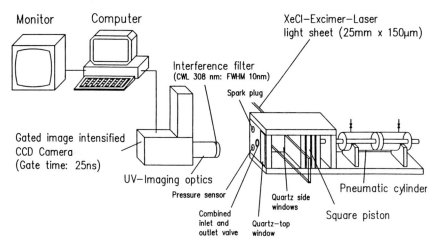

Figure 1.9: Experimental setup to measure the OH-radical concentration during combustion in an experimental engine with a square piston [*Suntz et al.*, 1988].

1.5 Hierarchy of Image Processing Operations

Image processing is not a one-step process. We are able to distinguish between several steps which must be performed one after the other until we can extract the data of interest from the observed scene. In this way a *hierarchical processing* scheme is built up as sketched in figure 1.10. As a conclusion to this introduction to image processing, an overview of the different phases of image processing is given, together with a summary outline of this book.

Image processing begins with the capturing of an image with a suitable, not necessarily optical, acquiring system. Then the image sensed must be brought into a form which can be treated with digital computers. This process is called *digitization*.

The first steps of digital processing may include a number of different operations. It may be necessary to correct known disturbances in the image, for instance caused by a defocused optics, motion blur, errors in the sensor, or errors in the transmission of image signals (*image restoration*). If the sensor has nonlinear characteristics, these need to be corrected. Likewise, brightness and contrast of the image can be optimized. Another important operation is noise reduction in noisy images. A regular task for satellite imagery are coordinate transformations to remove geometrical distortions.

The next phases depend on the aim of image processing. Sometimes only removing sensor-related errors from the image or enhancing the contrast is required. Effective transmission and storage of images necessitates a further step. In order to cope with the enormous amount of image data, the images must be stored and transmitted in the tightest possible code. Some types of images may allow errors in the coding process, other types may not.

A whole chain of processing steps is necessary to analyze and identify objects. First, adequate filtering procedures must be applied in order to distinguish the objects of interest from other objects and the background. Then the object has to be separated

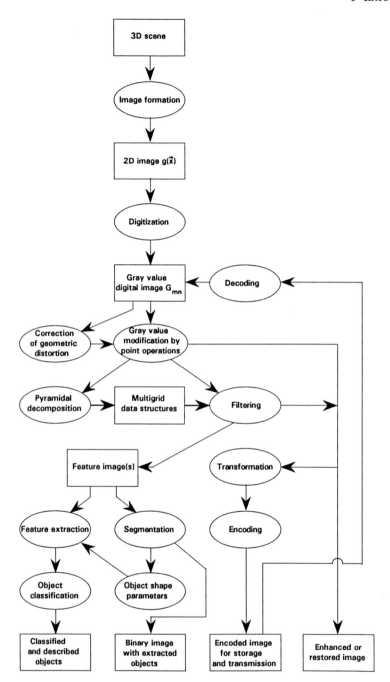

Figure 1.10: A hierarchy of digital image processing tasks from image formation to image comprehension.

Figure 1.11: By what means do we recognize that all objects, except for one, are lamps?

from the background (*segmentation*). This process leads to a binary image. Now that we know the exact geometrical shape of the object, we can extract further information as the mean gray value, the area, perimeter, and other parameters for the form of the object. These parameters can be used to classify objects (*classification*). This is an important step in many applications of image processing as the following examples show:

- In a satellite image which shows an agricultural area, we would like to distinguish fields with different fruits and obtain parameters to estimate the ripeness or to detect damage by parasites (see figure 1.2).
- There are many medical applications where the essential question is to detect pathological changes. A classical example is the analysis of aberrations of chromosomes.
- Character recognition in printed and handwritten text is another example which has been studied since image processing began and still poses significant difficulties. While you are reading this text, you are performing just this task.

You hopefully do more, namely to try to understand the meaning of what you are reading. This is also the final step of image processing which aims to understand the observed scene. We perform this task more or less unconsciously whenever we use our visual system. We recognize people, we can easily distinguish between the image of a scientific lab and that of a living room, or watch the traffic to cross a street safely. We all do this without knowing how the visual system works.

Take as another example the objects shown in figure 1.11. We will have no problem in recognizing that all objects but one are lamps. How could a machine vision system perform this task? It is obvious that it is a complex problem, which can only be solved if adequate representation of and access to previously gained knowledge is available. We can recognize a lamp because we have already seen many other lamps before and because we can draw conclusions not only from the geometric shape but also by considering the possible purpose of an object. Research on problems of this kind are part of a research area called *artificial intelligence*.

"Recognition" in scientific applications is often much easier to handle than in ordinary scenes. We can often describe the features of an object in which we are interested in a precise way. Thus scientific applications often do not include any methods of artificial intelligence but have an algorithmic approach. We will discuss this matter in more detail in chapter 12.

1.6   Image Processing and Computer Graphics

For some time, image processing and computer graphics have been treated as two different areas. Since then knowledge in both areas has increased considerably and more complex problems are able to be treated. Computer graphics is striving to achieve photorealistic computer generated images of a three-dimensional scene, while image processing is trying to reconstruct it from an image actually taken with a camera. In this sense, computer graphics performs the inverse procedure to that of image processing. We start with knowledge on the shape and features of an object, i.e., start at the bottom of figure 1.10 and work upwards until we yield a two-dimensional image. To handle image processing or computer graphics, we basically have to work from the same knowledge. We need to know the interaction between illumination and objects, how a three-dimensional scene is projected onto an image plane, etc.

There are still quite some differences between an image processing and a graphics workstation. But we can envisage that, when the similarities and interrelations between computer graphics and image processing are better understood and the proper hardware is developed, we will see some kind of general purpose workstation in the future which can handle computer graphics as well as image processing tasks.

2 Image Formation and Digitization

Image acquisition is the first step of digital image processing and is often not properly taken into account. However, quantitative analysis of any images requires a good understanding of the image formation process. Only with a profound knowledge of all the steps involved in image acquisition, is it possible to interpret the contents of an image correctly. The steps necessary for an object in the three-dimensional world to become a digital image in the memory of a computer are as follows:

- *Becoming visible*. An object becomes visible by the interaction with light or, more generally, electromagnetic radiation. The four basic types of interaction are reflection, refraction, absorption, and scattering. These effects depend on the optical properties of the material from which the object is made and on its surface structure. The light collected by a camera system is determined by these optical properties as well as by the illumination, i. e., position and nature of the light or, more generally, radiation sources.
- *Projection*. An optical system collects the light rays reflected from the objects and projects the three-dimensional world onto a two-dimensional image plane.
- *Digitization*. The continuous image on the image plane must be converted into image points on a discrete grid. Furthermore, the intensity at each point must be represented by a suitable finite number of gray values (*Quantization*).

These steps will be discussed in the following three sections. Quantization is the topic of section 4.2.2.

2.1 Interaction between Light and Matter

2.1.1 Introduction

The interaction between matter and radiation is the basis for all imaging. This is more a topic of physics rather than image processing. Knowledge about this subject, however, is very useful, especially in scientific and industrial applications, where we have control on how we set up our imaging system. An approach which integrates the optical setup and the processing of the resulting images is required in order to obtain the best and most cost effective solution. In other words, if we make a serious error in the imaging

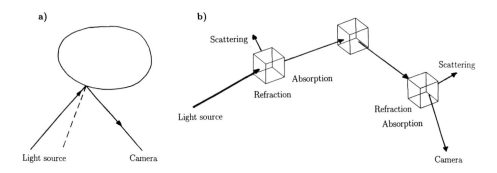

Figure 2.1: a) Sketch of the interaction between illumination and objects; a) objects with impermeable surfaces; b) more general arrangement showing reflection, absorption, scattering, and refraction of light from the light source to the object, the object of interest itself, and from the object back to the camera.

system, processing of the images may be costly and slow or, even worse, it might not be possible at all to correct for the resulting degradations.

Applications in image processing are so widespread that a complete discussion of this topic is not possible here. We should, however, be aware of some basic facts that enable us to consider the illumination arrangement in our application properly. Interaction between illumination and the observed scene has received much attention in computer graphics where researchers are trying to achieve more realistic computer generated images. In computer graphics the task is to determine the light intensity at the surface of the object, given the geometrical arrangement of objects and light sources and the optical properties of the objects. In image processing, we have to solve the inverse problem, namely, to infer the position of the objects in space and their optical properties from the image projected onto the image plane.

We can get a feeling of this complexity from the sequence shown in plate 3. It shows the same scene rendered with more and more sophisticated models of the interactions between the illumination and the illuminated objects.

2.1.2 Opaque Surfaces

The illumination problem is less complex if only opaque surfaces are considered (figure 2.1a). The problem can be divided into two parts. First we have to calculate the *illuminance* at the object's surface. In this simple case, only the light from the light sources may be considered. However, this is only a zero order approximation, since the object is also illuminated by light reflected from all the other object points in the scene. In other words, illuminances from the objects are coupled. As an example, consider the motion of a single object without any other changes in the scene including the setup of the light sources. Then many more things than just the position of the moving object change. The *shadow*, the moving object is casting, changes with the relative position of the object and the light sources. When the object comes close to other objects, the illuminance of these objects will change.

An exact solution to this problem can only be found by solving a huge linear equation system containing all object points and light sources. Solving such an equation system which takes into account the influence of other objects on the illumination of an object point is called *ray tracing* and is a computationally costly procedure. If finally we have obtained the correct object illumination, the second task is to use the optical properties of the object's surface again to calculate the light intensity which is collected by the camera lens.

2.1.3   Volumes

Opaque surfaces govern natural scenes. However, many scientific objects cannot be reduced to such a simple description, as much scientific data is three-dimensional. The most obvious example are all kinds of three-dimensional fields. We might, for example, have determined the three-dimensional current field from the analysis of flow visualization experiments or numerical calculations. Modern medical image techniques with penetrating radiation also yield volume data of the human body (sections 2.2.10 and 13.3).

In all these cases, not only the surfaces, i. e., planes of discontinuities in optical properties, are of importance, but also volume elements which scatter or absorb radiation. These effects have to be taken into account both for the generation of realistic computer images and for the reconstruction from projections. In contrast to *surface rendering*, the generation of computer images from volume data is called *volume rendering*.

If we take absorption and scattering processes into account imaging becomes much more complex (figure 2.1b). In general, we must consider refraction, absorption and scattering of light rays from the light source to each object point and back to the camera. This general situation is much too complex to be solvable practically. Fortunately, most practical situations are much easier in the sense that they include only a few of the possible interaction processes.

With respect to image processing, awareness of the complexity of illumination helps us in the design of a proper illumination system. Since in scientific applications object properties are inferred from optical properties, we need to know the illumination of the object's surface.

As an example, consider satellite images in the far infrared from the ocean surface. Without any other influences, the observed brightness would directly be related to the ocean's surface temperature. There are, however, many disturbances which must be properly corrected, if accessible, in order to determine accurate surface temperatures:

- The infrared radiation, emitted by the ocean's surface, is slightly absorbed in the atmosphere by water vapor and other trace gases.
- As in the visible range, water has a small reflectivity of about 2–3% at low angles of incidence. With this level of fraction, the measurement of the sea surface temperature is influenced by the temperatures of the sky and clouds.
- Clouds must be carefully detected and screened since they hinder the view onto the ocean surface. This is not difficult for thick clouds which are not penetrated at all, but it is for thin, partly transparent clouds.

2.1.4 Light Sources

The simplest model for a light source is the *point light source*. Any other light source can be built from point light sources. The total power emitted by a light source is called the *radiation flux*, Θ. A surface element, dA, whose normal is inclined at an angle ε with the incoming light ray, and which is r distant from a point source, receives the illuminance E:

$$E = \frac{\Theta \cos \varepsilon}{4\pi r^2}. \tag{2.1}$$

The illuminance of a point light source decreases quadratically with distance. We can regard all light sources as point sources whose size on the image plane is smaller than the resolution of the camera system. The illuminance of extended light sources is independent of the distance from the camera. The quadratic decrease in the intensity of a small element in the source is compensated exactly by the quadratic increase in the numbers of elements per surface unit on the image plane.

2.1.5 Reflection

Basically, we can distinguish between two types of reflection; those directed from mirrors and diffusive reflection.

Mirror surfaces reflect the incident light only in one direction. Many objects, for example, metallic and water surfaces, reflect partly or entirely in this manner. Directed reflection becomes visible in images as mirror images or, if the scene is illuminated with direct light, in the form of *specular reflexes* (see also plate 3). Specular reflexes constitute a serious problem for image processing. They are not fixed to the object's surface, i.e., they cannot be regarded as a valid feature, but depend solely on the angles between light sources, the object surface, and the camera.

In contrast, an ideal diffusively reflecting surface, called a *Lambertian radiator*, scatters light in all directions equally. Diffusively reflecting surfaces, which are not Lambertian radiators, must be characterized by the angular dispersion of the reflected light intensity. Many surfaces such as painted metallic surfaces, show a mixed reflectivity; here radiation is reflected partly diffusively and partly directedly.

2.2 Image formation

Nearly all imaging techniques essentially project three-dimensional space in one way or the other onto a two-dimensional image plane. Thus basically imaging can be regarded as a projection from 3-D into 2-D space. The essential point is the loss of one coordinate which constitutes a severe loss of information. Because we unconsciously and constantly experience that the human visual system performs this task in real time, we might be

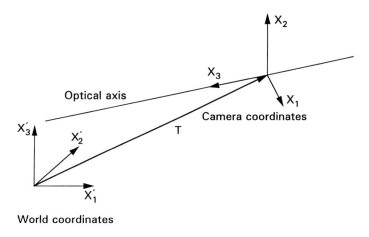

World coordinates

Figure 2.2: Illustration of world and camera coordinates.

tempted to think that the reconstruction of the three-dimensional world from two-dimensional images is quite a simple task. In this section, we analyze step by step the formation of an image from the three-dimensional world, and discover the complexity of the reconstruction task.

2.2.1 World and Camera Coordinates

The position of objects can be described in two different ways (figure 2.2). First, we can use a coordinate system which is related to the scene observed. These coordinates are called *world coordinates* and denoted as $\boldsymbol{X'} = (X_1', X_2', X_3')$. We use the convention that the X_1' and X_2' coordinates describe the horizontal and the X_3' the vertical positions, respectively. A second coordinate system, the *camera coordinates* $\boldsymbol{X} = (X_1, X_2, X_3)$, can be fixed to the camera observing the scene. The X_3 axis is aligned with the *optical axis* of the camera system (figure 2.2). Physicists are familiar with such considerations. It is common to discuss physical phenomena in different coordinate systems. In elementary mechanics, for example, motion is studied with respect to two observers, one at rest, the other moving with the object.

Transition from world to camera coordinates can be described by a *translation* and a *rotation* term. First, we shift the origin of the world coordinate system to the origin of the camera coordinate system by the translation vector $\boldsymbol{T}$ (figure 2.2). Then we change the orientation of the shifted system by rotations about suitable axes so that it coincides with the camera coordinate system. Mathematically, translation can be described by vector subtraction and rotation by the multiplication of the coordinate vector with a matrix:

$$\boldsymbol{X} = \boldsymbol{R}(\boldsymbol{X'} - \boldsymbol{T}). \tag{2.2}$$

Rotation does not change the length or *norm* of the vectors. Then basic matrix algebra

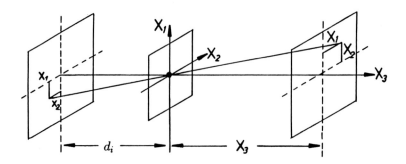

Figure 2.3: Image formation with a pinhole camera.

tells us that the matrix $\boldsymbol{R}$ must be orthogonal, i. e., it holds the condition

$$\boldsymbol{R}\boldsymbol{R}^T = \boldsymbol{I} \quad \text{or} \quad \sum_{m=1}^{3} r_{km}r_{lm} = \delta_{kl} \tag{2.3}$$

where $\boldsymbol{I}$ denotes the identity matrix, whose elements are one and zero on diagonal and non-diagonal positions, respectively. The orthogonality condition leaves three matrix elements independent out of nine. Unfortunately, the relationship between the matrix elements and sets of three such parameters turns out to be quite complex and nonlinear. A widely used set of parameters are the three Eulerian rotation angles. Any rotation can be decomposed into three consecutive rotations about the axes of the coordinate system with these angles. A more detailed discussion can be found in textbooks of classical mechanics such as *Goldstein* [1980]. Rotation and translation together constitute six independent parameters describing the general transition from world to camera coordinates.

2.2.2   Pinhole Camera Model: Perspective Projection

Once we know the camera coordinates of the scene, we can study the optical system of the camera. First we take the simplest possible camera, the *pinhole camera*. The imaging element of this camera is an infinitesimal small hole (figure 2.3). Only the light ray coming from a point of the object at (X_1, X_2, X_3) which passes through this hole meets the image plane at $(x_1, x_2, -d_i)$. Through this condition an image of the object is formed on the image plane. The relationship between the 3-D world and the 2-D *image coordinates* (x_1, x_2) is given by

$$x_1 = -\frac{d_i X_1}{X_3}, \quad x_2 = -\frac{d_i X_2}{X_3}. \tag{2.4}$$

The two world coordinates parallel to the image plane are scaled by the factor d_i/X_3. Therefore, the image coordinates (x_1, x_2) contain only ratios of world coordinates, from which neither the distance nor the true size of an object can be inferred.

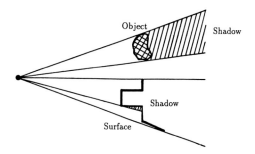

Figure 2.4: Occlusion of more distant objects and surfaces by perspective projection.

A straight line in the world space is projected onto a straight line at the image plane. This important feature can be proved by a simple geometric consideration. All light rays emitted from a straight line pass through the pinhole. Consequently they all lie on a plane which is spanned by the straight line and the pinhole. This plane intersects with the image plane in a straight line.

All object points on a ray through the pinhole are projected onto a single point in the image plane. In a scene with several transparent objects, the objects are projected onto each other. Then we cannot infer the three dimensional structure of the scene at all. We may not even be able to recognize the shape of individual objects. This example demonstrates how much information is lost by projection of a 3-D scene onto a 2-D image plane.

Most natural scenes, however, contain opaque objects. Here the observed 3-D space is essentially reduced to 2-D surfaces. These surfaces can be described by two two-dimensional functions $g(x_1, x_2)$ and $X_3(x_1, x_2)$ instead of the general description of a 3-D scalar gray value image $g(X_1, X_2, X_3)$. A surface in space is completely projected onto the image plane provided that not more than one point of the surface lies on the same ray through the pinhole. If this condition is not met, parts of the surface remain invisible. This effect is called *occlusion*. The occluded 3-D space can be made visible if we put a point light source at the position of the pinhole (figure 2.4). Then the invisible parts of the scene lie in the shadow of those objects which are closer to the camera.

As long as we can exclude occlusion, we only need the depth map $X_3(x_1, x_2)$ to reconstruct the 3-D shape of a scene completely. One way to produce it — which is also used by our visual system — is by stereo imaging, i. e., the observation of the scene with two sensors from different points of view (section 2.2.9).

Imaging with a pinhole camera is essentially a *perspective projection*, since all rays must pass through one central point, the pinhole. Thus the pinhole camera model is very similar to the imaging with penetrating rays, as X-rays, emitted from a point source (figure 2.5). In this case, the object lies between the central point and the image plane.

The projection equation corresponds to (2.4) except for the sign:

$$(X_1, X_2, X_3) \longmapsto (x_1, x_2) = \left(\frac{d_i X_1}{X_3}, \frac{d_i X_2}{X_3} \right). \tag{2.5}$$

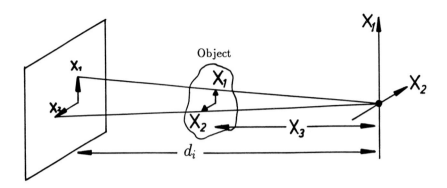

Figure 2.5: Perspective projection with X-rays.

Here *generalized* image coordinates are used. The image coordinates are divided by the image distance d_i

$$\frac{x_1}{d_i} \to x_1, \quad \frac{x_2}{d_i} \to x_2. \tag{2.6}$$

Generalized image coordinates are dimensionless. They are equal to the tangent of the angle with respect to the optical axis of the system under which the object is observed. These coordinates explicitly take the limitations of the projection onto the image plane into account. From these coordinates, we cannot infer absolute positions but know only the angle under which the object is projected onto the image plane. The same coordinates are used in astronomy. The general projection equation of perspective projection (2.5) then reduces to

$$\boldsymbol{X} = (X_1, X_2, X_3) \longmapsto \boldsymbol{x} = \left(\frac{X_1}{X_3}, \frac{X_2}{X_3}\right). \tag{2.7}$$

We will use this simplified projection equation in all further considerations. For optical imaging, we just have to include a minus sign or, if speaking geometrically, reflect the image at the origin of the coordinate system.

Perspective projection is only a model for imaging. It is a rather good approximation for X-ray imaging since the focus, i.e., the extension of the X-ray source, can be made quite small. However, it is less good for optical imaging. Real lens systems only image a certain distance range sharply onto the image plane because of the non-zero aperture. The images are degraded by lens aberrations causing limited sharpness and geometrical distortions. Even if these effects can be neglected, the sharpness of the images is limited by diffraction of the electromagnetic waves at the aperture of the lens. We will discuss these effects in further sections.

2.2.3   Homogeneous Coordinates

In computer graphics, the elegant formalism of *homogeneous coordinates* [*Maxwell*, 1951; *Watt*, 1989] is used to describe all the transformations we have discussed so far, i.e., translation, rotation, and perspective projection, with a matrix vector multiplication.

This formalism is significant, since the whole image formation process can be expressed in a single 4×4 matrix.

Homogeneous coordinates are a four-component row vector $\boldsymbol{X'} = (tX_1', tX_2', tX_3', t)$, from which the ordinary three-dimensional coordinates are obtained by dividing the first three components of the homogeneous coordinates by the fourth. Any arbitrary transformation can be obtained by postmultiplying the homogeneous coordinates with a 4×4 matrix $\boldsymbol{M}$. In particular, we can obtain the image coordinates $\boldsymbol{x} = (sx_1, sx_2, sx_3, s)$ by

$$\boldsymbol{x} = \boldsymbol{X'M}. \tag{2.8}$$

Since matrix multiplication is associative, we can view the matrix $\boldsymbol{M}$ as composed of many transformation matrices, performing such elementary transformations as translation, rotation around a coordinate axis, perspective projection, and scaling. The transformation matrices for the elementary transformations are readily derived:

$$\boldsymbol{T} = \begin{bmatrix} 1 & 0 & 0 & 0 \\ 0 & 1 & 0 & 0 \\ 0 & 0 & 1 & 0 \\ -T_1 & -T_2 & -T_3 & 1 \end{bmatrix} \quad \text{Translation by } (-T_1, -T_2, -T_3)$$

$$\boldsymbol{R}_x = \begin{bmatrix} 1 & 0 & 0 & 0 \\ 0 & \cos\Theta & \sin\Theta & 0 \\ 0 & -\sin\Theta & \cos\Theta & 0 \\ 0 & 0 & 0 & 1 \end{bmatrix} \quad \text{Rotation about } X_3 \text{ axis by } \Theta$$

$$\boldsymbol{R}_y = \begin{bmatrix} \cos\varphi & 0 & \sin\varphi & 0 \\ 0 & 1 & 0 & 0 \\ -\sin\varphi & 0 & \cos\varphi & 0 \\ 0 & 0 & 0 & 1 \end{bmatrix} \quad \text{Rotation about } X_2 \text{ axis by } \varphi$$

$$\boldsymbol{R}_z = \begin{bmatrix} \cos\psi & \sin\psi & 0 & 0 \\ -\sin\psi & \cos\psi & 0 & 0 \\ 0 & 0 & 1 & 0 \\ 0 & 0 & 0 & 1 \end{bmatrix} \quad \text{Rotation about } X_1 \text{ axis by } \psi$$

$$\boldsymbol{S} = \begin{bmatrix} s_1 & 0 & 0 & 0 \\ 0 & s_2 & 0 & 0 \\ 0 & 0 & s_3 & 0 \\ 0 & 0 & 0 & 1 \end{bmatrix} \quad \text{Scaling}$$

$$\boldsymbol{P} = \begin{bmatrix} 1 & 0 & 0 & 0 \\ 0 & 1 & 0 & 0 \\ 0 & 0 & 1 & -1/d_i \\ 0 & 0 & 0 & 1 \end{bmatrix} \quad \text{Perspective projection}$$

$$\tag{2.9}$$

Perspective projection is formulated slightly differently from the definition in (2.7). Postmultiplication of the homogeneous vector $\boldsymbol{X} = (tX_1, tX_2, tX_3, t)$ with $\boldsymbol{P}$ yields

$$\left(tX_1, tX_2, tX_3, t\frac{d_i - X_3}{d_i}\right), \tag{2.10}$$

from which we obtain the image coordinates by division through the fourth coordinate

$$(x_1, x_2) = \left(X_1 \frac{d_i}{d_i - X_3}, X_2 \frac{d_i}{d_i - X_3} \right). \qquad (2.11)$$

From this equation we can see that the image plane is positioned at the origin, since if $X_3 = 0$, both image and world coordinates are identical. The center of projection has been shifted to $(0, 0, -d_i)$.

Complete transformations from world coordinates to image coordinates can be composed of these elementary matrices. *Strat* [1984] proposed the following decomposition:

$$M = T R_x R_y R_z P S C. \qquad (2.12)$$

The scaling S and cropping (translation) C are transformations taking place in the two-dimensional image plane. *Strat* [1984] shows how the complete transformation parameters from camera to world coordinates can be determined in a noniterative way from a set of calibration points whose positions in the space is exactly known. In this way an absolute calibration of the camera parameters including position, orientation, piercing point (of the optical axis), and focal length can be obtained.

2.2.4   Geometric Distortion

A real optical system causes deviations from a perfect perspective projection. The most obvious distortions can be observed with simple spheric lenses as barrel- or cushion-shaped images of squares. Even with a corrected lens system these effects are not completely suppressed. This type of distortion can easily be understood by considerations of symmetry. Since lens systems show a cylinder symmetry, concentric circles only experience a distortion in the radius. This distortion can be approximated by

$$x' = \frac{x}{1 + k_3 |x|^2}. \qquad (2.13)$$

Depending on whether k_3 is positive or negative, barrel- and cushion shaped distortions in the images of squares will be observed. Commercial TV lenses show a radial deviation of several image points (pixels) at the edge of the sensor. If the distortion is corrected with (2.13), the residual error is less than 0.06 image points [*Lenz*, 1987]. This high degree of correction, together with the geometric stability of modern CCD-sensors, accounts for subpixel accuracy in distance and area measurements without using expensive special lenses.

Lenz [1988] discusses further details which influence the geometrical accuracy of CCD sensors. Reconstruction of the depth of objects from stereo images (section 2.2.9) also requires careful consideration of the geometrical distortions of the camera lenses.

Distortions also occur if non-planar surfaces are projected onto the image plane. These distortions prevail in satellite and aerial imagery. Thus correction of geometric distortion in images is a basic topic in remote sensing and photogrammetry [*Richards*, 1986]. Accurate correction of the geometrical distortions requires shifting of image points by fractions of the distance of two image points. We will deal with this problem later in section 8.2.4 after we have worked out the knowledge necessary to handle it properly.

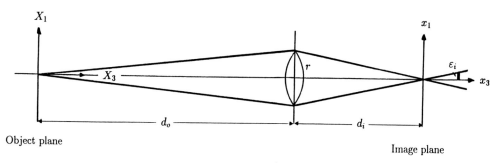

Object plane

Image plane

Figure 2.6: Illustration of the depth of focus of a thin lens.

2.2.5 Depth of Focus

The abstract model of a pinhole camera images every object, independent of its distance from the camera, without any loss of sharpness onto the image plane. A real optical system can only image objects at a certain distance from the camera onto the image plane. The further away the object is located from this plane, the less sharp is its image. For practical purposes, it is useful to define a range of distances as the *depth of focus* in which the unsharpness remains under a certain threshold. In this section we will consider the depth of focus within the range of geometrical optics, i.e., with a perfect lens system and no limits of sharpness due to diffraction.

First, we can conclude that the replacement of the pinhole by a lens does not change the principal imaging geometry. Although a point is no longer imaged onto a point, but — assuming a circular aperture — onto a small disc, (2.4) still holds for the center of the disc.

The depth of focus is illustrated in figure 2.6. We have placed the origins of the camera and image coordinate systems on the object and image plane, respectively. If the object distance is increasing, the corresponding image plane lies closer to the lens. The image of a point smears to a disc with radius ε at the original image plane. The relation between ε and the shift of the object plane X_3 can be calculated using the image equation for a thin lens

$$\frac{1}{f} = \frac{1}{d_o} + \frac{1}{d_i},$$
(2.14)

where d_o and d_i are the distance of the object and image from the lens, respectively. In case of an out-of-focus object, $d'_o = d_o + X_3$ and $d'_i = d_i - x_3$, a first order Taylor expansion in X_3 and x_3 (assuming that $X_3 \ll d_o$ and $x_3 \ll d_i$) yields

$$x_3 \approx \frac{d_i^2}{d_o^2} X_3.$$
(2.15)

Introducing the *f-number* as the ratio of the focal length f to the diameter of the lens aperture $2r$

$$n_f = \frac{f}{2r}$$
(2.16)

and using $\varepsilon \approx (r/d_i)x_3$ and (2.14), we can express the depth of focus X_3 as a function of the allowed radius of unsharpness ε:

$$X_3 \approx \frac{2n_f d_o (d_o - f)}{f^2} \varepsilon = \frac{2n_f d_o^2}{f d_i} \varepsilon. \tag{2.17}$$

The depth of focus is directly proportional to the f-number of the lens. The limit of $n_f \to \infty$ corresponds to the pinhole camera with an unlimited depth of focus.

We illustrate the depth of focus further with some practical examples.

- *Distant objects, $d_o \gg f$*

  This is the "normal" situation in photography. For this condition equation (2.17) approximately yields

$$X_3 \approx 2n_f \varepsilon \frac{d_o^2}{f^2}. \tag{2.18}$$

The depth of focus is inversely proportional to the square of the focal length. Consequently, smaller focal lengths result — despite the smaller image size — in a larger depth of focus. This fact is well known in photography. Tele lenses and large-image-size cameras have a considerably lower depth of focus than wide-angle lenses and small-image-size cameras. A typical high resolution CCD camera has 800×590 sensor elements, which are $11.5 \times 10 \, \mu m$ in size. Thus we can allow for a radius of the unsharpness disc of $5 \, \mu m$. Assuming a lens with an f-number of 2 and a focal length of $15 \, mm$, we have a depth of focus of $\pm \, 0.2 \, m$ at an object distance of $1.5 \, m$. This example illustrates that even with this small f-number and the relative low distance, we may obtain a large depth of focus.

- *Object-image scale 1:1, $d_o \approx d_i \approx 2f$*

  The image and object are of the same size. The depth of focus,

$$X_3 \approx 4n_f \varepsilon, \tag{2.19}$$

then does not depend on the focal length, and is only in the order of the unsharpness ε. With the same f-number of 2 as in the first example, we obtain a depth of focus of only $40 \, \mu m$. Only a small object zone can be imaged sharply.

- *Microscopy $d_o \approx f$, $d_i \gg f$*

  The depth of focus is even smaller in microscopy where the objects are significantly enlarged, since it is then given by

$$X_3 \approx \frac{2n_f \varepsilon d_o}{d_i}. \tag{2.20}$$

With a 50-fold enlargement, i.e., $d_i / d_o = 50$ and $n_f = 1$, we yield the extreme low depth of focus of only $0.2 \, \mu m$.

In conclusion, we can distinguish between two different types of imaging systems: with distant objects, we obtain a sufficient depth of focus to image a 3-D scene with considerable depth variations, without significant losses in sharpness. In microscopy, however, we only can focus a tiny depth zone of an object. Thus we can observe cross sections of an object.

This simple fact has critical consequences for 3-D reconstruction. In microscopy, we have no chance at all to reconstruct the 3-D structure of an object from a single image. Essentially, it contains information of only one depth, which is, however, distorted by

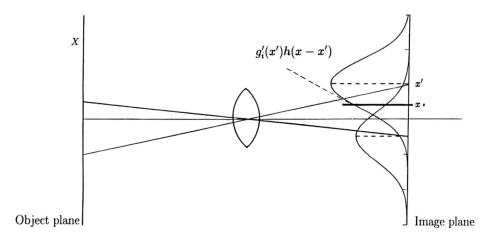

Figure 2.7: Image formation by integration of the point spread function $h(x)$. A point at X' in the object plane results in an intensity distribution with a maximum at the corresponding point x' on the image plane. At a point x on the image plane, the contributions from all points x', i.e., $g'_i(x')h(x-x')$, must be integrated.

unsharp contours from other depth ranges. Consequently, 3-D reconstruction requires a set of images, focused on different depths. Such an image sequence is called a *focus series* and already constitutes a 3-D dimensional image. Reconstruction of the 3-D object requires eliminating of any distortions caused by unsharp contours from defocused image planes which considerably limit the image quality.

The 3-D shape of distant objects and X-ray imaging cannot be reconstructed with this technique because of the large depth of focus. We will learn later in sections 2.2.10 and 13.3 how we can reconstruct the 3-D structure by projections from different directions.

2.2.6 3-D Point Spread Function

Previously it was seen that a point in the 3-D object space is not imaged onto a point in the image space but onto a more or less extended area with varying intensities. Obviously, the function which describes the imaging of a point is an essential feature of the imaging system which is called the *point spread function*, abbreviated as PSF. We assume that the PSF is not position dependent. Then the system is called *shift invariant*.

If we know the PSF, we can calculate how any arbitrary 3-D object will be imaged. To perform this operation, we think of the object to be decomposed into single points. Figure 2.7 illustrates this process. A point X' at the object plane is projected onto the image plane with an intensity distribution corresponding to the point spread function h. With $g'_i(\boldsymbol{x}')$ we denote the intensity values at the object plane $g'_o(\boldsymbol{X}')$ projected onto the image plane but without any defects through the imaging. Then the intensity of a point $\boldsymbol{x}$ at the image plane is computed by integrating the contributions from the point spread functions which have their maximums at x' (figure 2.7)

$$g_i(x) = \int\limits_{-\infty}^{\infty} \mathrm{d}^2 x' \; g_i'(x') h(x - x') = (g_i' * h)(x).\tag{2.21}$$

The operation in (2.21) is known as a *convolution*. Convolutions play an essential role in image processing. Convolutions are not only involved in image formation but also in many image processing operations. In case of image formation, a convolution obviously "smears" an image. Where points and lines are blurred, the resolution is reduced.

This effect of convolutions can be most easily demonstrated with image structures which show periodic gray value variations. As long as the repetition length, the *wavelength*, of this structure is larger than the width of the PSF, it will experience no significant changes. As the wavelengths decrease, however, the amplitude of the gray value variations will start to decrease. Fine structures will finally be smeared out to such an extent that they are no longer visible. These considerations emphasize the important role of periodic structures and lead naturally to the introduction of the *Fourier transform* which decomposes an image into the periodic gray value variations it contains.

In the following, it is assumed that the reader is familiar with the basic properties of the Fourier transform. (Appendix A.2 gives a brief summary with references for further reading.)

Previous considerations showed that formation of a two-dimensional image on the image plane is described entirely by its PSF. In the following we will extend this concept to three dimensions and explicitly calculate the point spread function within the limit of geometrical optics, i.e., with a perfect lens system and no diffraction. This approach is motivated by the need to understand three-dimensional imaging, especially in microscopy, i.e., how a point in the 3-D object space is imaged not only onto a 2-D image plane but onto a 3-D image space.

First, we consider how a fixed point in the object space is projected into the image space. From figure 2.6 we infer that the radius of the unsharpness disk is given by

$$\varepsilon_i = \frac{r x_3}{d_i}.\tag{2.22}$$

The index i of ε indicates the image space. Then we replace the radius of the aperture r by the maximum angle under which the lens collects light from the point considered and obtain

$$\varepsilon_i = \frac{d_o}{d_i} x_3 \tan \alpha.\tag{2.23}$$

This equation gives us the edge of the PSF in the image space. It is a double cone with the x_3 axis in the center. The tips of both the cones meet in the origin. Outside of the two cones, the PSF is zero. Inside the cone, we can infer the intensity from the conservation of the radiation energy. Since the radius of the cone increases linearly with the distance to the plane of focus, the intensity within the cone decreases quadratically. Thus the PSF $h_i(x)$ in the image space is given by

$$h_i(x) = \frac{I_0}{\pi(\frac{d_o}{d_i} x_3 \tan \alpha)^2} \Pi\left(\frac{(x_1^2 + x_2^2)^{1/2}}{2\frac{d_o}{d_i} x_3 \tan \alpha}\right) = \frac{I_0}{\pi(\frac{d_o}{d_i} z \tan \alpha)^2} \Pi\left(\frac{r}{2\frac{d_o}{d_i} z \tan \alpha}\right).\tag{2.24}$$

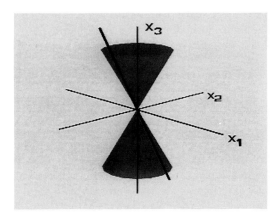

Figure 2.8: 3-D PSF of optical imaging with a lens, backprojected into the object space. Lens aberrations and diffraction effects are neglected.

I_0 is the light intensity collected by the lens from the point; Π is the *box function* which is defined as

$$\Pi(x) = \left\{ \begin{array}{ll} 1 & |x| \le 1/2 \\ 0 & \text{otherwise} \end{array} \right. . \tag{2.25}$$

The last expression in (2.24) is written in cylinder coordinates (r, ϕ, z) to take the rotation symmetry of the PSF about the x_3 axis into account.

In a second step, we discuss what the PSF in the image space refers to in the object space, since we are interested in how the effects of the imaging are projected back into the object space. We have to consider two effects. First, the image, and thus also ε, are larger than the object by the factor d_i/d_o. Second, we must find the planes in object and image space corresponding to each other. This problem has already been solved in section 2.2.5. Equation (2.15) relates the image to the camera coordinates. In effect, the backprojected radius of the unsharpness disk, ϵ_o, is given by

$$\varepsilon_o = X_3 \tan \alpha, \tag{2.26}$$

and the PSF, backprojected into the object space, by

$$h_o(\boldsymbol{X}) = \frac{I_0}{\pi (X_3 \tan \alpha)^2} \Pi \left(\frac{(X_1^2 + X_2^2)^{1/2}}{2 X_3 \tan \alpha} \right) = \frac{I_0}{\pi (Z \tan \alpha)^2} \Pi \left(\frac{R}{2 Z \tan \alpha} \right). \tag{2.27}$$

The double cone of the PSF backprojected into the object space, shows the same opening angle as the lens (figure 2.8).

2.2.7 Optical Transfer Function

Convolution with the PSF in the space domain is a quite complex operation. In Fourier space, however, it is performed as a multiplication of complex numbers. In particular, convolution of the 3-D object $g'_o(\boldsymbol{X})$ with the PSF $h_o(\boldsymbol{X})$ corresponds in Fourier space to a multiplication of the Fourier transformed object $\hat{g}'_o(\boldsymbol{k})$ with the Fourier transformed PSF, the *optical transfer function* or OTF $\hat{h}_o(\boldsymbol{k})$. In this section, we consider the optical transfer function in the object space, i. e., we project the imaged object back into the object space. Then the image formation can be described by:

$$
\begin{array}{ccccc}
 & \text{Imaged object} & & \text{Imaging} & \text{Object} \\
\text{Object space} & g_o(\boldsymbol{X}) & = & h_o(\boldsymbol{X}) & * & g_o'(\boldsymbol{X}) \\
 & \updownarrow & & \updownarrow & \updownarrow & (2.28) \\
\text{Fourier space} & \hat{g}_o(\boldsymbol{k}) & = & \hat{h}_o(\boldsymbol{k}) & \cdot & \hat{g}_o'(\boldsymbol{k}).
\end{array}
$$

Fourier transform pairs are denoted by the symbol ∘—● . This correspondence means that we can describe optical imaging either with the point spread function or the optical transfer function. Both descriptions are complete. As with the PSF, the OTF has an illustrative meaning. Since the Fourier transform decomposes an object into the periodic structures it contains, the OTF tells us how these periodic structures are changed by the optical imaging process. An OTF of 1 for a particular wavelength means that this periodic structure is not affected at all. If the OTF is 0, it completely disappears. For values between 0 and 1 it is attenuated correspondingly. Since the OTF is a complex figure, not only the amplitude of a periodic structure can be changed but also its phase.

Calculation of the OTF
Direct calculation of the OTF is complicated. Here several features of the Fourier transform are used, especially the linearity and separability, to decompose the PSF into suitable functions which can be transformed more easily. Two possibilities are demonstrated. They are also more generally instructive, since they illustrate some important features of the Fourier transform.

First, some remarks concerning the nomenclature are necessary. Unfortunately, two definitions of the wave number k are in use. In spectroscopy and mineralogy, k is defined as the reciprocal wavelength λ: $k = 1/\lambda$, i.e., it denotes the number of the wavelengths per unit length. In physics, however, the factor 2π is included: $k = 2\pi/\lambda$. Both definitions have disadvantages and advantages. We will use both definitions and denote them as follows: $k = 1/\lambda$ and $k = 2\pi/\lambda$. The corresponding quantities for time series are more familiar: the frequency $\nu = 1/T$ and the circular frequency $\omega = 2\pi/T$, where T is the period of oscillation.

The first method to calculate the OTF decomposes the PSF into a bundle of δ lines intersecting at the origin of the coordinate system. They are equally distributed in the cross section of the double cone (figure 2.9a). We can think of each δ line as being one light ray. Without further calculations, we know that this decomposition gives the correct quadratic decrease in the PSF, because the same number of δ lines intersect a quadratically increasing area. The Fourier transform of a δ line is a δ plane which is perpendicular to the line (see appendix A.2). Thus the OTF is composed of a bundle of δ planes. They intersect the $k_1 k_2$ plane at a line through the origin of the k space under an angle of at most α. Since Fourier transform preserves rotational symmetry, the OTF is also rotationally symmetric to the k_3 axis. The OTF fills the whole Fourier space except for a double cone with an angle of $\pi/2 - \alpha$. In this sector the OTF is zero. The exact values of the OTF in the non-zero part are difficult to obtain with this decomposition method. We will infer it with another approach which is based on the

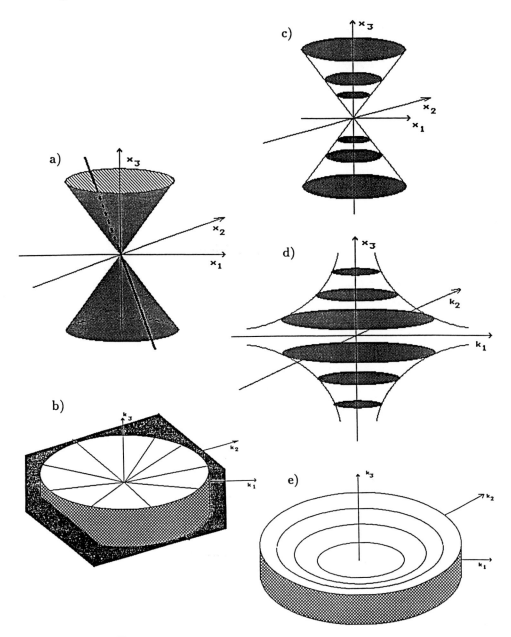

Figure 2.9: Calculation of the 3-D OTF from the 3-D PSF.

separability of the Fourier transform. We think of the double cone as layers of disks with varying radii which increase with $|x_3|$ (figure 2.9c). In the first step, we perform the Fourier transform only in the x_1x_2 plane. This transformation yields a function with two coordinates in the k space and one in the x space, (k_1, k_2, x_3), respectively (q, φ, z) in cylinder coordinates. Since the PSF (2.27) depends only on r (rotational symmetry around the z axis), the two-dimensional Fourier transform conforms with a one-dimensional *Hankel transform of zero order* [*Bracewell*, 1965]:

$$h(r, z) \quad = \quad \frac{I_0}{\pi (z \tan \alpha)^2} \Pi\left(\frac{r}{2z \tan \alpha}\right)$$

$$\updownarrow$$

$$\tag{2.29}$$

$$h'(q, z) \quad = \quad I_0 \frac{J_1(2\pi z q \tan \alpha)}{\pi z q \tan \alpha}.$$

The Fourier transform of the disk thus results in a function which contains the *Bessel function* J_1.

As a second step, we perform the missing one-dimensional Fourier transform in the z direction. Equation (2.29) shows that $h'(q, z)$ is also a Bessel function in z. This time, however, the Fourier transform is one-dimensional. Thus we obtain no disk function but

$$\frac{J_1(2\pi x)}{x} \quad \circ\!\!-\!\!\bullet \quad 2\left(1 - k^2\right)^{1/2} \Pi\left(\frac{k}{2}\right). \tag{2.30}$$

If we finally apply the *similarity theorem* of the Fourier transform

$$f(x) \quad \circ\!\!-\!\!\bullet \quad \hat{f}(k) \quad \rightsquigarrow$$

$$\tag{2.31}$$

$$f(ax) \quad \circ\!\!-\!\!\bullet \quad \frac{1}{|a|} \hat{f}\left(\frac{k}{a}\right),$$

we obtain

$$\hat{h}(q, k_3) = \frac{2I_0}{\pi |q \tan \alpha|} \left(1 - \frac{k_3^2}{q^2 \tan^2 \alpha}\right)^{1/2} \Pi\left(\frac{k_3}{2q \tan \alpha}\right). \tag{2.32}$$

Interpretation of the OTF

A large part of the OTF is zero. This means that spatial structures with the corresponding directions and wavelengths completely disappear. This is particularly the case for all structures in the z direction, i. e., perpendicularly to the image plane. Such structures get completely lost and cannot be reconstructed without additional knowledge.

3-D structures can only be seen if they also contain structures parallel to the image plane. It is, for example, possible to resolve points or lines which lie above each other. We can explain this in the x space as well as in the k space. The PSF blurs the points and lines, but they can still be distinguished if they are not too close to each other. Points or lines are extended objects in Fourier space, i. e., a constant or a plane. Such extended objects partly coincide with the non-zero parts of the OTF and thus will not vanish entirely. Periodic structures up to an angle of α to the k_1k_2 plane, which just corresponds to the opening angle of the lens, are not eliminated by the OTF. Intuitively, we can say that we are able to recognize all 3-D structures in which we actually can look into. All we need is at least one ray which is perpendicular to the structure.

Another important property of the OTF emerges which has not yet been considered so far. The OTF is inversely proportional to the radial wave number q (2.32). Consequently, the contrast of a periodic structure is attenuated proportionally to its wave number. Since this property of the OTF is valid for all optical imaging — as in the human visual system — the question arises why we can see fine structures at all.

The answer lies in a closer examination of the geometrical structure of the objects observed. Normally, we only see the surfaces of objects, i.e., we do not observe real 3-D objects but only 2-D surface structures. If we image a 2-D surface onto a 2-D image plane, the PSF also reduces to a 2-D function. Mathematically, this means a multiplication of the PSF with a δ plane parallel to the observed surface. Consequently, the 2-D PSF is now given by the unsharpness disk corresponding to the distance of the surface from the lens. The convolution with the 2-D PSF preserves the intensity of all structures with wavelengths larger than the disk.

We arrive at the same conclusion in Fourier space. Multiplication of the 3-D PSF with a δ plane in the x space corresponds to a convolution of the 3-D OTF with a δ line perpendicular to the plane, i.e., an integration in the corresponding direction. If we integrate the 3-D OTF along the k coordinate, we actually get a constant independent of the radial wave number q:

$$\frac{2I_0}{\pi} \int\limits_{-q\tan\alpha}^{q\tan\alpha} \mathrm{d}z' \, \frac{1}{|q\tan\alpha|} \left[1 - \left(\frac{z'}{q\tan\alpha} \right)^2 \right]^{1/2} = I_0. \tag{2.33}$$

(To solve the integral, we substitute $z'' = qz'\tan\alpha$; then we yield an integral over a half unit circle.)

In conclusion, the OTF for surface structures is independent of the wave number. However, for volume structures, we still have the problem of the decrease of the OTF with the radial wave number. Observing such structures by eye or with a camera, we will not be able to observe fine structures. Real 3-D, that is transparent objects, are much more common in scientific applications than in natural scenes. One prominent example is the wide area of flow visualization.

2.2.8 Cross Sectional Imaging

Because of the problems in imaging real 3-D structures, many scientific applications observe de facto 2-D objects. In microscopy, only flat objects or thin slits are used whose thickness lies within the narrow depth of focus of microscopes (see section 2.2.5). In a similar manner, mineralogists fabricate thin slits from mineral probes.

In flow visualization, it is also possible to observe cross sections of flow fields by proper illumination. Only a thin sheet is illuminated and observed with a camera perpendicularly to the light sheet. We have already discussed such a technique in section 1.4 (see also plate 2d). An example for flow visualization is shown in plate 4 [Wierzimok et al., 1989]. Here a thin vertical zone is illuminated. The flow is made

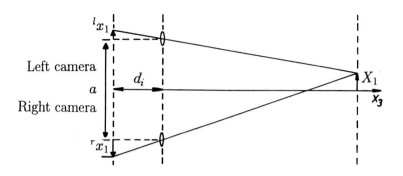

Figure 2.10: A stereo camera setup.

visible by small floating particles. Because of the illumination time of 40 ms, they appear as small streak lines. Twelve images of a sequence are superposed on this image. The streaks from the individual images are shown in a different color. The influence of the orbital motions of the waves on the flow field is clearly visible and increases towards the surface of the water.

All these techniques basically observe 2-D cross sections of 3-D objects. They allow for a proper imaging of the cross section — which would otherwise not be possible — but with a complete loss of information in the third dimension.

2.2.9 Stereoscopy

Observation of a scene from two different points of view allows the distance of objects to be determined. A setup with two imaging sensors is called a *stereo system*. In this way, many biological visual systems perform depth perception. Figure 2.10 illustrates how the depth can be determined from a stereo camera setup. Two cameras are placed close to each other with parallel optical axes. The distance vector a between the two optical axes is called the *stereoscopic basis*.

An object will be projected onto different positions of the image plane because it is viewed under slightly different angles. The difference in the position is denoted as the *parallax, p*. It is easily calculated from figure 2.10:

$$p = {}^r x_1 - {}^l x_1 = d_i \frac{X_1 + a/2}{X_3} - d_i \frac{X_1 - a/2}{X_3} = a \frac{d_i}{X_3}. \tag{2.34}$$

(Here we do not use generalized image coordinates; see section 2.2.2.) The parallax is inversely proportional to the distance X_3 of the object (zero for an object at infinity) and is directly proportional to the stereoscopic basis and the focal length of the cameras ($d_i \approx f$ for distant objects). In my research group, we use stereo imaging to observe the spatial structure of small-scale water surface waves on the ocean surface. The stereo system has a stereoscopic basis of 200 mm; the focal length of the lenses is 100 mm. With these figures, we calculate from (2.34) that the change in the parallax is about one sensor element of the CCD camera per 1 cm height change at a distance of 4 m. A stereo image taken with this system is shown in plate 6.

The parallax is a vector parallel to the stereoscopic basis a. On the one side, this has the advantage that if the two cameras are exactly orientated we know the direction of the parallax beforehand. On the other side, we cannot calculate the parallax in all cases. If an image sector does not show gray value changes in the direction of the stereo basis, then we cannot determine the parallax. This problem is a special case of the so-called *aperture problem* which occurs also in motion determination and will be discussed in detail in section 14.1.2.

In stereo imaging, this problem can partly be overcome by using a third camera [*Pietikäinen and Harwood*, 1986]. The three images result in the three stereo bases which lie in different directions. As long as there are gray value changes in the images, we can determine the parallax from at least two stereo bases.

Stereo images can be viewed with different methods. First, the left and right stereo image can be represented in one image, if one is shown in red and the other in green. The viewer uses a spectacle with a red filter for the right, and a green filter for the left eye. In this way, the right eye observes only the green, and the left eye only the red image. This method — called the *anaglyph method* — has the disadvantage that no color images can be used. However, this method needs no special hardware, can be projected, shown on any RGB monitor, or be printed out with standard printers. The stereo image shown in plate 6 is presented in this way.

Vertical stereoscopy also allows for the viewing of color stereo images [*Koschnitzke et al.*, 1983]. The two component images are arranged one upon the other. When viewed with a prism spectacle, which refracts the image of the right eye to the upper, and the image of the left eye to the lower image, both images fuse into a 3-D image.

Other stereoscopic imagers use dedicated hardware. A common principle is to show the left and right stereo image in fast alternation on a monitor. Synchronously, the polarization direction of the screen is switched. The viewer wears a polarization spectacle which filters the correct images out for the left and right eye.

However, the anaglyph method has the largest potential for most applications, since it can be used with almost any image processing workstation, the only additional piece of hardware needed being the red-green spectacle. A stimulating overview on scientific and technical applications of stereo images is given by *Lorenz* [1985].

2.2.10 Tomography

Tomographic methods do not generate a 3-D image of an object directly, but allow reconstruction of the three-dimensional shape of objects using suitable methods. Tomographic methods can be thought as an extension of stereoscopy. With stereoscopy the depth of surfaces is only inferred, but not the 3-D shape of transparent objects. Intuitively, we may assume that it is necessary to view such an object from as many directions as possible.

Tomographic methods use radiation which penetrates an object from different directions. If we use a point source (figure 2.11b), we observe a perspective or *fan-beam projection* on the screen behind the object just as in optical imaging (section 2.2.2).

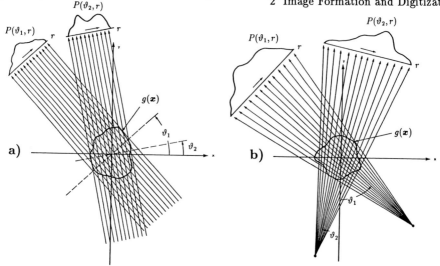

Figure 2.11: a) Parallel projection and b) fan-beam projection in tomography.

Such an image is taken from different projection directions by rotating the point source and the projection screen around the object. In a similar way, we can use parallel projection (figure 2.11a) which is easier to analyze but harder to realize. If the object absorbs the radiation, the intensity loss measured in the projection on the screen is proportional to the path length of the ray in the object. The 3-D shape of the object cannot be reconstructed from one projection. It is necessary to measure projections from all directions by turning the radiation source and projection screen around the object.

As in other imaging methods, tomography can make use of different interactions between matter and radiation. The most widespread application is transmission tomography. The imaging mechanism is by the absorption of radiation, e. g., X-rays. Other methods include emission tomography, reflection tomography, and time-of-flight tomography (especially with ultrasound), and complex imaging methods using nuclear magnetic resonance (NMR).

2.3 Digitization

2.3.1 Image matrix

Digitization means sampling the gray values at a discrete set of points, which can be represented by a matrix. Sampling may already be happening by use of the sensor which converts the collected photons into an electrical signal. In a conventional tube camera, the image is already sampled in lines, as an electron beam scans the imaging tube line by line. The number of lines per image is fixed by television standards (see appendix B). A CCD-camera already has a matrix of discrete sensors. Each sensor is a sampling point on a 2-D grid. The standard video signal is, however, an analog signal. Consequently, we lose the horizontal sampling again, as the signal from a line of sensors is converted into an analog signal. The problems associated with this conversion and redigitization are discussed in appendix B.

Mathematically, digitization is described as the mapping from a continuous function in $I\!R^2$ onto a matrix with a finite number of elements:

$$g(x_1, x_2) \stackrel{D}{\longmapsto} G_{m,n}$$
$$x_1, x_2 \in I\!R \qquad m, n \in Z \qquad . \tag{2.35}$$

The image matrix can take different geometries. Solid state physicists, mineralogists, and chemists are familiar with problems of this kind. Crystals show periodic 3-D patterns of the arrangements of their atoms, ions, or molecules which can be classified due to their symmetries. In 3-D this problem is quite complex. In 2-D we have fewer choices. For a two-dimensional grid of the image matrix, a rectangular basis cell is almost exclusively chosen. This is due to the fact that common image processing systems use square image matrices (typically 512×512), while the common image formats are rectangular (35 mm film: 24×36 mm; video images: length ratio 3:4).

Pixel or Pel
A point on the 2-D grid is called a *pixel* or *pel*. Both words are abbreviations of the word picture element. A pixel represents the gray value at the corresponding grid position. The position of the pixel is given in the common notation for matrices. The first index, m, denotes the position of the row, the second, n, the position of the column (figure 2.12a). If the image is represented by an $M \times N$ matrix, the index n runs from 0 to $N - 1$, the index m from 0 to $M - 1$. M gives the number of rows, N the number of columns.

Neighborhood Relations
On a rectangular grid, there are two possibilities to define neighboring pixels (figure 2.12b and c). We can either regard pixels as neighbors when they have a joint edge or when they have at least one joint corner. Thus four and eight neighbors exist, respectively, and we speak of a *4-neighborhood* or an *8-neighborhood*.

Both definitions are needed. This can be seen if we study *adjacent* objects. An object is called adjacent when we can reach any pixel in the object by walking to neighboring pixels. The black object shown in figure 2.12d is adjacent in the 8-neighborhood, but constitutes two objects in the 4-neighborhood. The white background, however, shows the same feature at the questionable position, where the object might either be adjacent or not. Thus the inconsistency arises, that we may have either two crossing adjacent objects in the 8-neigborhood or two separated objects in the 4-neighborhood. This difficulty can be overcome if we declare the objects as 4-neighboring and the background as 8-neighboring, or vice versa.

These complications are a special feature of the *rectangular grid*. They do not occur with a hexagonal grid (figure 2.12e). On a *hexagonal grid*, we can only define a *6-neighborhood*, since pixels which have a joint corner, but no joint edge, do not exist. Neighboring pixels have always one joint edge and two joint corners. Despite this advantage, hexagonal grids are hardly used in image processing, as the hardware does not support them.

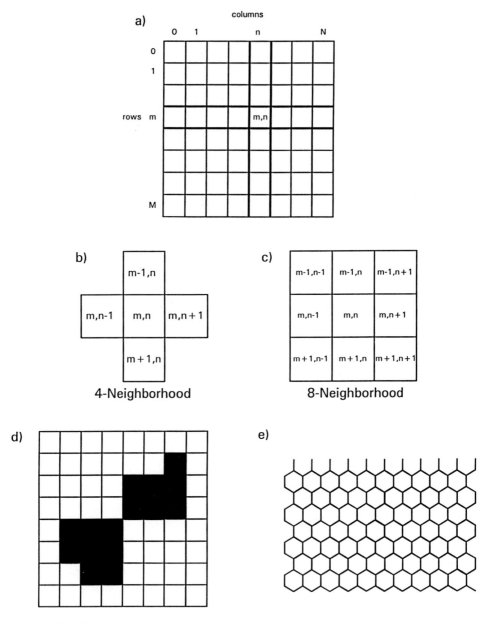

Figure 2.12: a) Each square in the image matrix represents a pixel; the pixel positions are numbered as denoted. b) 4-neighbors; c) 8-neighbors; d) Is the black object adjacent? e) A discrete hexagonal grid.

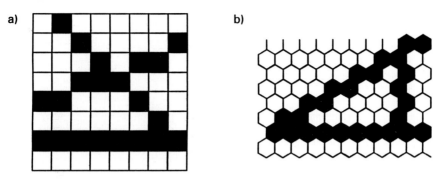

Figure 2.13: Straight lines on discrete geometries: a) square grid; b) hexagonal grid.

Discrete Geometry
The difficulties discussed in the previous section result from the fact that the image matrix constitutes a discrete structure where only points on the grid are defined. The discrete nature of the image matrix causes further problems.

Rotations on a discrete grid are defined only for certain angles, when all points of the rotated grid coincide with grid points. On a rectangular grid, only a rotation of 180° is possible, on a square grid in multiples of 90°, and on a hexagonal grid in multiples of 60°.

Equally difficult is the presentation of *straight lines*. Generally, a straight line can only be represented as a jagged, staircase-like sequence of pixels (figure 2.13). These difficulties lead not only to ugly images of lines and boundaries, but also force us to consider very carefully how we determine the direction of edges, the circumference and area of objects. In general that is how we handle all the questions concerning the *shape* of objects.

Problems related to the discrete nature of digitized images are common to both image processing and computer graphics. While the emphasis in computer graphics is on a better appearance of the images, e. g., to avoid jagged lines, researchers in image processing focus on accurate analysis of the form of objects. The basic knowledge worked out in this chapter will help to deal with both problems.

2.3.2 Moiré-Effect and Aliasing

Digitization of a continuous image constitutes an enormous loss of information, since we reduce the information about the gray values from an infinite to a finite number of points. Therefore the crucial question arises as to which condition we can ensure that the sampled points are a valid representation of the continuous image, i. e., there is no loss of information. We also want to know how we can reconstruct a continuous image from the sampled points. We will approach these questions by first studying the distortions which result from improper sampling.

Intuitively, it is clear that sampling leads to a reduction in resolution, i. e., structures of about the scale of the sampling distance and finer will be lost. It might come as a surprise to know that considerable distortions occur if we sample an image which

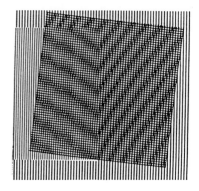

Figure 2.14: The Moiré-effect: the left image shows the original image, two linear grids with different grid constants. In the right image, digitization is simulated by overlaying a 2-D grid over part of the left image.

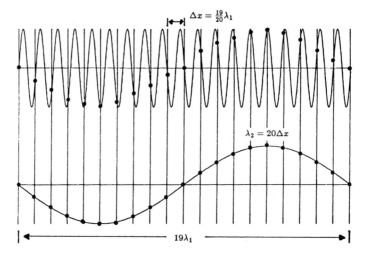

Figure 2.15: Demonstration of the aliasing effect: an oscilliatory signal is sampled with a sampling distance Δx equal to 19/20 of the wavelength. The result is an aliased wavelength which is 20 times the sampling distance.

contains fine structures. Figure 2.14 shows a simple example. Digitization is simulated by overlaying a 2-D grid on the object comprising two linear grids with different grid constants. After sampling, both grids appear to have grid constants with different periodicity and direction. This kind of image distortion is called the *Moiré-effect*.

The same phenomenon, called *aliasing*, is known for one-dimensional signals, especially time series. Figure 2.15 shows a signal with a sinusoidal oscillation. It is sampled with a sampling distance which is slightly smaller than its wavelength. As a result we can observe a much larger wavelength.

Whenever we digitize analog data, these problems occur. It is a general phenomenon of signal processing. In this respect, only image processing is a special case in the more general field of signal theory.

Since the aliasing effect has been demonstrated with periodic signals, the key to understand and thus to avoid it, is by an analysis of the digitization process in Fourier space. In the following, we will perform this analysis step by step. As a result, we can formulate the conditions under which the sampled points are a correct and complete representation of the continuous image in the so-called *sampling theorem*. The following considerations are not a strict mathematical proof of the sampling theorem but rather an illustrative approach.

2.3.3   The Sampling Theorem

Our starting point is an infinite, continuous image $g(\boldsymbol{x})$, which we want to map onto a finite matrix $G_{m,n}$. In this procedure we will include the image formation process, which we discussed in section 2.2. We can then distinguish three separate steps: imaging, sampling, and the limitation of a finite image matrix.

Image Formation
Digitization cannot be treated without the image formation process. The optical system, including the sensor, influences the image signal so that we should include the effect in this process.

Digitization means that we sample the image at certain points of a discrete grid, $\boldsymbol{x}_{m,n}$. If we restrict our considerations to rectangular grids, these points can be written as:

$$\boldsymbol{x}_{m,n} = (m\,\Delta x_1, n\,\Delta x_2)\,. \tag{2.36}$$

Generally, we do not collect the illumination intensity exactly at these points, but in a certain area around them. As an example, we take a CCD camera, which consists of a matrix of directly neighboring photodiodes without any light insensitive strips in between. We further assume that the photodiodes are uniformly and equally sensitive. Then $g'(\boldsymbol{x})$ at the image plane will be integrated over the area of the individual photodiodes. This corresponds to the operation

$$g(\boldsymbol{x}_{m,n}) = \int\limits_{(m-1/2)\Delta x_1}^{(m+1/2)\Delta x_1} dx_1 \int\limits_{(n-1/2)\Delta x_2}^{(n+1/2)\Delta x_2} dx_2\, g'(\boldsymbol{x})\,. \tag{2.37}$$

This operation includes convolution with a rectangular box function and sampling at the points of the grid. These two steps can be separated. We can first perform the continuous convolution and then the sampling. In this way we can generalize the image formation process and separate it from the sampling process. Since convolution is an associative operation, we can combine the averaging process of the CCD sensor with the PSF of the optical system (section 2.2.6) in a single convolution process. Therefore

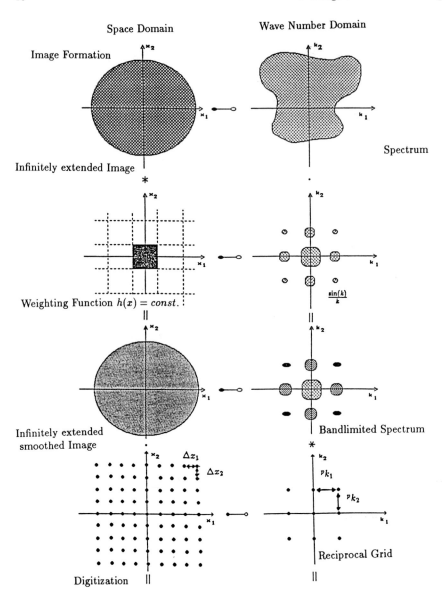

Figure 2.16: Derivation of the sampling theorem I: schematic illustration of the imaging and sampling process in the x and k spaces.

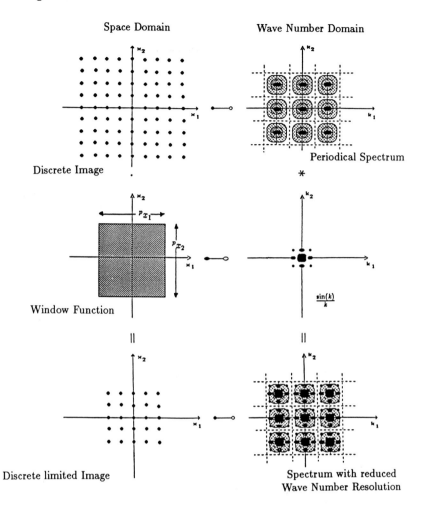

Figure 2.17: Derivation of the sampling theorem II: limited to a finite window.

we can describe the image formation process by the following operation:

$$g(\boldsymbol{x}) = \int\limits_{-\infty}^{\infty} \mathrm{d}^2 x' \; g'(\boldsymbol{x}')h(\boldsymbol{x} - \boldsymbol{x}') = g'(\boldsymbol{x}) * h(\boldsymbol{x})$$

$$\hat{g}(\boldsymbol{k}) = \hat{g}'(\boldsymbol{k})\hat{h}(\boldsymbol{k}),$$

(2.38)

where $h(\boldsymbol{x})$ and $\hat{h}(\boldsymbol{k})$ are the resulting PSF and OTF, respectively, and $g'(\boldsymbol{x})$ can be considered as the gray value image obtained with a perfect sensor, i. e., an optical system (including the sensor) whose OTF is identically 1 and whose PSF is a δ-function.

Generally, the image formation process results in a blurring of the image; fine details are lost. In Fourier space this leads to an attenuation of high wave numbers. The resulting gray value image is called *bandlimited*.

Sampling
Now we perform the sampling. Sampling means that all information is lost except at the grid points. Mathematically, this constitutes a multiplication of the continuous function which is zero everywhere except for the grid points. This operation can be performed by multiplying the image function $g(\boldsymbol{x})$ with the sum of δ functions located at the grid points $\boldsymbol{x}_{m,n}$ (2.36). This function is called the two-dimensional δ comb, or "nail-board function" (figure 2.16). Then sampling can be expressed as

$$g_s(\boldsymbol{x}) = g(\boldsymbol{x})\sum_{m,n}\delta(\boldsymbol{x} - \boldsymbol{x}_{m,n})$$

$$\hat{g}_s(\boldsymbol{k}) = \sum_{u,v}\hat{g}(\boldsymbol{k} - \boldsymbol{k}_{u,v}),$$

(2.39)

where

$$^p\boldsymbol{k}_{u,v} = \begin{bmatrix} u\,^p k_1 \\ v\,^p k_2 \end{bmatrix} = \begin{bmatrix} 2\pi u/\Delta x_1 \\ 2\pi v/\Delta x_2 \end{bmatrix}$$

(2.40)

are the points of the so-called *reciprocal grid*, which plays a significant role in solid state physics and crystallography. According to the convolution theorem, multiplication of the image with the 2-D δ comb corresponds to a convolution of the Fourier transform of the image, the image spectrum, with another 2-D δ comb, whose grid constants are reciprocal to the grid constants in x space (see (2.36) and (2.40)). A dense sampling in x space yields a wide mesh in the k space, and vice versa. Consequently, sampling results in a reproduction of the image spectrum at each point of the grid (figure 2.16).

Now we can formulate the condition where we get no distortion of the signal by sampling. If the image spectrum is so extended that parts of it overlap with the periodically repeated copies, then the overlapping parts are alternated. We cannot distinguish whether the spectral amplitudes come from the original spectrum at the center or from one of the copies. In order to obtain no distortions, we must avoid overlapping.

A safe condition to avoid overlapping is as follows: the spectrum must be restricted to the area which extends around the central grid point up to the lines parting the area

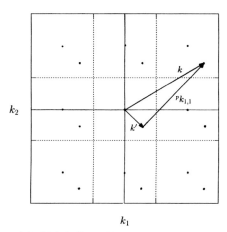

Figure 2.18: Explanation of the Moiré-effect with a periodic structure which does not meet the sampling condition.

between the central grid point and all other grid points (figure 2.16). (In solid state physics this zone is called the first Brillouin zone [*Kittel*, 1971].) On a rectangular grid, this results in the simple condition that the maximum wave number at which the image spectrum is not equal to zero, must be restricted to less than half of the grid constants of the reciprocal grid:

If the spectrum $\hat{g}(\mathbf{k})$ of a continuous function $g(\mathbf{x})$ is bandlimited, i. e.,

$$\hat{g}(\mathbf{k}) = 0 \ \ \forall |k_i| \geq {}^{P}k_i/2, \tag{2.41}$$

then it can be reconstructed exactly from samples with a distance

$$\Delta x_i = 2\pi/{}^{P}k_i. \tag{2.42}$$

In other words, we will obtain a periodic structure correctly only if we take at least two samples per wavelength. The maximum wave number which can be sampled without errors is called the *Nyquist* or *limiting* wave number. In the following, we will often use wave numbers which are scaled to the limiting wave number. We denote this scaling with a tilde:

$$\tilde{k}_i = \frac{k_i \Delta x_i}{\pi}. \tag{2.43}$$

In this scaling all components of the wave number $\tilde{k}_i$ fall into the $]-1, 1[$ interval.

Explanation of the Moiré-Effect
Considerations from the previous section can now be used to explain the Moiré- and aliasing effect. We start with a periodic structure which does not meet the sampling condition. The unsampled spectrum contains a single peak, which is marked with the long vector $\mathbf{k}$ in figure 2.18. Because of the periodic replication of the sampled spectrum, there is exactly one peak, at $\mathbf{k}'$, which lies in the central cell. Figure 2.18 shows that this peak does not only have another wavelength, but in general another direction, as observed in figure 2.14.

The observed wave number $\boldsymbol{k}'$ differs from the true wave number $\boldsymbol{k}$ by a grid translation vector $\boldsymbol{k}_{u,v}$ on the reciprocal grid. u and v must be chosen to meet the condition

$$|k_1 + u\,{}^p k_1| \quad < \quad {}^p k_1/2$$
$$|k_2 + v\,{}^p k_2| \quad < \quad {}^p k_2/2. \tag{2.44}$$

According to this condition, we yield an aliased wave number

$$k' = k - {}^p k = 19/20\,{}^p k - {}^p k = -1/20\,{}^p k \tag{2.45}$$

for the one-dimensional example in figure 2.15, as we just observed.

The sampling theorem, as formulated above, is actually too strict a requirement. A sufficient and necessary condition is that the periodic replications of the non-zero parts of the image spectra must not overlap.

Limitation to a Finite Window
So far, the sampled image is still infinite in size. In practice, we can only work with finite image matrices. Thus the last step is the limitation of the image to a finite window size. The simplest case is the multiplication of the sampled image with a box function. More generally, we can take any *window function* $w(\boldsymbol{x})$ which is zero for sufficient large $\boldsymbol{x}$ values:

$$g_l(\boldsymbol{x}) = g_s(\boldsymbol{x}) \cdot w(\boldsymbol{x})$$

$$\hat{g}_l(\boldsymbol{k}) = \hat{g}_s(\boldsymbol{k}) * \hat{w}(\boldsymbol{k}). \tag{2.46}$$

In Fourier space, the spectrum of the sampled image will be convolved with the Fourier transform of the window function (figure 2.17). Let us consider the example of the box window function in detail. If the window in the x space includes $M \times N$ sampling points, its size is $M\Delta x_1 \times N\Delta x_2$. The Fourier transform of the 2-D box function is the 2-D sinc function (see appendix A.2). The main peak of the sinc function has a half-width of $2\pi/(M\Delta x_1) \times 2\pi/(N\Delta x_2)$. A narrow peak in the spectrum of the image will become a 2-D sinc function. Generally, the resolution in the spectrum will be reduced to the order of the half-width of the sinc function.

In summary, sampling leads to a limitation of the wave number, while the limitation of the image size determines the wave number resolution. Thus the scales in x and k space are reciprocal to each other. The resolution in the x space determines the size in the k space, and vice versa.

2.3.4   Reconstruction from Samples

One task is missing. The sampling theorem ensures the conditions under which we can reconstruct a continuous function from sampled points, but we still do not know how to perform the reconstruction of the continuous image from its samples, i.e., the inverse operation to sampling.

Reconstruction is performed by a suitable *interpolation* of the sampled points. Generally, the interpolated points $g_r(\boldsymbol{x})$ are calculated from the sampled values $g(\boldsymbol{x}_{m,n})$

weighted with suitable factors depending on the distance from the interpolated point:

$$g_r(\boldsymbol{x}) = \sum_{m,n} g_s(\boldsymbol{x}_{m,n}) h(\boldsymbol{x} - \boldsymbol{x}_{m,n}). \tag{2.47}$$

Using the integral properties of the δ function, we can substitute the sampled points on the right side by the continuous values:

$$
\begin{aligned}
g_r(\boldsymbol{x}) &= \sum_{m,n} \int_{-\infty}^{\infty} d^2x' \; g(\boldsymbol{x}') h(\boldsymbol{x} - \boldsymbol{x}') \delta(\boldsymbol{x}_{m,n} - \boldsymbol{x}') \\
&= \int_{-\infty}^{\infty} d^2x' \; h(\boldsymbol{x} - \boldsymbol{x}') \left(\sum_{m,n} \delta(\boldsymbol{x}_{m,n} - \boldsymbol{x}') g(\boldsymbol{x}') \right).
\end{aligned}
$$

The last integral means a convolution of the weighting function h with a sum of the image function g replicated at each grid point in the x space. In Fourier space, convolution is replaced by complex multiplication:

$$\hat{g}_r(\boldsymbol{k}) = \hat{h}(\boldsymbol{k}) \sum_{u,v} \hat{g}(\boldsymbol{k} - \boldsymbol{k}_{u,v}). \tag{2.48}$$

The interpolated function cannot be equal to the original image, if the periodically repeated image spectra are overlapping. This is nothing new; it is exactly the statement of the sampling theorem. The interpolated image function is only equal to the original image function if the weighting function is a box function with the width of the elementary cell of the reciprocal grid. Then only one term unequal to zero remains at the right side of (2.48):

$$\hat{g}_r(\boldsymbol{k}) = \Pi(k_1 \Delta x_1/2\pi, k_2 \Delta x_2/2\pi) \hat{g}(\boldsymbol{k}). \tag{2.49}$$

The interpolation function is the inverse Fourier transform of the box function

$$h(\boldsymbol{x}) = \frac{\sin \pi x_1/\Delta x_1}{\pi x_1/\Delta x_1} \frac{\sin \pi x_2/\Delta x_2}{\pi x_2/\Delta x_2}. \tag{2.50}$$

This function performs only with $1/x$ towards zero. A correct interpolation requires a large image area; mathematically, it must be infinite large. This condition can be weakened if we "overfill" the sampling theorem, i.e., ensure that $\hat{g}(\boldsymbol{k})$ is already zero before we reach the Nyquist wave number. According to (2.48), we can then choose $\hat{h}(\boldsymbol{k})$ arbitrarily in the region where $\hat{g}$ vanishes. We can use this freedom to construct an interpolation function which decreases more quickly in the x space, i.e., it has a minimum-length interpolation mask. We can also start from a given interpolation formula. Then the deviation of its Fourier transform from a box function tells us to what extent structures will be distorted as a function of the wave number. Suitable interpolation functions will be discussed in detail in section 8.2.4.

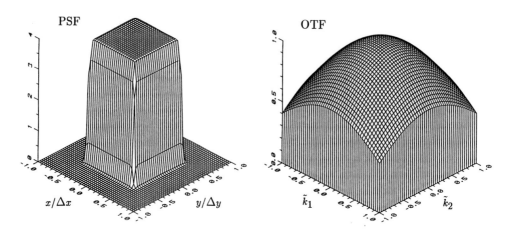

Figure 2.19: a) PSF and b) OTF of standard sampling.

2.3.5   Standard Sampling

The type of sampling discussed in section 2.3.3 using the example of the ideal CCD camera is called *standard sampling*. Here the mean value of an elementary cell is assigned to a corresponding sampling point. It is a kind of *regular* sampling, since each point in the continuous space is equally weighted. We might be tempted to assume that standard sampling conforms to the sampling theorem. Unfortunately, this is not the case (figure 2.19). To the Nyquist wave number, the Fourier transform of the box function is still $1/\sqrt{2}$. The first zero crossing occurs at double the Nyquist wave number. Consequently, Moiré effects will be observed with CCD cameras. The effects are even more pronounced since only a small fraction — typically 20% of the chip area for interline transfer cameras — are light sensitive [*Lenz*, 1988].

Smoothing over larger areas with a box window is not of much help since the Fourier transform of the box window only decreases with k^{-1} (figure 2.19). The ideal window function for sampling is identical to the ideal interpolation formula (2.50) discussed in section 2.3.4, since its Fourier transform is a box function with the width of the elementary cell of the reciprocal grid. However, this windowing is impracticable. We will consider this matter further in our discussion of smoothing filters in section 6.1.

3 Space and Wave Number Domain

3.1 Introduction

Fourier transform, i.e., decomposition of an image into periodic structures, proved to be an extremely helpful tool to understanding image formation and digitization. Throughout the whole discussion in the last chapter we used the continuous Fourier transform. Proceeding now to discrete imagery, the question arises whether there is a discrete analogue to the continuous Fourier transform. Such a transformation would allow us to decompose a discrete image directly into its periodic components.

In continuous space, the image is represented equivalently in the space and Fourier domain. As an introduction to a discrete Fourier space, we will first consider the effects of sampling in Fourier space. Since the back transformation is — except for the sign of the kernel — the same as for the forward transformation (see appendix A.2), we can follow the route as for sampling in the space domain. By interchanging the roles of space and wave number domain, we can write the sampling theorem for the wave number domain directly (compare equation (2.41)):

If a function $g(\boldsymbol{x})$ is finite, i. e.,

$$g(\boldsymbol{x}) = 0 \ \forall |x_i| \geq {}^P x_i/2, \tag{3.1}$$

then it can be reconstructed exactly from samples of its Fourier transform, $\hat{g}(\boldsymbol{k})$, with a distance

$$\Delta k_i = 2\pi/{}^P x_i. \tag{3.2}$$

As in the spatial domain, we limit the infinite Fourier domain by a window function. Multiplication in the Fourier domain corresponds to a convolution in the space domain with the inverse Fourier transform of the window function. This convolution process results in a smoothing, i.e., limitation of the resolution, an effect we expected since we attenuate or remove high wave numbers entirely by multiplication with the window function in the Fourier domain.

Comparing the effects of the limitation of a continuous function in either of the two domains, we conclude that they have a corresponding effect in the other domain. Thus we might suspect that a transformation on the discrete data, i.e., matrices, may exist which shows very similar features to the continuous Fourier transform. This transformation is called the *discrete Fourier transform*, or DFT. The relation between the grid constants and sizes in the space and wave number domains are given by

$$
\begin{aligned}
{}^{P}k_1 &= M\Delta k_1 = 2\pi/\Delta x_1 & {}^{P}x_1 &= M\Delta x_1 = 2\pi/\Delta k_1 \\
{}^{P}k_2 &= N\Delta k_2 = 2\pi/\Delta x_2 & {}^{P}x_2 &= N\Delta x_2 = 2\pi/\Delta k_2.
\end{aligned}
\tag{3.3}
$$

The subject of this chapter is rather mathematical, but is significant for a greater understanding of image processing. We will try to treat the subject illustratively and to focus on several aspects which are important for practical application. We will discuss in detail the special features of the DFT of *real-valued* images, the importance of *phase* and *amplitude* of the DFT, and several fast algorithms to calculate the DFT. The reader will find references to a more rigorous mathematical treatment in appendix A.3. This appendix also includes a ready-to-use summary of the theorems of DFT and important special functions used in image processing.

3.2   The Discrete Fourier transform (DFT)

3.2.1   The one-dimensional DFT

First, we will consider the one-dimensional Fourier transform. The DFT maps an ordered M-tupel of complex numbers g_i, the *complex-valued vector* $\boldsymbol{g}$,

$$
\boldsymbol{g} =
\begin{bmatrix}
g_0 \\
g_1 \\
\vdots \\
g_{M-1}
\end{bmatrix},
\tag{3.4}
$$

onto another vector $\hat{\boldsymbol{g}}$ of a vector space with the same dimension M.

$$
\hat{g}_u = \frac{1}{M} \sum_{m=0}^{M-1} g_m \exp\left(-\frac{2\pi i\, mu}{M}\right), \quad 0 \le u < M.
\tag{3.5}
$$

The back transformation is given by

$$
g_m = \sum_{u=0}^{M-1} \hat{g}_u \exp\left(\frac{2\pi i\, mu}{M}\right), \quad 0 \le m < M.
\tag{3.6}
$$

The expressions in (3.5) and (3.6) with which the vectors are multiplied are called the *kernel* of the DFT. We can consider the DFT as inner products of the vector $\boldsymbol{g}$ with a set of M vectors

$$
\boldsymbol{b}_u = \frac{1}{M}
\begin{bmatrix}
1 \\
\exp\left(\frac{2\pi i\, u}{M}\right) \\
\exp\left(\frac{2\pi i\, 2u}{M}\right) \\
\vdots \\
\exp\left(\frac{2\pi i\, (M-1)u}{M}\right)
\end{bmatrix}, \quad 0 \le u < M.
\tag{3.7}
$$

The elements of these vectors are conveniently abbreviated using

$$W_M = \exp\left(\frac{2\pi i}{M}\right). \tag{3.8}$$

Then we can write:

$$\boldsymbol{b}_u = \frac{1}{M} \begin{bmatrix} 1 \\ W_M^u \\ W_M^{2u} \\ \vdots \\ W_M^{(M-1)u} \end{bmatrix}. \tag{3.9}$$

Using the definition for the *inner product*

$$\langle \boldsymbol{g}, \boldsymbol{h} \rangle = \sum_{m=0}^{M-1} g_m h_m^* = \boldsymbol{g} \boldsymbol{h}^*, \tag{3.10}$$

the DFT reduces to

$$\hat{g}_u = \langle \boldsymbol{g}, \boldsymbol{b}_u \rangle = \underbrace{\boldsymbol{g}}_{1 \times M} \underbrace{\boldsymbol{b}_u^*}_{M \times 1}. \tag{3.11}$$

Used with a scalar, the superscript $*$ denotes the complex conjugate; used with a vector or matrix, it denotes the complex conjugate and transposed vector or matrix. Here we consider vectors as special cases of matrices. Column ($\boldsymbol{g}$) and row ($\boldsymbol{g}^T$ or $\boldsymbol{g}^*$) vectors are equivalent to $M \times 1$ and $1 \times M$ matrices, respectively.

Then the scalar product is a special matrix multiplication between a column and a row vector resulting in a scalar.

The M vectors $\boldsymbol{b}_u$ are orthogonal to each other

$$M \langle \boldsymbol{b}_u, \boldsymbol{b}_v \rangle = \boldsymbol{b}_u \boldsymbol{b}_v^* = \delta_{u,v}. \tag{3.12}$$

Consequently, the set $\boldsymbol{b}_u$ forms a basis for the *vector space*, which means that each vector of the vector space can be expressed as a linear combination of the basis vectors. The DFT calculates the projections of the vector $\boldsymbol{g}$ onto all the basis vectors directly, i.e., the components of $\boldsymbol{g}$ in the direction of the basis vectors. In this sense, the DFT is just a special type of coordinate transformation in an M-dimensional vector space. Mathematically, the DFT differs from more familiar coordinate transformations such as rotation in a three-dimensional vector space (section 2.2.1, see also section 2.2.3) only because the vector space is over the field of the complex instead of real numbers.

The real and imaginary part of the basis vectors are sampled sine and cosine functions of different wavelengths (figure 3.1). The index u denotes how often the wavelength of the function fits into the interval $[0, M]$. Only wavelengths with integer fractions of the interval length M occur. The basis vector $\boldsymbol{b}_0$ is a constant real vector.

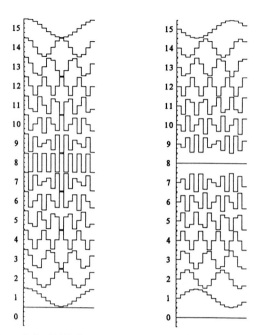

Figure 3.1: Basis functions of the DFT for $M = 16$; real part (cosine function) left, imaginary part (sine function) right.

3.2.2   The Two-Dimensional DFT

In two dimensions, the DFT maps an $M \times N$ matrix with complex components onto another matrix of the same size:

$$
\begin{aligned}
\hat{G}_{u,v} &= \frac{1}{MN} \sum_{m=0}^{M-1}\sum_{n=0}^{N-1} G_{m,n} \exp\left(-\frac{2\pi i\, mu}{M}\right) \exp\left(-\frac{2\pi i\, nv}{N}\right) \\
&= \frac{1}{MN} \sum_{m=0}^{M-1} \left(\sum_{n=0}^{N-1} G_{m,n} W_N^{-nv} \right) W_M^{-mu}.
\end{aligned}
\tag{3.13}
$$

In the second line, the abbreviation defined in (3.8) is used. As in the one-dimensional case, the DFT expands a matrix into a set of basis matrices which spans the $N \times M$-dimensional vector space over the field of complex numbers. The basis matrices are of the form

$$
\underbrace{\boldsymbol{B}_{u,v}}_{M \times N} = \frac{1}{MN}
\begin{bmatrix}
1 \\
W_M^{u} \\
W_M^{2u} \\
\vdots \\
W_M^{(M-1)u}
\end{bmatrix}
\left[1, W_N^{v}, W_N^{2v}, \ldots, W_N^{(N-1)v} \right]
\tag{3.14}
$$

$$
= \frac{1}{MN} \underbrace{\boldsymbol{b}_u}_{M \times 1} \underbrace{\boldsymbol{b}_v^{*}}_{1 \times N}.
$$

In this equation, the basis matrices are expressed as an *outer product* between a column and a row vector which are the basis vectors of the one-dimensional DFT. Kernels with this property are called *separable* kernels.

The inverse DFT is given by

$$G_{mn} = \sum_{u=0}^{M-1}\sum_{v=0}^{N-1} \hat{G}_{u,v} W_M^{mu} W_N^{nv}. \tag{3.15}$$

The theorems of the DFT are very similar to the corresponding theorems of the continuous Fourier transform and are summarized in appendix A.3. In this section we focus on additional properties of the DFT which are of importance when we want to apply the DFT to image data.

3.2.3   Periodicity

The kernel of the DFT shows a characteristic periodicity

$$\exp\left(-\frac{2\pi i\,(m+kM)}{M}\right) = \exp\left(-\frac{2\pi i\,m}{M}\right), \quad \forall k \in \mathbb{Z}. \tag{3.16}$$

The definitions of the DFT restrict the space and Fourier domain to an $M \times N$ matrix. If we do not care about this restriction and calculate the forward and back transformation for indices with unrestricted integer numbers, we find the same periodicities from (3.13) and (3.15):

$$\begin{array}{ll} \text{wave number domain} & \hat{G}_{u+kM,v+lN} = \hat{G}_{u,v}, \quad \forall k,l \in \mathbb{Z} \\ \text{space domain} & G_{m+kM,n+lN} = G_{m,n}, \quad \forall k,l \in \mathbb{Z}. \end{array} \tag{3.17}$$

These equations state a periodic extension in both domains beyond the original matrices. In sections 2.3.3 and 3.1 we obtained the very same result with our considerations about sampling in the space and wave number domain.

The periodicity of the DFT gives rise to an interesting geometric interpretation. In the one-dimensional case, the border points g_{M-1} and $g_M = f_0$ are neighboring points. We can meet this property geometrically if we draw the points of the vector not on a finite line but on a circle, the so-called *Fourier ring* (figure 3.2a). This representation has a deeper meaning when we consider the Fourier transform as a special case of the *z-transform* [*Oppenheim and Schafer, 1989*]. With two dimensions, this can lead to a mapping of the matrix onto a torus (figure 3.2b), the *Fourier torus*.

3.2.4   Symmetry

The study of symmetries is important for practical purposes. Careful consideration of symmetry allows storage space to be saved and algorithms to be speeded up. After a general introduction to symmetries with discrete functions, we discuss the DFT of real-valued images.

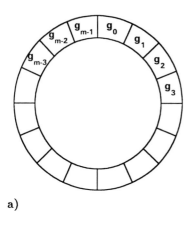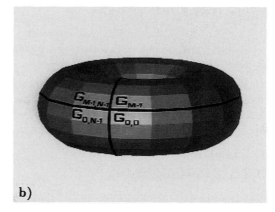

Figure 3.2: Geometric interpretation of the periodicity of the one- and two-dimensional DFT with a) the Fourier ring and b) the Fourier torus.

In continuous space, Fourier transform conserves the symmetry of functions. The Fourier transform of an *even* or *odd function*

$$g(\boldsymbol{x}) = \pm g(-\boldsymbol{x}) \tag{3.18}$$

remains even or odd. In the discrete and finite space, for which the DFT is defined, we first must find an appropriate definition for symmetries. The direct analogue,

$$G_{mn} = \pm G_{-m,-n}, \tag{3.19}$$

is not appropriate, because negative indices lie outside of definition range. However, we can make use of the periodicity property (3.17). Then we find the index $(-m, -n)$ at $(M - m, N - n)$ within the matrix and define the symmetry condition

$$G_{mn} = \pm G_{M-m,N-n}, \tag{3.20}$$

for even (+ sign) and odd (− sign) functions. The symmetry center lies at the point $(M/2, N/2)$.

The complex-valued basis vectors of the DFT also show symmetries. While the real part (cosine function) is even, the imaginary part (sine function) is odd [(figure 3.1), (3.7) and (3.14)]. This kind of symmetry for complex valued functions is called *Hermitian*.

After these general considerations, we can study the DFT of real-valued images in more detail. From the Hermitian symmetry of the basis vectors of the DFT, we can conclude that real-valued functions also exhibit a Hermitian DFT:

$$G_{mn} = G_{mn}^* \quad \circ\!\!-\!\!\bullet \quad \hat{G}_{M-u,N-v} = \hat{G}_{uv}^*. \tag{3.21}$$

Figure 3.3: Representation of the spectrum of an image: a) Fourier transformed image; b) original image; c) remapped spectrum to consider negative values of one component of the wave number.

The complex-valued DFT of real-valued matrices is therefore completely determined by the values in one half space. The other half space is obtained by mirroring at the symmetry center $(M/2, N/2)$. Consequently, we need the same amount of storage place for the DFT of a real image as for the image itself.

At first glance, the basis functions of the DFT in figure 3.1 seem to contradict the sampling theorem. The sampling theorem states that a periodic structure must be sampled at least twice per wavelength. This condition is only met for the first half of the basis functions (indices 0 to 8), but not for the second half. We can resolve this apparent discrepancy by reindexing the vector. Using the periodicity property (3.17), we can change the indices in the interval $[M/2, M-1]$ to $[-M/2, -1]$. Now the indices, except for the minus sign, directly reflect the period of the basis functions (figure 3.1). The indices now lie in the interval $[-M/2, M/2-1]$; all basis vectors meet the sampling theorem.

However, what is the meaning of negative frequencies and wave numbers, respectively? For real physical phenomena they make no sense. But as the spectrum of a real vector is Hermitian, we can just pick out the part with the positive wave numbers.

In two and higher dimensions, matters are slightly more complex. The spectrum of a real-valued image is determined completely by the values in one half space. This means that *one* component of the wave number can be negative, but that we cannot distinguish between k and $-k$, i.e., between wave numbers which only differ in sign. Therefore we can represent power spectra of real-valued images in a half space, where only one component of the wave number includes negative values. For proper representation of the spectra with zero values of this component in the middle of the image, it is necessary to interchange the upper (positive) and lower (negative) parts of the image (figure 3.3).

An image sequence can be regarded as a three-dimensional image with two space and one time coordinates. Consequently, the DFT results in a spectrum with two wave numbers and one frequency coordinate. For real-valued image sequences, again we need only a half space to represent the spectrum. Physically, it makes most sense to choose

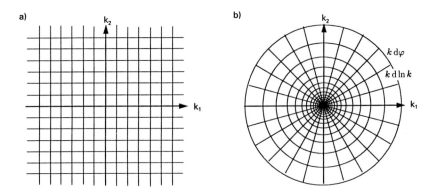

Figure 3.4: Representation of the Fourier domain in a) Cartesian and b) log-polar coordinate system.

the half space which contains positive frequencies. In contrast to a single image, we obtain the *full* wave number space. Now we can identify the spatially identical wave numbers k and $-k$ as structures propagating in opposite directions.

3.2.5 Dynamical Range of the DFT

While in most cases it is sufficient to represent an image with 256 quantization levels, i. e., one byte per pixel, the Fourier transform of an image needs a much larger dynamical range. Typically, we observe a strong decrease of the Fourier components with the magnitude of the wave number (figure 3.3). Consequently, at least 16-bit integers or 32-bit floating-point numbers are necessary to represent an image in the Fourier domain without significant rounding errors.

The reason for this behavior is not the insignificance of high wave numbers in images. If we simply omit them, we blur the image. The decrease is caused by the fact that the *relative* resolution is increasing. It is natural to think of relative resolutions, because we are better able to distinguish relative distance differences than absolute ones. We can, for example, easily see the difference of 10 cm in 1 m, but not in 1 km. If we apply this concept to the Fourier domain, it seems to be more natural to represent the images in a so-called *log-polar coordinate system* as illustrated in figure 3.4. A discrete grid in this coordinate system separates the space into angular and $\log k$ intervals. Thus the cell area is proportional to k^2. In order to preserve the norm, the Fourier components need to be multiplied by k^2 in this representation:

$$\int_{-\infty}^{\infty} dk_1 dk_2 \, |g(\boldsymbol{k})|^2 = \int_{-\infty}^{\infty} d\ln k \; d\varphi \; k^2 |g(\boldsymbol{k})|^2. \qquad (3.22)$$

If we assume that the power spectrum $|g(\boldsymbol{k})|^2$ is flat in the natural log-polar coordinate system, it will decrease with k^{-2} in the Cartesian coordinates.

For a display of power spectra, it is common to take the logarithm of the gray values in order to compress the high dynamic range. Our considerations in this section suggest that a multiplication with k^2 is a valuable alternative. Likewise, representation in the

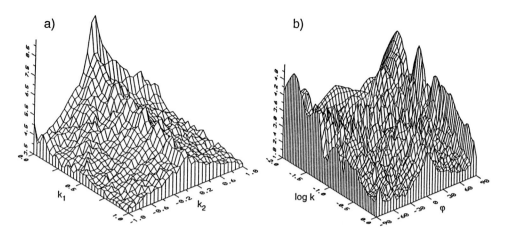

Figure 3.5: Power spectrum of an image in a) Cartesian and b) log-polar coordinate system.

log-polar coordinate systems allows a much better evaluation of the directions of the spatial structures and the smaller scales (figure 3.5).

3.2.6   Phase and Amplitude

As outlined above, the DFT can be regarded as a coordinate transformation in a finite-dimensional vector space. Therefore, the image information is completely conserved. We can perform the inverse transformation to obtain the original image. In Fourier space, we observe the image from another "point of view". Each point in the Fourier domain contains two pieces of information: the *amplitude* and the *phase*, i.e., relative position, of a periodic structure. Given this composition, we are confronted with the question as to whether the phase or amplitude contains more information of the structure in the image, or whether both are of equal importance. In order to answer this question, we perform a simple experiment. Figure 3.6a shows part of a building at Heidelberg University. We calculate the DFT of this image and then arbitrarily change either the phase or the amplitude of the Fourier component and then perform the inverse DFT.

First, we arbitrarily set the amplitude proportional to k^{-1} (figure 3.6b) or $k^{-3/2}$ (figure 3.6c), but leave the phase unchanged. The images become somewhat stained, and in case of $|\hat{g}(\boldsymbol{k})| \propto k^{-3/2}$ also blurred, but otherwise we can still recognize all the details.

Second, we keep the amplitude of the spectrum, but change the phase by replacing it with random numbers with the exception of the first row (figure 3.6d). Consequently, only the phase of horizontally orientated structures is kept unchanged. The arbitrary change causes significant effects: we can no longer recognize the image except for the coarse horizontal dark/bright pattern which corresponds to the Fourier components whose phase was not changed.

From this experiment, we can conclude that the phase of the Fourier transform carries essential information about the image structure. The amplitude alone implies

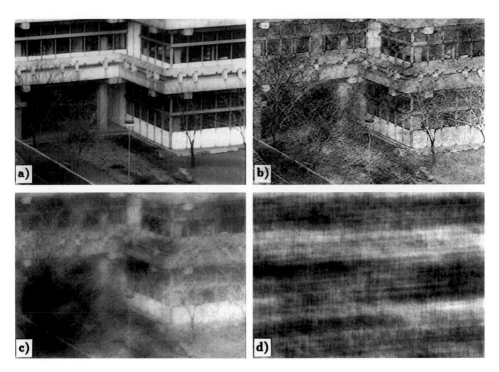

Figure 3.6: The importance of phase and amplitude for the image contents: a) original image; b) back transformed image with unchanged phase but an amplitude arbitrarily set to $|\hat{g}(\boldsymbol{k})| \propto k^{-1}$; c) as b), but with $|\hat{g}(\boldsymbol{k})| \propto k^{-3/2}$; d) unchanged amplitude and random phase.

only *that* such a periodic structure is contained in the image but not *where*. We can also illustrate this important fact with the shift theorem (see appendix A.3). A shift of an object in the space domain leads to a shift of the phase in the wave number domain. If we do not know the phase of its Fourier components, we know neither what the object looks like nor where it is located.

From these considerations we can conclude that the *power spectrum*, i. e., the squared amplitudes of the Fourier components, contains only very little information, since all the phase information is lost. The power spectrum only indicates the amplitude of the wave numbers. If the gray value can be associated with the amplitude of a physical process, say a harmonic oscillation, then the power spectrum gives us the distribution of the energy in the wave number domain.

3.3   Discrete Unitary Transforms

3.3.1   General Properties

In section 3.2.1, we learnt that the discrete Fourier transform can be regarded as a linear transformation in a vector space. Thus it is only an example of a large class of transformations, called *unitary transforms*. In this section, we discuss some of their general features which will be of help for a deeper insight into image processing. Furthermore, we give examples of other unitary transforms which have gained some importance in digital image processing.

Unitary transforms are defined for vector spaces over the field of complex numbers, for which an *inner product* is defined. Implicitly, we have already used the inner or dot product for vectors. Let g and h be two vectors of an M-dimensional vector space over the field of complex numbers. Then the *standard inner product* is defined as

$$\langle g, h \rangle = gh^* = \sum_{m=0}^{M-1} g_m h_m^*. \tag{3.23}$$

This definition can be extended for matrices with the following definition:

$$\langle G, H \rangle = \sum_{m=0}^{M-1}\sum_{n=0}^{N-1} G_{mn} H_{mn}^*. \tag{3.24}$$

The inner product for matrices is closely related to the *trace function*

$$tr(G) = \sum_{m=0}^{M-1} G_{mm} \tag{3.25}$$

by

$$\langle G, H \rangle = tr(GH^*) = tr(G^*H). \tag{3.26}$$

Now we can define the unitary transform:

Let V be a finite-dimensional inner product vector space. Let U be a one-one linear transformation of V onto itself. Then the following are equivalent.
1. U is unitary.
2. U preserves the inner product, i. e., $\langle g, h \rangle = \langle Ug, Uh \rangle$, $\forall g, h \in V$.
3. The inverse of U, U^{-1}, is the adjoint of U, U^*: $UU^* = I$.

In the definition given, the most important properties of a unitary transform are already incorporated: an unitary transform preserves the inner product. This includes that another important property, the *norm*, is also preserved

$$\|g\| = \langle g, g \rangle^{1/2} = \langle Ug, Ug \rangle^{1/2}. \tag{3.27}$$

It is appropriate to think of the norm as the *length* or *magnitude* of the vector. Rotation in $I\!R^2$ or $I\!R^3$ is an example for a unitary transform where the preservation of the length of the vectors is obvious (compare also the discussion of homogeneous coordinates in section 2.2.3).

The product of two unitary transforms, $U_1 U_2$, is unitary. Since the identity operator I is unitary as well as the inverse of a unitary operator, the set of all unitary transforms on an inner product space is a *group* under the operation of composition. In practice, this means that we can compose/decompose complex unitary transforms from/into simpler or elementary transforms.

We will illustrate some of the properties of unitary transforms discussed with the discrete Fourier transform. First we consider the one-dimensional DFT (3.5):

$$\hat{g}_u = \frac{1}{M} \sum_{m=0}^{M-1} g_m W_M^{-mu}.$$

This equation can be regarded as a multiplication of an $M \times M$ matrix W_M ($W_{mu} = W_M^{-mu}$) with the vector g:

$$\hat{g} = W_M g. \tag{3.28}$$

Explicitly, the DFT for an 8-dimensional vector is given by

$$
\begin{bmatrix} \hat{g}_0 \\ \hat{g}_1 \\ \hat{g}_2 \\ \hat{g}_3 \\ \hat{g}_4 \\ \hat{g}_5 \\ \hat{g}_6 \\ \hat{g}_7 \end{bmatrix}
=
\begin{bmatrix}
W^0 & W^0 & W^0 & W^0 & W^0 & W^0 & W^0 & W^0 \\
W^0 & W^7 & W^6 & W^5 & W^4 & W^3 & W^2 & W^1 \\
W^0 & W^6 & W^4 & W^2 & W^0 & W^6 & W^4 & W^2 \\
W^0 & W^5 & W^2 & W^7 & W^4 & W^1 & W^6 & W^3 \\
W^0 & W^4 & W^0 & W^4 & W^0 & W^4 & W^0 & W^4 \\
W^0 & W^3 & W^6 & W^1 & W^4 & W^7 & W^2 & W^5 \\
W^0 & W^2 & W^4 & W^6 & W^0 & W^2 & W^4 & W^6 \\
W^0 & W^1 & W^2 & W^3 & W^4 & W^5 & W^6 & W^7
\end{bmatrix}
\begin{bmatrix} g_0 \\ g_1 \\ g_2 \\ g_3 \\ g_4 \\ g_5 \\ g_6 \\ g_7 \end{bmatrix}. \tag{3.29}
$$

We omitted the subscript M for W to keep the matrix elements more simple and made use of the periodicity of the kernel of the DFT (3.16) to limit the exponents of W between 0 and 7. The transformation matrix for the DFT is symmetric ($W = W^T$), but not Hermitian ($W = W^*$).

For the two-dimensional DFT, we can write similar equations if we map the $M \times N$ matrix onto an MN-dimensional vector. There is, however, a simpler way if we make use of the separability of the kernel of the DFT as expressed in (3.13). Using the $M \times M$ matrix W_M and the $N \times N$ matrix W_N analogously as in the one-dimensional case, we can write (3.13) as

$$\hat{g}_{u,v} = \frac{1}{MN} \sum_{m=0}^{M-1} \sum_{n=0}^{N-1} g_{mn} W_{mu} W_{nv}, \tag{3.30}$$

or, in matrix notation,

$$\underbrace{\hat{G}}_{M \times N} = \underbrace{W_M^T}_{M \times M} \underbrace{G}_{M \times N} \underbrace{W_N}_{N \times N} = W_M G W_N. \tag{3.31}$$

Physicists will be reminded of the theoretical foundations of *quantum mechanics* which are formulated in an inner product vector space of infinite dimension, the *Hilbert space*. In digital image processing, the difficulties associated with infinite-dimensional vector spaces can be avoided. A detailed discussion of the mathematics of unitary transforms with respect to digital image processing can be found in *Jaroslavskij* [1985]. *Hoffmann and Kunze* [1971] discuss inner product spaces and unitary operators in detail in their classic textbook on the foundations of linear algebra.

3.3.2 Further Examples for Unitary Transforms

After discussing the general features of unitary transforms, some illustrative examples will be given. They will be brief as they are not as important as the discrete Fourier transform in digital image processing.

Cosine and Sine Transform
It is often inconvenient that the DFT transforms real-valued to complex-valued images. We can derive a real transformation if we decompose the complex DFT into its real and imaginary parts:

$$K_{mu} = \cos\left(-\frac{2\pi mu}{M}\right) + i\sin\left(-\frac{2\pi mu}{M}\right). \tag{3.32}$$

Neither the cosine nor the sine part is useful as a transformation kernel, since these functions do not form a basis for the vector space. The cosine and sine functions only span the subspaces of the even and odd functions, respectively. We can, however, artificially define even or odd vectors if we double the dimension of the vector space and extend the upper half of the vector so that the vector becomes even or odd, i.e., $g_{2M-m} = \pm g_m$, $0 < m \le M$. The doubling of the dimension means that the periods of the kernels double. The transform, however, only needs to be calculated for the lower half, i.e., the dimension of the original vector, since the other part is given by symmetry. The kernels for the cosine and sine transforms in an M-dimensional vector space are

$$\begin{aligned}
K_{mu} &= \cos\left(\frac{\pi mu}{M}\right), \\
K_{mu} &= \sin\left(\frac{\pi mu}{M}\right).
\end{aligned} \tag{3.33}$$

Figure 3.7a and b show the basis functions of the 1-D cosine and sine functions. From the graphs, it is easy to imagine that all the basis functions are orthogonal to each other. Because of the doubling of the periods, both transforms now contain even and odd functions. The basis functions with half integer wavelengths fill in the functions with the originally missing symmetry.

The cosine transform has gained importance for *image data compression* [*Jain*, 1989]. It is included into the standard high-compression algorithm proposed by the Joint Photographic Experts Group (JPEG).

Hadamard Transform
The basis functions of the Hadamard transform are orthogonal binary patterns (figure 3.7c). Some of these patterns are regular rectangular waves, others are not. The Hadamard transform is computationally efficient, since its kernel contains only the figures 1 and -1. Thus only additions and subtractions are necessary to compute the transform.

If we compare the basis functions of the DFT with the cosine, sine, and Hadamard transforms, we might be tempted to assume that these transforms still decompose the vector in larger and smaller scales. This is only partly true. Imagine that we shift the basis function with the largest scale (index 1) one position. It will then become a linear combination of many basis vectors, including those with the smallest

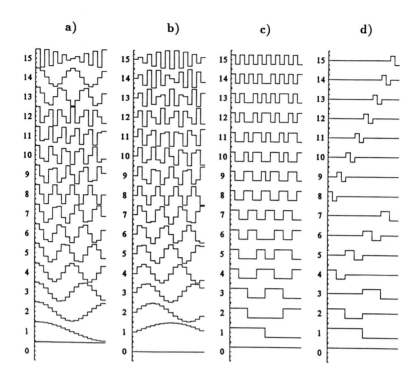

Figure 3.7: Basis functions of one-dimensional unitary transforms for $M = 16$-dimensional vectors: a) cosine transform; b) sine transform; c) Hadamard transform; d) Haar transform.

scales. This example demonstrates the importance of the shift theorem of the DFT (see appendix A.3). Changes in position do not change the amplitude of the basis vectors, but only its phase.

Haar Transform

The basis vectors of all the transforms considered so far are characterized by the fact that they spread out over the whole vector or image. In this sense we may denote these transforms as *global*. All locality is lost. If we have, for example, two independent objects in our image, then they will be simultaneously decomposed into these global patterns and will no longer be recognizable as two individual objects in the new representation.

The Haar transform is the first example of a unitary transform which partly preserves some local information, since its basis functions are pairs of impulses which are non-zero only at the position of the impulse (figure 3.7d). With the Haar transform the position resolution is better for smaller structures.

As in the Hadamard transform, the Haar transform is computational efficient, since its kernel only includes the figures -1, 0 and 1.

3.4 Fast Algorithms for Unitary Transforms

3.4.1 Importance of Fast Algorithms

Without an effective algorithm to calculate the discrete Fourier transform, it would not be possible to use the Fourier transform in image processing. Applied directly, (3.13) is prohibitively expensive. Each point in the transformed image requires M^2 complex multiplications and $M^2 - 1$ complex additions (not counting the calculation of the cosine and sine functions in the kernel). In total, we need M^4 complex multiplications and $M^2(M^2 - 1)$ complex additions.

Counting only the multiplications, a PC performing 40 000 real multiplications per second would need about two months to transform a single 512×512 image. Even on a super computer with a computational power of 1000 MFLOPS (million floating point operations per second) the computation would take about three minutes. These figures emphasize the urgent need to minimize the number of computations by choosing a suitable algorithm. This is an important topic in computer science. In order to do so we must study the inner structure of a given task, its *computational complexity*, and try to find out how it may be solved with the minimum number of operations.

As an example, consider the following simple *search* problem. A friend lives in a high-rise building with M floors. We want to find out on which floor his apartment is located. Our questions will only be answered with yes or no. How many questions must we pose to find out where he lives? The simplest and most straightforward approach is to ask "Do you live on floor m?". In the best case, our initial guess might be right, but it is more likely to be wrong so that the same question has to be asked with other floor numbers again and again. In the worst case, we must ask exactly $M - 1$ questions, in the mean $M/2$ questions. With each question, we can only rule out one out of M possibilities. With the question "Do you live in the top half of the building?", however, we can rule out half of the possibilities with just one question. After the answer, we know that he either lives in the top or bottom half, and can continue our questioning in the same manner by splitting up the remaining possibilities into two halves. With this strategy, we need fewer questions. If the number of floors is a power of two, say 2^l, we need exactly l questions. Thus for M floors, we need ld$M$ questions, where ld denotes the logarithm to the base of two. The strategy which has been applied recursively for a more efficient solution to the search problem is called *divide and conquer*.

One measure of the computational complexity of a problem with M components is the largest power of M that occurs in the count of operations necessary to solve it. This approximation is useful, since the largest power in M dominates the number of operations necessary for large M. We speak of a zero-order problem $O(M^0)$, if the number of operations does not depend on its size, or a linear order problem $O(M^1)$, if the number of computations increases linearly with the size. The straightforward solution of the search problem discussed in the previous example is that of $O(M)$, the divide-and-conquer strategy of $O(\text{ld}M)$.

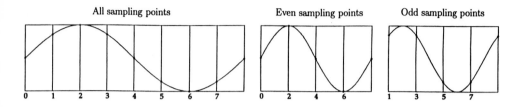

Figure 3.8: Decomposition of a vector into two vectors containing the even and odd sampling points.

3.4.2   The 1-D Radix-2 FFT Algorithms

First we consider fast algorithms for the one-dimensional DFT, commonly abbreviated as FFT algorithms for *fast Fourier transform*. We assume that the dimension of the vector is a power of two, $M = 2^l$. Since the direct solution according to (3.5) is that of $O(M^2)$ it seems useful to use the divide-and-conquer strategy. If we can split the transformation into two parts with vectors the size of $M/2$, we reduce the number of operations from M^2 to $2(M/2)^2 = M^2/2$. This procedure can be recursively applied ld$M$ times, until we obtain a vector the size of 1, whose DFT is trivial. Of course, this procedure only works if the partitioning is possible and the number of additional operations is not of a higher order than $O(M^1)$.

We part the vector into two vectors by choosing the even and odd elements separately (figure 3.8):

$$
\begin{aligned}
\hat{g}_u &= \sum_{m=0}^{M-1} g_m \exp\left(-\frac{2\pi i\, mu}{M}\right) \\
&= \sum_{n=0}^{M/2-1} g_{2n} \exp\left(-\frac{2\pi i\, 2nu}{M}\right) + \sum_{n=0}^{M/2-1} g_{2n+1} \exp\left(-\frac{2\pi i\,(2n+1)u}{M}\right) \\
&= \sum_{n=0}^{M/2-1} g_{2n} \exp\left(-\frac{2\pi i nu}{M/2}\right) + \exp\left(-\frac{2\pi i u}{M}\right) \sum_{n=0}^{M/2-1} g_{2n+1} \exp\left(-\frac{2\pi i nu}{M/2}\right).
\end{aligned}
\tag{3.34}
$$

Both sums constitute a DFT with $M' = M/2$. The second sum is multiplied with a phase factor which depends only on the wave number u. This phase factor results from the shift theorem (see appendix A.3), since the odd elements are shifted one place to the left. As an example, we take the basis vector with $u = 1$ and $M = 8$ (figure 3.8). Taking the odd sampling points, the function shows a phase shift of $\pi/4$. This phase shift is exactly compensated by the phase factor $\exp(-2\pi i u/M) = \exp(-\pi/4)$ in (3.34).

So far the partitioning seems to be successful. The operations necessary to combine the partial Fourier transforms is just one complex multiplication and addition, i.e., $O(M^1)$. Some more detailed considerations are necessary, however, since the DFT over the half-sized vectors only yields $M/2$ values. In order to see how the composition of the M values works, we study the values for u from 0 to $M/2 - 1$ and $M/2$ to

$M - 1$ separately. The partial transformations over the even and odd sampling points are abbreviated by ${}^e\hat{g}_u$ and ${}^o\hat{g}_u$, respectively. For the first part, we can just take the partitioning as expressed in (3.34). For the second part, $u' = u + M/2$, only the phase factor changes. The addition by $M/2$ results in a change of the sign:

$$\exp\left(-\frac{2\pi i\, u'}{M}\right) = \exp\left(-\frac{2\pi i\, (u + M/2)}{M}\right) = \exp\left(-\frac{2\pi i\, u}{M}\right)\exp(-\pi i) = -\exp\left(-\frac{2\pi i\, u}{M}\right)$$

or

$$W_M^{-(u+M/2)} = -W_M^{-u}.$$

Making use of this symmetry we can write

$$\left.\begin{array}{rcl}\hat{g}_u &=& {}^e\hat{g}_u + W_M^{-u}\,{}^o\hat{g}_u \\[2mm] \hat{g}_{u+M/2} &=& {}^e\hat{g}_u - W_M^{-u}\,{}^o\hat{g}_u.\end{array}\right\} \quad 0 \le u < M/2. \qquad (3.35)$$

The Fourier transforms for the indices u and $u + M/2$ only differ by the sign of the second term. Thus for the composition of *two* terms we only need *one* complex multiplication. The partitioning is now applied recursively. The two transformations of the $M/2$-dimensional vectors are parted again into two transformations each. We obtain similar expressions as in (3.34) with the only difference being that the phase factor has doubled to $\exp[-(2\pi i u)/(M/2)]$. The even and odd parts of the even vector contain the points $\{0, 4, 8, \cdots, M/2 - 4\}$ and $\{2, 6, 10, \cdots, M/2 - 2\}$, respectively.

In the last step, we decompose a vector with two elements into two vectors with one element. Since the DFT of a single-element vector is an identical operation (3.5), no further calculations are necessary.

After the decomposition is complete, we can use (3.35) recursively with appropriate phase factors to compose the original vector step by step in the inverse order. In the first step, we compose vectors with just two elements. Thus we only need the phase factor for $u = 0$ which is equal to one. Consequently, the first composition step has a very simple form:

$$\begin{array}{rcl}\hat{g}_0 &=& g_0 + g_1 \\[2mm] \hat{g}_{0+M/2} = \hat{g}_1 &=& g_0 - g_1.\end{array} \qquad (3.36)$$

The algorithm we have discussed is called a *decimation-in-space* FFT algorithm, since the signal is decimated in the space domain. All steps of the FFT algorithm are shown in the signal flow diagram in figure 3.9 for $M = 8$. The left half of the diagram shows the decimation steps. The first column contains the original vector, the second the result of the first decomposition step into two vectors. The vectors with the even and odd elements are put in the lower and upper halves, respectively. This decomposition is continued until we obtain vectors with one element. As a result of the decomposition, the elements of the vectors are arranged in a new order. We can easily understand the new ordering scheme if we represent the indices of the vector with dual numbers. In the first decomposition step we order the elements according to the least significant bit, first the even elements (least significant bit is zero), then the odd elements (least significant bit is one). With each further decomposition step, the bit which governs the sorting is shifted one place to the left. In the end, we obtain a sorting in which the ordering of the bits is completely reversed. The element with the index

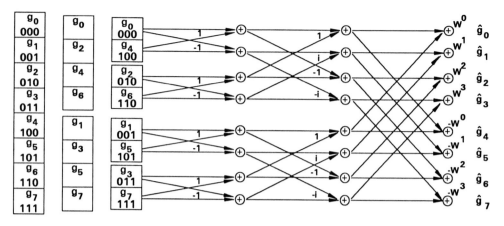

Figure 3.9: Signal flow diagram of the radix-2 decimation-in-time Fourier transform algorithm for $M = 8$; for further explanations, see text.

$1 = 001_2$, for example, will be at the position $4 = 100_2$, and vice versa. Consequently, the chain of decomposition steps can be performed with one operation by interchanging the elements at the normal and bit-reversed positions.

Further steps on the right side of the signal flow diagram show the stepwise composition to vectors of double the size. The composition to the 2-dimensional vectors is given by (3.36). The operations are pictured with arrows and points which have the following meaning: points represent a figure, an element of the vector. These points are called the *nodes* of the signal flow graph. The arrows transfer the figure from one point to another. During the transfer the figure is multiplied by the factor written close to the arrow. If the associated factor is missing, no multiplication takes place. A value of a knot is the sum of the values transferred from the previous level.

The elementary operation of the FFT algorithm involves only two knots. The lower knot is multiplied with a phase factor. The sum and difference of the two values are then transferred to the upper and lower knot, respectively. Because of the cross over of the signal paths, this operation is denoted as a *butterfly operation*.

We gain further insight into the FFT algorithm if we trace back the calculation of a single element. Figure 3.10 shows the signal paths for $\hat{g}_0$ and $\hat{g}_4$. For each level we go back the number of knots which contribute to the calculation doubles. In the last stage all the elements are involved. The signal path for $\hat{g}_0$ and $\hat{g}_4$ are identical but for the last stage, thus nicely demonstrating the efficiency of the FFT algorithm.

All phase factors in the signal path for $\hat{g}_0$ are one. As expected from (3.5), $\hat{g}_0$ contains the sum of all the elements of the vector

$$\hat{g}_0 = [(g_0 + g_4) + (g_2 + g_6)] + [(g_1 + g_5) + (g_3 + g_7)],$$

while in the last stage the addition is replaced by a subtraction for $\hat{g}_4$

$$\hat{g}_4 = [(g_0 + g_4) + (g_2 + g_6)] - [(g_1 + g_5) + (g_3 + g_7)].$$

After this detailed discussion of the algorithm, we can now estimate the number of necessary operations. At each stage of the composition, $M/2$ complex multiplications

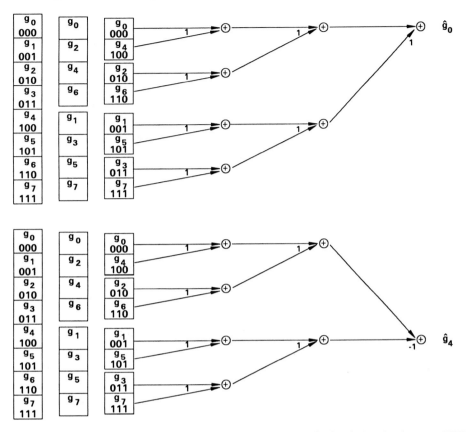

Figure 3.10: Signal flow path for the calculation of $\hat{g}_0$ and $\hat{g}_4$ with the decimation-in-space FFT algorithm for an M-dimensional vector.

and M complex additions are carried out. In total we need $M/2\,\mathrm{ld}\,M$ complex multiplications and $M\,\mathrm{ld}\,M$ complex additions. A deeper analysis shows that we can save even more multiplications. In the first two composition steps only trivial multiplications by 1 or i occur (compare figure 3.10). For further steps the number of trivial multiplications decreases by a factor of two. If our algorithm could avoid all the trivial multiplications, the number of multiplications would be reduced to $(M/2)(\mathrm{ld}\,M - 3)$.

The FFT algorithm is a classic example of a *fast algorithm*. The computational savings are enormous. For a 512-element vector, only 1536 instead of 262 144 complex multiplications are needed compared to the direct calculation according to (3.5); thus figures for an 8192-element vector need 73 728 instead of 67 108 864 complex multiplications. The number of multiplications has been reduced by a factor 170 and 910, respectively.

Using the FFT algorithm, the discrete Fourier transform can no longer be regarded as a computationally expensive operation, since only a few operations are necessary per element of the vector. For a vector with 512 elements, only 3 complex multiplications and 8 complex additions, corresponding to 12 real multiplications and 24 real additions, need to be computed.

In section 3.3, we learnt that the DFT is an example of a unitary transform which is generally performed by multiplying a unitary matrix with the vector. What does the FFT algorithm mean in this context? The signal flow graph in figure 3.9 shows that the vector is transformed in several steps. Consequently, the unitary transformation matrix is broken up into several partial transformation matrices which are applied one after the other. If we take the algorithm for $M = 8$ as shown in figure 3.9, the unitary matrix is split up into three simpler transformations with spare unitary transformations:

$$
\begin{bmatrix} \hat{g}_0 \\ \hat{g}_1 \\ \hat{g}_2 \\ \hat{g}_3 \\ \hat{g}_4 \\ \hat{g}_5 \\ \hat{g}_6 \\ \hat{g}_7 \end{bmatrix}
=
\begin{bmatrix}
1 & 0 & 0 & 0 & 1 & 0 & 0 & 0 \\
0 & 1 & 0 & 0 & 0 & W^{-1} & 0 & 0 \\
0 & 0 & 1 & 0 & 0 & 0 & W^{-2} & 0 \\
0 & 0 & 0 & 1 & 0 & 0 & 0 & W^{-3} \\
1 & 0 & 0 & 0 & -1 & 0 & 0 & 0 \\
0 & 1 & 0 & 0 & 0 & -W^{-1} & 0 & 0 \\
0 & 0 & 1 & 0 & 0 & 0 & -W^{-2} & 0 \\
0 & 0 & 0 & 1 & 0 & 0 & 0 & -W^{-3}
\end{bmatrix}
\begin{bmatrix}
1 & 0 & 1 & 0 & 0 & 0 & 0 & 0 \\
0 & 1 & 0 & i & 0 & 0 & 0 & 0 \\
1 & 0 & -1 & 0 & 0 & 0 & 0 & 0 \\
0 & 1 & 0 & -i & 0 & 0 & 0 & 0 \\
0 & 0 & 0 & 0 & 1 & 0 & 1 & 0 \\
0 & 0 & 0 & 0 & 0 & 1 & 0 & i \\
0 & 0 & 0 & 0 & 1 & 0 & -1 & 0 \\
0 & 0 & 0 & 0 & 0 & 1 & 0 & -i
\end{bmatrix}
$$
$$
\begin{bmatrix}
1 & 0 & 0 & 0 & 1 & 0 & 0 & 0 \\
1 & 0 & 0 & 0 & -1 & 0 & 0 & 0 \\
0 & 0 & 1 & 0 & 0 & 0 & 1 & 0 \\
0 & 0 & 1 & 0 & 0 & 0 & -1 & 0 \\
0 & 1 & 0 & 0 & 0 & 1 & 0 & 0 \\
0 & 1 & 0 & 0 & 0 & -1 & 0 & 0 \\
0 & 0 & 0 & 1 & 0 & 0 & 0 & 1 \\
0 & 0 & 0 & 1 & 0 & 0 & 0 & -1
\end{bmatrix}
\begin{bmatrix} g_0 \\ g_1 \\ g_2 \\ g_3 \\ g_4 \\ g_5 \\ g_6 \\ g_7 \end{bmatrix}.
$$

The reader can verify that these transformation matrices reflect all the properties of a single level of the FFT algorithm. The matrix decomposition emphasizes that the FFT algorithm can also be considered as a clever method to decompose the unitary transformation matrix into spare partial unitary transforms.

3.4.3 Other 1-D FFT Algorithms

Having worked out one fast algorithm, we still do not know whether the algorithm is optimal or if even more efficient algorithms can be found. Actually, we have applied only one special case of the divide-and-conquer strategy. Instead of parting the vector in two pieces, we could have chosen any other partition, say PQ-dimensional vectors, if $M = PQ$. This type of algorithms is called a Cooley-Tukey algorithm [Blahut, 1985].

Radix-4 Decimation-in-Time FFT
Another partition often used is the *radix-4 FFT algorithm*. We can decompose a vector into four components

$$
\hat{g}_u = \sum_{n=0}^{M/4-1} g_{4n} W_M^{-4nu} + W_M^{-u} \sum_{n=0}^{M/4-1} g_{4n+1} W_M^{-4nu}
$$
$$
+ W_M^{-2u} \sum_{n=0}^{M/4-1} g_{4n+2} W_M^{-4nu} + W_M^{-3u} \sum_{n=0}^{M/4-1} g_{4n+3} W_M^{-4nu}.
$$

For simpler equations, we will use similar abbreviations as for the radix-2 algorithm and denote the partial transformations by $^0\hat{g}, \cdots, ^3\hat{g}$. Making use of the symmetry of W_M^u, the transformations into quarters of each of the vectors are given by

$$
\begin{aligned}
\hat{g}_u &= {}^0\hat{g}_u + W_M^{-u}\,{}^1\hat{g}_u + W_M^{-2u}\,{}^2\hat{g}_u + W_M^{-3u}\,{}^3\hat{g}_u \\
\hat{g}_{u+M/4} &= {}^0\hat{g}_u - iW_M^{-u}\,{}^1\hat{g}_u - W_M^{-2u}\,{}^2\hat{g}_u + iW_M^{-3u}\,{}^3\hat{g}_u \\
\hat{g}_{u+M/2} &= {}^0\hat{g}_u - W_M^{-u}\,{}^1\hat{g}_u + W_M^{-2u}\,{}^2\hat{g}_u - W_M^{-3u}\,{}^3\hat{g}_u \\
\hat{g}_{u+3M/4} &= {}^0\hat{g}_u + iW_M^{-u}\,{}^1\hat{g}_u - W_M^{-2u}\,{}^2\hat{g}_u - iW_M^{-3u}\,{}^3\hat{g}_u
\end{aligned}
$$

or, in matrix notation,

$$
\begin{bmatrix}
\hat{g}_u \\
\hat{g}_{u+M/4} \\
\hat{g}_{u+M/2} \\
\hat{g}_{u+3M/4}
\end{bmatrix}
=
\begin{bmatrix}
1 & 1 & 1 & 1 \\
1 & -i & -1 & i \\
1 & -1 & 1 & -1 \\
1 & i & -1 & -i
\end{bmatrix}
\begin{bmatrix}
{}^0\hat{g}_u \\
W_M^{-u}\,{}^1\hat{g}_u \\
W_M^{-2u}\,{}^2\hat{g}_u \\
W_M^{-3u}\,{}^3\hat{g}_u
\end{bmatrix}.
$$

12 complex additions and 3 complex multiplications are needed to compose 4-tupel elements of the vector. We can reduce the number of additions further when we decompose the matrix into two simpler matrices:

$$
\begin{bmatrix}
\hat{g}_u \\
\hat{g}_{u+M/4} \\
\hat{g}_{u+M/2} \\
\hat{g}_{u+3M/4}
\end{bmatrix}
=
\begin{bmatrix}
1 & 0 & 1 & 0 \\
0 & 1 & 0 & -i \\
1 & 0 & -1 & 0 \\
0 & 1 & 0 & i
\end{bmatrix}
\begin{bmatrix}
1 & 0 & 1 & 0 \\
1 & 0 & -1 & 0 \\
0 & 1 & 0 & 1 \\
0 & 1 & 0 & -1
\end{bmatrix}
\begin{bmatrix}
{}^0\hat{g}_u \\
W_M^{-u}\,{}^1\hat{g}_u \\
W_M^{-2u}\,{}^2\hat{g}_u \\
W_M^{-3u}\,{}^3\hat{g}_u
\end{bmatrix}.
\tag{3.37}
$$

The first matrix multiplication yields intermediate results which can be used for several operations in the second stage. In this way, we save four additions. We can apply this decomposition recursively $\log_4 M$ times. As for the radix-2 algorithm, only trivial multiplications in the first composition step are needed. At all other stages, multiplications occur for 3/4 of the points (3.37). In total, $3/4M(\log_4 M - 1) = 3/8M(\mathrm{ld}\,M - 2)$ complex multiplications and $2M \log_4 M = M \mathrm{ld} M$ complex additions are necessary for the radix-4 algorithm. While the number of additions remains equal, 25 % less multiplications are required than for the radix-2 algorithm.

Radix-2 decimation-in-frequency FFT

The *decimation-in-frequency FFT* is another example of a Cooley-Tukey algorithm. This time, we break the M-dimensional input vector into first $M/2$ and second $M/2$ components. This partition breaks the output vector into its even and odd components:

$$
\begin{aligned}
\hat{g}_{2u} &= \sum_{m=0}^{M/2-1} (g_m + g_{m+M/2}) W_{M/2}^{-mu} \\
\hat{g}_{2u+1} &= \sum_{m=0}^{M/2-1} W_M^{-m}(g_m - g_{m+M/2}) W_{M/2}^{-mu}.
\end{aligned}
\tag{3.38}
$$

A recursive application of this partition results in a bit reversal of the elements in the output vector, but not the input vector. As an example, the signal flow graph for $M = 8$ is shown in figure 3.11. A comparison with the decimation-in-time flow graph (figure 3.9) shows that all steps are performed in inverse order. Even the elementary butterfly operations of the decimation-in-frequency algorithm are the inverse of the butterfly operation in the decimation-in-time algorithm.

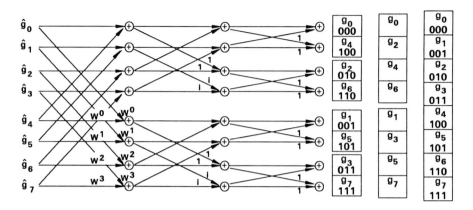

Figure 3.11: Signal flow diagram of the radix-2 decimation-in-frequency Fourier transform algorithm for $M = 8$.

Measures for Fast Algorithms

According to the number of arithmetic operations required, there are many other fast Fourier transform algorithms which are more effective. Most of them are based on polynomial algebra and the number theory. An in-depth discussion of these algorithms is given by *Blahut* [1985].

However, the mere number of arithmetic operations is not the only measure for an efficient algorithm. We must also consider a number of other factors.

- Access to the data requires additional operations. Consider the simple example of the addition of two vectors. There, besides the addition, the following operations are performed: the addresses of the appropriate elements must be calculated; the two elements are read into registers, and the result of these additions is written back to the memory. Depending on the architecture of the hardware used, these five operations constitute a significant overhead which may take much more time than the addition itself. Consequently, an algorithm with a complicated scheme to access the elements of a vector might add a considerable overhead to the arithmetic operations. In effect, a simpler algorithm with more arithmetic operations but less algorithmic overhead, may be faster.

- Another factor to rate algorithms is the amount of storage space needed. This not only includes the space for the code but also storage space required for intermediate results or tables for constants. For example, an in-place FFT algorithm, which can perform the Fourier transform on an image without using an intermediate storage area for the image, is very advantageous. Often there is a trade off between storage space and speed. Many integer FFT algorithms, for example, precalculate the complex phase factors W_m and store it in statically allocated tables.

- To a large extend the efficiency of algorithms depends on the computer architecture where it is to be implemented. If the multiplication is performed either in software or by a microcoded instruction, it is much slower than addition or memory access. In this case, the aim of fast algorithms is to reduce the number of multiplications even at the cost of more additions or a more complex memory access. Such a strategy makes no sense on some modern high-speed RISC architectures, as with the Intel i860 microprocessor, where pipelined floating point addition and multiplication take just one clock cycle. The faster the operations on the processor, the more the memory access becomes the bottleneck. Fast algorithms must now consider effective memory access schemes ensuring a high data cache hit rate. *Margulis* [1990] discusses the implementation of the FFT on the Intel i860 RISC processor. An optimized radix-2 decimation-in-frequency butterfly code, consisting of 4 real multiplications, 3 additions, 3 subtractions, 3 8-byte fetches, and 2 8-byte stores, takes just 6 processor cycles by making use of the fact that the i860 can perform several instructions in parallel.

3.4.4 Multidimensional FFT Algorithms

Generally, there are two possibilities to develop fast algorithms for multidimensional discrete Fourier transforms. Firstly, we can decompose the multidimensional DFT into 1-D DFTs and use fast algorithms for them. Secondly, we can generalize the approaches of the 1-D FFT for multidimensional spaces. In this section, we show examples for both possibilities.

Decomposition into 1-D Transforms
A two-dimensional DFT can be broken up in one-dimensional DFTs because of the separability of the kernel. In the 2-D case (3.13), we yield

$$\hat{G}_{u,v} = \frac{1}{MN} \sum_{m=0}^{M-1} \left[\sum_{n=0}^{N-1} G_{m,n} \exp\left(-\frac{2\pi i \, nv}{N} \right) \right] \exp\left(-\frac{2\pi i \, mu}{M} \right). \qquad (3.39)$$

The inner summation forms M 1-D DFTs of the rows, the outer N 1-D DFTs of the columns, i.e., the 2-D FFT is computed as M row transformations followed by N column transformations

$$\text{row transformations} \qquad \tilde{G}_{m,v} = \frac{1}{N} \sum_{n=0}^{N-1} G_{m,n} \exp\left(-\frac{2\pi i \, nv}{N} \right)$$

$$\text{column transformations} \quad \hat{G}_{u,v} = \frac{1}{M} \sum_{m=0}^{M-1} \tilde{G}_{m,v} \exp\left(-\frac{2\pi i \, mu}{M} \right).$$

In an analogous way, a k-dimensional DFT can be composed of k 1-dimensional DFTs.

Multidimensional Decomposition
A decomposition is also directly possible in multidimensional spaces. We will demonstrate such algorithms with the simple case of a 2-D radix-2 decimation-in-time algorithm.

We decompose an $M \times N$ matrix into four submatrices by taking only every second pixel in every second line (figure 3.12). This decomposition yields

$$\begin{bmatrix} \hat{G}_{u,v} \\ \hat{G}_{u,v+N/2} \\ \hat{G}_{u+M/2,v} \\ \hat{G}_{u+M/2,v+N/2} \end{bmatrix} = \begin{bmatrix} 1 & 1 & 1 & 1 \\ 1 & -1 & 1 & -1 \\ 1 & 1 & -1 & -1 \\ 1 & -1 & -1 & 1 \end{bmatrix} \begin{bmatrix} {}^{0,0}\hat{G}_{u,v} \\ W_N^{-v}\, {}^{0,1}\hat{G}_{u,v} \\ W_M^{-u}\, {}^{1,0}\hat{G}_{u,v} \\ W_M^{-u}W_N^{-v}\, {}^{1,1}\hat{G}_{u,v} \end{bmatrix}.$$

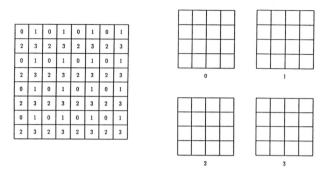

Figure 3.12: Composition of an image matrix into four partitions for the 2-D radix-2 FFT algorithm.

The superscripts in front of $\hat{G}$ denote the corresponding partial transformation. The 2-D radix-2 algorithm is very similar to the 1-D radix-4 algorithm (3.37). In a similar manner as for the 1-D radix-4 algorithm, we can reduce the number of additions from 12 to 8 by factorizing the matrix:

$$
\begin{bmatrix}
\hat{G}_{u,v} \\
\hat{G}_{u,v+N/2} \\
\hat{G}_{u+M/2,v} \\
\hat{G}_{u+M/2,v+N/2}
\end{bmatrix}
=
\begin{bmatrix}
1 & 0 & 1 & 0 \\
0 & 1 & 0 & 1 \\
1 & 0 & -1 & 0 \\
0 & 1 & 0 & -1
\end{bmatrix}
\begin{bmatrix}
1 & 1 & 0 & 0 \\
1 & -1 & 0 & 0 \\
0 & 0 & 1 & 1 \\
0 & 0 & 1 & -1
\end{bmatrix}
\begin{bmatrix}
{}^{0,0}\hat{G}_{u,v} \\
W_N^{-v}\, {}^{0,1}\hat{G}_{u,v} \\
W_M^{-u}\, {}^{1,0}\hat{G}_{u,v} \\
W_M^{-u}W_N^{-v}\, {}^{1,1}\hat{G}_{u,v}
\end{bmatrix}
.
$$
$$(3.40)$$

The 2-D radix-2 algorithm of an $M \times M$ requires $(3/4M^2)\mathrm{ld}\,M$ complex multiplications, 25 % less than the separation into two 1-D radix-2 FFTs.

4 Pixels

4.1 Introduction

Discrete images are composed of individual image points, which we denoted in section 2.3.1 as *pixels*. Pixels are the elementary units in digital image processing. The simplest processing is to handle these pixels as individual objects or measuring points. This approach enables us to regard image formation as a measuring process which is corrupted by noise and systematic errors. Thus we learn to handle image data as statistical quantities. As long as we are confined to individual pixels, we can apply the classical concepts of statistics which are used to handle point measurements, e. g., the measurement of meteorological parameters at a weather station such as air temperature, wind speed and direction, relative humidity, and air pressure.

Statistical quantities are found in image processing in many respects:
- The imaging sensor introduces electronic noise into the light intensities measured.
- In low-light level application, we are no longer measuring a continuous stream of light, but rather single photons.
- The process or object observed may exhibit a statistical nature. An evident example are images of turbulent flows (see section 1.4 and plate 4).

4.2 Random Variables

4.2.1 Basics

We consider an experimental setup in which we are measuring a certain process. In this process we also include the noise introduced by the sensor. The measured quantity is the light intensity or gray value of a pixel. Because of the statistical nature of the process, each measurement will give a different value. This means that the observed process is not characterized by a single gray value but rather a probability density function $p(g)$ indicating how often we observe the gray value g. A measurable quantity which is governed by a random process — such as the gray value g of a pixel in image processing — is denoted as a *random variable*.

In the following, we discuss both continuous and discrete random variables and probability functions. We need discrete probabilities as only discrete gray values can be handled by a digital computer. Discrete gray values are obtained after a process called quantization, which is discussed in section 4.2.2. All formulas in this section contain continuous formulation on the left side and their discrete counterparts on the right side. In the continuous case, a gray value g is measured with the probability $p(g)$. In the discrete case, we can only measure a finite number, Q, of gray values g_q ($q = 0, 1, \ldots, Q - 1$) with the probability p_q. Normally, the gray value of a pixel is stored in one byte so that we can measure $Q = 256$ different gray values. Since the total probability to observe any gray value is 1, the probability meets the requirement

$$\int_{-\infty}^{\infty} dg\, p(g) = 1, \quad \sum_{q=0}^{Q-1} p_q = 1. \tag{4.1}$$

The *expected* or *mean* gray value μ is defined as

$$\mu = \langle g \rangle = \int_{-\infty}^{\infty} dg\, p(g)g, \quad \mu = \sum_{q=0}^{Q-1} p_q g_q. \tag{4.2}$$

The computation of the expectation value is denoted — as in quantum mechanics — by a pair of angle brackets $\langle \cdots \rangle$. The *variance* is a measure to which extent the measured values deviate from the mean value

$$\sigma^2 = \left\langle (g - \langle g \rangle)^2 \right\rangle = \int_{-\infty}^{\infty} dg\, p(g)(g - \langle g \rangle)^2, \quad \sigma^2 = \sum_{q=0}^{Q-1} p_q(g_q - \langle g \rangle)^2. \tag{4.3}$$

The probability function can be characterized in more detail by similar quantities as the variance, the *moments*:

$$m_n = \langle (g - \langle g \rangle)^n \rangle = \int_{-\infty}^{\infty} dg\, p(g)(g - \langle g \rangle)^n, \quad m_n = \sum_{q=0}^{Q-1} p_q(g_q - \langle g \rangle)^n. \tag{4.4}$$

The first moment is — by definition — zero. The second moment corresponds to the variance. The third moment, the *skewness*, is a measure for the asymmetry of the probability function around the mean value. If a distribution function is symmetrical with respect to the mean value, the third and all higher-order odd moments vanish.

The probability function depends on the nature of the underlying process. Many processes with continuous random variables can be adequately described by the *normal* or *Gaussian* probability distribution

$$p(g) = \frac{1}{\sqrt{2\pi}\sigma} \exp\left(-\frac{(g - \langle g \rangle)^2}{2\sigma^2}\right). \tag{4.5}$$

The normal distribution is completely described by the two elementary statistical parameters, mean and variance. Many physical random processes are governed by the normal distribution, because they are a *linear* superimposition of many (n) individual processes. The *central limit theorem* of statistics states that in the limit $n \to \infty$ the

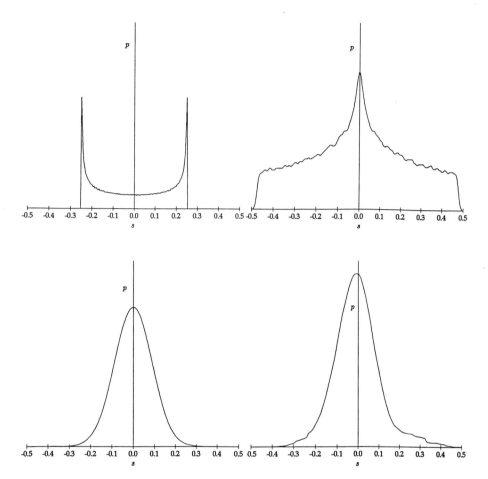

Figure 4.1: Illustration of the superimposition of the probability functions with the slope distribution on the undulated ocean surface: a) slope distribution of a single sinusoidal wave; b) slope distribution of the superposition of two statistically independent sinusoidal waves; c) Gaussian distribution as the theoretical limit for the linear superimposition of many sinusoidal waves; d) slope distribution as measured in a wind-wave facility [*Jähne*, unpublished data].

distribution tends to a normal distribution, provided certain conditions are met by the individual processes [*Reif*, 1985].

As an example, we consider the distribution of the slope of the ocean surface. The ocean surface is undulated by surface waves which incline the water surface. As elementary processes, we can regard sinusoidal waves as propagating on the ocean surface. Such a single wave shows a slope distribution very different from that of a normal distribution (figure 4.1a). The maximum probability occurs with the maximum slopes of the wave. Let us assume that waves with different wavelengths and direction superimpose on each other without any disturbance and that the slope of the individual wave trains is small. The slopes can then be added up. The resulting probability distribution is given by convolution of the individual distributions, since, at each probable slope of the first wave, the second can have all slopes according to its own probability distribution. The superimposition of two waves results in a distribution with the maximum at slope zero (figure 4.1b). Even for quite a small number of superimpositions, we can expect a normal distribution (figure 4.1c).

A measured slope distribution looks very similar to a normal distribution, but also shows some significant deviations (figure 4.1d). The distribution is slightly asymmetric. The maximum is shifted to small negative slopes, high positive slope values are much more likely than high negative slopes and than those expected from a normal distribution.

The deviations from a normal distribution occur because water surface waves violate one of the requirements for a normal distribution. They do not superimpose without interactions because of their non-linear nature. In consequence, deviations from the normal distribution provide some clues about the strength and the kind of nonlinear interactions.

For discrete values, the Gaussian distribution is replaced by the *binomial distribution* [*Reif*, 1985]

$$p_q = \frac{Q!}{q!\,(Q-q)!}p^q(1-p)^{Q-q}, \quad \text{with } 0 < p < 1. \tag{4.6}$$

Again Q denotes the number of quantization levels. The parameter p determines the mean and the variance

$$\mu = Qp \tag{4.7}$$

$$\sigma^2 = Qp(1-p). \tag{4.8}$$

For large Q, the binomial distribution quickly converges to the Gaussian distribution. For $Q = 8$, the differences are already quite small, as is shown by the following table ($p = 1/2$, $\sigma^2 = 2$, $\mu = 4$):

q	0	1	2	3	4	5	6	7	8
Binomial distribution	1	8	28	56	70	56	28	8	1
Gaussian distribution	1.3	7.6	26.6	56.2	72.2	56.2	26.6	7.6	1.3

An application of this simple statistics is shown in the handling of noisy images. There are a number of imaging sensors available which show a considerable noise level. The most prominent example is *thermal imaging*. Such a sensor collects thermal radiation in the far infrared with wavelengths between 3 and 14 μm and thus can measure the temperature of objects. Figure 4.2a shows the temperature of the water surface. We can hardly detect the small temperature fluctuations which indicate the turbulent mixing close to the water surface. We can however take the mean of several images, just as we would take several measurements to obtain a better estimate of the mean. An estimate of the error of the mean taken from N samples is given by

$$\sigma^2_{\langle g \rangle} \approx \frac{1}{(N-1)}\sigma^2_g = \frac{1}{N(N-1)}\sum_{n=0}^{N}(g - \langle g \rangle)^2. \tag{4.9}$$

If we take the average of N images, the noise level is already reduced by a factor $\sqrt{N}$ compared to a single image. Figure 4.2b shows how much better the pattern can be observed in the average image.

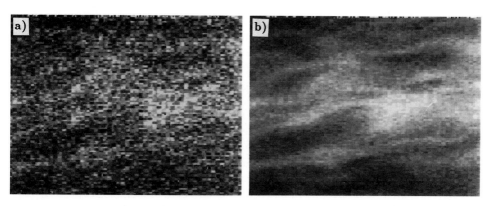

Figure 4.2: Noise reduction by image averaging: a) single thermal image of small temperature fluctuations on a water surface; b) same, averaged over 16 images; temperature range corresponding to full gray value range: 1.25 K.

4.2.2 Quantization

As another application of statistical handling of data we consider quantization. After digitization (section 2.3), the pixels still show continuous gray values. For use with a computer we must map them onto a limited number Q of discrete gray values:

$$[0, \infty[\xrightarrow{Q} \{g_0, g_1, \ldots, g_{Q-1}\} = G.$$

This process is called *quantization*. The number of quantization levels in image processing should meet two criteria.

First, no gray value steps should be recognized by our visual system. Figure 4.3 shows images quantized with 2 to 16 levels of gray values. It can be clearly seen that a low number of gray values leads to false edges and makes it very difficult to recognize objects which show no uniform gray values. In printed images, 16 levels of gray values seem to be sufficient, but on a monitor we would still be able to see the gray value steps. Generally, image data are quantized into 256 gray values. Then each pixel occupies 8 bit or one byte. This bit size is well adapted to the architecture of standard computers which can address memory bytewise. Furthermore, the resolution is good enough that we have the illusion of a continuous change in the gray values, since the relative intensity resolution of our visual system is only about 2 % (see section 1.3).

The other criterion is related to the imaging task. For a simple application in machine vision, where the objects show a uniform brightness which is different from the background, or for particle tracking in flow visualization (section 1.4 and plate 4), two quantization levels, i. e., a *binary image*, might be sufficient. Other applications might require the resolution of faint changes in the intensity. Then an 8-bit resolution would be too coarse.

Quantization always introduces errors, since the true value g is replaced by one of the quantization levels g_q. If the quantization levels are equally spaced with a distance Δg and all gray values are equally probable, the variance introduced by the quantization

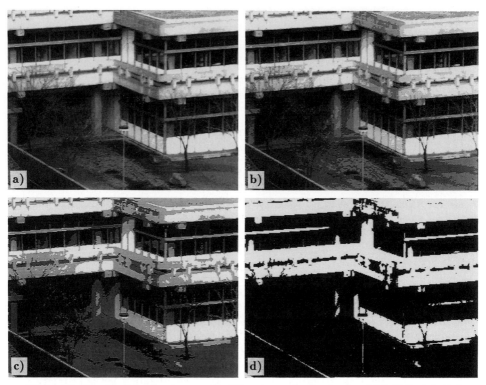

Figure 4.3: Quantization of an image with different quantization levels: a) 16; b) 8; c) 4; d) 2.

is given by

$$\sigma_q^2 = \frac{1}{\Delta g} \int\limits_{g_q-\Delta g/2}^{g_q+\Delta g/2} (g - g_q)^2 \mathrm{d}g = \frac{1}{12}(\Delta g)^2. \qquad (4.10)$$

This equation shows how we select a quantization level. We take the level g_q for which the distance from the gray value g, $|g - g_q|$, is smaller than the neighboring quantization levels q_{k-1} and q_{k+1}. The standard deviation σ_q^2 is about 0.3 times the distance of the quantization levels Δg.

Quantization with unevenly spaced quantization levels is discussed in detail by *Rosenfeld and Kak* [1982]. Unevenly spaced quantization levels are hard to realize in any image processing system. An easier way to yield unevenly spaced levels is to use equally spaced quantization but to transform the intensity signal before quantization with a non-linear amplifier, e. g., a logarithmic amplifier. In case of a logarithmic amplifier we would obtain levels whose widths increase proportionally with the gray value.

Algorithm 1: C subroutine to calculate the histogram of an image stored row by row in video memory. The offset between the lines allows that the histogram of only a subimage (area-of-interest) can be calculated. This program has been written to run on the TMS 34010 graphics processor of the VISTA frame buffer (see appendix B).

```
/*
** Compute histogram in vector l1 for the byte image i1 in memory
** Explanation of variables:
** v1:      pointer to LVEC structure
** i1:      pointer to BMAT structure
** pv:      pointer to begin of histogram vector
** pi:      pointer to image data
** dx:      number of columns
** dy:      number of rows
** loffs:   offset between end of previous and beginning of next line
*/
void vml1b1hist(v1,i1) LVEC *v1; BMAT *i1; {
    long *pv=v1->dat;
    unsigned char *pi=(unsigned char*)i1->dat;
    long dy=i1->dy, dx=i1->dx, i;
    long loffs=i1->offs-(long)i1->dx;

    /* clear histogram */
    vl1clr(v1);

    /* compute histogram */
    while (dy--) {
        for (i=dx; i > 0; i--) pv[*pi++]++;
        pi += loffs;
    }
}
```

4.2.3 Histograms

Generally, the probability distribution is not known a priori. Rather it is estimated from measurements. If the observed process is *homogeneous*, that is, it does not depend on the position of the pixel in the image, there is a simple way to estimate the probability distribution with the so-called *histogram*.

A histogram of an image is a vector which contains one element for each quantization level. Each element contains the number of pixels whose gray value corresponds to the index of the element. Histograms can be calculated straightforwardly (algorithm 1). First we set the whole histogram vector to zero. Then we scan all pixels of the image, take the gray value as the index to the vector, and increment the corresponding element of the vector by one. The actual scanning algorithm depends on how the image is stored. Algorithm 1 assumes that the image is stored row by row in the memory, where an arbitrary offset between the lines is allowed.

Histograms allow a first examination of the images acquired. A surprising property of the acquisition hardware is revealed in figure 4.4a. We might have expected a smooth histogram from an image which just contains gradual changes in the gray values. However, the histogram shows large variations from gray value to gray value. These variations cannot be caused by statistical variations: a 512×512 image has 1/4 million

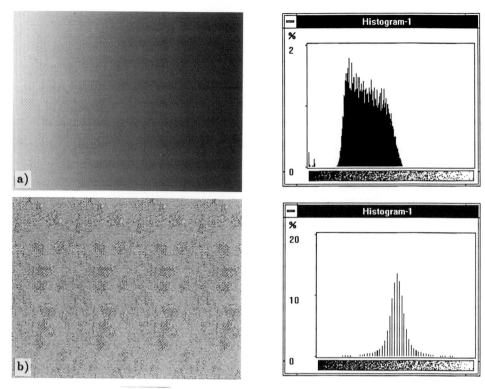

Figure 4.4: Images and their gray value histograms I; a) quality control of the analog-digital-converter (ADC); b) contrast enhanced difference of two consecutive images to show the camera noise.

pixels, so that on average 1000 pixels show the same gray values. Consequently, the statistical fluctuations even in a total random image should only be $\sqrt{1000}$ or about 3 %. The reason lies rather in the varying widths of the quantization levels. Imagine that the decision levels of the video analog-digital converter are accurate to 1/8 least significant bit. Then the widths of a quantization level might vary from 3/4 to 5/4 least significant bit. Consequently, the probability distribution may vary by ±25 %.

Figure 4.4b gives an impression of the noise of CCD cameras. It shows the difference between two consecutive images taken from the same static scene. The histogram gives a clear indication whether an image is too dark or too bright (figure 4.5). As we know from our discussion on the human visual system in section 1.4, it is very difficult to estimate absolute intensities just by eye. Therefore, it is strongly recommended to use objective tools such as histograms to rate image intensities. Especially dangerous are under- or overflows in the gray values, since they are deceiving areas of constant brightness, where there may actually be considerable gray value variation. Over- or underflow can be recognized in the histogram by a strong peak at gray values 255 and 0, respectively. Under optimal conditions, the histogram should fill the whole gray value range, but go to zero at the edges. We should adjust our imaging system in such a way that this condition is met.

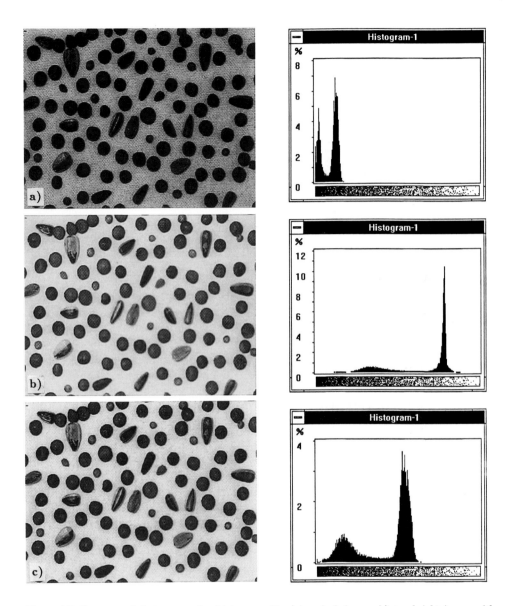

Figure 4.5: Images and their gray value histograms II; a) too dark image; b) too bright image with overflow in gray values; c) correctly illuminated image.

4.3   Point Operations

4.3.1   Homogeneous Point Operations

Point operations are a class of very simple image processing operations. The gray values at individual pixels are modified depending on the gray value and the position of the pixel. Generally, such a kind of operation is expressed by

$$G'_{mn} = P_{mn}(G_{mn}). \qquad (4.11)$$

The indices at the function P denote the explicit dependence on the position of the pixel. If the point operation is independent of the position of the pixel, we speak of it as being an *homogeneous point operation* and can write

$$G'_{mn} = P(G_{mn}). \qquad (4.12)$$

Point operations are used to perform such simple image processing tasks as
- Compensation of non-linear camera characteristics. Generally, the gray value is not directly proportional to the brightness in the image.
- Correction and optimization of the brightness and contrast.
- Highlighting of image parts with a certain range of gray values; detection of small intensity differences.
- Balancing of illumination differences caused by the uneven sensitivity of the image sensors or intensity drop towards the edge of the images.

It is important to note that the result of the point operation does not depend at all on the gray value of neighboring pixels. A point operation maps the set of gray values onto itself. Generally, point operations are not invertible, since two different gray values may be mapped onto one. Thus a point operation generally results in a loss of information which cannot be recovered. The point operation

$$P(g_q) = \begin{cases} 0 & g_q < t \\ 255 & g_q \geq t \end{cases}, \qquad (4.13)$$

for example, performs a simple threshold evaluation. All gray values below the threshold are set to zero (black), all above and equal to the threshold to 255 (white).

Only a point operation with a one-one mapping of the gray values is invertible.

4.3.2   Look-Up Tables

The direct computation of homogeneous point operations, according to (4.12), is very costly. Imagine that we intend to present a 512×512 image in a logarithmic gray value scale with the point operation $P(g_q) = 25.5 \log g_q$. We would have to calculate the logarithm $262\,144$ times. The key point for a more efficient implementation lies in the observation that the definition range of any point operation consists of only very few gray values, typically 256. Thus we would have to calculate the very same values many times. We can avoid this if we precalculate $P(g_q)$ for all 256 possible gray values and store the computed values in a 256-element table. Then the computation of the point operation is reduced to a replacement of the gray value by the element in the table with an index corresponding to the gray value.

Such a table is called a *look-up table* or LUT. As a result, homogeneous point operations are equivalent to *look-up table operations*.

In most image processing systems, look-up tables are implemented in hardware. Generally, one look-up table, the *input LUT*, is located between the analog-digital converter and the frame buffer. Another, the *output LUT*, is located between the frame buffer and the digital-analog converter for output of the image in the form of an analog video signal, e. g., to a monitor. (Technical details are described in appendix B.) The input LUT allows a point operation to be performed *before* the image is stored in the frame buffer. With the output LUT, a point operation can be performed and observed on the monitor. In this way, we can interactively perform point operations *without* modifying the stored image.

As a first example of LUT operations, we will consider contrast stretching and brightness optimization. Because of poor lighting conditions and the offset level of the video amplifier being too low, an image will be too dark and of low contrast (figure 4.6a). The histogram shows that the image contains only a low range of gray values at low gray values. We can improve the appearance of the image considerably if we apply a point operation which shows a steep line from 0–255 only over a small gray value range and is 0 below and 255 above the selected range. This operation stretches the small range of gray values over the full range from 0 to 255 (figure 4.6a). It is important to recognize that we only improve the appearance of the image with this operation but not the image *quality* itself. The gray value resolution is still the same.

The right way to improve the image quality is to optimize the lighting conditions. If this is not possible, we can increase the gain of the analog video amplifier. Many modern image processing boards include an amplifier whose gain and offset can be set by software (see appendix B). Increasing the gain we can improve the brightness and resolution of the image but only at the expense of an increased noise level.

The point operation which yields the digital negative of an image,

$$N(g_q) = Q - 1 - g_q, \qquad (4.14)$$

is one of the few examples of a reversible point operation (figure 4.6b).

A logarithmic transformation of the gray values allows a larger dynamic range to be recognized at the cost of resolution in the bright parts of the image. The dark parts become brighter and show more details (figure 4.7a). The image is better adapted to the logarithmic characteristics of the human visual system which can detect relative intensity differences over a wide range of intensities (section 1.4). The last example in figure 4.7b shows a *clipping* operation of the bright parts of the image. High gray values above a threshold are set to 255. This operation maps the gray values of the background to a constant value and thus is useful to suppress background noise while leaving the darker gray values in the objects unchanged.

A cautionary note is necessary for all kinds of LUT operations. As we have already discussed in contrast stretching, any LUT operation makes the images look better, but does not actually improve them. This is why we should use them thoughtfully. A careful

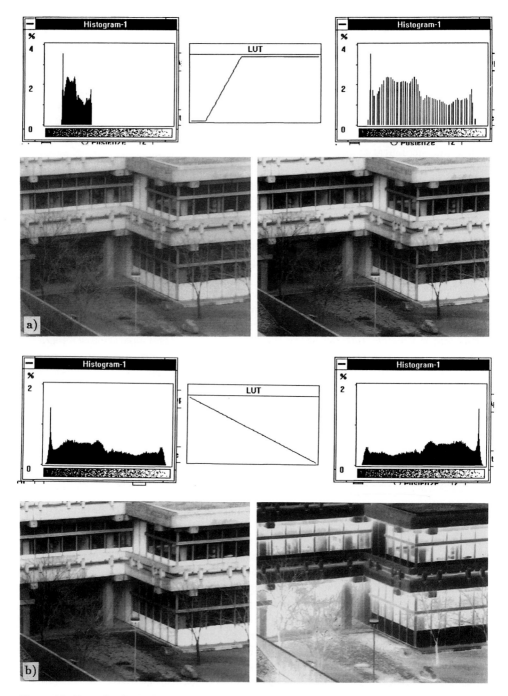

Figure 4.6: Examples for LUT operations I: a) contrast stretching of a low-contrast image; b) digital negative.

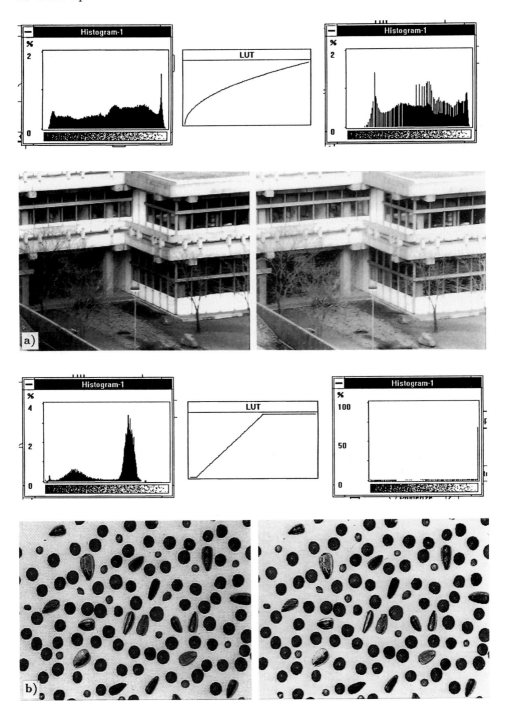

Figure 4.7: Examples for LUT operations II: a) range compression; b) background clipping.

preparation of images using an LUT operation is very important for printouts which have a lower contrast range than images on monitors. It may also be appropriate to use more advanced methods such as histogram equalization [*Jain*, 1989]. However, for further processing of images, especially if we are interested in a *quantitative* analysis of gray values, they are not of much help. On the contrary, they may introduce additional errors, because of the rounding errors introduced by non-linear LUT functions. They may lead to missing gray values in the output or mapping of two consecutive gray values onto one. These problems are apparent in the histogram of the processed image in figure 4.7a.

In conclusion, the use of input LUTs is limited. Input LUTs would be a valuable processing element if the digitization precision were higher than the storage precision. Imagine that we digitize with 12 bit, pass the data through a 12-bit input LUT, and store them with 8 bit. Then we would not see rounding errors. In addition, we could compress a larger dynamic range with a logarithmic LUT onto 8 bit.

In contrast to the input LUT, the output LUT is a much more widely used tool, since it does not change the stored image. With LUT operations we can also convert a gray-value image into a *pseudo-color image*. Again, this technique is common even with the simplest image processing boards, since not much additional hardware is needed. Three digital analog converters are used for the primary colors red, green, and blue. Each channel has its own LUT. In this way, we can map each individual gray value g_q to any color by assigning a color triple to the corresponding LUT addresses $r(g_q)$, $g(g_q)$, and $b(g_q)$. Formally, we now have a *vector* point operation

$$\boldsymbol{P}(g_q) = \begin{bmatrix} r(g_q) \\ g(g_q) \\ b(g_q) \end{bmatrix}. \tag{4.15}$$

As long as all three point functions $r(g_q)$, $g(g_q)$, and $b(g_q)$ are identical, a gray value image will be displayed. If two of them vanish, the image will appear in the remaining color. RGB output LUTs find a wide variety of applications:

- Small gray value differences can be recognized much better if they are transformed into color differences. We can mark gray value ranges of interest with a certain color. In this way we can also overcome the incapability of the human visual system to recognize absolute gray values. Some examples of pseudo-coloring of gray value images are shown in plate 7.

- Recognized objects — as the result of a *segmentation* (chapter 10) — can be marked by coloring without changing the gray values if we reserve another bit plane of the frame buffer to store the binary image generated by segmentation. This bit can then be used to switch to another set of RGB output LUTs which, for example, show the gray values of the image in yellow instead of white, if it belongs to the object. Since the original gray values can still be seen, we can study the quality of the segmentation in detail.

- In the same manner, we can visualize the result of a *classification* (chapter 12). Now we can use a different color for objects belonging to different classes.

- Histograms, LUTs, markers and grids can be superimposed in color over the gray value image and can thus be recognized much better as if we had overlaid them in black-and-white.

- A more complex application is the representation of stereo images (see section 2.2.9 and plate 6a). We either need two frame buffers, or must split the bit planes of a frame buffer in two parts to store the left and right stereo image with half the resolution, e. g., 4 bit = 16 gray values, instead of 8 bit = 256 gray values. With two frame buffers, we just need to associate the red and green color channel to the first and second frame buffer, respectively. If we store the red and green component images in the 4 lower and higher bit planes, the RGB LUTs would contain the following values:

$$\begin{aligned} r(g_p) &= (g_q \bmod 16)16 \\ g(g_p) &= (g_q/16)16 \\ b(g_p) &= 0. \end{aligned} \tag{4.16}$$

The LUT for the red channel sets the output gray value according to the four lowest bits, while the green channel ignores these bits and only takes the 4 most significant bits.

- In a similar manner, we can represent multi-channel images. An interesting example is shown in plate 4a. This color image is composed of eight binary images. Each bit plane is shown in a different color to identify the individual images.
- Finally, we can code vectorial image features in color, as we will discuss in section 7.1.2.

A final remark concerns the representation of gray values. Normally we think of them as unsigned numbers ranging from 0 to 255 in 8 bit values. As soon as we perform operations with images, e. g., if we subtract two images, negative gray values may appear which cannot be represented. Thus we are confronted with the problem of two different representations of gray values, as unsigned and signed 8 bit numbers. Correspondingly, we must have two versions of algorithms, one for unsigned and one for signed gray values.

A simple solution to this problem is to handle gray values principally as signed numbers. This can be simply done by subtracting 128. Then the mean gray value intensity of 128 would become the gray value zero. Gray values lower than this mean value are negative. Subtraction by 128 can be easily implemented with the input LUT

$$p(g_q) = (g_q - 128) \bmod 256, \quad 0 \le g_q < 256. \tag{4.17}$$

This point operation converts unsigned gray values to signed gray values which are stored and manipulated in the frame buffer. For display, we must convert the gray values again to unsigned values by the inverse point operation

$$p(g_q) = (g_q + 128) \bmod 256, \quad 0 \le g_q < 256, \tag{4.18}$$

which is the same point operation since all calculations are performed modulo 256.

4.3.3 Inhomogeneous Point Operations

Computation of an *inhomogeneous point operation* is much more time consuming. We cannot use look-up tables since the point operation depends on the pixel position and we are forced to calculate the function for each pixel. Despite the effort involved, inhomogeneous point operations are used quite often. Here we will discuss two important applications.

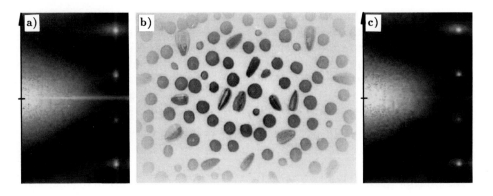

Figure 4.8: Effect of windowing on the discrete Fourier transform: a) DFT of b) without using a window function; b) image multiplied with a cosine window; c) DFT of b) using a cosine window.

Window Operations

Before we can calculate the DFT of an image, the image must be multiplied with a *window function*. If we omit this step, the spectrum will be distorted by the convolution of the image spectrum with the Fourier transform of the box function, the sinc function (see appendix A.3), which causes spectral peaks to become star-like patterns along the coordinate axes in Fourier space (figure 4.8a). We can also explain these distortions with the periodic repeat of finite area images (see section 2.3.3). The periodic repeat leads to discontinuities in horizontal and vertical directions which cause corresponding high spectral densities along the axes in the k space. In order to avoid these disturbances, we must multiply the image with a window function which approaches zero towards the edges of the image. An optimum window function should a) preserve a high spectral resolution and b) show minimum distortions in the spectrum, that is, its DFT should fall off as fast as possible. These are two contradictory requirements. A good spectral resolution requires a broad window function. Such a window, however, falls off steeply at the edges causing a slow fall-off of the sidelopes of its spectrum.

A carefully chosen window is very crucial for a spectral analysis of time series [*Marple*, 1987; *Oppenheim and Schafer*, 1989]. However, in digital image processing it is not so critical, because of the much lower dynamic range of the gray values. A simple cosine window

$$w'_{mn} = \cos\left(\frac{2\pi m}{M}\right)\cos\left(\frac{2\pi n}{N}\right)\cdot w_{mn}, \quad -M/2 \le m < M/2, \ -N/2 \le n < N/2 \quad (4.19)$$

performs this task well (figure 4.8b). The indices in (4.19) are centered around zero.

A direct implementation of the windowing operation is very time consuming, because we would have to calculate the cosine function MN times. It is much more efficient to perform the calculation of the window function once, store it in the frame buffer, and use it for the calculation of many DFTs. The computational efficiency can be further improved by recognizing that the window function (4.19) is separable, i. e., a product of two functions $w_{m,n} = {}^c w_m \cdot {}^r w_n$. Then we need to calculate only the M plus N values for the column and row function ${}^c w_m$ and ${}^r w_n$, respectively. As a result there

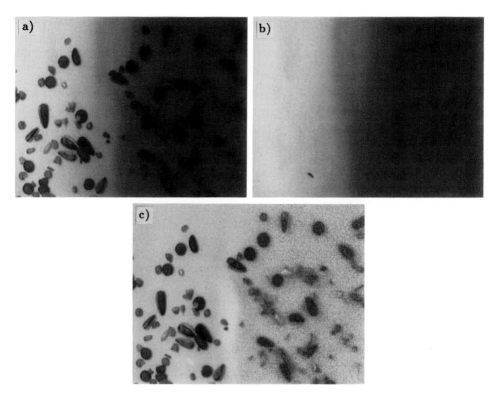

Figure 4.9: Correction of uneven illumination with an inhomogeneous point operation: a) original image; b) background image; c) division of the image by the background image. Computations performed with BioScan OPTIMAS.

is no need to store the whole window image. It is sufficient to store only the row and column functions at the expense of an additional multiplication per pixel when using the window operation.

Correction of Uneven Illumination
Every real-world application has to contend with *uneven illumination* of the observed scene. Even if we spend a lot of time optimizing the lighting system, it is still very hard to obtain a perfect even illumination. A more difficult problem are small dust particles in the optical path especially on the glass window close to the CCD sensor. These particles are not sharply imaged but absorb some light and thus cause a drop in the illumination level in a small area. These effects are not easily visible in a scene with high contrast and many details, but become very apparent in a scene with a uniform background (figure 4.9a and b). CCD sensors also illustrate the problem of uneven sensitivity of the individual photo receptors. These distortions severely limit the quality of the images. Additional noise is introduced, it is more difficult to separate an object from the background, and additional systematic errors have to be considered concerning the accuracy of gray values.

Nevertheless, it is possible to correct these effects if we can take a background image. We might either be able to take a picture without the objects, or, if they are distributed randomly, we can calculate a mean image from the many different images. This background image b_{mn} can be used to correct the uneven illumination and sensitivity of our sensor. We just divide the image by the background image:

$$g'_{mn} = c g_{mn}/b_{mn}. \tag{4.20}$$

Since the gray values of the divided image again have to be represented by integers, multiplication with an appropriate constant is necessary. Figure 4.9c demonstrates that an effective suppression of an uneven illumination is possible using this simple method.

4.4   Dyadic LUT Operations

The window operations and corrections of uneven illumination discussed in the last section are two examples of operations in which two images are involved, termed *dyadic image operations*. In those two examples only simple operations, multiplication and division, were involved. In this section we discuss how dyadic image operations can be implemented as LUT operations and consider some further examples. Generally, any dyadic image operation can be expressed as

$$g'_{mn} = P(g_{mn}, h_{mn}) \tag{4.21}$$

and performed as an LUT operation. Let the gray values of each parameter in P take Q different values. In total we have to calculate Q^2 combinations of parameters and thus different values of the LUT table L. For 8-bit images, 64k values need to be calculated, that is still a quarter less then with a direct computation for each pixel in a 512×512 image. We can store all the results of the dyadic operation in a large LUT with $Q^2 = 64k$ entries in the following manner:

$$L(2^8 g_p + h_q) = P(g_p, h_q), \quad 0 \le g_p, h_q < Q. \tag{4.22}$$

High and low bytes of the LUT address are given by the gray values in the images G and H, respectively.

More advanced image processing systems, such as the Series 151 (see appendix B), contain a 16-bit LUT as a modular processing element. With such an LUT processor any dyadic LUT operation with two 8-bit images can be performed in video time, i.e., 33 ms for a 512×512 image, once the 64k LUT has been programmed. This is much faster than a direct computation of a dyadic operation using the PC hardware, especially if the operation is complex. One such example is the calculation of phase and magnitude from a complex-valued image, such as the DFT of an image. We can perform both operations simultaneously with one LUT operation if we restrict the output to 8 bit:

$$L(2^8 r_p + i_q) = 2^8 \sqrt{r_p^2 + i_q^2} + \frac{128}{\pi} \arctan\left(\frac{i_p}{r_q}\right), \quad 0 \le r_p, i_q < Q. \tag{4.23}$$

The magnitude is returned in the high byte and the phase, scaled to ± 128, in the low byte.

4.5 Correlations and Spectra

4.5.1 Random Fields

The statistics developed so far, notably histograms, does not contain any information on the image content, i. e., the relations between the pixels. Let us illustrate this important fact by a simple example. Take the image shown in figure 4.5 with a bimodal histogram. This histogram could belong to many different images. We do not know anything about the size and number of the objects. The histogram could be from an image with a single dark and white area. Or, even more complicated, a bimodal histogram does not mean at all that we can separate an object from the background. It could result, for example, from an image where the objects show a pattern with dark and light stripes and the background shows white dots on a black background.

If we want to analyze the contents of images statistically, we must consider the whole image as a statistical quantity, known as a *random field*. In case of an $M \times N$ image, a random field consists of an $M \times N$ matrix whose elements are random variables. This means that a different probability distribution belongs to each individual pixel. The mean of a random field is then given by

$$\langle G_{m,n} \rangle = \sum_{q=0}^{Q} p_q(m,n) g_q. \qquad (4.24)$$

We can make an estimate of the mean, just as we would do for a single value, by taking N measurements under the same conditions and computing the average image

$$\langle G \rangle_E = \frac{1}{N} \sum_{n=1}^{N} G_n. \qquad (4.25)$$

The index E indicates that we compute the mean by averaging over several members of the ensemble of possible random fields belonging to a given experimental setup (*ensemble mean*). The estimate of the *variance* is given by

$$\sigma^2_G = \frac{1}{N-1} \sum_{n=1}^{N} (G_n - \langle G \rangle)^2. \qquad (4.26)$$

4.5.2 Correlations and Covariances

Now we can relate the gray values at two different positions with each other. One measure for the correlation of the gray values is the expectation value for the product of the gray values at the two positions, the *autocorrelation function*

$$R_{gg}(m,n;m',n') = \langle G_{mn} G_{m'n'} \rangle = \sum_{q=0}^{Q-1} \sum_{r=0}^{Q-1} g_q g_r p(q,r;m,n;m',n'). \qquad (4.27)$$

The probability function has six parameters and tells us the probability that we simultaneously measure the gray value q at the point (m,n) and r at the point (m',n'). The autocorrelation function is four-dimensional. Therefore this general statistics is hardly ever used. Things become easier, if the statistics does not explicitly depend on the position of the pixel. Such a random field is called *homogeneous*. The mean value is then constant over the whole image

$$\langle G \rangle = \text{const}, \tag{4.28}$$

and the autocorrelation function becomes *shift invariant*

$$\begin{aligned} R_{gg}(m+k, n+l; m'+k, n'+l) &= R_{gg}(m, n; m', n') \\ &= R_{gg}(m-m', n-n'; 0, 0) \\ &= R_{gg}(0, 0; m'-m, n'-n). \end{aligned} \tag{4.29}$$

The last two identities are obtained when we set $(k, l) = -(m', n')$ and $(k, l) = -(m, n)$. Since the autocorrelation function depends only on the distance between point, it reduces from a four- to a two-dimensional function. Fortunately, many stochastic processes are homogeneous. A deterministic image which additively contains *zero-mean noise*,

$$G' = G + R, \quad \langle G' \rangle = G, \tag{4.30}$$

is not a homogeneous field, because the mean is not constant. By subtraction of the mean, however, we yield a homogeneous random field. Some processes show *multiplicative noise*. Multiplicative noise can be converted to additive noise by taking the logarithm of the gray values. The autocorrelation function for a homogeneous random field takes a much simpler form, since it depends only on the distance between the pixels:

$$R_{gg}(kl) = \sum_{m=0}^{M-1} \sum_{n=0}^{N-1} G_{mn} G_{m+k, n+l}. \tag{4.31}$$

This expression includes spatial averaging. For a general homogeneous random field it is not certain that spatial averaging leads to the same mean as the ensemble mean. A random field which meets this criterion is called an *ergodic random field*. Another difficulty concerns indexing. As soon as $(m, n) \neq (0, 0)$, the indices run over the range of the matrix. We then have to consider the periodic extension of the matrix, as discussed in section 3.2.3. This is known as *cyclic autocorrelation*.

As discussed above, many processes consist of a deterministic and a zero-mean random process. Therefore it is helpful first to subtract the mean and then to calculate the correlation

$$C_{gg}(kl) = \sum_{m=0}^{M-1} \sum_{n=0}^{N-1} (G_{mn} - \langle G_{mn} \rangle)(G_{m+k, n+l} - \langle G_{m+k, n+l} \rangle). \tag{4.32}$$

This function is called the *autocovariance*. The autocovariance for zero-shift ($(k, l) = (0, 0)$) is equal to the variance.

Now we illustrate the meaning of the autocorrelation function with some examples. First we consider an image containing only zero-mean homogeneous noise. The fluctuations at the individual pixels should be independent of each other. Autocorrelation (and autocovariance) then vanishes except for zero shift. For zero shift it is equal to the variance of the noise. This means that the autocorrelation is unequal to zero if the fluctuations at neighboring pixels are not independent. If the autocorrelation gradually decreases with the distance of the pixels, the pixels become more and more statistically independent. We can then define a characteristic length scale over which the gray values at the pixels are correlated to each other. In this sense the autocorrelation function is a description of the interrelation between the gray values of neighboring pixels.

In a similar manner as we correlate one image with itself, we can correlate images from two different homogeneous stochastic processes G and H. The *cross correlation* function is defined as

$$R_{gh}(k,l) = \sum_{m=0}^{M-1}\sum_{n=0}^{N-1} G_{mn} H_{m+k,n+l} \tag{4.33}$$

and the *cross covariance* as

$$C_{gh}(kl) = \sum_{m=0}^{M-1}\sum_{n=0}^{N-1} (G_{mn} - \langle G_{mn}\rangle)(H_{m+k,n+l} - \langle H_{m+k,n+l}\rangle). \tag{4.34}$$

The cross correlation operation is very similar to the convolution operation (see appendix A.3). The only difference is the sign of the indices (m,n) in the second term.

4.5.3   Spectra and Coherence

Now we consider random fields in the Fourier space. In the previous section we learnt that they are characterized by the auto- and cross correlation functions. Correlation in the space domain corresponds to multiplication in the Fourier space with the complex conjugate functions

$$\langle G \star G \rangle \quad \circ\!\!-\!\!\bullet \quad P_{gg}(\boldsymbol{k}) = \langle \hat{g}(\boldsymbol{k})\hat{g}^*(\boldsymbol{k})\rangle \tag{4.35}$$

and

$$\langle G \star H \rangle \quad \circ\!\!-\!\!\bullet \quad P_{gh}(\boldsymbol{k}) = \left\langle \hat{g}(\boldsymbol{k})\hat{h}^*(\boldsymbol{k})\right\rangle. \tag{4.36}$$

In these equations, correlation is abbreviated with the $\star$ symbol, similar to convolution for which we use the $*$ symbol. For a simpler notation, the spectra are written as continuous functions. The Fourier transform of the autocorrelation function is the *power spectrum P_{gg}*. The Fourier transform of the cross-correlation function is called the *cross-correlation spectrum P_{gh}*. In contrast to the power spectrum, it is a complex quantity, the real and imaginary parts being termed the co- and quad-spectrum, respectively. To understand the meaning of the cross-correlation function, it is useful to define another quantity, the *coherence function* Φ:

$$\Phi^2(\boldsymbol{k}) = \frac{|P_{gh}(\boldsymbol{k})|^2}{P_{gg}(\boldsymbol{k})P_{hh}(\boldsymbol{k})}. \tag{4.37}$$

Basically, the coherence function contains information on the similarity of two images. We illustrate this by assuming that the spectrum of image H is a shifted copy of the image G, $\hat{h} = \hat{g}\exp(-\mathrm{i}\boldsymbol{k}\boldsymbol{x}_s)$. In this case, the coherence function is one and the cross-correlation spectrum P_{gh} reduces to

$$P_{gh}(\boldsymbol{k}) = P_{gg}(\boldsymbol{k})\exp(\mathrm{i}\boldsymbol{k}\boldsymbol{x}_s). \tag{4.38}$$

Since P_{gg} is a real quantity, we can compute the shift $\boldsymbol{x}_s$ between the two images from the phase factor $\exp(\mathrm{i}\boldsymbol{k}\boldsymbol{x}_s)$.

If there is no fixed phase relationship of a periodic component between the two images, then the coherency decreases. We can easily see this if we think of several independent components with different phase shifts. If the phase shift of these components is randomly distributed, the cross-correlation vectors in the complex plane point into random directions and add up to zero. A more detailed discussion of cross-spectral analysis can be found in *Marple* [1987].

An illustrative example is seen in cross-spectral image analysis of water surface waves (see section 1.4). As two different random fields, we take images which have been acquired shortly after each other with a time interval of t_0. During this time a wave with the wave number $\boldsymbol{k}$ travels a certain distance so that it shows a phase lag in the second image which is given by

$$\phi = \omega t_0, \tag{4.39}$$

where ω is the circular frequency of the wave. This phase shift is measured with the coherence function and allows us to determine the phase speed $\boldsymbol{c}$ of the wave by the simple relation

$$\boldsymbol{c} = \frac{\phi}{k^2 t_0}\boldsymbol{k}. \tag{4.40}$$

The coherence function tells us whether all waves with the same wave number $\boldsymbol{k}$ have the same phase speed. The larger the fluctuations of the phase speed, the lower is the coherence. Figure 4.10 shows the power spectrum, the coherency function, and the phase speed averaged over 258 images as a function of the wave number in a log-polar wave number coordinate system (section 3.2.5). Even if we are not familiar with the physics of water surface waves, the apparent differences in the phase speed and the coherence function observed under the two different conditions tell us that cross-spectral analysis is a useful tool.

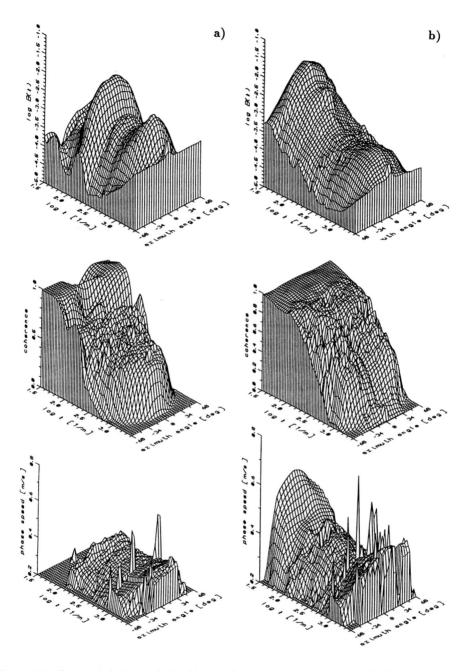

Figure 4.10: Cross-correlation analysis of images from water surface waves at 3 m/s wind speed to determine the phase speed and the coherence of the wave field: a) 6.2 m fetch; b) 21.3 m fetch. Unpublished data of the author from measurements in the wind-wave facility IMST, University of Marseille, France.

5 Neighborhoods

5.1 Combining Pixels

The contents of an image can only be revealed when we analyze the spatial relations of the gray values. If the gray value does not change in a small neighborhood, we are within an area of constant gray values. This could mean that the neighborhood is included in an object. If the gray value changes, we might be at the edge of an object. In this way, we recognize areas of constant gray values and edges.

Point operations do not provide this type of information. New classes of operations are necessary which combine the pixels of a small neighborhood in an appropriate manner and yield a result which forms a new image. The meaning of the gray values in such an image has changed. If we apply an operation to detect the edges, a bright gray value at a pixel may now indicate that an edge runs across the pixel.

Point operations are a very simple class of operations which are basically used for *image enhancement*; in other words, to make images look better. It is obvious that operations combining neighboring pixels to form a new image are much more diversified and complex. They can perform quite different image processing tasks:

- Suppression of noise.
- Correction of disturbances caused by errors in image acquisition or transmission. Such errors will result in incorrect gray values for a few individual pixels.
- Compensation of incorrect focusing, motion blur or similar errors during image acquisition. Such operations are called *image restoration* operations since they try to restore the original from a degraded image.
- Enhancement or suppression of fine details in images.
- Detection of simple local structures as edges, corners, lines and areas of constant gray values.

In this chapter we will discuss linear shift-invariant and rank value filters as two principal possibilities for combining pixels in a local neighborhood. Then we have to work out the base from which to handle a wide range of image processing tasks starting with simple smoothing and edge detection operations (chapter 6). These two chapters are central to this book as simple filter operations are the building blocks for more complex operations discussed in chapters 6 through 9 and 17. Optimum filter design and fast algorithms for filter operations are also discussed in chapter 6.

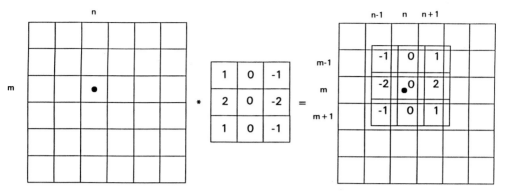

Figure 5.1: Illustration of the discrete convolution operation with a 3×3 filter mask.

5.1.1 Linear Filtering

First we focus on the question as to how we can combine the gray values of pixels in a small neighborhood. The first characteristic is the size of the neighborhood, which we call the *window* or *filter mask*. The window size may be rectangular or of any other form. We must also specify the position of the pixel relative to the window which will receive the result of the operation. With regard to symmetry, the most natural choice is to place the result of the operation at the pixel in the center of an odd-sized mask.

The most elementary combination of the pixels in the window is given by an operation which multiplies each pixel in the range of the filter mask with the corresponding weighting factor of the mask, adds up the products, and writes the result to the position of the center pixel:

$$G'_{mn} = \sum_{k=-r}^{r} \sum_{l=-r}^{r} H_{kl} G_{m-k,n-l} = \sum_{k=-r}^{r} \sum_{l=-r}^{r} H_{-k,-l} G_{m+k,n+l}. \tag{5.1}$$

This equation assumes an odd-sized mask with $(2r + 1) \times (2r + 1)$ coefficients. It describes a *discrete convolution* operation. In comparison to the continuous convolution, the integral is replaced by a sum over discrete elements (compare appendices A.2 and A.3).

The convolution operation is such an important operation that it is worth studying it in detail to see how it works. First, we might be confused by the negative signs of the indices k and l either for the mask or the image in (5.1). This just means that we either rotate the mask or the image around its symmetry center by 180° before we put the mask over the image. (We will learn the reason for this rotation in section 5.2.) If we want to calculate the result of the convolution at the point (m,n), we center the rotated mask at this point, perform the convolution, and write the result back to position (m, n) (figure 5.1). This operation is performed for all pixels of the image. Close to the edges of the image, when the filter mask ranges over the edge of the image, we run into difficulties as we are missing some image points. The *correct* way to solve

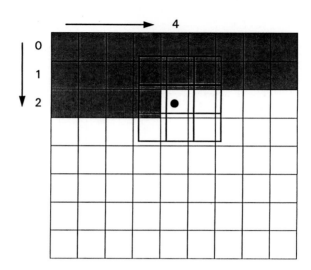

Figure 5.2: Image convolution by scanning the convolution mask line by line over the image. At the shaded pixels the gray value is already been replaced by the convolution sum. Thus the gray values at the shaded pixels falling within the filter mask need to be stored in an extra buffer.

this problem according to our summations in section 2.3, especially equation (3.17), is to take into account that finite image matrices must be thought of as being repeated periodically. Consequently, when we arrive at the left edge of the image, we take the missing points from the right edge of the image. We speak of a *cyclic convolution*. Only this type of convolution will reduce to a simple multiplication in the Fourier space (see appendix A.3). In practice, this approach is seldom chosen. Instead we add a border to the image with half the width of the filter mask. In this border either zeros are written, or we extrapolate in one way or the other the gray values from the gray values at the edge of the image. The simplest type of extrapolation is to write the gray values of the edge pixels into the border.

Although this approach gives less visual distortion at the edge of the image than cyclic convolution, we do introduce errors at the edge of the image with a width of half the size of the filter mask. If we choose the extrapolation method, the edge pixels are overweighted.

Equation (5.1) indicates that none of the calculated gray values G'_{mn} will flow into the computation at other neighboring pixels. This means that the result of the convolution operation, i.e., a complete new image, has to be stored in a separate memory area. If we want to perform the filter operation in-place, we run into a problem. Let us assume that we perform the convolution line by line and from left to right. Then the gray values at all pixel positions above and to the left of the current pixel are already overwritten by the previously computed results (figure 5.2). Consequently, we need to store the gray values at these positions in an appropriate buffer.

Now, the question arises whether it is possible or even advantageous to include the already convolved neighboring gray values into the convolution at the next pixel. In this way, we might be able to do a convolution with fewer operations since we include the previously computed results. In effect, we are able to perform convolutions with much less computational effort and also more flexibility. However, these filters, which are called *recursive filters*, are much more difficult to understand and to handle — especially in the two-dimensional case.

For a first impression, we consider a very simple one-dimensional example. The simplest recursive filter we can think of has the general form

$$g'_m = (1 - \alpha)g'_{m-1} + \alpha g_m. \tag{5.2}$$

This filter takes the fraction $1 - \alpha$ from the previously calculated value and the fraction α from the current pixel. Recursive filters, in contrast to non-recursive filters, work in a certain direction, in our example from left to right. For time series, the preferred direction seems natural, since the current state of a signal depends only on previous values. Filters, which depend only on the previous values of the signal, are called *causal filters*. For images, however, no preferred direction exists. This is the first principal problem posed by recursive filters for spatial data. Consequently, we have to search for ways to construct noncausal and symmetric filters from recursive filters.

From (5.2), we can calculate the response of the filter to the *discrete delta function*

$$\delta_k = \begin{cases} 1 & k = 0 \\ 0 & k \neq 0 \end{cases}, \tag{5.3}$$

i.e., the *point spread function* or *impulse response* of the filter (compare section 2.2.6). Recursively applying (5.2) to the discrete delta function, we obtain

$$\begin{aligned} g'_{-1} &= & 0 \\ g'_0 &= & \alpha \\ g'_1 &= & \alpha(1 - \alpha) \\ g'_m &= & \alpha(1 - \alpha)^m. \end{aligned} \tag{5.4}$$

This equation shows several typical general properties of recursive filters:

- First, the impulse response is infinite, despite the finite number of coefficients. For $|\alpha| < 1$ it decays but never becomes exactly zero. In contrast, the impulse response of non-recursive convolution filters is always finite. It is equal to the size of the filter mask. Therefore the two types of filters are sometimes named *finite impulse response filters* (FIR filters) and *infinite impulse response filters* (IIR filters).
- FIR filters are always *stable*. This means that they always give a finite response to a finite signal. This is not the case for IIR filters. The stability of recursive filters depends on the filter coefficients. The filter in (5.2) is instable for $|\alpha| \geq 1$ since even the impulse response diverges. In the simple case of (5.2) it is easy to recognize the instability of the filter. Generally, however, it is much more difficult to analyze the stability of a recursive filter, especially in dimensions which are two and higher.

5.1.2 Recursive Filters and Linear Systems

Recursive filters can be regarded as the discrete counterpart of *analog filters*. A simple analog filter for electrical signals contains resistors, capacitors, and inductors. As an

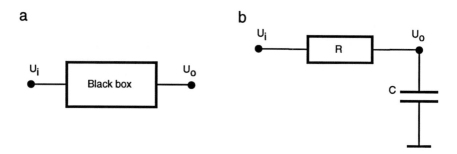

Figure 5.3: Analog filter for time series: a) black-box model: a signal U_i is put into an unknown system. At the output we measure the signal U_o. b) a resistor-capacitor circuit as a simple example for an analog lowpass filter.

example, we take the simple resistor-capacitor circuit shown in figure 5.3b. The differential equation for this filter can easily be derived from Kirchhoff's current-sum law. The current flowing through the resistor from U_i to U_o must be equal to the current flowing into the capacitor. Since the current flowing into a capacitor is proportional to the temporal derivative of the potential $\dot{U}_o$, we end up with the first order differential equation

$$\frac{U_i - U_o}{R} = C\dot{U}_o. \tag{5.5}$$

This equation represents a very important general type of process called a *relaxation process*, which is governed by a time constant τ. In our case, the time constant is given by $\tau = RC$. Generally, we can write the differential equation of a relaxation process as

$$\tau \dot{U}_o + U_o = U_i. \tag{5.6}$$

The impulse response $h(t)$ of this system (in case of an RC-circuit the reaction to a short voltage impulse) is given by

$$h(t) = \begin{cases} 0 & t < 0 \\ (1/\tau)\exp(-t/\tau) & t \geq 0. \end{cases} \tag{5.7}$$

In case of a continuous function the impulse response is also known as *Green's function*. Once we know the impulse response of the filter, we can calculate the response to any arbitrary signal by

$$U_o(t) = \int_0^\infty dt'\, U_i(t')h(t - t'), \tag{5.8}$$

since (5.6) is linear in U. Because the impulse response is zero for $t < 0$ (*causal* filter), the integration limits extend from 0 to ∞ only.

A discrete approximation of the analog RC filter can be derived by transforming the differential equation (5.6) into a finite difference equation

$$U_o(t) = \frac{\tau}{\tau + \Delta t}U_o(t - \Delta t) + \frac{\Delta t}{\tau + \Delta t}U_i(t). \tag{5.9}$$

This equation is equivalent to the simple recursive filter (5.2). We have already seen this identity when comparing the discrete and continuous impulse responses in (5.4) and (5.7). Since the difference equation is only an approximation of the differential equation, discrete and continuous filters are better called equivalent when the sampled continuous impulse response is equal to the discrete impulse response. In this way, we can derive the relationship between the constant α and the time constant τ. It is sufficient to compare the exponential terms. From

$$\exp(-t/\tau) = \exp(-m\Delta t/\tau) = (1 - \alpha)^m = \exp[m \ln(1 - \alpha)], \qquad (5.10)$$

we derive

$$\tau = -\frac{\Delta t}{\ln(1 - \alpha)} \quad \text{or} \quad \alpha = 1 - \exp(-\Delta t/\tau). \qquad (5.11)$$

With these equations, we obtain a relationship between a continuous process and its discrete counterpart. Since the discrete samples resemble the analog process exactly, it is not only an approximation. This means that we can exactly simulate analog filters with discrete filters, provided we meet the sampling theorem.

Another example also demonstrates the relationship between recursive filters and linear systems. Let us consider the next more complex recursive filter, a *second-order* filter, which relates the current output to the output of the two last samples:

$$g'_m = 2r \cos \Theta g'_{m-1} - r^2 g'_{m-2} + g_m. \qquad (5.12)$$

The impulse response of this filter can be shown to be [*Oppenheim and Schafer*, 1989]

$$h_m = \begin{cases} \dfrac{r^m \sin[\Theta(m + 1)]}{\sin \Theta} & m \geq 0 \\ 0 & m < 0. \end{cases} \qquad (5.13)$$

The transfer function of this asymmetric causal filter is complex:

$$\hat{h}(\tilde{k}) = \frac{1}{\left(e^{-i\Theta} - e^{-\pi i k}\right)\left(e^{i\Theta} - e^{-\pi i k}\right)}, \qquad (5.14)$$

with the magnitude

$$|\hat{h}(\tilde{k})|^2 = \frac{1}{\left(r^2 + 1 - 2r \cos(\pi \tilde{k} - \Theta)\right)\left(r^2 + 1 - 2r \cos(\pi \tilde{k} + \Theta)\right)}. \qquad (5.15)$$

At first glance, these formulas might look not familiar, but closer examination reveals that they describe the discrete analogue to a very important physical system, the *damped harmonic oscillator*. The impulse response describes a sampled damped harmonic oscillation which has been excited at time zero:

$$h(t) = \begin{cases} \exp(-t/\tau) \sin(\omega_0 t) & t \geq 0 \\ 0 & t < 0 \end{cases} . \qquad (5.16)$$

The transfer function (5.14) contains the physical meaning of the *resonance curve* for the oscillator. If $r = 1$, the oscillator is undamped, and the transfer function has two *poles* at $\tilde{k} = \pm \Theta/\pi$. If $r > 1$, the resonator is unstable; even the slightest excitement will cause infinite amplitudes of the oscillation. Only for $r < 1$, the system is stable; the oscillation is damped. Comparing (5.13) and (5.16), we can determine the relationship of the eigenfrequency ω_0 and the time constant τ of a real-world oscillator to the parameters of the discrete oscillator, r and Θ

$$r = \exp(-\Delta t/\tau) \quad \text{and} \quad \Theta = \omega_0 \Delta t. \tag{5.17}$$

The last example of the damped oscillator illustrates that there is a close relationship between discrete filter operations and analog physical systems. Thus filters may be used to represent a real-world physical process. They model how the corresponding system would respond to a given input signal g. Actually, we have already made use of this equivalence in our discussion of optical imaging in section 2.2.6. There we found that imaging with a homogeneous optical system is completely described by its point spread function and that the image formation process can be described by convolution. Optical imaging together with physical systems such as electrical filters and oscillators of all kinds, can thus be regarded as representing an abstract type of processes or systems, called *linear shift-invariant systems*.

This generalization is very useful for image processing, since we can describe both the image formation and image processing as convolution operations with the same formalism. Moreover, the images observed may originate from a physical process which can be modelled by a linear shift-invariant system. Then an experiment to find out how the system works can be illustrated using the black-box model (figure 5.3a). The black box means that we do not know the composition of the system observed or, physically speaking, the laws which govern it. We can find them out by probing the system with certain signals (input signals) and watching the response by measuring some other signals (output signals). If it turns out that the system is linear, it will completely be described by the impulse response. Many biological and medical experiments are performed in this way. Biological systems are typically so complex that the researchers often stimulate them with signals and watch for responses in order to be at least able to make a model. From this model more detailed research may start to investigate how the observed system functions might be realized. In this way many properties of biological visual systems have been discovered. But be careful — a model is not the reality! It pictures only the aspect that we probed with the applied signals.

Oppenheim et al. [1983] give a thorough and coherent treatment of linear system theory. *Marple* [1987] discusses in detail digital spectral analysis with emphasis on model-based approaches.

5.1.3   Rank Value Filtering

The considerations on how to combine pixels have resulted in the powerful concept of linear shift-invariant systems. Thus we might be tempted to think that we have learnt all we need to know for this type of image processing operations. This is not the case. There is another class of operations which works on a quite different concept.

We might characterize a convolution with a filter mask by weighting and summing up. The class of operations to combine neighboring pixels we are considering now may be characterized by comparing and selecting. They are called *rank value filters*. For this

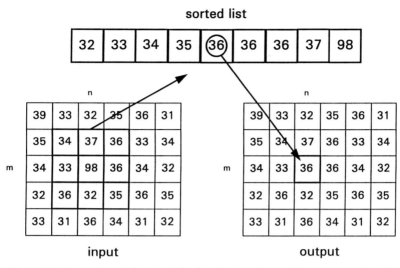

Figure 5.4: Illustration of the principle of rank value filters with a 3×3 median filter.

we take all the gray values of the pixels which lie within the filter mask and sort them by ascending gray value. This sorting is common to all rank value filters. They only differ by the position in the list from which the gray value is picked out and written back to the center pixel. The filter operation which selects the medium value is called the *median filter*. Figure 5.4 illustrates how the median filter works. The filters choosing the minimum and maximum values are denoted as the minimum and maximum filter, respectively.

There are a number of significant differences between linear convolution filters and rank value filters. First of all, rank value filters are *nonlinear* filters. Consequently, it is much more difficult to understand their general properties. We will discuss the consequences in detail throughout this chapter in comparison with the convolution filters. Since rank value filters do not perform arithmetic operations but select pixels, we will never run into rounding problems. These filters map a discrete set of gray values onto themselves.

5.2 Linear Shift-Invariant Filters

In this section we discuss the general properties of filters which are both linear and shift-invariant. We denote this filter type as *LSI filters*. The theoretical foundations laid down in this section will help us enormously for practical application. In the previous section we discussed convolution as a natural way to combine neighboring pixels. Here we will go the other way round. We start with a discussion of linearity and shift invariance and end up with the conclusion that convolution is the only class of operation meeting these properties. Instead of filters, we will speak of *operators* which map or transform an image onto itself. In the following we will denote these operators with calligraphic symbols and write

$$\mathbf{G}' = \mathcal{H}\mathbf{G} \tag{5.18}$$

for an operator $\mathcal{H}$ which transforms the image $\mathbf{G}$ into the image $\mathbf{G}'$. Such a general notation is very helpful, since it allows us to write complex operations easily comprehensible. Furthermore, it does not matter whether the image is represented by an $M \times N$ matrix in the space or the Fourier domain. The reason for this *representation indepen-dent notation* lies in the fact that the general properties of operations do not depend on the actual representation. The mathematical foundation is composed of inner product vector spaces, which we discussed in section 3.3.1. In this sense, we regard an image as an element in a complex-valued $M \times N$-dimensional vector space.

5.2.1 Linearity

Linear operators are defined by the principle of *superposition*. If $\mathbf{G}$ and $\mathbf{G}'$ are two $M \times N$ images, a and b two complex-valued scalars, and $\mathcal{H}$ is an operator which maps an image onto another image of the same dimension, then the operator is linear if and only if

$$\mathcal{H}(a\mathbf{G} + b\mathbf{G}') = a\mathcal{H}\mathbf{G} + b\mathcal{H}\mathbf{G}'. \tag{5.19}$$

We can generalize (5.19) to the superposition of many inputs

$$\mathcal{H}\left(\sum_k a_k \mathbf{G}_k\right) = \sum_k a_k \mathcal{H}\mathbf{G}_k. \tag{5.20}$$

The superposition property makes linear operators very useful. We can decompose a complex image into simpler components for which we can easily derive the response of the operator and then compose the resulting response from that of the components.

It is especially useful to decompose an image into its individual elements. Formally, this means that we compose the image with the base images of the chosen representation, which is a series of shifted discrete δ or impulse images $\mathbf{D}$

$$^{kl}\mathbf{D} = \begin{cases} 1 & k = k', l = l' \\ 0 & \text{otherwise} \end{cases}. \tag{5.21}$$

Thus we can write

$$\mathbf{G} = \sum_{m=0}^{M-1}\sum_{n=0}^{N-1} G_{mn}\,{}^{mn}\mathbf{D}. \tag{5.22}$$

As an example for a nonlinear operator, we take the *median filter* $\mathcal{M}$, which has been introduced in section 5.1.3. For the sake of simplicity, we consider a one-dimensional case with a 3-element median filter. It is easy to find two vectors for which the median filter is not linear:

$$\begin{aligned} &\mathcal{M}\left(\left[\cdots\ 0\ 1\ 0\ -1\ 0\ 1\ \cdots\right] + \left[\cdots\ 1\ 1\ 0\ 0\ -1\ -1\ \cdots\right]\right) \\ =\ &\left[\cdots\ 1\ 0\ -1\ -1\ \cdots\right] \neq \\ &\mathcal{M}\left[\cdots\ 0\ 1\ 0\ -1\ 0\ 1\ \cdots\right] + \mathcal{M}\left[\cdots\ 1\ 1\ 0\ 0\ -1\ -1\ \cdots\right] \\ =\ &\left[\cdots\ 1\ 0\ 0\ -1\ \cdots\right]. \end{aligned} \tag{5.23}$$

5.2.2   Shift Invariance

Another important property of an operator is shift invariance or homogeneity. It means that the response of the operator does not explicitly depend on the position in the image. If we shift an image, the output image is the same but for the shift applied. We can formulate this property more elegantly if we define a *shift operator* ^{kl}S which is defined as

$$^{kl}SG_{mn} = G_{m-k,n-l}. \tag{5.24}$$

Then we can define a *shift-invariant* operator in the following way: an operator is shift invariant if and only if it commutes with the shift operator, i.e.,

$$\mathcal{H}\left(^{kl}SG\right) = {}^{kl}S\left(\mathcal{H}G\right). \tag{5.25}$$

It is important to note that the shift operator ^{kl}S itself is a linear shift-invariant operator.

5.2.3   Impulse Response, Transfer Function, and Eigenfunctions

From our considerations in sections 2.2.6 and 5.1.1, we are already familiar with the *point spread function* or *impulse response* of either a continuous or a discrete operator. Here we introduce the formal definition of the point spread function for an operator $\mathcal{H}$ onto an $M \times N$-dimensional vector space

$$\boldsymbol{H} = \mathcal{H}^{00}\boldsymbol{D}. \tag{5.26}$$

Now we can use the linearity (5.20) and shift invariance (5.25) of the operator $\mathcal{H}$ and the definition of the impulse response (5.26) to calculate the result of the operator on any arbitrary image $\boldsymbol{G}$ in the space domain

$$
\begin{aligned}
(\mathcal{H}G)_{mn} &= \left(\mathcal{H}\left(\sum_{k=0}^{M-1}\sum_{l=0}^{N-1}G_{kl}\,{}^{kl}\boldsymbol{D}\right)\right)_{mn} && \text{with (5.20)} \\
&= \left(\sum_{k=0}^{M-1}\sum_{l=0}^{N-1}G_{kl}\mathcal{H}\,{}^{kl}\boldsymbol{D}\right)_{mn} && \text{linearity} \\
&= \left(\sum_{k=0}^{M-1}\sum_{l=0}^{N-1}G_{kl}\mathcal{H}\,{}^{kl}S\,{}^{00}\boldsymbol{D}\right)_{mn} && \text{with (5.24)} \\
&= \left(\sum_{k=0}^{M-1}\sum_{l=0}^{N-1}G_{kl}\,{}^{kl}S\mathcal{H}\,{}^{00}\boldsymbol{D}\right)_{mn} && \text{shift invariance} \qquad (5.27) \\
&= \left(\sum_{k=0}^{M-1}\sum_{l=0}^{N-1}G_{kl}\,{}^{kl}S\boldsymbol{H}\right)_{mn} && \text{with (5.26)} \\
&= \sum_{k=0}^{M-1}\sum_{l=0}^{N-1}G_{kl}H_{m-k,n-l} && \text{with (5.24)} \\
&= \sum_{k'=0}^{M-1}\sum_{l'=0}^{N-1}G_{m-k',n-l'}H_{k',l'} && \text{using } k'=m-k, l'=n-l.
\end{aligned}
$$

These calculations prove that a linear shift-invariant operator must *necessarily* be a convolution operation in the space domain. There is *no* other operator type which is both linear and shift-invariant.

Next we are interested in the question whether special types of image E exist which are preserved except for multiplication with a scalar by a linear shift-invariant operator, i. e.,

$$\mathcal{H}E = \lambda E. \tag{5.28}$$

A vector (image) which meets this condition is called an *eigenvector* or *characteristic vector* of the operator, the scaling factor λ an *eigenvalue* or *characteristic value* of the operator.

As a simple linear shift-invariant operator, we first consider the shift operator $\mathcal{S}$. It is quite obvious that for real images only a trivial eigenimage exists, namely a constant image. For complex images, however, a whole set of eigenimages exists. We can find it when we consider the shift property of the *complex exponentials*

$$^{uv}W_{mn} = \exp\left(\frac{2\pi \mathrm{i}\, mu}{M}\right) \exp\left(\frac{2\pi \mathrm{i}\, nv}{N}\right), \tag{5.29}$$

which is given by

$$^{kl}\mathcal{S}\,^{uv}W = \exp\left(-\frac{2\pi \mathrm{i}\, ku}{M}\right) \exp\left(-\frac{2\pi \mathrm{i}\, lv}{N}\right)\,^{uv}W. \tag{5.30}$$

The latter equation directly states that the complex exponentials ^{uv}W are eigenfunctions of the shift operator. The eigenvalues are complex phase factors which depend on the wave number indices (u, v) and the shift (k, l). When the shift is one wavelength, $(k, l) = (M/u, N/v)$, the phase factor reduces to 1 as we would expect.

Now we are curious to learn whether any linear shift-invariant operator has such a handy set of eigenimages. It turns out that all linear shift-invariant operators have the same set of eigenimages. We can prove this statement by referring to the *convolution theorem* (see appendix A.3) which states that convolution is a point-wise multiplication in the Fourier space:

$$G' = H * G \quad \circ\!\!-\!\!\bullet \quad \hat{G}' = \hat{H} \cdot \hat{G}. \tag{5.31}$$

The element-wise multiplication of the two matrices H and G in the Fourier space is denoted by a centered dot to distinguish this operation from matrix multiplication which is denoted without any special sign. Equation (5.31) tells us that each element of the image representation in the Fourier space $\hat{G}_{uv}$ is multiplied by the complex scalar $\hat{H}_{uv}$. Since each point $\hat{G}_{uv}$ in the Fourier space represents a base image, namely the complex exponential ^{uv}W in (5.29) multiplied with the scalar $\hat{G}_{uv}$, they are eigenfunctions of any convolution operator. The eigenvalues are then the elements of the transfer function, $\hat{H}_{uv}$. In conclusion, we can rewrite (5.31)

$$\mathcal{H}(\hat{G}_{uv}\,^{uv}W) = \hat{H}_{uv}\hat{G}_{uv}\,^{uv}W. \tag{5.32}$$

Another proof is based on the theorem that two commutable operators have the same set of eigenvectors [*Grawert*, 1973].

5.2.4 Symmetry

In section 5.1.1 we have already pointed out that for the sake of symmetry, filter masks with an odd number of pixels are preferred. In this section we will continue the discussion on symmetry of LSI filters and how it effects the representations of the operators in the space and wave number domain.

Representation in the Space Domain
In section 5.2.3 (5.27) we found that an LSI filter can be represented in the space domain as a convolution of the operator image H with the image G

$$G'_{mn} = \sum_{k=0}^{M-1}\sum_{l=0}^{N-1} H_{k,l} G_{m-k,n-l}. \tag{5.33}$$

In section 5.1.1 (5.1) we wrote it as the convolution with a small filter mask centered around the index $(0,0)$

$$G'_{mn} = \sum_{k=-r}^{r}\sum_{l=-r}^{r} H_{-k,-l} G_{m+k,n+l}. \tag{5.34}$$

Both representations are equivalent if we consider the periodicity in the space domain (section 3.2.3). The restriction of the sum in (5.34) reflects the fact that the impulse response or PSF of the filter is zero except for the few points around the center pixel. Thus the latter representation is much more practical and gives a better comprehension of the PSF. For example, the filter mask

$$\begin{bmatrix} 0 & -1 & -2 \\ 1 & 0_{\bullet} & -1 \\ 2 & 1 & 0 \end{bmatrix} \tag{5.35}$$

written as an $M \times N$ matrix reads as

$$\begin{bmatrix} 0_{\bullet} & -1 & 0 & \ldots & 0 & 1 \\ 1 & 0 & 0 & \ldots & 0 & 2 \\ 0 & 0 & 0 & \ldots & 0 & 0 \\ \vdots & \vdots & \vdots & \vdots & \vdots & \vdots \\ 0 & 0 & 0 & \ldots & 0 & 0 \\ -1 & -2 & 0 & \ldots & 0 & 0 \end{bmatrix}. \tag{5.36}$$

In the following we will write all filter masks in the much more comprehensive first notation where the filter mask is centered around the point H_{00}.

Concerning symmetry, we can distinguish two important classes of filters: even and odd filters with the following condition

$$H_{-m,-n} = \pm H_{mn}, \tag{5.37}$$

where the $+$ and $-$ signs stand for *even* and *odd* symmetry. From this definition we can immediately reduce (5.34) to make the computation of filters more efficient

$$G'_{mn} = H_{00}G_{mn} + \sum_k \sum_l H_{kl}(G_{m-k,n-l} + G_{m+k,n+l}) \quad \text{even}$$

$$G'_{mn} = \sum_k \sum_l H_{kl}(G_{m-k,n-l} - G_{m+k,n+l}) \quad \text{odd}$$

$$G'_{mn} = H_0G_{m,n} + \sum_{l=1}^{r} H_l(G_{m,n-l} + G_{m,n+l}) \quad \text{even, 1-D horizontal} \tag{5.38}$$

$$G'_{mn} = \sum_{l=1}^{r} H_l(G_{m,n-l} - G_{m,n+l}) \quad \text{odd, 1-D horizontal.}$$

The double sums now only run over half of the filter mask, excluding the center pixel which must be treated separately because it has no symmetric counterpart. It can be omitted for the odd filter since the coefficient at the center pixel is zero. In these equations we also include the special case of a one-dimensional horizontal filter mask of size $1 \times (2r + 1)$. Corresponding equations can be written for 1-D vertical masks.

For FIR filters, the filter mask is equal to the point spread function, as we can easily verify by convolving the filter mask with an impulse image. Geometrically, we can rotate the filter mask by 180°, and then scan the mask over the image. Now we understand the reason for the inversion of the sign in the indices k, l in (5.34). If the change in the sign were omitted, the point spread function would be a 180° rotated copy of the filter mask.

Now let us study *recursive* or *IIR filters*. Generally, we can write

$$G'_{mn} = \underbrace{\sum_{k=0}^{K} \sum_{l=0,k+l\neq0}^{L} R_{kl}G'_{m\pm k,n\pm l}}_{\text{IIR part}} + \underbrace{\sum_{k=-r}^{r} \sum_{l=-r}^{r} H_{kl}G_{m-k,n-l}}_{\text{FIR part}}. \tag{5.39}$$

The filter contains two parts, a conventional FIR part with a $(2r + 1) \times (2r + 1)$ filter mask and an IIR part which takes the coefficients from only one quadrant except for the origin. Such a restriction is necessary, since the recursive part falls back upon previously calculated pixels. The sign of the indices (k, l) in G determines the general direction in which the recursive filter is applied. There are four principal directions in a two-dimensional image: a) from left to right and top to bottom, b) from right to left and top to bottom, c) from left to right and bottom to top, and d) from right to left and bottom to top.

The point spread function of these filters is not given directly by the filter mask, but must be calculated recursively as demonstrated in section 5.1.1 (5.4). Two problems arise. First, the PSF does not show any symmetry but generally lags behind in the direction of the filter. Second, the PSF is infinite. Thus IIR filters are in principle only suitable for infinite images. In practice, we must ensure that the PSF is significantly low in a distance which is small compared to the size of the image. Otherwise we run into similar border problems as with large FIR filters (see section 5.1.1).

Asymmetrical filters are not of much use for image processing, since they shift the image structures. An even filter only blurs a point but does not shift its center of gravity. If we use filters which shift points, the exact position measurements will not be possible.

We can, however, still use recursive filters if we run the *same* filter in two opposite directions or in all the directions possible over the image and add or subtract the filter results. With this operation, the point spread functions add to an even and odd point spread function. Let $^iH, i = 1, 2, 3, 4$ be the point spread functions of the four different directions in which an IIR filter can propagate on an image. The following symmetries are then valid:

$$^iH_{mn} = {}^{i+2}H_{mn},\tag{5.40}$$

where the addition in the superscript is performed modulo 4. Consequently, we can obtain the following symmetrical PSFs

$$\begin{aligned} &^iH_{mn} \pm {}^{i+2}H_{mn}\\ &({}^1H_{mn} \pm {}^3H_{mn}) \pm ({}^2H_{mn} \pm {}^4H_{mn}), \end{aligned}\tag{5.41}$$

which are of use in digital image processing. For further details see section 6.1.3.

Representation in the Wave Number Domain

In the wave number domain, an LSI filter is represented by its transfer function. The transfer function directly expresses how periodic structures change in amplitude and phase as a function of the wave number $\mathbf{k}$. In this section we consider the influence of the symmetry of the filter masks on the transfer function. The relationship between the transfer function and the point spread function is given by the discrete Fourier transform. For correct scaling of the transfer function, the factor $1/NM$ is omitted:

$$\hat{H}_{uv} = \sum_{m=0}^{M-1}\sum_{n=0}^{N-1} H_{mn} \exp\left(-\frac{2\pi i\, mu}{M}\right)\exp\left(-\frac{2\pi i\, nv}{N}\right).\tag{5.42}$$

This relation can be considerably simplified for even and odd filters. We can then combine the corresponding symmetric terms $H_{m,n}$ and $H_{M-m,N-n}$ in the sum and write

$$\begin{aligned} \hat{H}_{uv} = H_{00} + \underbrace{\sum\sum}_{(m,n)\in S_h} &\left[H_{mn}\exp\left(-\frac{2\pi i\, mu}{M}\right)\exp\left(-\frac{2\pi i\, nv}{N}\right)\right.\\ &\left.+ H_{M-m,N-n}\exp\left(\frac{2\pi i\, mu}{M}\right)\exp\left(\frac{2\pi i\, nv}{N}\right)\right]. \end{aligned}\tag{5.43}$$

Now the sum runs over one half space S_h only. The origin is handled in addition since no symmetric point exists for it. Using the symmetry properties for even and odd filter masks, we obtain the following equations for these even and odd filter masks:

$$\begin{aligned} \hat{H}_{uv} &= H_{00} + \underbrace{\sum\sum}_{(m,n)\in S_h} 2H_{mn}\cos\left(\frac{2\pi mu}{M} + \frac{2\pi nv}{N}\right) \quad\text{even}\\ \hat{H}_{uv} &= -i\underbrace{\sum\sum}_{(m,n)\in S_h} 2H_{mn}\sin\left(\frac{2\pi mu}{M} + \frac{2\pi nv}{N}\right) \quad\text{odd.} \end{aligned}\tag{5.44}$$

These equations can be written more conveniently if we express the wave number by the scaled wave number $\tilde{\mathbf{k}} = (2u/M, 2v/N)$ as introduced in section 2.3.3, whose components $\tilde{k}_i$ lie in the $]-1, 1[$ interval. Then we obtain for even filters

$$\hat{H}_{uv} = H_{00} + \underbrace{\sum\sum}_{(m,n)\in S_h} 2H_{mn}\cos[\pi(m\tilde{k}_1 + n\tilde{k}_2)],\tag{5.45}$$

and for odd filters

$$\hat{H}_{uv} = -i \underbrace{\sum \sum}_{(m,n) \in S_h} 2H_{mn} \sin[\pi(m\tilde{k}_1 + n\tilde{k}_2)]. \tag{5.46}$$

These equations are very useful, since they give a straightforward relationship between the coefficients of the filter masks and the transfer function. They will be our main tool to study the properties of filters for specific image processing tasks. They are also valid for sets of even or odd IIR filters as described above provided we have calculated the point spread function.

5.2.5   General Properties of Linear Shift-Invariant Operators

We now introduce an operator notation which helps us to describe composite image processing operations. All operators will be written with calligraphic letters, as $\mathcal{B}, \mathcal{D}, \mathcal{H}, \mathcal{S}$. We will systematically reserve special letters for certain operators. For example, $\mathcal{S}$ always means a shift operator. Superscripts in front of the operator will be used to specify the operator in more detail, as $^{kl}\mathcal{S}$ denotes a shift operator which shifts the image by k pixels to the right, and l pixels down.

Consecutive application is denoted by writing the operators one after the other. The right operator is applied first. Consecutive application of the same operator is denoted by the exponents

$$\underbrace{\mathcal{H}\mathcal{H}\ldots\mathcal{H}}_{m-times} = \mathcal{H}^m. \tag{5.47}$$

If the operator acts on a single image, the operand, which stands to the right in the equations, we will omit the operand. In this way we can write operator equations. In (5.47), we already made use of this notation. Furthermore, we will use braces in the usual way to control the order of execution.

Using this operator notation, we will now summarize the general properties of linear shift-invariant image processing operators. This notation and the general properties of convolution filters will be a valuable help in understanding complex image processing operations.

Linearity; Principle of Superposition
$$\mathcal{H}(a\boldsymbol{G} + b\boldsymbol{G}') = a\mathcal{H}\boldsymbol{G} + b\mathcal{H}\boldsymbol{G}'. \tag{5.48}$$

Commutativity
We can change the order of operators:

$$\mathcal{H}\mathcal{H}' = \mathcal{H}'\mathcal{H}. \tag{5.49}$$

This property is easy to prove in the Fourier domain, since there the operators reduce to an element-wise scalar multiplication which is commutative.

Associativity

$$\mathcal{H}'\mathcal{H}'' = \mathcal{H}. \tag{5.50}$$

Since LSI operations are associative, we can compose a complex operator out of simple operators. Likewise, we can try to decompose a given complex operator into simpler operators. This feature is essential for an effective implementation of convolution operators. As an example, consider the operator

$$\begin{bmatrix} 1 & 4 & 6 & 4 & 1 \\ 4 & 16 & 24 & 16 & 4 \\ 6 & 24 & 36 & 24 & 6 \\ 4 & 16 & 24 & 16 & 4 \\ 1 & 4 & 6 & 4 & 1 \end{bmatrix}. \tag{5.51}$$

We need 25 multiplications and 24 additions per pixel with this convolution mask. We can easily verify, however, that we can decompose this mask into two simpler masks:

$$\begin{bmatrix} 1 & 4 & 6 & 4 & 1 \\ 4 & 16 & 24 & 16 & 4 \\ 6 & 24 & 36 & 24 & 6 \\ 4 & 16 & 24 & 16 & 4 \\ 1 & 4 & 6 & 4 & 1 \end{bmatrix} = [1\ 4\ 6\ 4\ 1] * \begin{bmatrix} 1 \\ 4 \\ 6 \\ 4 \\ 1 \end{bmatrix}. \tag{5.52}$$

Applying the two convolutions with the smaller masks one after the other, we need only 10 multiplications and 8 additions. Filter masks which can be decomposed into one-dimensional masks along the axes are called *separable masks*. We will denote one-dimensional operators with an index indicating the axis. We are then able to write a separable operator $\mathcal{B}$ in a three-dimensional space

$$\mathcal{B} = \mathcal{B}_x\mathcal{B}_y\mathcal{B}_z. \tag{5.53}$$

In case of one-dimensional masks directed in orthogonal directions, the convolution reduces to an outer product. Separable filters are more efficient the higher the dimension of the space. Let us consider a $9 \times 9 \times 9$ filter mask as an example. A direct implementation would cost 729 multiplications and 728 additions per pixel, while a separable mask of the same size would just need 27 multiplications and 24 additions, about a factor of 30 fewer operations.

Distributivity over Addition

Since LSI operators are elements of the same vector space on which they can operate, we can define addition of the operators by the addition of the vector elements. We then find that LSI operators distribute over addition

$$\mathcal{H}'\boldsymbol{G} + \mathcal{H}''\boldsymbol{G} = (\mathcal{H}' + \mathcal{H}'')\boldsymbol{G} = \mathcal{H}\boldsymbol{G}. \tag{5.54}$$

Because of this property we can also integrate operator additions into our general operator notation.

Inverse Operators

Can we invert a filter operation? This question is significant since degradations such as image blurring by motion or by defocused optics can also be regarded as a filter operation. If an inverse operator exists and if we know the point spread function of the degradation, we can reconstruct the original, undisturbed image. The problem of inversing a filter operation is known as *deconvolution* or *inverse filtering*.

By considering the filter operation in the Fourier domain, we immediately recognize that we can only reconstruct those wave numbers for which the transfer function of the filter does not vanish. In practice, we are much more limited because of quantization and additional noise in the image. If a wave number is attenuated below a critical level which depends on the noise and quantization levels, it will not be recoverable. It is obvious that these conditions limit the power of a straightforward inverse filtering considerably. The problem of inverse filtering is considered further in section 13.3.2.

6 Mean and Edges

In this chapter we will apply neighborhood operations to analyze two elementary structures: the mean gray value and changes in the gray values. The determination of
a correct mean value also includes the suppression of distortions in the gray values
caused by sensor noise or transmission errors. Changes in the gray value mean, in the
simplest case, the edges of objects. Thus *edge detection* and *smoothing* are complementary operations. While smoothing gives adequate averages for the gray values within
the objects, edge detection aims at estimating the boundaries of objects.

6.1 Smoothing

The mean gray value is obtained by a filter operation which "somehow" smooths the
image. Such an operation also suppresses noise or individual pixels which are distorted
by transmission errors. Generally, these operations can be characterized by attenuating
fine-scale features, i. e., high wave numbers. This class of filters is called *smoothing* or
lowpass filters. We will describe these filters in detail, since they are elementary filters
which will be used to compose more complex filter operations (see, for example, sections
7.3, 8.2.2, 15.3.2, and 17.4).

6.1.1 Box Filters

It is obvious that smoothing filters will average pixels within a small neighborhood.
The simplest method is to add all the pixels within the filter mask and to divide the
sum by the number of pixels. Such a simple filter is called a *box filter*. Box filters are
an illustrative example as to how to design a filter properly. As an introduction, we
consider a 3×3 box filter

$$^3 R = \frac{1}{9} \cdot \begin{bmatrix} 1 & 1 & 1 \\ 1 & 1 & 1 \\ 1 & 1 & 1 \end{bmatrix}. \tag{6.1}$$

The factor $1/9$ scales the result of the convolution sum. For any smoothing filter, the
sum of all the coefficients should be one. Otherwise the gray value in a region with

constant gray values is not preserved. We apply this mask to a vertical edge

$$
\begin{array}{cccc}
\vdots & \vdots & \vdots & \vdots \\
\cdots\ 0 & 0 & 1 & 1\ \cdots \\
\cdots\ 0 & 0 & 1 & 1\ \cdots \\
\cdots\ 0 & 0 & 1 & 1\ \cdots \\
\vdots & \vdots & \vdots & \vdots
\end{array}
\ *\ \frac{1}{9} \cdot
\begin{bmatrix} 1 & 1 & 1 \\ 1 & 1 & 1 \\ 1 & 1 & 1 \end{bmatrix}
\ =\
\begin{array}{cccc}
\vdots & \vdots & \vdots & \vdots \\
\cdots\ 0 & 1/3 & 2/3 & 1\ \cdots \\
\cdots\ 0 & 1/3 & 2/3 & 1\ \cdots \\
\cdots\ 0 & 1/3 & 2/3 & 1\ \cdots \\
\vdots & \vdots & \vdots & \vdots
\end{array}
$$

As expected for a smoothing operation, the sharp edge is transformed into a smoother ramp with a gradual transition from 0 to 1. Smoothing filters attenuate structures with high wave numbers. Let us first try to convolve a vertical structure with a wavelength of 3 pixel distance by the 3×3 box filter

$$
\begin{array}{cccccc}
\vdots & \vdots & \vdots & \vdots & \vdots & \vdots \\
\cdots\ 1 & -2 & 1 & 1 & -2 & 1\ \cdots \\
\cdots\ 1 & -2 & 1 & 1 & -2 & 1\ \cdots \\
\cdots\ 1 & -2 & 1 & 1 & -2 & 1\ \cdots \\
\vdots & \vdots & \vdots & \vdots & \vdots & \vdots
\end{array}
\ *\ \frac{1}{9} \cdot
\begin{bmatrix} 1 & 1 & 1 \\ 1 & 1 & 1 \\ 1 & 1 & 1 \end{bmatrix}
\ =\
\begin{array}{cccccc}
\vdots & \vdots & \vdots & \vdots & \vdots & \vdots \\
\cdots\ 0 & 0 & 0 & 0 & 0 & 0\ \cdots \\
\cdots\ 0 & 0 & 0 & 0 & 0 & 0\ \cdots \\
\cdots\ 0 & 0 & 0 & 0 & 0 & 0\ \cdots \\
\vdots & \vdots & \vdots & \vdots & \vdots & \vdots
\end{array}
$$

It turns out that the 3×3 box filter completely removes a structure with the wavelength 3. From a good smoothing filter we expect that all structures with a wave number above a certain threshold are removed. This is not the case for the 3×3 box filter. As an example, we take a structure with the wavelength 2:

$$
\begin{array}{cccccc}
\vdots & \vdots & \vdots & \vdots & \vdots & \vdots \\
\cdots\ 1 & -1 & 1 & -1 & 1 & -1\ \cdots \\
\cdots\ 1 & -1 & 1 & -1 & 1 & -1\ \cdots \\
\cdots\ 1 & -1 & 1 & -1 & 1 & -1\ \cdots \\
\vdots & \vdots & \vdots & \vdots & \vdots & \vdots
\end{array}
\ *\ \frac{1}{9} \cdot
\begin{bmatrix} 1 & 1 & 1 \\ 1 & 1 & 1 \\ 1 & 1 & 1 \end{bmatrix}
\ =\
\begin{array}{cccccc}
\vdots & \vdots & \vdots & \vdots & \vdots & \vdots \\
\cdots\ -1/3 & 1/3 & -1/3 & 1/3 & -1/3 & 1/3 \\
\cdots\ -1/3 & 1/3 & -1/3 & 1/3 & -1/3 & 1/3\ \cdots \\
\cdots\ -1/3 & 1/3 & -1/3 & 1/3 & -1/3 & 1/3\ \cdots \\
\vdots & \vdots & \vdots & \vdots & \vdots & \vdots
\end{array}
$$

Obviously, the box filter is not a good lowpass filter. Directly convolving the filter with test images containing periodic structures of different wavelength to study its wave number response is a ponderous method. The attenuation of periodic structures as a function of the wave number is directly given by the transfer function. The box filter is an even filter. Thus we can apply (5.45). First we consider a one-dimensional 1×3 box filter. Its mask is given by

$$
{}^{3}\boldsymbol{R}_x = \begin{bmatrix} 1/3 & 1/3 & 1/3 \end{bmatrix}.
\tag{6.2}
$$

Thus only the coefficients $H_{00} = H_{01} = 1/3$ are unequal to zero and the transfer function reduces, according to (5.45), to

$$
\hat{\boldsymbol{R}}_x = \frac{1}{3} + \frac{2}{3} \cos(\pi \tilde{k}_x).
\tag{6.3}
$$

The even filter masks result in a real transfer function. This means that for positive values no phase shift occurs, while for negative values the signal is inverted. The transfer function is shown in figure 6.1a. Our exemplary computations are verified. The transfer

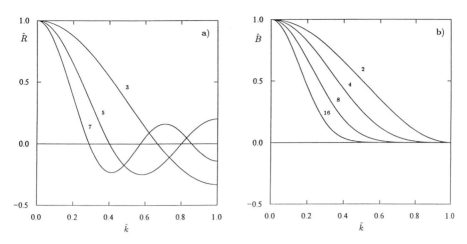

Figure 6.1: Transfer functions of one-dimensional smoothing filters: a) box filters of size 3, 5, and 7; b) binomial filters as indicated.

function shows a zero at $\tilde{k} = 2/3$. This corresponds to a wave number which is sampled 3 times per wavelength. The smallest possible wavelength ($\tilde{k} = 1$), which is sampled twice per wavelength, is only damped by a factor of three. The negative sign indicates an interchange of minima and maxima. In conclusion, the 3×3 box filter is not a good lowpass filter. It is disturbing that the attenuation does not increase monotonously with the wave number but tends to oscillate. Even worse, structures with the largest wave number are not attenuated strongly enough.

Larger box filters do not show a significant improvement (figure 6.1a). On the contrary, the oscillatory behavior is more pronounced and the attenuation is only proportional to the wave number. For large filter masks, we can approximate the discrete with m coefficients by a continuous box function of width $m - 1$. The transfer function is then given by a sinc function (see appendix A.2):

$$^m\boldsymbol{R}_x \approx \frac{\sin(2\pi(m-1)\tilde{k})}{2\pi(m-1)\tilde{k}}. \tag{6.4}$$

Now we turn to two-dimensional box filters. To simplify the arithmetic, we utilize the fact that the box filter is a separable filter and decompose it into 1-D vertical and horizontal components, respectively:

$$^3\boldsymbol{R} = {}^3\boldsymbol{R}_x * {}^3\boldsymbol{R}_y = \frac{1}{9}\begin{bmatrix} 1 & 1 & 1 \\ 1 & 1 & 1 \\ 1 & 1 & 1 \end{bmatrix} = \frac{1}{3}\begin{bmatrix} 1 & 1 & 1 \end{bmatrix} * \frac{1}{3}\begin{bmatrix} 1 \\ 1 \\ 1 \end{bmatrix}.$$

The transfer function of the one-dimensional filters is given by (6.3) (replacing $\tilde{k}_x$ by $\tilde{k}_y$ for the vertical filter). Since convolution in the space domain corresponds to multiplication in the wave number domain, the transfer function of $\boldsymbol{R}$ is

$$^3\hat{\boldsymbol{R}} = \left(\frac{1}{3} + \frac{2}{3}\cos(\pi\tilde{k}_x)\right)\left(\frac{1}{3} + \frac{2}{3}\cos(\pi\tilde{k}_y)\right). \tag{6.5}$$

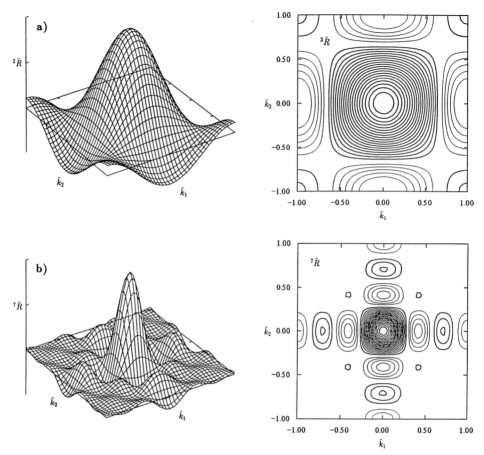

Figure 6.2: Transfer function of two-dimensional box filters shown in a pseudo 3-D plot and a contour plot. a) 3×3 box filter; b) 7×7 box filter; distance of the contour lines: 0.05.

From this equation and from figure 6.2a, we can conclude that this 2-D box filter is a poor lowpass filter. A larger box filter, for example one with a 7×7 mask (figure 6.2b), does not perform any better. Besides the disadvantages already discussed for the one-dimensional case, we are faced with the problem that the transfer function is not *isotropic*, i.e., it depends, for a given wave number, on the direction of the wave number.

When we apply a box filter to an arbitrary image, we hardly observe these effects (figure 6.6). They are only revealed if we use a carefully designed *test image*. This image contains concentric sinusoidal rings. Their wavelength increases with the distance from the center. When we convolve this image with a 7×7 or 9×9 box filter, the deviations from an isotropic transfer function become readily visible (figure 6.3). We can observe the wave numbers which entirely vanish and the change of gray value maxima in gray value minima and vice versa in some regions, indicating the 180° phase shift caused by negative values in the transfer function.

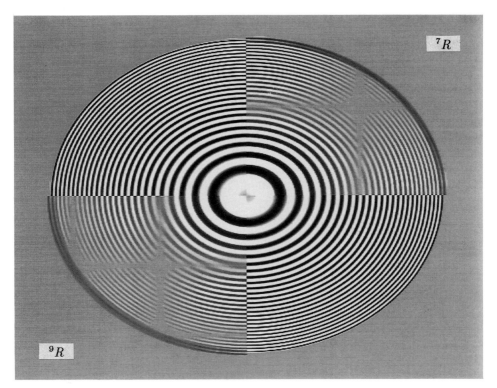

Figure 6.3: Test of the smoothing with a 7 × 7 and a 9 × 9 box filter using a test image with concentric sinusoidal rings.

From this experience, we can learn an important lesson. We must not rate the properties of a filter operation from its effect on arbitrary images, even if we think that they seem to work correctly. Obviously, the eye perceives a rather qualitative impression (see section 1.3). For quantitative scientific applications we need a quantitative analysis of the filter properties. A careful analysis of the transfer function and the use of carefully designed test images are appropriate here.

Now we turn back to the question of what went wrong with the box filter. We might try to design a better smoothing filter directly in the wave number space. An ideal smoothing filter would cut off all wave numbers above a certain threshold value. We could use this ideal transfer function and compute the filter mask by an inverse Fourier transform. However, we run into two problems which can be understood without explicit calculations. The inverse Fourier transform of a box function is a sinc function. This means that the coefficients decrease only proportionally to the distance from the center pixel. We would be forced to work with large filter masks. Furthermore, the filter has the disadvantage that it overshoots at the edges.

6.1.2   Binomial Filters

From our experience with box filters, we conclude that the design of filters is a difficult optimization problem. If we choose a small rectangular filter mask, we get a poor transfer function. If we start with an ideal transfer function, we get large filter masks and overshooting filter responses. The reason for this behavior is because of a fundamental property of Fourier transform called the *classical uncertainty relation* in physics or the *time-bandwidth product* in the signal processing literature [*Marple*, 1987]. Here we briefly discuss what the uncertainty relation means for a steep edge. An edge constitutes a discontinuity or an impulse in the first derivative. The Fourier transform of an impulse is evenly spread over the whole Fourier domain. Using the integral property of the Fourier transform (appendix A.2), an integration of the derivative in the space domain means a division by k in the Fourier domain. Then we know without any detailed calculation that in the one-dimensional case the envelope of the Fourier transform of a function which shows discontinuities in the space domain will go with k^{-1} in the wave number domain. This was exactly what we found for the Fourier transform of the box function, the sinc function.

Considering this basic fact, we can design better smoothing filters. One condition is that the filter masks should gradually approach zero.

Here we will introduce a class of smoothing filters which meets this criterion and can be calculated very efficiently. Furthermore these filters are an excellent example of how more complex filters can be built from simple components. The simplest and most elementary smoothing mask we can think of for the one-dimensional case is

$$\boldsymbol{B}_x = \frac{1}{2} [1\ 1],\qquad(6.6)$$

which averages the gray values of two neighboring pixels. We can use this mask m times in a row on the same image. This corresponds to the filter mask

$$\underbrace{[1\ 1] * [1\ 1] * \ldots * [1\ 1]}_{m\ \text{times}},\qquad(6.7)$$

or written as an operator equation

$$\mathcal{B}_x^m = \underbrace{\mathcal{B}_x\mathcal{B}_x\ldots\mathcal{B}_x}_{m\ \text{times}}.\qquad(6.8)$$

Some examples of the resulting filter masks are:

$$\begin{aligned}
\boldsymbol{B}_x^2 &= 1/4\,[1\ 2\ 1]\\
\boldsymbol{B}_x^3 &= 1/8\,[1\ 3\ 3\ 1]\\
\boldsymbol{B}_x^4 &= 1/16\,[1\ 4\ 6\ 4\ 1]\\
\boldsymbol{B}_x^8 &= 1/256\,[1\ 8\ 28\ 56\ 70\ 56\ 28\ 8\ 1].
\end{aligned}\qquad(6.9)$$

Because of symmetry, only the odd-sized filter masks are of interest. In order to perform a convolution with the asymmetric mask $1/2\,[1\ 1]$ correctly, we store the result in the right and left pixel alternately.

The masks contain the values of the discrete *binomial distribution*. Actually, the iterative composition of the mask by consecutive convolution with the $1/2\,[1\ 1]$ mask is equivalent to the computation scheme of *Pascal's triangle*:

n	f		σ^2
0	1	1	0
1	1/2	1 1	1/4
2	1/4	1 2 1	1/2
3	1/8	1 3 3 1	3/4
4	1/16	1 4 6 4 1	1
5	1/32	1 5 10 10 5 1	5/4
6	1/64	1 6 15 20 15 6 1	3/2
7	1/128	1 7 21 35 35 21 7 1	7/4
8	1/256	1 8 28 56 70 56 28 8 1	2

$$(6.10)$$

n denotes the order of the binomial, f the scaling factor 2^{-n}, and σ^2 the variance, i.e., effective width, of the mask. We can write the values for the coefficients of an odd-sized $(2R+1)$ binomial mask directly using the binomial distribution (4.6)

$$B_r^{2R+1} = \frac{1}{2^{2R+1}} \frac{(2R+1)!}{(R-r)!(R+r)!} \qquad r = -R, \cdots, R. \tag{6.11}$$

The computation of the transfer function of a binomial mask is also very simple, since we only need to know the transfer function of $\mathcal{B}^2$. The transfer function of $\mathcal{B}^{2R}$ is then given as the Rth power. With the help of (5.45) we obtain

$$\hat{B}_x^{2R} = \frac{1}{2^R} \left[1 + \cos(\pi\tilde{k})\right]^R \approx 1 - R\frac{\pi^2}{4}\tilde{k}^2 + O(\tilde{k}^4). \tag{6.12}$$

The graphical representation of the transfer function in figure 6.1b reveals that binomial filters are much better smoothing filters. The transfer function decreases monotonically and approaches zero at the largest wave number. The smallest mask, $\mathcal{B}^2$, has a halfwidth of $\tilde{k}/2$ or discrete $u = M/4$. This is a periodic structure which is sampled four times per wavelength. For larger masks, both the transfer function and the filter masks approach the Gaussian distribution with an equivalent variance. Larger masks result in smaller half-width wave numbers in agreement with the uncertainty relation.

Two-dimensional binomial filters can be composed from a horizontal and a vertical 1-D filter

$$\mathcal{B}^n = \mathcal{B}_x^n \mathcal{B}_y^n. \tag{6.13}$$

The smallest mask of this kind is a 3×3-binomial filter ($R = 1$):

$$\mathcal{B}^2 = \frac{1}{4}\begin{bmatrix} 1 & 2 & 1 \end{bmatrix} * \frac{1}{4}\begin{bmatrix} 1 \\ 2 \\ 1 \end{bmatrix} = \frac{1}{16}\begin{bmatrix} 1 & 2 & 1 \\ 2 & 4 & 2 \\ 1 & 2 & 1 \end{bmatrix}. \tag{6.14}$$

The transfer function of a $(2R+1) \times (2R+1)$-sized binomial filter is given by

$$\hat{B}^{2R} = \frac{1}{2^{2R}} \left[\left(1 + \cos(\pi\tilde{k}_x)\right)\left(1 + \cos(\pi\tilde{k}_y)\right)\right]^R. \tag{6.15}$$

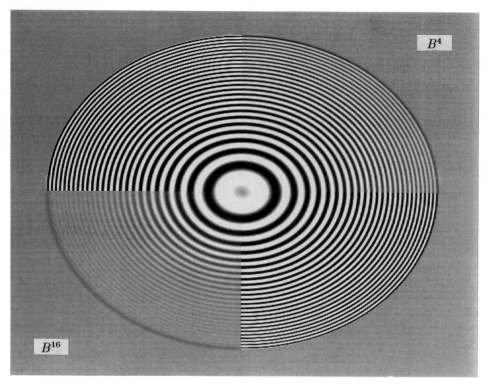

Figure 6.4: Test of the smoothing with a $\mathcal{B}^4$ and $\mathcal{B}^{16}$ binomial filter using a test image with concentric sinusoidal rings.

The transfer functions of $\mathcal{B}^2$ and $\mathcal{B}^4$ are shown in figure 6.5. Already the small 3×3 filter is remarkably isotropic. Larger deviations from the circular contour lines can only be recognized for larger wave numbers, when the transfer function has dropped to 0.3 (figure 6.5a). Generally, the transfer function (6.15) is not isotropic. A Taylor expansion in $\tilde{k}$ for $n = 1$

$$\hat{\mathcal{B}}^2 \approx 1 - \frac{\pi^2}{4}\tilde{k}^2 + \frac{\pi^4}{48}\tilde{k}^4 + \frac{\pi^4}{48}\tilde{k}_x^2\,\tilde{k}_y^2 + O(\tilde{k}^6)$$

shows that the second order term is isotropic. Only the fourth order term contains an anisotropic term which increases the transfer function in the directions of the diagonals (figure 6.5a). In the graph for the 5×5 filter (figure 6.5b), we notice that the residual anisotropy is even smaller. The insignificant anisotropy of the binomial filters also becomes apparent when applied to the test image in figure 6.4.

Figures 6.6b and c show smoothing with two different binomial filters. There we observe that the edges get blurred. Fine structures as in the branches of the tree become lost. Smoothing is one technique to suppress *Gaussian noise*. Binomial filters can reduce the noise level considerably but only at the price of blurred details (figure 6.7a and c). *Binary noise*, i. e., totally wrong gray values for a few randomly distributed pixels (figure 6.7b), which is typically caused by transmission errors, is handled poorly

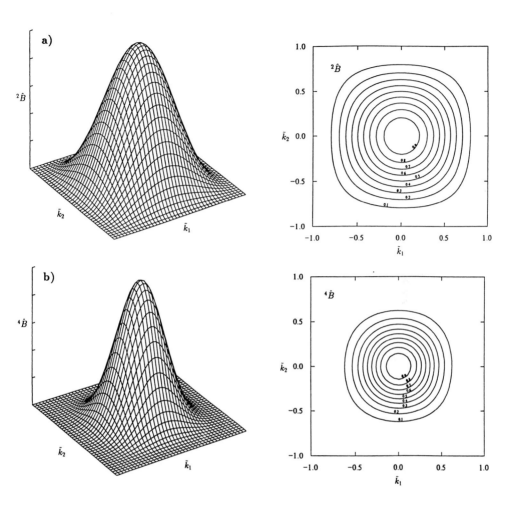

Figure 6.5: Transfer function of two-dimensional binomial filters: a) 3×3, $R = 1$; b) 5×5, $R = 2$; distance of the contour lines: 0.1.

by linear filters. The images become blurred, but we still see the effect of the binary noise.

We close our considerations about binomial filters with some remarks on fast algorithms. A direct computation of a $(2R + 1) \times (2R + 1)$ filter mask requires $(2R + 1)^2$ multiplications and $(2R + 1)^2 - 1$ additions. If we decompose the binomial mask in the elementary smoothing mask $1/2\,[1\ 1]$ and apply this mask in horizontal and vertical directions $2R$ times each, we only need $4R$ additions. All multiplications can be handled much more efficiently as shift operations. For example, the computation of a 17×17 binomial filter requires only 32 additions and some shift operations compared to 289 multiplications and 288 additions needed for the direct approach.

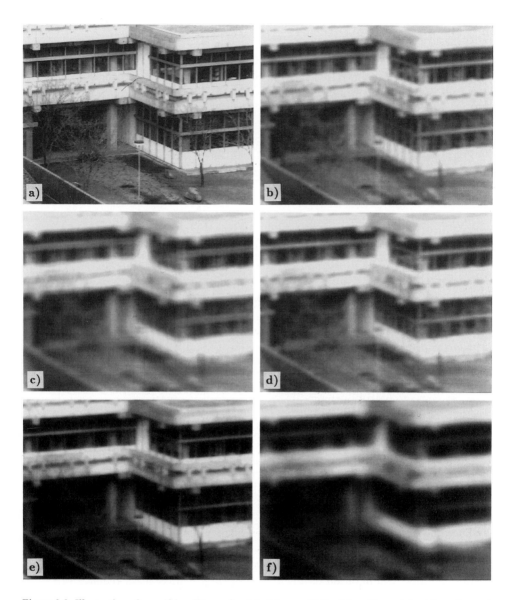

Figure 6.6: Illustration of smoothing filters: a) original image; b) 5×5 box filter; c) 9×9 box filter; d) 17×17 binomial filter ($\mathcal{B}^{16}$); a set of recursive filters (6.19) running in horizontal and vertical direction; e) $p = 2$; f) $p = 32$.

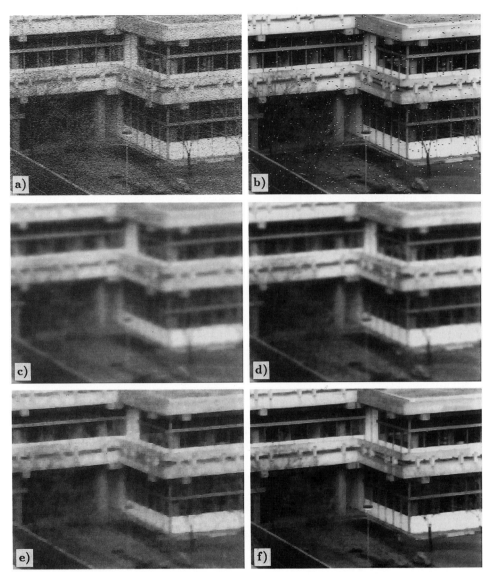

Figure 6.7: Suppression of noise with smoothing filters: a) image from figure 6.6 with Gaussian noise; b) image with binary noise; c) image a) filtered with a 17×17 binomial filter ($\mathcal{B}^{16}$); d) image b) filtered with a 9×9 binomial filter ($\mathcal{B}^8$); e) image a) filtered with a 5×5 median filter; f) image b) filtered with a 3×3 median filter.

6.1.3 Recursive Smoothing Filters

Now we turn to recursive smoothing filters. Basically, they work the same as non-recursive filters. Principally, we can replace any recursive filter with a non-recursive filter whose filter mask is identical to the point spread function of the recursive filter. The real problem is the design of the recursive filter, i.e., the determination of the filter coefficients for a desired transfer function. While the theory of one-dimensional recursive filters is standard knowledge in digital signal processing (see, for example, *Oppenheim and Schafer* [1989]), the design of two-dimensional filters is still not adequately understood. The main reason are the fundamental differences between the mathematics of one- and higher-dimensional z-transforms and polynomials [*Lim*, 1990].

Despite these theoretical problems, recursive filters can be applied successfully in digital image processing. In order to avoid the filter design problems, we will use only very simple recursive filters which are easily understood and compose them to more complex filters, similar to the way we constructed the class of binomial filters from the elementary smoothing mask $1/2 \begin{bmatrix} 1 & 1 \end{bmatrix}$. In this way we will obtain a class of recursive filters which are not optimal from the point of view of filter design but which are useful in practical applications.

In the first composition step, we combine causal recursive filters to symmetric filters. We start with a general one-dimensional recursive filter with the transfer function

$$^{+}\hat{A} = a(\tilde{k}) + ib(\tilde{k}). \tag{6.16}$$

The index $+$ denotes the run direction of the filter. The transfer function of the same filter but running in the opposite direction is

$$^{-}\hat{A} = a(\tilde{k}) - ib(\tilde{k}). \tag{6.17}$$

Only the sign of the imaginary part of the transfer function changes, since it corresponds to the uneven part of the point spread function, while the real part corresponds to the even part. We now have several possibilities to combine these two filters to symmetrical filters which are useful for image processing:

$$\text{addition} \qquad ^{e}\hat{A} = \frac{1}{2}\left(^{+}\hat{A} + ^{-}\hat{A}\right) \quad = a(\tilde{k})$$

$$\text{subtraction} \qquad ^{o}\hat{A} = \frac{1}{2}\left(^{+}\hat{A} - ^{-}\hat{A}\right) \quad = ib(\tilde{k}) \tag{6.18}$$

$$\text{multiplication} \quad \hat{A} = {}^{+}\hat{A}{}^{-}\hat{A} \qquad \qquad = a^{2}(\tilde{k}) + b^{2}(\tilde{k}).$$

Addition and multiplication (consecutive application) of the left and right running filter yields even filters, while subtraction results in an odd filter. For smoothing filters, which have even masks, we can only use addition and multiplication.

As the elementary smoothing filter, we use the two-element lowpass filter we have already studied in section 5.1.1:

$$\mathcal{A}_{x}: \ G'_{mn} = \frac{1}{p}\left[(p-1)G'_{m,n\pm1} + G_{mn}\right], \quad p \in \mathbb{Z}, \ p > 1, \tag{6.19}$$

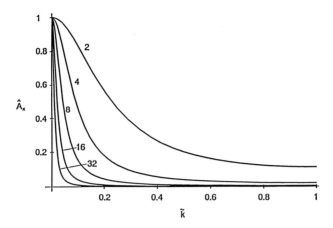

Figure 6.8: Transfer function of the recursive lowpass filter (6.22) for different values of p as indicated.

where we replaced α by p with $\alpha = (p-1)/p$ for the sake of an efficient implementation of the filter. The impulse response is then given by

$$^{\pm}A_x = \frac{1}{p}\sum_{m=0}^{\pm\infty}\left(\frac{p-1}{p}\right)^{\pm m}. \tag{6.20}$$

The transfer function of this filter can easily be calculated by taking into account that the Fourier transform of (6.20) forms a *geometric series*:

$$^{\pm}\hat{A}_x(\tilde{k}) \approx \frac{1}{p-(p-1)\exp(\mp\pi\tilde{k})}. \tag{6.21}$$

This relation is valid only approximately, since we broke off the infinite sum in (6.20) at $p = N$ because of the limited size of the image.

Consecutive filtering with a left and right running filter corresponds to a multiplication of the transfer function

$$\hat{A}_x(\tilde{k}) = {}^{+}\hat{A}_x(\tilde{k})\,{}^{-}\hat{A}_x(\tilde{k}) \approx \frac{1}{1+2p(p-1)(1-\cos(\pi\tilde{k}))}. \tag{6.22}$$

The transfer function shows the characteristics expected for a lowpass filter (figure 6.8). At $\tilde{k} = 0$, $\hat{A}_x(\tilde{k}) = 1$; for small $\tilde{k}$, the transfer function falls off proportional to $\tilde{k}^2$:

$$\hat{A}_x \approx 1 - p(p-1)(\pi\tilde{k})^2 \quad \tilde{k} \ll 1, \tag{6.23}$$

and has a cut-off wave number $\tilde{k}_c$ ($\hat{A}_x(\tilde{k}) = 1/2$) of

$$\tilde{k}_c = \frac{1}{\pi}\arccos\left[\,1 - \frac{1}{2p(p-1)}\,\right] \approx \frac{1}{\pi}\frac{1}{\sqrt{p(p-1)}}. \tag{6.24}$$

At the highest wave number, $\tilde{k} = 1$, the transfer function has dropped off to

$$\hat{A}_x(1) \approx \frac{1}{1+4p(p-1)}. \tag{6.25}$$

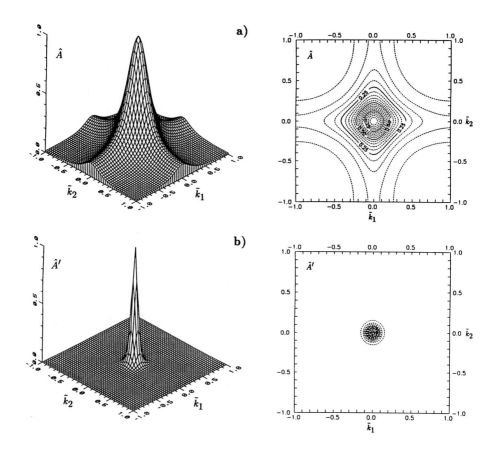

Figure 6.9: Transfer functions of two-dimensional recursive low-pass filters: a) $\mathcal{A}$ with $p = 2$; b) $\mathcal{A}'$ with $p = 4$.

It is not exactly zero as for binomial filters, but sufficiently small even for small values of p (figure 6.8).

Two-dimensional filters can be composed from one-dimensional filters running in the horizontal and vertical directions:

$$\mathcal{A} = \mathcal{A}_x \mathcal{A}_y = {}^+\mathcal{A}_x {}^-\mathcal{A}_x {}^+\mathcal{A}_y {}^-\mathcal{A}_y. \qquad (6.26)$$

This filter (figure 6.9) is considerably less isotropic than binomial filters (figure 6.5). The anisotropy of the recursive filter is also visible in figures 6.10 and 6.6f. However, recursive filters show the big advantage that the computational effort does not depend on the cut-off wave numbers. With the simple first-order recursive filter, we can adjust a wide range of cut-off wave numbers with an appropriate choice of the filter parameter p (6.24). The isotropy of recursive filters can be further improved by running additional filters along the diagonals:

$$\mathcal{A}' = \mathcal{A}_x \mathcal{A}_y \mathcal{A}_{x-y} \mathcal{A}_{x+y}. \qquad (6.27)$$

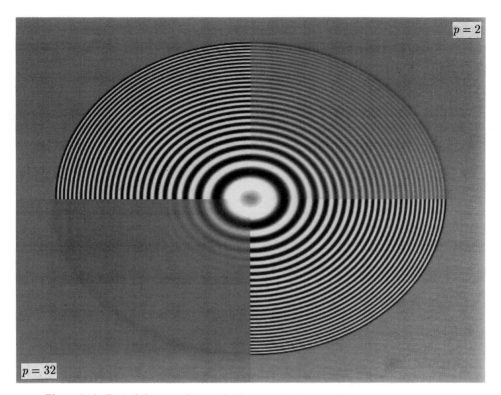

Figure 6.10: Test of the smoothing with the recursive lowpass filter $\mathcal{A}$, $p = 2$ and $p = 32$.

The subscripts $x - y$ and $x + y$ denote the main and second diagonal, respectively. The transfer function of such a filter is shown in figure 6.9b.

Finally, here are a few considerations on computational efficiency. In contrast to non-recursive filters, the computational effort does not depend on the cut-off wave number. If $p = 2^l$ in (6.19), the filter can be computed without any multiplication:

$$G'_{mn} = \left[G'_{m,n\pm1} \cdot 2^l - G'_{m,n\pm1} + G_{mn} \right] \cdot 2^{-l}, \quad l > 1, \tag{6.28}$$

The two-dimensional filter $\mathcal{A}$ then needs only 8 additions and shift operations per pixel, while the $\mathcal{A}'$ filter, running in four directions, needs twice as many operations. An example program is given in algorithm 2.

6.1.4   Median Filter

Linear filters effectively suppress Gaussian noise but perform very poorly in case of binary noise (figure 6.7). Using linear filters which weigh and sum up, we assume that each pixel carries some useful information. Pixels which are distorted by transmission errors have lost their original gray value. Linear smoothing does not eliminate this information but carries it on to neighboring pixels. Thus the only right operation to process such distortions is to detect these pixels and to eliminate them.

Algorithm 2: C subroutine to perform the one-dimensional noncausal recursive lowpass filtering in an arbitrary direction over one line in an image.

```
/*
** Recursive noncausal lowpass filter for an image of type short
** m1[i]=1/2**l((2**l-1)m1[i-inc]+m1[i]), running cnt times forwards and backwards
*/
void ms1lowp(ptr,len,inc,cnt,l) short *ptr; short len, inc, cnt, l; {
    unsigned int i;
    int s1;
    short *m1p;

    while (cnt--) {
/*
** forward direction
*/
        m1p=ptr;
        s1 = *m1p;   /* m1[0] > s1 */
        for (i = len; i > 0; i--) {
            s1 = ((s1<<l)-s1 + *m1p)>>l;
            *m1p = s1;
            m1p += inc;
        }
/*
** backward direction
*/
        m1p -= inc;
        s1 = 0;   /* m1[n-1] > s1 */
        for (i = len; i > 0; i--) {
            s1 = ((s1<<l)-s1 + *m1p)>>l;
            *m1p = s1;
            m1p -= inc;
        }
    }
}
```

This is exactly what a rank value filter does (section 5.1.3). The pixels within the mask are sorted and one pixel is selected. In particular, the *median filter* selects the medium value. Since binary noise completely changes the gray value, it is very unlikely that it will show the medium gray value in the neighborhood. In this way, the medium gray value of the neighborhood is used to restore the gray value of the distorted pixel.

The following examples illustrate the effect of a 1×3 median filter $\mathcal{M}$:

$$\mathcal{M}\left[\,\cdots\,1\,2\,3\,7\,8\,9\,\cdots\,\right] = \left[\,\cdots\,1\,2\,3\,7\,8\,9\,\cdots\,\right]$$

$$\mathcal{M}\left[\,\cdots\,1\,2\,102\,4\,5\,6\,\cdots\,\right] = \left[\,\cdots\,1\,2\,4\,5\,5\,6\,\cdots\,\right]$$

$$\mathcal{M}\left[\,\cdots\,0\,0\,0\,9\,9\,9\,\cdots\,\right] = \left[\,\cdots\,0\,0\,0\,9\,9\,9\,\cdots\,\right]$$

As expected, the median filter eliminates runaways. The two other gray value structures — a monotonously increasing ramp and an edge between two plateaus of constant gray values — are preserved. In this way a median filter effectively eliminates binary noise without significantly blurring the image (figure 6.7b and f). Gaussian noise is less effectively eliminated (figure 6.7a and e).

The more important deterministic properties of a one-dimensional $2N + 1$ median filter can be formulated using the following definitions.

- A *constant neighborhood* is an area with $N + 1$ equal gray values.
- An *edge* is a monotonously in- or decreasing area between two constant neighborhoods.
- An *impulse* is an area of at most N points surrounded by constant neighborhoods with the same gray value.
- A *root* or *fix point* is a signal which is preserved under the median filter operation.

With these definitions, the deterministic properties of a median filter can be described very compactly:

- Constant neighborhoods and edges are fix points.
- Impulses are eliminated.

Iterative filtering of an image with a median filter results in an image containing only constant neighborhoods and edges. If only single pixels are distorted, a 3×3 median filter is sufficient to eliminate them. If clusters of distorted pixels occur, larger median filters must be used.

The statistical properties of the median filter can be illustrated with an image containing only constant neighborhoods, edges and impulses. The power spectrum of impulses is flat (*white noise*). Since the median filter eliminates impulses, the power spectrum decreases homogeneously. The contribution of the edges to a certain wave number is not removed. This example also underlines the non-linear nature of the median filter. A detailed description of the deterministic and statistic properties of median filters can be found in *Huang* [1981] and *Arce* [1986].

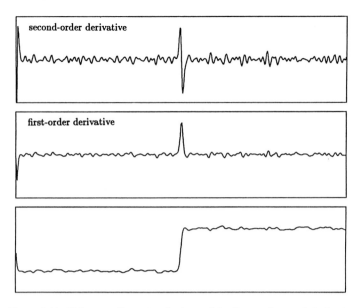

Figure 6.11: Noisy one-dimensional edge and its first and second derivative.

6.2 Edge Detection

Smoothing filters suppress structures with high wave numbers. If we want to detect edges, a filter operation is necessary which emphasizes the changes in gray values and suppresses areas with constant gray values. Figure 6.11 illustrates that derivative operators are suitable for such an operation. The first derivative shows an extremum at the edge, while the second derivative crosses zero where the edge has its steepest ascent. Both criteria can be used to detect edges.

A nth-order derivative operator corresponds to multiplication by $(\mathrm{i}k)^n$ in the wave number space (appendix A.2). In two dimensions, derivative operators are represented by

$$
\begin{array}{ccc}
\dfrac{\partial}{\partial x_1} & \circ\!\!-\!\!\bullet & \mathrm{i}k_1 \\[2mm]
\dfrac{\partial}{\partial x_2} & \circ\!\!-\!\!\bullet & \mathrm{i}k_2 \\[2mm]
\Delta = \dfrac{\partial^2}{\partial x_1^2} + \dfrac{\partial^2}{\partial x_2^2} & \circ\!\!-\!\!\bullet & -(k_1^2 + k_2^2)
\end{array}
\tag{6.29}
$$

in the space and wave number domain. The sum of the two second partial derivatives is called the *Laplace operator* and is denoted by Δ.

6.2.1 First-Order Derivative Operators

On a discrete grid, a derivative operator can only be approximated. In case of the first partial derivative in the x-direction, one of the following approximations may be used:

$$\frac{\partial f(x_1, x_2)}{\partial x_1} \approx \frac{f(x_1, x_2) - f(x_1 - \Delta x_1, x_2)}{\Delta x_1} \quad \text{Backward difference}$$

$$\approx \frac{f(x_1 + \Delta x_1, x_2) - f(x_1, x_2)}{\Delta x_1} \quad \text{Forward difference} \quad (6.30)$$

$$\approx \frac{f(x_1 + \Delta x_1, x_2) - f(x_1 - \Delta x_1, x_2)}{2\Delta x_1} \quad \text{Symmetric difference.}$$

These approximations correspond to the filter masks

$$
\begin{aligned}
{}^{-}\boldsymbol{D}_x &= [1_\bullet \ -1] \\
{}^{+}\boldsymbol{D}_x &= [1 \ -1_\bullet] \\
{}^{s}\boldsymbol{D}_x &= 1/2 \ [1 \ 0 \ -1].
\end{aligned}
\qquad (6.31)
$$

The subscript $\bullet$ denotes the central pixel of the asymmetric masks with two elements. We should keep in mind that these masks need to be inverted when the convolution is performed (compare (5.1) in section 5.1.1). Only the last mask shows a symmetry; it is odd. We may also consider the two-element mask as an odd mask provided that the result is not stored at the position of the right or left pixel but at a position halfway between the two pixels. This corresponds to a shift of the grid by half a pixel distance. The transfer function for the backward difference is then

$$^{-}\hat{D}_x = \exp(\mathrm{i}\pi \tilde{k}_x/2)\left[\,1 - \exp(-\mathrm{i}\pi \tilde{k}_x)\,\right] = \mathrm{i}\sin(\pi\tilde{k}_x/2), \qquad (6.32)$$

where the first term results from the shift by half a grid point. Using (5.46), the transfer function of the symmetric difference operator reduces to

$$^{s}\hat{D}_x = \mathrm{i}\sin(\pi\tilde{k}_x). \qquad (6.33)$$

At high wave numbers, both operators show considerable deviations from the ideal transfer function of a derivative operator, $-\mathrm{i}\pi\tilde{k}_x$. For wave numbers $\tilde{k}_x > 1/2$, the symmetric difference operator works even like a lowpass filter. Indeed, we can think of this operator as a combination of a smoothing and a difference operator:

$$^{s}\boldsymbol{D}_x = {}^{-}\boldsymbol{D}_x \,{}^{1}\boldsymbol{B}_x = [1_\bullet \ -1] * 1/2 \ [1 \ 1_\bullet] = 1/2 [1 \ 0 \ -1].$$

In two dimensions, edge detection is more complex. One-dimensional difference operators such as

$$^{s}\boldsymbol{D}_x = \frac{1}{2}\begin{bmatrix} 1 & 0 & -1 \end{bmatrix} \quad \text{and} \quad {}^{s}\boldsymbol{D}_y = \frac{1}{2}\begin{bmatrix} 1 \\ 0 \\ -1 \end{bmatrix}$$

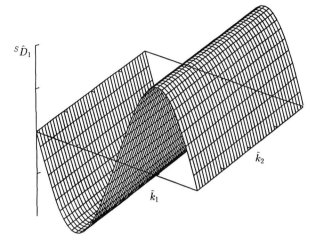

$${}^s\hat{D}_1$$

$\tilde{k}_2$

$\tilde{k}_1$

Figure 6.12: Imaginary part of the transfer function of derivative operators. a) 1-D transfer function of ${}^-\mathcal{D}_x$ and ${}^s\mathcal{D}_x$; b) 2-D transfer function of ${}^s\mathcal{D}_x$.

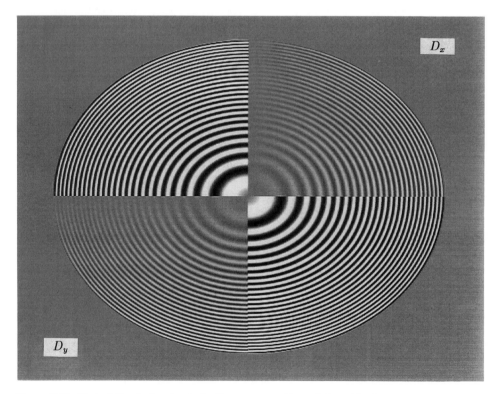

Figure 6.13: Test of the first-order derivative operators $\mathcal{D}_x$ and $\mathcal{D}_y$ with the test image shown in figure 6.4.

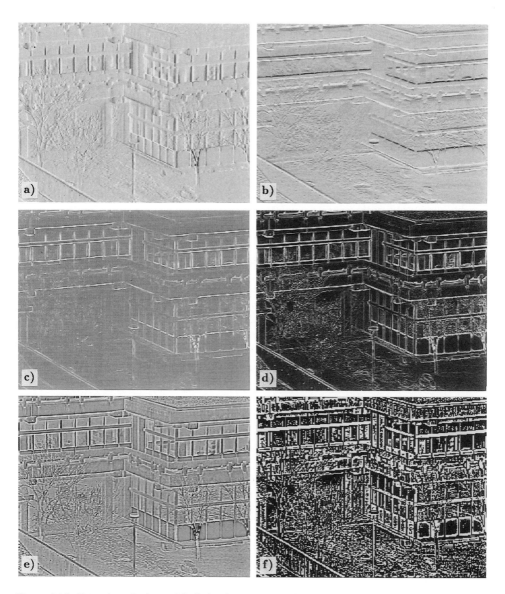

Figure 6.14: Detection of edges with derivative operators shown at image figure 6.6a: a) horizontal derivative ${}^s\mathcal{D}_x$; b) vertical derivative ${}^s\mathcal{D}_y$; c) magnitude-of-gradient $|{}^s\mathcal{D}|$; d) sum-of-magnitudes (6.36); e) Laplace operator $\mathcal{L}$; f) signum of the Laplace operator.

predominantly detect edges which lie perpendicular to the direction of the operator (figure 6.14a and b). However, we are seeking a filter operator which detects edges *independent* of their orientation, i.e., an *isotropic* edge detector. From the two spatial derivatives, we can form a vector operator, the *gradient operator*

$$\mathcal{D} = \begin{bmatrix} \mathcal{D}_x \\ \mathcal{D}_y \end{bmatrix}. \tag{6.34}$$

The magnitude of the gradient operator is invariant under a rotation of the coordinate system. The computation of the magnitude of the gradient can be expressed by the operator equation

$$|\mathcal{D}| = [\boldsymbol{D}_x \cdot \boldsymbol{D}_x + \boldsymbol{D}_y \cdot \boldsymbol{D}_y]^{1/2}. \tag{6.35}$$

Some comments on the notation of this operator equation follow. The symbol $\cdot$ denotes a point-wise multiplication of the image matrices which result from the filtering with the operators $\mathcal{D}_x$ and $\mathcal{D}_y$, respectively. This is a *nonlinear* point operation which must not be commuted with linear convolution operators. The operator $\mathcal{D} \cdot \mathcal{D}$ must be distinguished from $\mathcal{D}\mathcal{D} = \mathcal{D}^2$. The latter means the twofold application of $\mathcal{D}$ on the operant. Likewise the square root in (6.35) is performed point-wise in the space domain. To get used to this helpful and brief notation we explicitly express the meaning of the operation $|\mathcal{D}|G$:

1. filter the image independently with $\boldsymbol{D}_x$ and $\boldsymbol{D}_y$,
2. square the gray values of the two resulting images,
3. add them, and
4. compute the square root of the sum.

In the course of this book, we will learn about many operators which contain a mixture of linear convolution operators and point operations in the space domain. Point-wise multiplication is denoted by $\cdot$ to distinguish it from consecutive application of two linear operators. All other point operations, as addition, division, or any other point operation $P()$, can be denoted unambiguously in standard notations.

The magnitude-of-gradient operator $|\mathcal{D}|$ is another example of a nonlinear operator. It has the disadvantage that it is computationally expensive. Therefore it is often approximated by

$$|\mathcal{D}| \approx |\mathcal{D}_x| + |\mathcal{D}_y| = \mathcal{D}'. \tag{6.36}$$

However, this operator is anisotropic even for small wave numbers. It detects edges along the diagonals more sensitively than along the principal axes.

6.2.2 Laplace Filter

With second derivatives, we can easily form an isotropic linear operator, the *Laplace operator*. We can directly derive second-order derivative operators by a twofold application of first-order operators

$$\boldsymbol{D}_x^2 = {}^-\boldsymbol{D}_x \, {}^+\boldsymbol{D}_x. \tag{6.37}$$

This means in the spatial domain

$$[1 \; -2 \; 1] = [1_\bullet \; -1] * [1 \; -1_\bullet]. \tag{6.38}$$

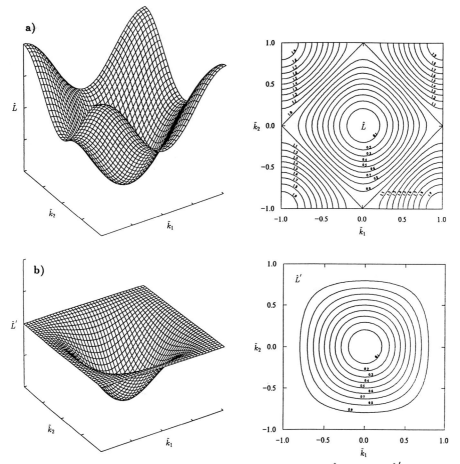

Figure 6.15: Transfer functions of discrete Laplace operators: a) $\hat{L}$ (6.39); b) $\hat{L}'$ (6.43).

The discrete Laplace operator $\mathcal{L} = \mathcal{D}_x^2 + \mathcal{D}_y^2$ has the filter mask

$$\boldsymbol{L} = \begin{bmatrix} 1 & -2 & 1 \end{bmatrix} + \begin{bmatrix} 1 \\ -2 \\ 1 \end{bmatrix} = \begin{bmatrix} 0 & 1 & 0 \\ 1 & -4 & 1 \\ 0 & 1 & 0 \end{bmatrix} \tag{6.39}$$

and the transfer function

$$\hat{L} = 2\cos(\pi\tilde{k}_x) + 2\cos(\pi\tilde{k}_y) - 4. \tag{6.40}$$

As in other discrete approximations of operators, the Laplace operator is only isotropic for small wave numbers (figure 6.15a):

$$\hat{L} \approx -(\pi\tilde{k})^2 + \frac{1}{12}(\pi\tilde{k})^4 - \frac{1}{6}(\pi^2\tilde{k}_x\tilde{k}_y)^2 + O(\tilde{k}^6). \tag{6.41}$$

There are many other ways to construct a discrete approximation for the Laplace operator. An interesting possibility is the use of binomial masks. With (6.15) we can approximate all binomial masks for sufficiently small wave numbers by

$$\hat{\boldsymbol{B}}^{2R} \approx 1 - R\frac{\pi^2}{4}|\tilde{\boldsymbol{k}}|^2 + O(\tilde{k}^4). \tag{6.42}$$

From this equation we can conclude that any operator $\mathcal{I} - \mathcal{B}^n$ constitutes a Laplace operator for small wave numbers. For example,

$$\boldsymbol{L}' = 4(\boldsymbol{B}^2 - \boldsymbol{I}) = \frac{1}{4}\left[\begin{bmatrix} 1 & 2 & 1 \\ 2 & 4 & 2 \\ 1 & 2 & 1 \end{bmatrix} - \begin{bmatrix} 0 & 0 & 0 \\ 0 & 16 & 0 \\ 0 & 0 & 0 \end{bmatrix}\right] = \frac{1}{4}\begin{bmatrix} 1 & 2 & 1 \\ 2 & -12 & 2 \\ 1 & 2 & 1 \end{bmatrix} \tag{6.43}$$

with the transfer function

$$\hat{\boldsymbol{L}}' = \cos(\pi\tilde{k}_x) + \cos(\pi\tilde{k}_y) + \frac{1}{2}\cos[\pi(\tilde{k}_x - \tilde{k}_y)] + \frac{1}{2}\cos[\pi(\tilde{k}_x + \tilde{k}_y)] - 3, \tag{6.44}$$

which can be approximated for small wave numbers by

$$\hat{\boldsymbol{L}}' \approx -(\pi\tilde{k})^2 + \frac{1}{12}(\pi\tilde{k})^4 + \frac{1}{12}(\pi^2\tilde{k}_x\tilde{k}_y)^2 + O(\tilde{k}^6). \tag{6.45}$$

For large wave numbers, the transfer functions of both Laplace operators show considerable deviations from an ideal Laplacian, $-(\pi\tilde{k})^2$ (figure 6.15). $\mathcal{L}'$ is slightly less anisotropic than $\mathcal{L}$.

6.3 Filter Design

So far in this chapter, we have discussed the elementary properties of smoothing and edge detecting filters. In this last section we will add some details. In the examples discussed so far we were confronted with the recurring questions: how can we find a filter which performs the given task a) as correctly as possible and b) in the most efficient way. These are the central questions of a special discipline called *filter design*. As we noted already in section 6.1.3, filter design has been well established for one-dimensional signals, i. e., time series. Excellent text books available for this topic, for example, *Oppenheim and Schafer* [1989]. However, multidimensional filter design is much less established. We do not want to follow the classical avenues here. Rather we will continue with the approach to combine more complex filter operations from the elementary operators which we have found useful so far. This approach also shows the advantage that we obtain effective implementations of the filters. Emphasis in this section will also be on more accurate derivative filters, since these filters determine the accuracy of more complex image processing operations such as the determination of local orientation (chapter 7) and the estimation of motion in image sequences (chapter 17). Examples of effective implementations will also be discussed.

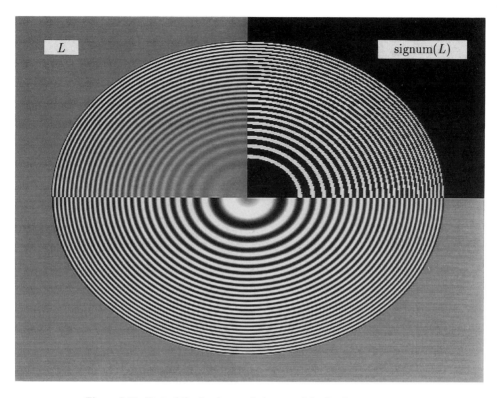

Figure 6.16: Test of the Laplace and signum of the Laplace operators.

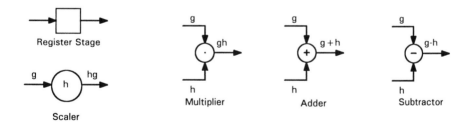

Figure 6.17: Elementary circuits to perform discrete filter operations.

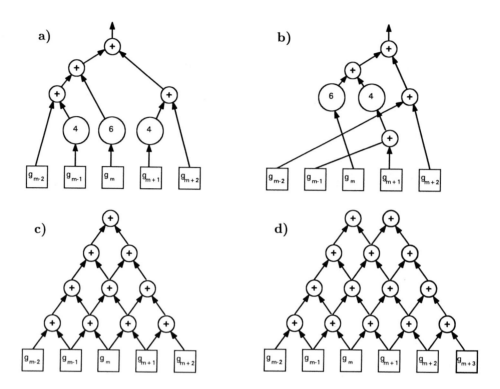

Figure 6.18: Different circuit nets to perform the binomial smoothing filter operation $B^4 = 1/16\,[1\;4\;6\;4\;1]$: a) direct implementation; b) saving multiplications; c) composition with the elementary filter $B = 1/2\,[1\;1]$; d) computation for the next pixels.

6.3.1 Filter Nets

The filters we have discussed so far are built from the simplest elementary operations we can think of: scaling of pixels and the addition of neighboring pixels. For each of these operations we can construct a circuit element which performs the corresponding operation. Figure 6.17 shows a *scaler*, an *adder*, a *subtractor*, a *multiplier*, and a *shift-register stage*. The circuit elements perform the operation either analogously or digitally.

With these circuit elements, we can view FIR filters in an instructive way. As a first example, we consider the one-dimensional binomial mask $B^4 = 1/16\,[1\;4\;6\;4\;1]$. Figure 6.18 shows different implementations to compute the filter output for one pixel. While direct implementations result in irregular-shaped circuit nets, the composition of the filter with the $B = 1/2\,[1\;1]$ mask gives a regular mesh of operations. For the calculation of a single output pixel, we need 10 additions, more than for the direct implementation. To calculate the filter output of the next pixel, we only need four additions if we store the intermediate results on each level of the filter net from the computations of the previous pixel (figure 6.18d).

Actually, we could build a net of these circuits, spanning the whole vector to compute

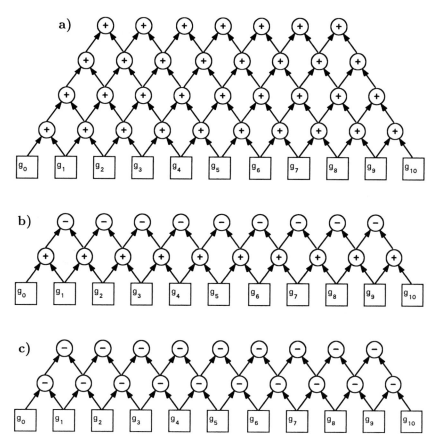

Figure 6.19: Circuit net to compute the several convolution operations in parallel: a) binomial smoothing filter $\mathcal{B}_x^4$; b) symmetric first-order derivative $^s\mathcal{D}_x$; c) second-order derivative $\mathcal{D}_x^2$.

the binomial smoothing in parallel (figure 6.19). Such a net has a number of interesting properties. Each level of the net corresponds to a filtering of the image with the elementary smoothing mask $1/2\,[1\ 1]$. Thus not only do we yield the final result, but all intermediate smoothing results. The grid points of the individual layers change from regular grid points to intermediate grid points in a natural way. With such filter nets we can also easily build derivative operators. For the first-order derivative operator, we need one layer with adders and one layer with subtracters (figure 6.19b), for the second-order derivative, we need two layers with subtracters (figure 6.19c).

The filter-net model also allows a straightforward approach to the boundary problems of filtering. We could close the net into a ring. This corresponds to a *cyclic convolution*. Or we could extend the net beyond the edges of the vector, so that we get all knots to calculate the first and last point. Then we can fill the grid points in the lowest levels which lie outside the vector either with zeros or we can extrapolate them in an appropriate manner from the points within the vector.

Algorithm 3: C subroutine to perform the one-dimensional binomial filtering with $B = 1/4\,[1\ 2\ 1]$ of a vector.

```c
/*
** Binomial filter of second order: 1/4 [1 2 1]
*/
void vs1bin2(v1) SVEC *v1; {
    register unsigned int i;
    register int s1, s2;
    register short *v1s, *v1d;
/*
** first loop from left to right
*/
    v1s = v1d = v1->dat;
    s1 = *v1s++;      /* v1[0] > s1 */
    for (i = v1->dx-1; i > 0; i--) {
        s2 = *v1s++;
        *v1d++ = (s2+s1)>>1; /* v[i]=(v[i+1]+v[i])/2 */
        s1 = s2; /* v[i] > v[i-1] */
    }
/*
** second loop from right to left
*/
    v1s = v1d = v1->dat + v1->dx;
    s1 = --*v1s;
    for (i = v1->dx-1; i > 0; i--) {
        s2 = --*v1s;
        --*v1d = (s2+s1)>>1; /* v[i]=(v[i-1]+v[i])/2 */
        s1 = s2; /* v[i-1] > v[i] */
    }
}
```

The extension of filter nets to two dimensions is straightforward for separable filters. The nets are then composed of nets alternately connecting the pixels in the horizontal or vertical direction. Generally, each such directional net contains two layers so that the filter results remain positioned on the original grid.

The filter nets are valuable tools for algorithm design. As we have seen, they are especially useful to make efficient use of intermediate results and to get a clear idea of the boundary problems at the edges of images. As an example, we discuss two different implementations of binomial filters. Algorithm 3 computes only one level per loop. First it runs forward, storing the result of the addition in the left pixel and then it runs backwards storing the result in the right pixel. For each level one addition, one shift operation, one memory read, and one memory write operation are necessary. In contrast, algorithm 4 computes four levels at once. Though the algorithm is more complex, the advantages are obvious. To compute four levels, we need four additions, but only one memory read and one memory write operation. The other memory read and write operations are replaced by faster register transfer operations. Only one shift operation is performed before we store the final result in the memory. This approach also leads to less rounding errors.

Algorithm 4: C subroutine to perform the one-dimensional binomial filtering with $B = 1/16 \, [1 \; 4 \; 6 \; 4 \; 1]$ in an arbitrary direction over the image.

```
/*
** Filtering of a line in an image starting at ptr with len pixels in an
** aritrary direction (determined by inc) by a 1/16(1 4 6 4 1) binomial filter.
** The filter is applied cnt times. If ZERO is defined, points outside the image
** are assumed to be zeros; otherwise they get the gray value of the edge pixels
*/
void ms1bin4(ptr,len,inc,cnt) short *ptr; short len,inc,cnt; {
    register long acc, s0, s1, s2, s3, s4, rinc=inc;
    register short *m1p;
    unsigned short i,j;
    for (j=cnt; j > 0; j--) {
    /* Preparation of the convolution loop */
        m1p=ptr;
        s0 = (long)*m1p; m1p += rinc; /* s0 = m1[0] */
        s1 = (long)*m1p; m1p += rinc; /* s1 = m1[1] */
        s2 = s0 + s1;                 /* s2 = m1[0]+m1[1] */
#ifndef ZERO
        s0 <<= 1;          /* extrapolate with edge pixel */
#endif
        s3 = s0 + s2;                      /* s3 = 2|3*m1[0]+m1[1] */
#ifndef ZERO
        s0 <<= 1;          /* extrapolate with edge pixel */
#endif
        s4 = s0 + s3;                      /* s4 = 3|7*m1[0]+m1[1] */
    /* Convolution loop for pixels 0 bis len-3 */
        for (i = len-2; i > 0; i--) {
            acc = (long)*m1p;                /* m1[i+2] */
            s0 = acc; acc += s1; s1 = s0; /* level 1 */
            s0 = acc; acc += s2; s2 = s0; /* level 2 */
            s0 = acc; acc += s3; s3 = s0; /* level 3 */
            s0 = acc; acc += s4; s4 = s0; /* level 4 */
            *(m1p-(rinc<<1)) = (short)(acc>>4); m1p += rinc;
        }
    /* Second last pixel m1[len-2] */
        m1p -= rinc; /* point to m1[len-1] */
#ifdef ZERO
        acc = 0;
#else
        acc = (long)*m1p;
#endif
        s0 = acc; acc += s1; s1 = s0;
        s0 = acc; acc += s2; s2 = s0;
        s0 = acc; acc += s3; s3 = s0;
        s0 = acc; acc += s4; s4 = s0;
        *(m1p-rinc) = (short)(acc>>4);
    /* Last pixel m1[len-1] */
#ifdef ZERO
        acc = 0;
#else
        acc = (long)*m1p;
#endif
        acc += s1; acc += s2; acc += s3; acc += s4; *m1p = (short)(acc>>4);
    }
}
```

6.3.2 Filter Decomposition

In the filter nets we discussed so far, it was possible to build up more complex filters such as larger binomial smoothing masks and derivative operators just by applying elementary filter masks which repeatedly combine neighboring pixels. Now we turn to the important question whether it is possible to decompose *every* convolution mask in a cascade of convolution operations with such elementary masks. The existence of such a decomposition would have far-reaching consequences. First, we could build simple filter nets for any type of convolution operations. Second, many modern image processing systems include high-performance hardware to perform convolutions with small convolution kernels (typically 4×4 or 8×8, see appendix B) very efficiently. If we can decompose any filter mask in a set of small filter masks, we can also make use of this hardware for large kernels. Third, the decomposition often reduces the computation, as we have already demonstrated with the binomial filter kernels.

Simonds [1988] proved that each two-dimensional filter kernel could be built up with the basic kernels

$$^1\boldsymbol{E}_x = \begin{bmatrix} 1 & 0 & 1 \end{bmatrix} \quad {}^1\boldsymbol{O}_x = \begin{bmatrix} 1 & 0 & -1 \end{bmatrix}$$

$$^1\boldsymbol{E}_y = \begin{bmatrix} 1 \\ 0 \\ 1 \end{bmatrix} \quad {}^1\boldsymbol{O}_y = \begin{bmatrix} 1 \\ 0 \\ -1 \end{bmatrix} \tag{6.46}$$

and the identity mask $\boldsymbol{I} = [1]$.

Simonds' decomposition is based on symmetry. First he shows that every convolution mask $\boldsymbol{H}$ can be decomposed into four kernels with show the following symmetry properties:

1. horizontally and vertically even ($^{ee}\boldsymbol{H}$),
2. horizontally even and vertically odd ($^{oe}\boldsymbol{H}$),
3. horizontally odd and vertically even ($^{eo}\boldsymbol{H}$), and
4. both directions odd ($^{oo}\boldsymbol{H}$),

$$
\begin{aligned}
^{ee}H_{m,n} &= (H_{m,n} + H_{m,-n} + H_{-m,n} + H_{-m,-n})/4 \\
^{oe}H_{m,n} &= (H_{m,n} + H_{m,-n} - H_{-m,n} - H_{-m,-n})/4 \\
^{eo}H_{m,n} &= (H_{m,n} - H_{m,-n} + H_{-m,n} - H_{-m,-n})/4 \\
^{oo}H_{m,n} &= (H_{m,n} - H_{m,-n} - H_{-m,n} + H_{-m,-n})/4.
\end{aligned}
\tag{6.47}
$$

It is easy to prove this lemma by adding the lines in (6.47). Next, we conclude that the four elementary masks in (6.46) and the four combinations of the horizontal and vertical masks just show these symmetry properties. Together with the identity mask $\boldsymbol{I}$, we have 9 independent masks, i.e., just as many independent elements as in a general 3×3 mask. Consequently, we can compose any 3×3 mask with these nine masks. For a general mask which does not show symmetry properties, this decomposition is computationally ineffective since it requires 9 more additions then a direct computation. However, since all useful image processing filters show certain symmetry properties, only a partial set of the elementary masks is needed.

Such a decomposition is especially useful if a set of similar masks has to be calculated. As an example, we take the *generalized Sobel operators*

$$
S_1 = \frac{1}{8}\begin{bmatrix} 1 & 0 & -1 \\ 2 & 0 & -2 \\ 1 & 0 & -1 \end{bmatrix} \quad S_3 = \frac{1}{8}\begin{bmatrix} 0 & -1 & -2 \\ 1 & 0 & -1 \\ 2 & 1 & 0 \end{bmatrix}
$$
$$
S_2 = \frac{1}{8}\begin{bmatrix} 1 & 2 & 1 \\ 0 & 0 & 0 \\ -1 & -2 & -1 \end{bmatrix} \quad S_4 = \frac{1}{8}\begin{bmatrix} 2 & 1 & 0 \\ 1 & 0 & -1 \\ 0 & -1 & -2 \end{bmatrix},
$$

(6.48)

which are sometimes used as simple operators to detect edges in the direction of the two axes and diagonals. Simultaneously, they perform some smoothing perpendicular to the direction of the edge.

These operators can be computed as follows:

$$
\begin{aligned}
{}^{eo}S &= (1 + {}^{1}E_y)^1 O_x \\
{}^{oe}S &= (1 + {}^{1}E_x)^1 O_y \\
S_1 &= 1/8({}^{1}O_x + {}^{eo}S) \\
S_2 &= 1/8({}^{1}O_y + {}^{oe}S) \\
S_3 &= 1/8({}^{eo}S - {}^{oe}S) \\
S_4 &= 1/8({}^{eo}S + {}^{oe}S).
\end{aligned}
$$

(6.49)

In total, we need only 12 additions and 4 shift operations to calculate the four 3×3 Sobel operators.

In order to decompose larger kernels, we need additional masks of the length $2k + 1$

$$
{}^{k}E = [1\ 0\ \cdots\ 0\ 1], \quad {}^{k}O = [1\ 0\ \cdots\ 0\ -1]. \tag{6.50}
$$

These masks can be computed iteratively from the masks of size one, ${}^{1}E$ and ${}^{1}O$

$$
\begin{aligned}
{}^{k}E &= \begin{cases} {}^{1}E^{k-1}E - {}^{k-2}E, & k > 2 \\ {}^{1}E^{1}E - 2, & k = 2 \end{cases} \\
{}^{k}O &= \begin{cases} {}^{1}E^{k-1}O - {}^{k-2}O, & k > 2 \\ {}^{1}E^{1}O, & k = 2. \end{cases}
\end{aligned}
$$

(6.51)

6.3.3 Smoothing Operators

In this section we discuss the filter design of smoothing filters. In contrast to classical approaches in filter design, we will try to develop filters with the desired characteristics from the elementary B operator. We will learn two design principles which will guide our search for composite filters.

The binomial smoothing filters B^n discussed in section 6.1.2 optimally balance wave number resolution and kernel size. Common to all of them is the rather gradual decrease of the transfer function with the wave number (figure 6.1b). For small wave numbers, all binomial filters decrease with $\tilde{k}^2$ (6.12). This property is the basic reason for the rather gradual decrease of the transfer function. A smoothing filter that decreases with a higher power in $\tilde{k}$ should first maintain a flat response. At the cut-off wave number, it should fall-off steeply towards zero. We can construct such filters by observing that the operator $\mathcal{I} - \mathcal{B}^n$ goes with $\tilde{k}^2$. If we apply this operator several times and subtract it from the original image, we obtain a smoothing operator which decreases with a higher power in $\tilde{k}$. The simplest operator of this type is

$$^{(2,1)}\mathcal{B} = \mathcal{I} - (\mathcal{I} - \mathcal{B}^2)^2 = 2\mathcal{B}^2 - \mathcal{B}^4. \tag{6.52}$$

The corresponding filter coefficients are

$$^{(2,1)}\mathbf{B}_x = \frac{1}{16}[-1\ 4\ 10\ 4\ -1] \tag{6.53}$$

in one dimension and

$$^{(2,1)}\mathbf{B} = \frac{1}{256} \begin{bmatrix} -1 & -4 & -6 & -4 & -1 \\ -4 & 16 & 40 & 16 & -4 \\ -6 & 40 & 92 & 40 & -6 \\ -4 & 16 & 40 & 16 & -4 \\ -1 & -4 & -6 & -4 & -1 \end{bmatrix} \tag{6.54}$$

in two dimensions. In this way, we can define an entire new class of smoothing filters:

$$^{(n,l)}\mathcal{B} = \left[\mathcal{I} - \left(\mathcal{I} - \mathcal{B}^2\right)^n\right]^l \tag{6.55}$$

with the transfer function

$$^{(n,l)}\hat{B} = \left\{1 - \left\{1 - \frac{1}{2^{2n}}\left[1 + \cos(\pi\tilde{k}_x)\right]\left[1 + \cos(\pi\tilde{k}_y)\right]\right\}^n\right\}^l. \tag{6.56}$$

We denote the order, i. e., the steepness of the transition, with n, while l controls the cut-off wave number of the filter. A Taylor expansion yields for small $\tilde{k}_x$, $\tilde{k}_y$

$$^{(n,l)}\hat{B} \approx 1 - \frac{l}{2^{2n}}\left(\pi\tilde{k}\right)^{2n}. \tag{6.57}$$

Figure 6.20 shows transfer functions for a number of filters of this type. The higher the order of the filter, the more the cut-off wave number is shifted to higher wave numbers. The minimum mask length increases proportionally with the order of the filter. The smallest smoothing mask of second order has five coefficients, the smallest filter of third order

$$^{(3,1)}\mathcal{B} = \mathcal{I} - (\mathcal{I} - \mathcal{B}^2)^3 = 3\mathcal{B}^2 - 3\mathcal{B}^4 + \mathcal{B}^6 \tag{6.58}$$

has seven coefficients in one dimension:

$$^{(3,1)}\mathbf{B}_x = \frac{1}{64}[1\ -6\ 15\ 44\ 15\ -6\ 1]. \tag{6.59}$$

This class of filters shares many important properties of the binomial filters $\mathcal{B}^n$:
• The transfer function decreases monotonically and vanishes at $\tilde{k}_x = 1$ and $\tilde{k}_y = 1$.

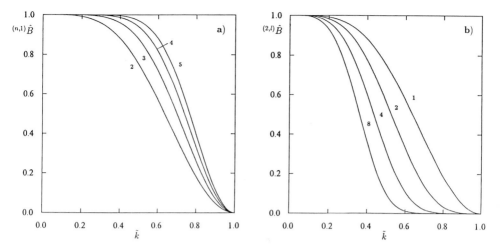

Figure 6.20: Transfer functions of one-dimensional smoothing filters of higher order according to (6.56): a) smallest masks of order n ($l = 1$); b) second-order filters with l as indicated.

- Since the filter is composed of (approximately) isotropic filters, the resulting filters are also isotropic (figure 6.21a and b). This is an important design issue in two dimensions. We cannot construct a higher-order smoothing filter from one-dimensional higher-order filters in a simple way. These filters tend to show square-like contour lines in the transfer function (figure 6.21c).

With these examples, we have learnt some advantages of the composition method for filter design:

- The filter coefficients and transfer functions can be expressed in analytical formulas. This allows us to analyze the properties of the filters directly.
- The design method coincides with an effective implementation.
- As demonstrated, we can incorporate such features as isotropy and behavior at low wave numbers into the composition rules.

Despite the very efficient implementation of the binomial smoothing filter $\mathcal{B}^n$, the computation required increases dramatically for smoothing masks with low cut-off wave numbers, because the standard deviation of the filters only coordinates with the square root of n according to (4.8): $\sigma = \sqrt{n}/2$. Let us consider a smoothing operation over a distance of only 5 pixels, i.e., $\sigma = 5$. Then we need to apply $\mathcal{B}^{100}$ which requires 200 additions for each pixel even with the most effective implementation. The linear dimensions of the mask size increase with the square of the standard deviation σ as does the computation required.

The problem originates in the small distance of the pixels averaged in the elementary $\mathbf{B} = 1/2\,[1\ 1]$ mask. The repetitive application of this mask is known as a *diffusion process* for gray values. The half width of the distribution is only proportional to the square root of the time, i.e., the number of iteration steps (see (16.25) in section 16.3.3). In order to overcome this problem, we may use the same elementary averaging process

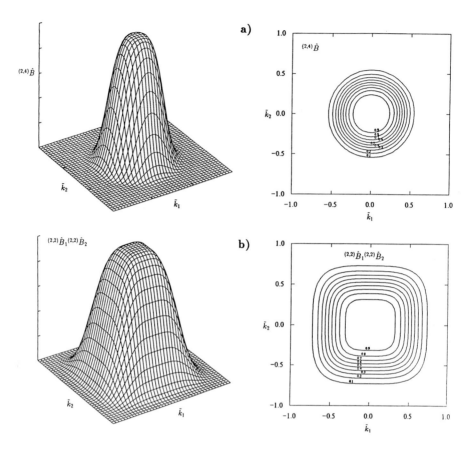

Figure 6.21: Transfer functions of two-dimensional smoothing filters of higher-order smoothing filters according to (6.56): a) $^{(2,4)}\hat{B}$; b) separable second-order filter $^{(2,4)}\hat{B}_x{}^{(2,4)}\hat{B}_y$.

but with more distant pixels, for example

$$
\begin{array}{ll}
\boldsymbol{B}_{x-y} = \begin{bmatrix} 1 & 0 \\ 0 & 1 \end{bmatrix} & \boldsymbol{B}_{x+y} = \begin{bmatrix} 0 & 1 \\ 1 & 0 \end{bmatrix} \\[2ex]
\boldsymbol{B}_{2x} = \begin{bmatrix} 1 & 0 & 1 \end{bmatrix} & \boldsymbol{B}_{2y} = \begin{bmatrix} 1 \\ 0 \\ 1 \end{bmatrix} \\[3ex]
\boldsymbol{B}_{x-2y} = \begin{bmatrix} 1 & 0 & 0 \\ 0 & 0 & 1 \end{bmatrix} & \boldsymbol{B}_{2x-y} = \begin{bmatrix} 1 & 0 \\ 0 & 0 \\ 0 & 1 \end{bmatrix} \\[3ex]
\boldsymbol{B}_{2x+y} = \begin{bmatrix} 0 & 0 & 1 \\ 1 & 0 & 0 \end{bmatrix} & \boldsymbol{B}_{x+2y} = \begin{bmatrix} 0 & 1 \\ 0 & 0 \\ 1 & 0 \end{bmatrix}.
\end{array}
\tag{6.60}
$$

The subscripts in these elementary masks denote the distance and direction of the pixels which are averaged. The subscript can be read as the equation for the line connecting the two pixels. $\boldsymbol{B}_{x-y}$ (plane equation $x - y = 0$) averages two neighbored pixels in the direction of the main diagonal. $\boldsymbol{B}_{x-2y}$ averages a pixel and its neighbor which is located two grid constants to the right and one to the top. The standard deviation of these filters is proportional to the distance of the pixels.

The problem with these filters is that they perform a subsampling. Consequently, they are no longer a good smoothing filter for larger wave numbers. If we take, for example, the symmetric 2-D $\boldsymbol{B}_{2x}^2\boldsymbol{B}_{2y}^2$ filter, we effectively work on a grid which is twice as large in the spatial domain. Hence, the reciprocal grid in the wave number is half the size, and we see the periodic replication of the transfer function (figure 6.22b, see also the discussion in section 2.3.3). The zero lines of the transfer function show the reciprocal grid for the corresponding subsample grids. For convolution with two neighboring pixels in the direction of the two diagonals, the reciprocal grid is turned by 45°. The grid constant of the reciprocal grid is $\sqrt{2}$ smaller than that of the original grid.

Used individually, these filters are not of much help. But we can use them in cascade, starting with directly neighboring pixels. Then the zero lines of the transfer functions, which lie differently for each pixel distance, efficiently force the transfer function close to zero for large wave numbers. In the filter combination $\boldsymbol{B}_x^2\boldsymbol{B}_y^2\boldsymbol{B}_{x-y}^2\boldsymbol{B}_{x+y}^2$ the non-zero high parts in the corners of $\boldsymbol{B}_{x-y}^2\boldsymbol{B}_{x+y}^2$ are nearly vanished since the transfer function $\boldsymbol{B}_x^2\boldsymbol{B}_y^2$ filter is close to zero in this part (figure 6.22a, b, and e). As a final example, we consider the filter

$$\boldsymbol{B}^{26'} = \boldsymbol{B}_x^2\boldsymbol{B}_y^2\boldsymbol{B}_{x-y}^2\boldsymbol{B}_{x+y}^2\boldsymbol{B}_{2x-y}^2\boldsymbol{B}_{2x+y}^2\boldsymbol{B}_{x-2y}^2\boldsymbol{B}_{x+2y}^2. \tag{6.61}$$

Its standard deviation is $\sqrt{6.5} \approx 2.5$, i.e., it corresponds to the $\boldsymbol{B}^{26}$ operator. The transfer function is shown in figure 6.22f. With only 16 additions and one shift operation we can convolve the image with the 19×19 kernel

$$\boldsymbol{B}^{26'} = \frac{1}{2^{16}}[1\ 2\ 1] * \begin{bmatrix} 1 \\ 2 \\ 1 \end{bmatrix} * \begin{bmatrix} 1 & 0 & 0 \\ 0 & 2 & 0 \\ 0 & 0 & 1 \end{bmatrix} * \begin{bmatrix} 0 & 0 & 1 \\ 0 & 2 & 0 \\ 1 & 0 & 0 \end{bmatrix}$$

$$* \begin{bmatrix} 1 & 0 & 0 & 0 & 0 \\ 0 & 0 & 2 & 0 & 0 \\ 0 & 0 & 0 & 0 & 1 \end{bmatrix} * \begin{bmatrix} 1 & 0 & 0 \\ 0 & 0 & 0 \\ 0 & 2 & 0 \\ 0 & 0 & 0 \\ 0 & 0 & 1 \end{bmatrix}$$

$$* \begin{bmatrix} 0 & 0 & 0 & 0 & 1 \\ 0 & 0 & 2 & 0 & 0 \\ 1 & 0 & 0 & 0 & 0 \end{bmatrix} * \begin{bmatrix} 0 & 0 & 1 \\ 0 & 0 & 0 \\ 0 & 2 & 0 \\ 0 & 0 & 0 \\ 1 & 0 & 0 \end{bmatrix} = \tag{6.62}$$

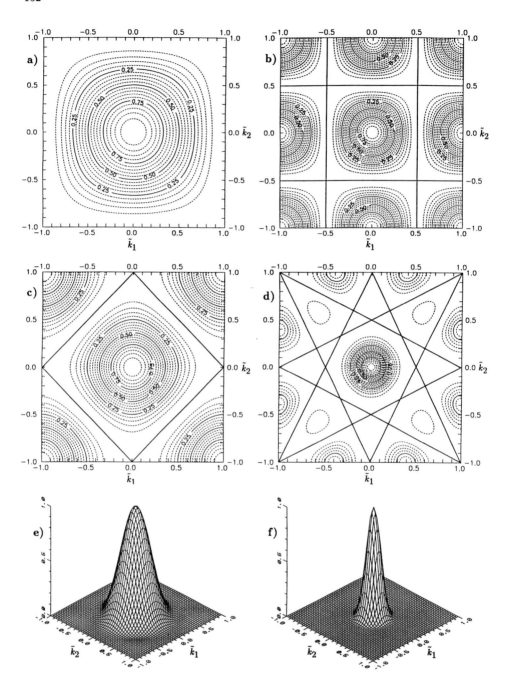

Figure 6.22: Transfer functions of the elementary binomial filter $\mathcal{B}^2$ used to average pixels with different distances shown as contour plots. The thick lines show the zeros of the transfer function. a) $\mathcal{B}_x^2\mathcal{B}_y^2$; b) $\mathcal{B}_{2x}^2\mathcal{B}_{2y}^2$; c) $\mathcal{B}_{x-y}^2\mathcal{B}_{x+y}^2$; d) $\mathcal{B}_{2x-y}^2\mathcal{B}_{2x+y}^2\mathcal{B}_{x-2y}^2\mathcal{B}_{x+2y}^2$; e) $\mathcal{B}_x^2\mathcal{B}_y^2\mathcal{B}_{x-y}^2\mathcal{B}_{x+y}^2$; f) $\mathcal{B}^{26'}$, see (6.61).

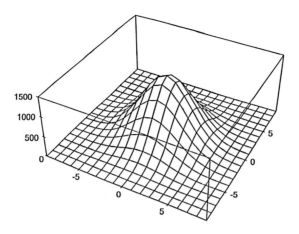

Figure 6.23: Convolution mask of the $\mathcal{B}^{26'}$ binomial smoothing operator (6.61).

$$= \frac{1}{2^{16}}$$

0	0	0	0	0	0	0	0	1	2	1	0	0	0	0	0	0	0	0
0	0	0	0	0	0	2	6	8	8	8	6	2	0	0	0	0	0	0
0	0	0	0	1	6	14	24	34	38	34	24	14	6	1	0	0	0	0
0	0	0	2	8	24	50	78	102	112	102	78	50	24	8	2	0	0	0
0	0	1	8	30	68	124	190	241	260	241	190	124	68	30	8	1	0	0
0	0	6	24	68	146	254	372	464	500	464	372	254	146	68	24	6	0	0
0	2	14	50	124	254	430	612	756	812	756	612	430	254	124	50	14	2	0
0	6	24	78	190	372	612	866	1062	1132	1062	866	612	372	190	78	24	6	0
1	8	34	102	241	464	756	1062	1294	1380	1294	1062	756	464	241	102	34	8	1
2	8	38	112	260	500	812	1132	1380	1480	1380	1132	812	500	260	112	38	8	2
1	8	34	102	241	464	756	1062	1294	1380	1294	1062	756	464	241	102	34	8	1
0	6	24	78	190	372	612	866	1062	1132	1062	866	612	372	190	78	24	6	0
0	2	14	50	124	254	430	612	756	812	756	612	430	254	124	50	14	2	0
0	0	6	24	68	146	254	372	464	500	464	372	254	146	68	24	6	0	0
0	0	1	8	30	68	124	190	241	260	241	190	124	68	30	8	1	0	0
0	0	0	2	8	24	50	78	102	112	102	78	50	24	8	2	0	0	0
0	0	0	0	1	6	14	24	34	38	34	24	14	6	1	0	0	0	0
0	0	0	0	0	0	2	6	8	8	8	6	2	0	0	0	0	0	0
0	0	0	0	0	0	0	0	1	2	1	0	0	0	0	0	0	0	0

This kernel is also shown in figure 6.23. It would take 52 additions with the equivalent $\mathcal{B}^{26}$ operator. Straightforward convolution with the 27×27 mask of $\mathcal{B}^{26}$ would take 729 multiplications and 728 additions. Again this example illustrates that good kernel design and extremely high efficiency go hand in hand with the composition method.

6.3.4   Bandpass Filters; DoG and LoG Filter

Bandpass filters select a range of wave numbers. Again, it is possible to construct them from simple binomial smoothing masks. To do so, we take two smoothing filters with different cut-off wave numbers. When we subtract the results of these two operations, we obtain an image which contains the range of wave numbers between the two cut-off wave numbers. A simple one-dimensional example is

$$\mathcal{P}_1 = 4(\mathcal{B}_1^2 - \mathcal{B}_1^4)$$

with the convolution mask

$$\boldsymbol{P}_1 = \begin{bmatrix} 1 & 2 & 1 \end{bmatrix} - \frac{1}{4}\begin{bmatrix} 1 & 4 & 6 & 4 & 1 \end{bmatrix} = \frac{1}{4}\begin{bmatrix} -1 & 0 & 2 & 0 & -1 \end{bmatrix}$$

and the transfer function

$$\hat{P}_1 = 1 - \cos^2(\pi\tilde{k}) = \frac{1 - \cos(2\pi\tilde{k})}{2}.$$

The transfer function shows a maximum at $\tilde{k} = 1/2$ and is zero at $\tilde{k} = 0$ and $\tilde{k} = 1$. With similar combinations of other binomial operators, we can construct bandpass operators with different a bandwidth and different a bandpass wave number. In a similar manner we can also construct isotropic two-dimensional bandpass filters.

Since the discrete binomial operators converge rapidly against the Gaussian function (section 4.2.1), we can use them to describe some general features for larger kernels. The continuous convolution mask

$$1/\sigma\sqrt{2/\pi}\exp(-\boldsymbol{x}^2/2\sigma^2) \tag{6.63}$$

has the transfer function

$$\exp(-\boldsymbol{k}^2\sigma^2/2). \tag{6.64}$$

Thus the difference filter, which is abbreviated to DoG (*Difference of Gaussian*) yields the transfer function

$$\widehat{\mathrm{DoG}} = \exp\frac{-\boldsymbol{k}^2\sigma_1^2}{2}\left(1 - \exp\frac{-\boldsymbol{k}^2(\sigma_2^2 - \sigma_1^2)}{2}\right). \tag{6.65}$$

For small wave numbers, the transfer function is proportional to $|\boldsymbol{k}|^2$

$$\widehat{\mathrm{DoG}} \approx \frac{\boldsymbol{k}^2(\sigma_2^2 - \sigma_1^2)}{2}. \tag{6.66}$$

The decrease towards high wave numbers is determined by the first exponential in (6.65). The wave number for the maximum response, $k_{\mathrm{max}} = |\boldsymbol{k}_{\mathrm{max}}|$, is given by

$$k_{\mathrm{max}} = \frac{2}{\sigma_2^2 - \sigma_1^2}\ln\frac{\sigma_2}{\sigma_1}. \tag{6.67}$$

Since DoG filters increase quadratically for small wave numbers, they behave like a Laplace operator in this region. Consequently, they are similar to an operator which first smooths the image with a Gauss operator and then applies the Laplace operator. Such a filter is called a *Laplace of Gaussian*, or LoG for short. A LoG filter has the transfer function

$$\widehat{\mathrm{LoG}} = \alpha\boldsymbol{k}^2\exp\frac{\boldsymbol{k}^2\sigma^2}{2}. \tag{6.68}$$

LoG and DoG filter operations are believed to have significant importance in low-level image processing in the human visual system [*Marr*, 1982]. Methods for fast computation of these filter operations have been discussed by *Chen et al.* [1987] and *Crowley and Stern* [1984].

6.3.5   Derivative Operators

We have already discussed discrete derivative operators in section 6.2 with respect to edge detection. Now we focus on the question of the accuracy of these operators. So far we have only used very crude approximations of the derivatives (6.30) which show considerable deviations from an ideal derivation operator (6.33) even for small wave numbers: $-36\,\%$ for $\tilde{k} = 1/2$, $-10\,\%$ for $\tilde{k} = 1/4$ and only $-2,6\,\%$ for $\tilde{k} = 1/8$. These deviations are too large to be tolerated for a number of complex filter operations which we will discuss in section 7.3 and chapter 17. Therefore, we now review improved approximations of derivative operators in this section.

We start with the fact that any derivative operator of odd or even order has a filter kernel with the corresponding symmetry. In the following we restrict our considerations to the first-order derivative operator. Generally, it has the mask

$$^{(R)}D = 1/2\,[d_R \; \ldots \; d_2 \; d_1 \; 0 \; -d_1 \; -d_2 \; \ldots \; -d_R] \tag{6.69}$$

and the transfer function

$$^{(r)}\hat{D} = \mathrm{i}\sum_{u=1}^{R} d_u \sin(u\pi\tilde{k}). \tag{6.70}$$

For a given filter length R, we now have to choose a set of coefficients, so that the sum in (6.70) approximates the ideal derivative operator $\mathrm{i}\pi\tilde{k}$ in an optimum way. We can do this by expanding the sine function in $u\pi\tilde{k}$ and then choose the coefficients d_u so that as many terms as possible vanish except for terms linear in $\tilde{k}$. Before we write the general mathematical formalism, we consider the simple example with $R = 2$. If we expand the transfer function in (6.70) to the third order in $\tilde{k}$, we obtain

$$
\begin{aligned}
^{(2)}\hat{D}_x \;=\;& d_1\pi\tilde{k} \;-\; d_1/6(\pi\tilde{k})^3 \\
&+\; 2d_2\,\pi\tilde{k} \;-\; 8d_2/6(\pi\tilde{k})^3
\end{aligned}
$$

or

$$^{(2)}\hat{D}_x = (d_1 + 2d_2)\pi\tilde{k} - 1/6(d_1 + 8d_2)(\pi\tilde{k})^3.$$

Since the factor of the $\tilde{k}^3$ should vanish and the factor for the $\tilde{k}$ term be equal to one, we have two equations with the two unknowns d_1 and d_2. The solution is $d_1 = 4/3$ and $d_2 = -1/6$. According to (6.69) we yield the filter mask

$$^{(2)}D_x = \frac{1}{12}[-1 \; 8 \; 0 \; -8 \; 1].$$

Now we use the same principle to compute an optimum derivative operator with $2r + 1$ elements. We expand the sine function up to the order $2r + 1$. Then we obtain r coefficients for the r powers in $\tilde{k}$ and thus r equations for the r unknowns d_u. The general form of the linear equation system is

$$
\begin{bmatrix}
1 & 2 & 3 & \cdots & R \\
1 & 8 & 27 & \cdots & R^3 \\
1 & 32 & 243 & \cdots & R^5 \\
\vdots & \vdots & \vdots & \ddots & \vdots \\
1 & 2^{2R-1} & 3^{2R-1} & \cdots & R^{2R-1}
\end{bmatrix}
\begin{bmatrix}
d_1 \\ d_2 \\ d_3 \\ \vdots \\ d_R
\end{bmatrix}
=
\begin{bmatrix}
1 \\ 0 \\ 0 \\ \vdots \\ 0
\end{bmatrix}. \tag{6.71}
$$

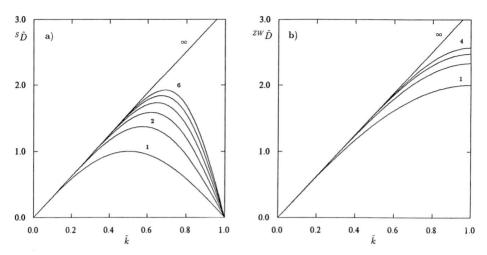

Figure 6.24: Optimized derivative operators for a given filter length: a) with odd number of coefficients $2R + 1$ according to (6.71); b) with even number of coefficients $2R$.

As examples of the solutions, we show the filter masks for $R = 3$

$$^{(3)}\boldsymbol{D}_x = \frac{1}{60}\,[1\ \text{-}9\ 45\ 0\ \text{-}45\ 9\ \text{-}1]$$

and $R = 4$

$$^{(4)}\boldsymbol{D}_x = \frac{1}{840}\,[\text{-}3\ 32\ \text{-}168\ 672\ 0\ \text{-}672\ 168\ \text{-}32\ 3]\,.$$

Figure 6.24 shows how the transfer function of these optimized kernels converges to the ideal derivative operator with increasing R. Convergence is slow, but the transfer function remains monotonous. No additional errors are introduced for small $\tilde{k}$. A filter of length 7 ($R = 3$) reduces the deviation for $\tilde{k} = 1/2$ to only $-2.4\,\%$ compared to $-36\,\%$ for the simple derivative operator with $R = 1$.

The linear equation system (6.71) can also be used to optimize other odd-order derivative operators. We must only change the vector on the right side of (6.71) accordingly. A similar equation system can be used to optimize even-order derivative operators as well as first-order derivative operators with an even number of coefficients (see figure 6.24b). The latter places the filter results between the grid points.

7 Local Orientation

7.1 Introduction

In the last chapter we became acquainted with neighborhood operations. In fact, we only studied very simple structures in a local neighborhood, namely the edges. We concentrated on the detection of edges, but we did not consider how to determine their *orientation*. Orientation is a significant property not only of edges but also of any pattern that shows a preferred direction. The *local orientation* of a pattern is the property which leads the way to a description of more complex image features. Local orientation is also a key feature in motion analysis (chapter 17). Furthermore, there is a close relationship between orientation and projection (section 13.4.2).

Our visual system can easily recognize objects which do not differ from a background by the mean gray value but only by the orientation of a pattern as demonstrated in figure 7.1. To perform this recognition task with a digital image processing system, we need an operator which determines the orientation of the pattern. After such an operation, we can distinguish differently oriented patterns in the same way we can distinguish gray values.

For a closer mathematical description of local orientation, we use continuous gray value functions. With continuous functions, it is much easier to formulate the concept of local orientation. As long as the corresponding discrete image meets the sampling theorem, all the results derived from continuous functions remain valid, since the sam-

Figure 7.1: Objects can not only be recognized because of differences in gray values but also because of the orientation of patterns.

pled image is an exact representation of the continuous gray value function. A local neighborhood with *ideal* local orientation is characterized by the fact that the gray value only changes in one direction, in the other direction it is constant. Since the curves of constant gray values are lines, local orientation is also denoted as *linear symmetry* [*Bigün and Granlund*, 1987]. If we orient the coordinate system along these two principal directions, we can write the gray values as a one-dimensional function of only one coordinate. Generally, we will denote the direction of local orientation with a vector $\bar{k}$ which is perpendicular to the lines of constant gray values. Then we can write for a local neighborhood with an ideal local orientation:

$$g(\boldsymbol{x}) = g(\boldsymbol{x}^T \bar{\boldsymbol{k}}). \tag{7.1}$$

We can easily verify that this representation is correct, since the gradient of the gray value structure

$$\nabla g(\boldsymbol{x}^T \bar{\boldsymbol{k}}) = \begin{bmatrix} \dfrac{\partial g(\boldsymbol{x}^T \bar{\boldsymbol{k}})}{\partial x_1} \\[2mm] \dfrac{\partial g(\boldsymbol{x}^T \bar{\boldsymbol{k}})}{\partial x_2} \end{bmatrix} = \begin{bmatrix} \bar{k}_1 g'(\boldsymbol{x}^T \bar{\boldsymbol{k}}) \\[2mm] \bar{k}_2 g'(\boldsymbol{x}^T \bar{\boldsymbol{k}}) \end{bmatrix} = \bar{\boldsymbol{k}} g'(\boldsymbol{x}^T \bar{\boldsymbol{k}}) \tag{7.2}$$

lies in the direction of $\bar{\boldsymbol{k}}$. (With g' we denote the derivative of g with respect to the scalar variable $\boldsymbol{x}^T \bar{\boldsymbol{k}}$.) From this coincidence we might conclude that we can easily determine local orientation with the *gradient operator*. We could use the magnitude of the gradient as an orientation-independent certainty measure

$$|\nabla g| = \left[\left(\frac{\partial g}{\partial x_1} \right)^2 + \left(\frac{\partial g}{\partial x_2} \right)^2 \right]^{1/2} \tag{7.3}$$

and determine the direction of the orientation by

$$\phi = \arctan \left(\frac{\partial g}{\partial x_2} \bigg/ \frac{\partial g}{\partial x_1} \right). \tag{7.4}$$

Unfortunately this simple approach does not lead to an adequate orientation determination because:

- The gradient is a too local feature. Even if we have a random pattern, the gradient will give us well defined orientations at each point. Consequently, an appropriate orientation operator must include some averaging in order to detect whether or not a local neighborhood shows local orientation.
- The gradient does not deliver the correct angular range for orientation. To describe orientation, a range of 180° is sufficient, since the rotation of a pattern by 180° does not change its orientation.
- It is not directly possible to average the orientation angle because of the 180° ambiguity and because the angle shows a discontinuity. For example, two structures with orientation angles of -89° and 87° lie in very similar directions despite the very different values of the angles. Direct averaging of the two orientations would yield the wrong mean value of -1°.

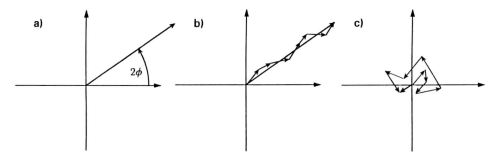

Figure 7.2: Representation of local orientation as a vector: a) the orientation vector: b) averaging of orientation vectors from a region with homogeneous orientation; c) same for a region with randomly distributed orientation.

7.1.1 Vectorial Representation of Local Orientation

The introduction made us think about an adequate representation of orientation. Such a representation needs to take into account the *circular* property of the orientation angle. Thus we are forced to represent orientation by an angle. Because its range is limited to 180°, we must double the angle. We then can think of orientation as a *vector* pointing in the direction 2ϕ (figure 7.2). The magnitude of the vector can be set to the certainty of the orientation determination. As a result any averaging means vector addition. In case of a region which shows a homogeneous orientation, the vectors line up to a large vector (figure 7.2c). However, in a region with randomly distributed orientation the resulting vector becomes very small, indicating that no significant local orientation is present (figure 7.2c).

7.1.2 Color Coding of Vectorial Image Features

We cannot display orientation adequately with a gray value image. We can either display the certainty or the orientation angle, but not both. The latter cannot be properly displayed at all, as we get a discontinuity in the representation with the jump from the smallest to the largest angle. However, both features can be displayed in a color image. It appears natural to code the certainty measure in the luminance and the orientation angle in color. Our attention is then drawn to the light parts of the image where we can determine the orientation angle with good accuracy. The darker a region becomes, the more difficult it will be for us to distinguish different colors visually. In this way, our visual impression coincides with the orientation contents in the image. Representing the orientation angle as a color means that it adapts well to its own cyclic behavior. There is no gap at a certain angle. Perpendicular orientations are shown in complementary colors (plate 8).

In the following two sections, we will introduce two different concepts to determine local orientation. First, we discuss the use of a set of directional filters. The second method is based on the Fourier space and allows a direct determination of local orientation with simple derivative operators.

7.2   The Quadrature Filter Set Method

In chapter 5 we learnt that we can use filter operations to select any wave number range which is contained in an image. In particular we could choose a filter that selects only wave numbers of a certain direction. In this way, we can extract those structures which are oriented in the same direction. Such an extraction, however, does not yield a determination of local orientation. We must use a whole set of directionally sensitive filters. We will then obtain a maximum filter response from the directional filter whose direction coincides best with that of local orientation. In order to determine local orientation we must apply a number of directional filters. Then we have to compare the filter results. If we get a clear maximum in one of the filters but only little response in the others, the local neighborhood contains a locally oriented pattern. If a large fraction of the filters gives a comparable response, the neighborhood contains a distribution of oriented patterns. So far, the concept seems to be straightforward, but a number of tricky problems needs to be solved. Which properties have to be met by the directional filters in order to ensure an exact determination of local orientation, if at all possible? For computational efficiency, we need to use a minimal number of filters to interpolate the angle of the local orientation. What is this minimum number?

The concepts introduced in this section are based on the work of *Granlund* [1978], *Knutsson* [1982], and *Knutsson et al.* [1983].

7.2.1   Directional Quadrature Filters

First we will discuss the selection of appropriate directional filters. Finally, our filters should give an exact orientation estimate. We can easily see that simple filters cannot be expected to yield such a result. A simple first-order derivative operator, for example, would not give any response at local minima and maxima of the gray values and thus will not allow determination of local orientation in these places. There is a special class of operators, called *quadrature filters*, which perform better. They can be constructed in the following way. Imagine we have a certain directional filter $\hat{h}(\boldsymbol{k})$. We calculate the transfer function of this filter and then rotate the phase of the transfer function by 90°. By this action, the wave number components in the two filter responses differ by a shift of a quarter of a wavelength for every wave number. Where one filter response shows zero crossings, the other shows extremes. If we now square and add the two filter responses, we actually obtain an estimate of the *spectral density*, or physically speaking, the *energy*, of the corresponding periodic image structure. We can best demonstrate this property by applying the two filters to a periodic structure $a\cos(\boldsymbol{kx})$. We assume that the first filter does not cause a phase shift, but the second causes a phase shift of 90°. Then

$$\begin{aligned} h_1 &= \hat{h}(\boldsymbol{k})a\cos(\boldsymbol{kx}) \\ h_2 &= \hat{h}(\boldsymbol{k})a\sin(\boldsymbol{kx}). \end{aligned}$$

Squaring and adding the filter results, we get a constant *phase-independent* response of $\hat{h}^2a^2$. We automatically obtain a pair of quadrature filters if we choose an even real and an odd imaginary transfer function with the same magnitude.

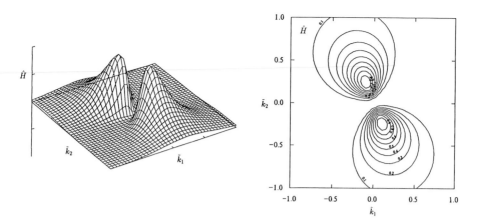

Figure 7.3: Transfer function of the directional quadrature filter according to (2.43) with $l = 2$ and $B = 2$ in $112.5°$ direction.

Returning to the selection of an appropriate set of directional filters, we can state further that they should be similar to each other. Thus the resulting filter's transfer function can be separated into an angular and a wave number part. Such a filter is called *polar separable* and may be conveniently expressed in polar coordinates

$$\hat{h}(q, \phi) = \hat{l}(q)\hat{k}(\phi), \tag{7.5}$$

with $q^2 = k_1^2 + k_2^2$ and $\tan \phi = k_2/k_1$.

Knutsson [1982] suggested the following directional quadrature filters:

$$
\begin{aligned}
\hat{l}(q) &= \exp\left[-\frac{\ln^2(q/q_0)}{(B/2)^2 \log 2}\right] \\
\hat{k}_e(\phi) &= \cos^{2l}(\phi - \phi_k) \\
\hat{k}_o(\phi) &= i\cos^{2l}(\phi - \phi_k)\, \text{signum}\,[\cos(\phi - \phi_k)].
\end{aligned}
\tag{7.6}
$$

q denotes the magnitude of the wave number; q_0 and ϕ_k are the peak wave number and the direction of the filter, respectively. The indices e and o indicate the even and odd component of the quadrature pair. The constant B determines the half-width of the wave number in the number of octaves and l the angular resolution of the filter. In a logarithmic wave number scale, the filter has the shape of a Gaussian function. Figure 7.3 shows the transfer function of such a filter.

A set of directional filters is obtained by a suitable choice of different ϕ_k:

$$\phi_k = \frac{\pi k}{K} \quad k = 0, 1, \cdots, K - 1. \tag{7.7}$$

Knutsson used four filters with $45°$ increments in the directions $22.5°$; $67.5°$; $112.5°$ and $157.5°$. These directions have the advantage that only *one* filter kernel has to be

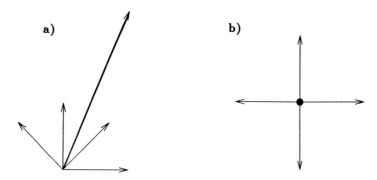

Figure 7.4: Computation of local orientation by vector addition of the four filter responses. Shown is an example where the neighborhood is isotropic concerning orientation: all filter responses are equal. The angles of the vectors are equal to the filter directions in a) and double the filter directions in b).

designed. The kernels for the filter in the other directions are obtained by mirroring the kernels at the axes and diagonals. These filters have been designed in the wave number space. The filter coefficients are obtained by inverse Fourier transform. If we choose a reasonably small filter mask, we will cut-off a number of non-zero filter coefficients. This causes deviations from the ideal transfer function. Therefore, Knutsson modified the filter kernel coefficient using an optimization procedure, in such a way that it approaches the ideal transfer function as close as possible. It turned out that at least a 15×15 filter mask is necessary to get a good approximation of the anticipated transfer function.

7.2.2   Vectorial Filter Response Addition

The local orientation can be computed from the responses of the four filters by vector addition if we represent them as an orientation vector: the magnitude of the vector corresponds to the filter response, while the direction is given by double the filter direction.

Figure 7.4 illustrates again why the angle doubling is necessary. An example is taken where the responses from all four filters are equal. In this case the neighborhood contains structures in all directions. Consequently, we observe no local orientation and the vector sum of all filter responses vanishes. This happens if we double the orientation angle (figure 7.4b), but not if we omit this step (figure 7.4a).

After these more qualitative considerations, we will prove that we can compute the local orientation exactly when the local neighborhood is ideally oriented in an arbitrary direction ϕ_0. As a result, we also know how many filters we need at least. We can simplify the computations by only considering the angular terms, since the filter responses show the same wave number dependence. We can also consider the two-dimensional vector of the filter response as a complex number. Using (7.7) we can write the angular part of the filter response as

$$\hat{h}_k(\phi_0) = \exp\left(2\pi ik/K\right) \cos^{2l}(\phi_0 - \pi k/K).$$

The factor two in the complex exponential results from the angle doubling. The cosine function is decomposed into the sum of two complex exponentials:

$$
\begin{aligned}
\hat{h}_k(\phi_0) &= \frac{1}{2^{2l}} \exp\left(2\pi i k/K\right) \left[\exp\left(i(\phi_0 - \pi k/K)\right) + \exp\left(-i(\phi_0 - \pi k/K)\right)\right]^{2l} \\
&= \frac{1}{2^{2l}} \exp\left(2\pi i k/K\right) \sum_{j=0}^{2l} \binom{2l}{j} \exp\left(ij(\phi_0 - \pi k/K)\right) \exp\left(-i(2l - j)(\phi_0 - \pi k/K)\right) \\
&= \frac{1}{2^{2l}} \sum_{j=0}^{2l} \binom{2l}{j} \exp\left(i(j - l)2\phi_0\right) \exp\left(2\pi i(1 + l - j)(k/K)\right).
\end{aligned}
$$

Now we sum up the vectors of all the K directional filters:

$$
\sum_{k=0}^{K-1} \hat{h}_k = \frac{1}{2^{2l}} \sum_{j=0}^{2l} \binom{2l}{j} \exp\left(i(j - l)2\phi_0\right) \sum_{k=0}^{K-1} \exp\left(2\pi i(1 + l - j)(k/K)\right).
$$

The complex double sum can be solved if we carefully analyze the inner sum over k. If $j = l + 1$ the exponent is zero. Consequently, the sum is K. Otherwise, the sum represents a geometric series with the factor $\exp\left(2\pi i(1 + l - j)(k/K)\right)$ and the sum

$$
\sum_{k=0}^{K-1} \exp\left(2\pi i(1 + l - j)(k/K)\right) = \frac{1 - \exp\left(2\pi i(1 + l - j)\right)}{1 - \exp\left(2\pi i(1 + l - j)/K\right)}. \tag{7.8}
$$

We can use this formula only if the denominator $\neq 0$ $\forall j = 0, 1, \cdots, 2l$; consequently $K > 1 + l$. With this condition the sum vanishes. This result has a simple geometric interpretation. The sum consists of vectors which are equally distributed on the unit circle. The angle between two consecutive vectors is $2\pi k/K$.

In conclusion, the inner sum in (7.8) reduces to K for $j = l + 1$, otherwise it is zero. Therefore the sum over j contains only the term with $j = l + 1$. The final result

$$
\sum_{k=0}^{K-1} \hat{h}_k = \frac{K}{2^{2l}} \binom{2l}{j} \exp\left(i2\phi_0\right) \tag{7.9}
$$

shows a vector with the angle of the local orientation doubled. This concludes the proof.

From $l > 0$ and $K > l + 1$ we conclude that at least $K = 3$ directional filters are necessary. If we have only two filters ($K = 2$), the vector responses of these two filters lie on a line (figure 7.5a). Thus orientation determination is not possible. Only with three or four filters, can the sum vector point in all directions (figure 7.5b and c).

With a similar derivation, we can prove another important property of the directional filters (7.6). The sum over the transfer functions of the K filters results in an isotropic function for $K > l$:

$$
\sum_{k=0}^{K-1} \cos^{2l}(\phi - \pi k/K) = \frac{K}{2^{2l}} \binom{2l}{l}. \tag{7.10}
$$

In other words: a preferred direction does not exist. This is the reason why we can determine local orientation exactly with a very limited number of filters and a simple linear procedure such as vector addition.

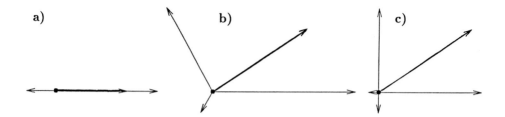

Figure 7.5: Vector addition of the filter responses from K directional filters to determine local orientation; a) $K = 2$; b) $K = 3$; c) $K = 4$; sum vector shown thicker.

7.3   The Tensor Method

In this section we discuss the question whether we can determine local orientation more directly. As a starting point, we consider what an ideally oriented gray value structure (7.1) looks like in the wave number domain. We can compute the Fourier transform of (7.1) more readily if we rotate the x_1 axis in the direction of $\bar{k}$. Then the gray value function is constant in the x_2 direction. Consequently, the Fourier transform reduces to a δ line in the direction of $\bar{k}$.

It seems promising to determine local orientation in the Fourier domain, since all we have to compute is the orientation of the line on which the spectral densities are non-zero. *Bigün and Granlund* [1987] devised the following procedure:

• With a window function, we select a small local neighborhood from an image.
• We Fourier transform the windowed image. The smaller the selected window, the more blurred the spectrum will be (*uncertainty relation*, see appendix A.2). This means that even with ideal local orientation we will obtain a rather band-shaped distribution of the spectral energy.
• Local orientation is then determined by fitting a straight line to the spectral density distribution. We yield the angle of the local orientation from the slope of the line.

The critical step of this procedure is fitting a straight line to the spectral densities in the Fourier domain. We cannot solve this problem exactly since it is generally *overdetermined*, but only minimize the measure of error. A standard error measure is the square of the magnitude of the vector (see (3.27) in section 3.3.1). When fitting a straight line, we minimize the sum of the squares of the distances of the data points to the line

$$ J = \int_{-\infty}^{\infty} \mathrm{d}^2 k \; d^2(\boldsymbol{k}, \bar{\boldsymbol{k}}) |\hat{g}(\boldsymbol{k})|^2 \rightarrow \text{minimum}. \tag{7.11} $$

For the sake of simplicity, $\bar{\boldsymbol{k}}$ is assumed to be a unit vector. The distance function is abbreviated using $d(\boldsymbol{k}, \bar{\boldsymbol{k}})$. The integral runs over the whole k space; the wave numbers are weighted with the spectral density $|\hat{g}(\boldsymbol{k})|^2$. Equation (7.11) is not restricted to two dimensions, but is generally valid for local orientation or linear symmetry in an n-dimensional space. Since we discuss local orientation in three dimensions in chapter 17,

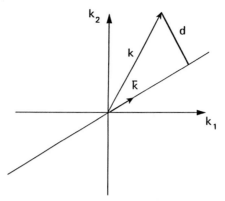

Figure 7.6: Distance of a point in k-space from the line in the direction of the unit vector $\bar{k}$.

we will solve (7.11) for an n-dimensional space.

The distance vector d can be inferred from figure 7.6 to be

$$d = k - (k^T \bar{k})\bar{k}. \tag{7.12}$$

The expression in brackets denotes the scalar product of $\bar{k}$ and k, and the superscript T the transposed vector. ($k^T k$ and kk^T denote an inner and outer product, respectively.) The square of the distance is then given by

$$|d|^2 = [k - (k^T \bar{k})\bar{k}]^T [k - (k^T \bar{k})\bar{k}] = k^T k - (k^T \bar{k})^2. \tag{7.13}$$

In order to express the distance more clearly as a function of the vector $\bar{k}$, we write it in the following manner

$$|d|^2 = \bar{k}^T (I(k^T k) - kk^T)\bar{k}. \tag{7.14}$$

Substituting this expression into (7.11) we obtain

$$J = \bar{k}^T J \bar{k}, \tag{7.15}$$

where J is a symmetric *tensor* with the diagonal elements

$$J_{pp} = \sum_{q \neq p} \int_{-\infty}^{\infty} d^n k \; k_q^2 |\hat{g}(k)|^2 \tag{7.16}$$

and the off-diagonal elements

$$J_{pq} = - \int_{-\infty}^{\infty} d^n k \; k_p k_q |\hat{g}(k)|^2. \tag{7.17}$$

In the two-dimensional case we can write

$$J(\bar{k}) = \begin{bmatrix} \bar{k}_1 & \bar{k}_2 \end{bmatrix} \begin{bmatrix} J_{11} & J_{12} \\ J_{12} & J_{22} \end{bmatrix} \begin{bmatrix} \bar{k}_1 \\ \bar{k}_2 \end{bmatrix}. \tag{7.18}$$

From this equation, we can readily find $\bar{k}$ so that J shows a minimum value. The key to the solution lies in the fact that every symmetric matrix reduces to a diagonal matrix by a suitable coordinate transformation (see appendix A.1):

$$J(\bar{k}) = \begin{bmatrix} \bar{k}'_1 & \bar{k}'_2 \end{bmatrix} \begin{bmatrix} J_1 & 0 \\ 0 & J_2 \end{bmatrix} \begin{bmatrix} \bar{k}'_1 \\ \bar{k}'_2 \end{bmatrix} = J_1 \bar{k}'^2_1 + J_2 \bar{k}'^2_2. \qquad (7.19)$$

If $J_1 < J_2$, we can immediately see that J is minimal in the k_1 direction.

In this way, the problem finally turns out to be an *eigenvalue problem* for the tensor J which can be calculated from the spectral densities via (7.16) and (7.17). The direction of the oriented pattern is given by the *eigenvector* k_1 to the smallest eigenvalue J_1

$$J k_1 = J_1 k_1. \qquad (7.20)$$

7.3.1   Analogy: The Inertia Tensor

Before we solve the two-dimensional eigenvalue problem, it is helpful to recognize that it is analogous to a well-known physical quantity, namely, the *inertia tensor*. If we replace the wave number coordinates by space coordinates and the spectral density $|\hat{g}(k)|^2$ by the specific density ρ, (7.11) constitutes the integral to compute the inertia of a rotary body rotating around the $\bar{k}$ axis. The tensor in (7.15) becomes the inertia tensor.

With this analogy, we can reformulate the problem to determine local orientation. We must find the axis about which the rotary body, formed from the spectral density in Fourier space, rotates with minimum inertia. The rotary body might have different shapes. We can relate the shape of the two-dimensional rotary body to the different solutions we get for the eigenvalues of the inertia tensor and thus for the solution of the local orientation problem.

1. *Ideal local orientation.* The rotary body is a line. For a rotation around this line, the inertia vanishes. Consequently, the eigenvector to the eigenvalue zero coincides with the direction of the line. The other eigenvector is orthogonal to the line, and the corresponding eigenvalue is unequal to zero. This eigenvector gives the rotation axis for the maximum inertia.

2. *Isotropic gray value structure.* In this case, the rotary body is a kind of a flat isotropic disk. A preferred direction does not exist. Both eigenvalues are equal, the inertia is the same for rotations around all axes. We cannot find a minimum.

3. *Constant gray values* (special case of one and two). The rotary body degenerates to a point at the origin of the k space. The inertia is zero for rotation around any axis. Therefore both eigenvalues vanish.

From this qualitative discussion, we can conclude that the tensor method to estimate local orientation provides more than just a value for the orientation. Using an analysis of the eigenvalues of the inertia tensor, we can separate the local neighborhood precisely into three classes: a) constant gray values, b) local orientation, and c) distributed orientation.

7.3.2   Eigenvalue Analysis of the 2-D Inertia Tensor

In the two-dimensional space, we can readily solve the eigenvalue problem. However, the solution is not reached in the standard way by solving the characteristic polynomial to determine the eigenvalues. It turns out that it is easier to rotate the inertia tensor to the principal axes coordinate system. The rotation angle ϕ then corresponds to the angle of the local orientation:

$$
\begin{bmatrix} J_1 & 0 \\ 0 & J_2 \end{bmatrix} = \begin{bmatrix} \cos\phi & \sin\phi \\ -\sin\phi & \cos\phi \end{bmatrix} \begin{bmatrix} J_{11} & J_{12} \\ J_{12} & J_{22} \end{bmatrix} \begin{bmatrix} \cos\phi & -\sin\phi \\ \sin\phi & \cos\phi \end{bmatrix}.
$$

Using the trigonometric identities $\sin 2\phi = 2\sin\phi\cos\phi$ and $\cos 2\phi = \cos^2\phi - \sin^2\phi$, the matrix multiplications result in

$$
\begin{bmatrix} J_1 & 0 \\ 0 & J_2 \end{bmatrix} = \begin{bmatrix} \cos\phi & \sin\phi \\ -\sin\phi & \cos\phi \end{bmatrix} \begin{bmatrix} J_{11}\cos\phi + J_{12}\sin\phi & -J_{11}\sin\phi + J_{12}\cos\phi \\ J_{22}\sin\phi + J_{12}\cos\phi & J_{22}\cos\phi - J_{12}\sin\phi \end{bmatrix}
$$

$$
= \begin{bmatrix} J_{11}\cos^2\phi + J_{22}\sin^2\phi + J_{12}\sin 2\phi & 1/2(J_{22} - J_{11})\sin 2\phi + J_{12}\cos 2\phi \\ 1/2(J_{22} - J_{11})\sin 2\phi + J_{12}\cos 2\phi & J_{11}\sin^2\phi + J_{22}\cos^2\phi - J_{12}\sin 2\phi \end{bmatrix}.
$$

Now we can compare the matrix coefficients on the left and right side of the equation. Because the matrices are symmetric, we have three equations with three unknowns, ϕ, J_1 and J_2. Though the equation system is nonlinear, it can be readily solved for ϕ. Addition of the diagonal elements yields

$$
J_1 + J_2 = J_{11} + J_{22}, \tag{7.21}
$$

i.e., the conservation of the trace of the tensor under a coordinate transformation. Subtraction of the diagonal elements results in

$$
J_1 - J_2 = (J_{11} - J_{22})\cos 2\phi + 2J_{12}\sin 2\phi, \tag{7.22}
$$

while from the off-diagonal element

$$
1/2(J_{22} - J_{11})\sin 2\phi + J_{12}\cos 2\phi = 0 \tag{7.23}
$$

we obtain the orientation angle as

$$
\tan 2\phi = \frac{2J_{12}}{J_{11} - J_{22}}. \tag{7.24}
$$

Without any presumptions we obtained the angle doubling anticipated. In this sense, the tensor method is much more elegant than the filter set method discussed in section 7.2. Since $\tan 2\phi$ is gained from a quotient, we can regard the dividend as the y and the divisor as the x component of a vector which we call the *orientation vector o*:

$$
o = \begin{bmatrix} J_{11} - J_{22} \\ 2J_{12} \end{bmatrix}. \tag{7.25}
$$

This vector has the magnitude $4J_{12} + J_{11}^2 + J_{22}^2 - 2J_{11}J_{22}$. In case of isotropically distributed orientation ($J_{11} = J_{22}$, $J_{12} = 0$), the magnitude of the orientation vector is zero.

7.3.3   Computing the Inertia Tensor in the Space Domain

So far, the tensor method to determine local orientation completely took place in the Fourier space. Now we will show that we can compute the coefficients of the inertia tensor easier in the space domain.

The integrals in (7.16) and (7.17) contain terms of the form

$$k_q^2 |\hat{g}(\boldsymbol{k})|^2 = |\mathrm{i}k_q \hat{g}(\boldsymbol{k})|^2$$

and

$$k_p k_q |\hat{g}(\boldsymbol{k})| = \mathrm{i}k_p \hat{g}(\boldsymbol{k})[\mathrm{i}k_q \hat{g}(\boldsymbol{k})]^*.$$

Integrals over these terms are *inner* or *scalar products* of the functions $\mathrm{i}k_l \hat{g}(\boldsymbol{k})$. Since the inner product is preserved under the Fourier transform (section 3.3.1), we can compute the corresponding integrals in the spatial domain as well. Multiplication of $\hat{g}(\boldsymbol{k})$ with $\mathrm{i}k_l$ in the wave number domain corresponds to performing the first spatial derivative in the same coordinate in the space domain:

$$
\begin{aligned}
\text{diagonal elements} \quad & J_{pp} = \sum_{q \neq p} \int_{\text{window}} \left(\frac{\partial g}{\partial x_q} \right)^2 \mathrm{d}^2 x \\
\text{off-diagonal elements} \quad & J_{pq} = - \int_{\text{window}} \frac{\partial g}{\partial x_p} \frac{\partial g}{\partial x_q} \mathrm{d}^2 x.
\end{aligned}
\tag{7.26}
$$

The integration area corresponds to the window we use to select a local neighborhood. On a discrete image matrix, the integral can be entirely performed by convolution. Integration over a window limiting the local neighborhood means convolution with a smoothing mask $\mathcal{B}$ of the corresponding size. The partial derivatives are computed with the derivative operators $\mathcal{D}_x$ and $\mathcal{D}_y$. Consequently the elements of the inertia tensor are essentially computed with nonlinear operators

$$\mathcal{J}_{pq} = \mathcal{B}(\mathcal{D}_p \cdot \mathcal{D}_q). \tag{7.27}$$

In two dimensions, the vectorial *orientation operator* is then given by

$$\mathcal{O} = \left[\begin{array}{c} \mathcal{J}_{22} - \mathcal{J}_{11} \\ 2\mathcal{J}_{12} \end{array} \right]. \tag{7.28}$$

It is important to note that the operators $\mathcal{J}_{kl}$ and $\mathcal{O}$ are nonlinear operators containing both linear convolution operations and nonlinear point operations (multiplications) in the space domain. In particular this means that we must not interchange the multiplication of the partial derivatives with the smoothing operations.

In their paper on "Analyzing oriented patterns", *Kass and Witkin* [1985] arrived at exactly the same expression for the orientation vector. Interestingly, they started entirely differently using directional derivatives. Since it now turns out that derivative operators are central to the orientation problem, we may wonder what went wrong with our initial idea to use the gradient operator for orientation analysis in section 7.1. The basic difference is that we now multiply the spatial derivatives and then average them, before we compute the orientation. This means that instead of the vector gradient operator a symmetric tensor operator of the form

$$\mathcal{J}' = \begin{bmatrix} \mathcal{J}_{11} & \mathcal{J}_{12} \\ \mathcal{J}_{12} & \mathcal{J}_{22} \end{bmatrix} \tag{7.29}$$

contains the appropriate description for the gray value changes in a local neighborhood. This tensor is sometimes called the *scatter matrix*. It is different from the two-dimensional inertia tensor

$$\mathcal{J} = \begin{bmatrix} \mathcal{J}_{22} & -\mathcal{J}_{12} \\ -\mathcal{J}_{12} & \mathcal{J}_{11} \end{bmatrix}. \tag{7.30}$$

However, these two tensors are closely related

$$\mathcal{J} = \text{trace}(\mathcal{J}') \begin{bmatrix} I & 0 \\ 0 & I \end{bmatrix} - \mathcal{J}', \ \mathcal{J}' = \text{trace}(\mathcal{J}) \begin{bmatrix} I & 0 \\ 0 & I \end{bmatrix} - \mathcal{J}. \tag{7.31}$$

From this relationship it is evident that both matrices have the same set of eigenvectors. The eigenvalues are related by

$$J_p = \sum_{q=1}^{n} J_q - J'_p, \ J'_p = \sum_{q=1}^{n} J'_q - J_p. \tag{7.32}$$

Consequently, we can perform the eigenvalue analysis with any of the two matrices. We will obtain the same set of eigenvectors. For the inertia tensor, the direction of local orientation is given by the minimum eigenvalue, but for the scatter matrix it is given by the maximum eigenvalue.

Finally, we discuss the interpretation of the estimated orientation information. Both the scatter and the inertia matrix contain three independent coefficients. In contrast, the orientation vector contains only two parameters (7.28) and thus does not include the entire information. The direction of the vector is twice the angle of the orientation and the magnitude of the vector is a measure of the *certainty* of the estimated orientation. There are, however, two reasons for failure of the orientation measure. The neighborhood may contain a constant gray value area or an isotropic gray value structure without a preferred orientation (see also classification of orientation in section 7.3.1). To distinguish these two cases we need to compare the magnitude of the orientation vector with the mean square magnitude of the gradient

$$B[(\mathcal{D}_1 \cdot \mathcal{D}_1) + (\mathcal{D}_2 \cdot \mathcal{D}_2)] = \mathcal{J}_{11} + \mathcal{J}_{22} = J_1 + J_2 \tag{7.33}$$

which is essentially the trace of both the inertia tensor (7.30) and the scatter matrix (7.29). A zero orientation vector combined with a non-zero mean square magnitude of the gradient indicate an isotropic gray value structure. If both are zero, a constant gray value structure is given. Consequently, we may express a *coherence measure* for local orientation by

$$C = \frac{(\mathcal{J}_{11} - \mathcal{J}_{22})^2 + 4\mathcal{J}_{12}^2}{(\mathcal{J}_{11} + \mathcal{J}_{22})^2} = \left(\frac{J_1 - J_2}{J_1 + J_2}\right)^2. \tag{7.34}$$

The coherence ranges from 0 to 1. For ideal local orientation ($J_1 = 0, J_2 > 0$) it is one, for an isotropic gray value structure ($J_1 = J_2 > 0$) it is zero.

7.3.4   Examples and Applications

In the final section of this chapter, we show several examples and applications of orientation analysis. The image with the concentric rings (figure 6.4) is an excellent test pattern for orientation analysis with which we now demonstrate the computation of the orientation vector step by step. First we calculate the horizontal and vertical spatial derivatives with the $[1\ 0\ -1]$ mask (figure 7.7a and b). Then we perform the point-wise multiplications of the two resulting images with each other and by themselves. After smoothing these images with a $\mathcal{B}^{16}$ binomial filter and another subtraction, we obtain the two components of the orientation vector (figure 7.7c and d). The magnitude (figure 7.7e) and phase (figure 7.7f) of the orientation vector are computed by a Cartesian to polar coordinate transformation (for a fast implementation see section 4.4).

Representing the orientation vector with two gray value images, either in Cartesian or polar representation, does not give a good impression of the orientation. Moreover, mapping the cyclic orientation angle onto a gray value scale results in a discontinuity and gives a wrong visual impression. Orientations which are mapped to the minimal and maximal gray values and which are in fact only slightly different, visually appear as completely different values. A much better representation of the vectorial orientation is the color coding technique discussed in section 7.1.2 and shown in plate 8b. There is a gradual change in color for all orientations and perpendicular orientations are shown in complementary colors. Plate 8 also shows that the orientation estimate is quite noise insensitive. The accuracy of orientation analysis will be discussed in detail in section 17.4.5.

The test image discussed so far contains only ideally orientated patterns. The examples in plate 9 give an impression of the orientation analysis with real-world images. The edges show up as colored lines, so that differentially oriented patterns can immediately be recognized by the colors. The certainty and coherency measures of the orientation analysis for the image in plate 9a are shown in figure 7.8. We recognize that the certainty measure does not drop at the intersections of lines, while the coherency measure does, indicating that a coherent local orientation does not exist at corners.

Plate 10 demonstrates how orientation analysis can be integrated into a hierarchy of simple processing steps to solve complex tasks. The original image contains a piece of calfskin from which a circular sector was rotated (plate 10a). From this image, the local orientation is computed (plate 10b). After smoothing the orientation image (plate 10c), the edge of the rotated sector can be computed with derivative operators in a similar manner as from a simple gray value image.

Orientation constitutes an important property for *image enhancement* (plate 10e–g). The original shows a distorted fingerprint image with partly disrupted lines (plate 10e). With the help of the orientation field (plate 10f), we can use a technique, called *adaptive filtering* to restore the image. We use the orientation field to smooth the image along the lines, and to sharpen it in the normal direction. The two steps, orientation determination and adaptive filtering, can be repeated iteratively. After only two iterations, a considerably improved fingerprint is obtained (plate 10g).

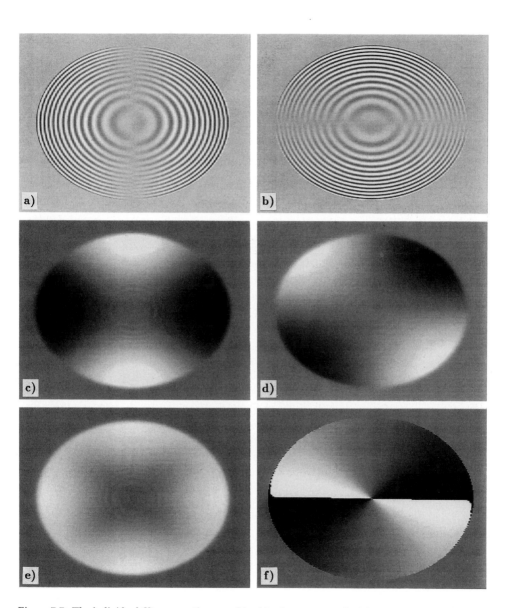

Figure 7.7: The individual filter operations combined in the tensor method for orientation analysis are demonstrated with a test image: a) $\mathcal{D}_x$; b) $\mathcal{D}_y$; c) $\mathcal{B}(\mathcal{D}_y \cdot \mathcal{D}_y - \mathcal{D}_x \cdot \mathcal{D}_x)$; d) $\mathcal{B}(\mathcal{D}_x \cdot \mathcal{D}_y)$; e) magnitude and f) phase of the orientation vector.

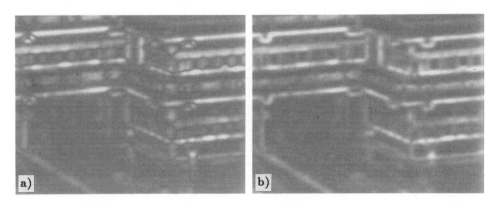

Figure 7.8: Orientation analysis of the image plate 9a: a) coherency measure; b) certainty measure.

8 Scales

8.1 Multigrid Data Structures

The effect of all the operators discussed so far — except for recursive filters — is restricted to local neighborhoods which are significantly smaller than the size of the image. This inevitably means that they can only extract local features. We have already seen a tendency that analysis of a more complex feature such as local orientation (chapter 7) requires larger neighborhoods than computing, for example, a simple property such as the Laplacian (section 6.2). It is quite obvious that a larger neighborhood can show a larger set of features which requires more complex operations to reveal them. If we extrapolate our approach by analyzing larger scales in the image with larger filter kernels, we inevitably run into a dead end. The computation of the more complex operators will become so tedious that they are not longer useful.

We can also run into problems computing even very simple operations. Imagine that we intend to calculate the first horizontal derivative of an image which shows only slowly varying gray values, i.e., large-scale features. Here only small gray value differences will exist between neighboring pixels. Because of the limited resolution of the gray values, the result of the operation will contain significant inaccuracies. The problem is caused by a *scale mismatch*: the gray values only vary on large scales, while the derivative operator operates on much finer scales, subtracting the neighboring pixels.

From these remarks we can conclude that we need new data structures to separate the information in the image into different "scale channels". The fine structures which are contained in an image must still be represented on a fine grid, whereas the large scales can be represented on a much coarser grid. On the coarse grid, the large scales come within the range of effective neighborhood operators with small kernels. In this way, we represent the image on a *multigrid* or *multiscale* data structure.

If we represent an image on a grid in the spatial domain, we do not have any access to the scales at all. This fact results from the *uncertainty relation*. We know the position with an accuracy of the grid constant Δx, but the local wave number at this position may be any out of the range of the wave numbers from 0 to $M\Delta k = 2\pi M/\Delta x$ (figure 8.1a). The other extreme is given by representing the image in the wave number domain. Each pixel in this domain represents one wave number with the highest resolution possible given for an image, but any positional information is lost since these periodic structures are spread over the whole image (figure 8.1b).

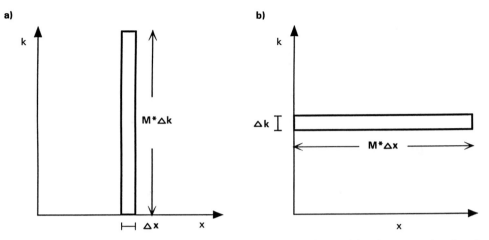

Figure 8.1: Illustration of the interdependence of resolution in the spatial and wave number domain in one dimension: a) representation of the image in the space domain; b) representation of the image in the wave number domain.

Under these considerations, the representation of an image in either the spatial or wave number domain describes opposite extremes. Between these extremes there should exist many other possibilities to represent image data. These data structures illustrate the fact that the image is separated into different ranges of wave numbers, but still preserves some spatial resolution.

8.2   Gauss and Laplace Pyramids

8.2.1   Introduction

In this section we discuss the transformation of an image which is represented on a grid in the spatial domain into a multigrid data structure. From what we have learnt so far, it is obvious that we cannot just *subsample* the image by taking, for example, every second pixel in every second line. If we did so, we would disregard the *sampling theorem* (see section 2.3.3). For example, a structure which is sampled three times per wavelength in the original image would only be sampled one and a half times in the subsampled image and thus appear as a Moiré pattern. Consequently, we must ensure that all wave numbers which are sampled less than four times per wavelength are suppressed by an appropriate smoothing filter to ensure a proper subsampled image. Generally, the requirement for the smoothing filter can be formulated as

$$\hat{B}(\tilde{\boldsymbol{k}}) = 0 \quad \forall \tilde{k}_i \geq \frac{1}{p_i}, \tag{8.1}$$

where p_i is the subsampling rate in the ith coordinate.

 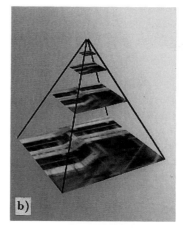

Figure 8.2: Gauss pyramid: a) schematic representation, the squares of the checkerboard correspond to pixels; b) example.

If we repeat the smoothing and subsampling operations iteratively, we obtain a series of images, which is called the *Gauss pyramid*. From level to level, the resolution decreases by a factor of two; the size of the images is decreasing correspondingly. Consequently, we can think of the series of images as being arranged in the form of a pyramid as illustrated in figure 8.2a.

The pyramid does not require much storage space, since the number of pixels in one direction decreases by a factor of two from level to level. Generally, if we consider the formation of a pyramid from a p-dimensional image with a subsampling factor of two and M pixels in each coordinate direction, the total number of pixels is given by

$$M^p \left(1 + \frac{1}{2^p} + \frac{1}{2^{2p}} + \ldots\right) < M^p \frac{2^p}{2^p - 1}. \tag{8.2}$$

For a two-dimensional image, the whole pyramid only needs one third more space than the original image. Likewise, the computation of the pyramid is equally effective. The *same* smoothing filter is applied to each level of the pyramid. Thus the computation of the *whole* pyramid only needs four thirds of the operations necessary for the first level.

The pyramid brings large scales into the range of local neighborhood operations with small kernels. Moreover, these operations are performed efficiently. Once the pyramid has been computed, we can perform neighborhood operations on large scales in the upper levels of the pyramid — because of the smaller image sizes — much more efficiently than for finer scales. The Gauss pyramid constitutes a series of lowpass filtered images in which the cut-off wave numbers decrease by a factor of two (an octave) from level to level. Thus only more and more coarse details remain in the image (figure 8.2b). Only a few levels of the pyramid are necessary to span a wide range of wave numbers. From a 512×512 image we can usefully compute only a seven-level pyramid. The smallest image is then 8×8.

From the Gauss pyramid, another pyramid type can be derived, the *Laplace pyramid*, by subtracting the smoothed from the unsmoothed image on each level (figure 8.3). In

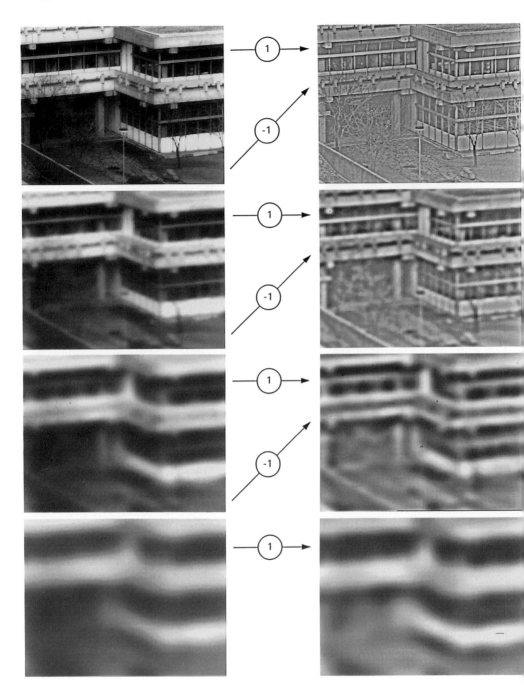

Figure 8.3: Construction of the Laplace pyramid from the Gauss pyramid. The left and right column show the Gauss and Laplace pyramid, respectively. The images at all levels have been enlarged to the original size by appropriate interpolation.

this way, only the fine scales, removed by the smoothing operation, remain in the finer level. The name Laplace pyramid results from the fact that subtracting an image smoothed by an isotropic operator from its original corresponds to a Laplace operator (section 6.2.2). The Laplace pyramid is an effective scheme for a *bandpass decomposition* of the image. The center wave number is halved from level to level. The last image of the Laplace pyramid is a lowpass-filtered image containing only the coarsest structures. If we add up the images at the different levels of the Laplace pyramid, starting with the highest level, we obtain the Gauss pyramid again. With the addition of each level of the Laplace pyramid, finer details become visible.

In contrast to the Fourier transform, the Laplace pyramid only leads to a coarse wave number decomposition and not to a directional decomposition. All wave numbers, independent of their direction, within the range of about an octave (factor of two) are contained in one level of the pyramid. Because of the coarse wave number resolution, we can preserve a good spatial resolution. Each level of the pyramid only contains matching scales which are sampled a few times (two to six) per wavelength. In this way, the Laplace pyramid is adapted to the *uncertainty relation*.

The Gauss and Laplace pyramids are examples of multigrid data structures which have been introduced into digital image processing in the early 1980s and have led to considerable progress in digital image processing since then. A new research area, *multiresolutional image processing*, has been established [*Rosenfeld*, 1984]. We will discuss a number of applications using pyramids in further chapters.

In this chapter we will continue our discussion on pyramids. First we will describe several algorithms to compute the Gauss and Laplace pyramids. Then we will discuss optimal smoothing filters for pyramids. Special attention will also be paid to the interpolation problem which arises when we enlarge an image to the next finer grid.

8.2.2 Algorithms for Pyramidal Decomposition

First we will discuss the original Gauss and Laplace pyramids as suggested by *Burt and Adelson* [1983] and *Burt* [1984]. They used an even, *separable, symmetric* 5×5 smoothing mask $\mathcal{G} = \mathcal{G}_x \mathcal{G}_y$ with the filter kernel

$$G_{x,y} = (\gamma/2 \quad \beta/2 \quad \alpha \quad \beta/2 \quad \gamma/2) \tag{8.3}$$

and the transfer function

$$\hat{G}_{x,y} = \alpha + \beta \cos(\pi \tilde{k}_{x,y}) + \gamma \cos(2\pi \tilde{k}_{x,y}). \tag{8.4}$$

Burt and Adelson tried to infer the proper coefficients α, β, and γ from the following principles:

1. *Normalization.* A proper smoothing mask requires preservation of the mean gray values, i.e., $\hat{G}_{x,y}(0) = 1$. From (8.4) we obtain

$$\alpha + \beta + \gamma = 1. \tag{8.5}$$

2. *Equal contribution.* All points should equally contribute to the next higher level. Each even point is one time central (factor α) and two times edge point (factor $\gamma/2$),

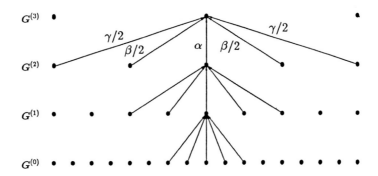

Figure 8.4: Graphical illustration of the generation of a one-dimensional Gauss pyramid after *Burt* [1984]: each dot row represents a level of the pyramid. The pixels of the lowest level are the gray values of the original. One point of the next level is computed from five points from the lower level with the same filter kernels on each level. The pixel distance doubles from layer to layer.

each odd point is weighted two times by $\beta/2$. Hence

$$\alpha + \gamma = \beta. \qquad (8.6)$$

3. *Adequate smoothing.* Condition (8.6) coincides with another requirement: a useful
   smoothing mask should make the highest wave number vanish, i. e., $\hat{G}_{x,y}(1) = 0$.
Equations (8.5) and (8.6) leave one degree of freedom in the choice of the filter coefficients. Subtracting both equations yields

$$\begin{aligned} \beta &= 1/2 \\ \alpha + \gamma &= 1/2. \end{aligned} \qquad (8.7)$$

Masks which meet these requirements are the binomial filter $\mathcal{B}^4$ (section 6.1.2, $\alpha = 6/16$)

$$\mathcal{B}_x^4 = 1/16\,[1\ 4\ 6\ 4\ 1]$$

and a more box-like filter ($\alpha = 1/4$)

$$1/8\,[1\ 2\ 2\ 2\ 1] = 1/4\,[1\ 1\ 1\ 1] * 1/2\,[1\ 1]\,.$$

The lowest level of the Gauss pyramid consists of the original image $G^{(0)}$. We denote the level of the pyramid with a braced superscript. This image will be smoothed with the operator $\mathcal{B}^{(0)}$. The braced superscript again denotes the level on which the operator is applied. We obtain the first level of the Gauss pyramid if we apply a *subsampling operator* $\mathcal{R}^{(0)}$ onto the smoothed image which picks out every second pixel in every second line

$$G_{m,n}^{(1)} = (\mathcal{B}G)_{2m,2n}^{(0)}. \qquad (8.8)$$

In summary, the first level of the Gauss pyramid is given by

$$G^{(1)} = (\mathcal{R}\mathcal{B})^{(0)}G^{(0)}. \qquad (8.9)$$

The same operations are performed with the new image $G^{(1)}$ and all subsequent levels of the pyramid. Generally,

$$G^{(p+1)} = (\mathcal{R}\mathcal{B})^{(p)} G^{(p)} \tag{8.10}$$

and

$$G^{(P)} = \left(\prod_{p=0}^{P-1} (\mathcal{R}\mathcal{B})^{(p)} \right) G^{(0)}. \tag{8.11}$$

With the operator product, we have to be careful with the order of the indices, since the operators are not commutative. Thus the indices increase from right to left.

The Laplace pyramid is formed by subtracting the images between consecutive levels in the Gauss pyramid. In order to perform this operation, we first must expand the image from the higher level to the double size so that both images show the same resolution. This operation is performed by an *expansion operator*, $\mathcal{E}$, which is the inverse of the reduction operator $\mathcal{R}$. Essentially, the expansion operator puts the known image points from the coarser image onto the even pixel positions at the even rows and interpolates the missing other points from the given points. Thus the first level of the Laplace pyramid is formed by the following operation:

$$L^{(0)} = G^{(0)} - \mathcal{E}^{(1)} G^{(1)} = \left[\mathcal{I} - \mathcal{E}^{(1)} (\mathcal{R}\mathcal{B})^{(0)} \right] G^{(0)}. \tag{8.12}$$

In a similar manner, we obtain the higher levels of the Laplace pyramid

$$L^{(P)} = G^{(P)} - \mathcal{E}^{(P+1)} G^{(P+1)} = \left[\mathcal{I}^{(P+1)} - \mathcal{E}^{(P+1)} (\mathcal{R}\mathcal{B})^{(P)} \right] \left(\prod_{p=0}^{P-1} (\mathcal{R}\mathcal{B})^{(p)} \right) G^{(0)}. \tag{8.13}$$

Reconstruction of the original image from its representation in a Laplace image starts at the highest level. There, we have a smoothed image, $G^{(P+1)}$. From (8.13) we see that we obtain the next lower level of the Gauss pyramid by expanding $G^{(P+1)}$ and adding $L^{(P)}$

$$G^{(P)} = L^{(P)} + \mathcal{E}^{(P+1)} G^{(P+1)}. \tag{8.14}$$

We continue this operation, until we obtain the original image at the lowest level

$$G = G^{(0)} = L^{(0)} + \sum_{p=0}^{P} \left(\prod_{q=1}^{p} \mathcal{E}^{(q)} \right) L^{(p)} + \left(\prod_{q=1}^{P+1} \mathcal{E}^{(q)} \right) G^{(P+1)}. \tag{8.15}$$

It is important to note that the reconstruction of the original image is exact except for round-off errors. This is no longer the case if we introduce a slight modification which makes computation of the Laplace pyramid easier. In (8.12), we first reduce the smoothed image and then expand it again. Actually, we can avoid this operation provided that no errors are introduced by the expansion operation, i.e., that the expansion operator $\mathcal{E}$ is the exact inverse of the reduction operator $\mathcal{R}$. Then we can simply compute a level of the Laplace pyramid by subtracting the smoothed from the original image on the same level

$$L^{(p)} = G^{(p)} - \mathcal{B}^{(p)} G^{(p)}, \tag{8.16}$$

or in operator notation

$$\mathcal{L} = \mathcal{I} - \mathcal{B}. \tag{8.17}$$

8.2.3   Filters for Pyramid Formation

As we already discussed in section 8.2.1, the subsampling operation is only error free if we meet the sampling theorem (section 2.3.3). Thus the smoothing filter must remove all the wave numbers $\tilde{k} \geq 1/2$. Figure 8.5 shows the transfer functions of the first level of the Laplace pyramid for different types of smoothing filters. The egg-cup shaped form results from the difference of the two smoothing filters in the first and zero level of the pyramid $({}^{(1)}\mathcal{L} = (\mathcal{I} - {}^{(1)}\mathcal{B}){}^{(0)}\mathcal{B})$. The decrease towards the higher wave numbers is caused by the smoothing filter at level zero.

Smoothing by the 5×5 binomial mask, as suggested by Burt, is insufficient, since the transfer function goes down to zero at the highest wave numbers. The results are significant Moiré patterns in the pyramid if the image contains periodic structures as in the test image figure 8.6. At least a 9×9 binomial filter $(\mathcal{B}^8)$ is required (figure 8.5b), although a 17×17 filter $(\mathcal{B}^{16})$ is better (figure 8.5c).

Radial cross sections through the transfer functions show that the binomial smoothing filters result in a rather wide bandpass decomposition in the Laplace pyramid. The maximum of the transfer function in one plane is just about 50 %. Each wave number is distributed over about three levels. A wave number which has a maximum response in one level also occurs with a response of about 28 %, 8 %, and 14 % in the levels one below, two below, and one above, respectively. Especially disturbing is the fact that low wave numbers are filtered out only proportionally to $\tilde{k}^2$.

Steeper smoothing filters result in a sharper separation of the wave numbers. In section 6.3.3 we have discussed a class of smoothing operators which fall off with higher powers in $\tilde{k}$. With these filters, the maximum of the transfer function increases and a wave number is only distributed over two levels of the Laplace pyramid.

In conclusion, we can state that use of different smoothing filters gives control when optimizing the Laplace pyramid for a given image processing task. By varying the cut-off wave number of the smoothing filter, we can adjust where the peak of the wave number occurs in the pyramid, and by the steepness of the smoothing filter, we can set the range of wave numbers contained in one level.

8.2.4   Interpolation

In section 2.3.4 we said that reconstruction of a continuous function from sampled points can be considered as a convolution operation

$$g_i(\boldsymbol{x}) = \sum_{m,n} g(\boldsymbol{x}_{m,n}) h(\boldsymbol{x} - \boldsymbol{x}_{m,n}), \tag{8.18}$$

where h is the continuous interpolation mask

$$h(\boldsymbol{x}) = \frac{\sin \pi x_1/\Delta x_1}{\pi x_1/\Delta x_1} \frac{\sin \pi x_2/\Delta x_2}{\pi x_2/\Delta x_2} \tag{8.19}$$

with the transfer function

$$\hat{h}(\boldsymbol{k}) = \Pi(k_1 \Delta x_1/2\pi, k_2 \Delta x_2/2\pi). \tag{8.20}$$

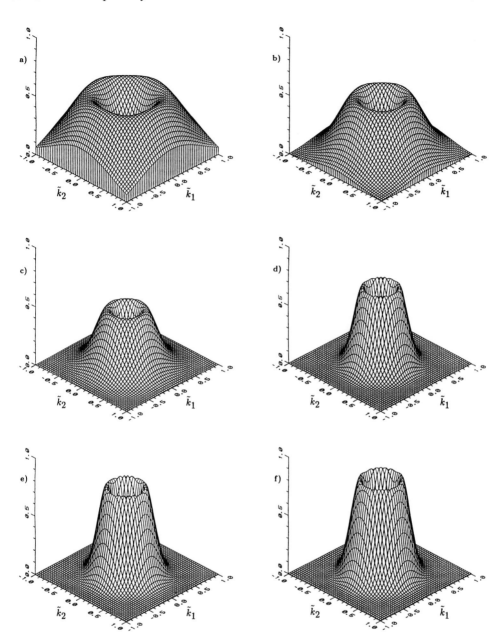

Figure 8.5: Transfer functions of the first level of the Laplace pyramid using different smoothing filters: a) $\mathcal{B}^4$; b) $\mathcal{B}^8$; c) $\mathcal{B}^{16}$; d) second-order smoothing filter; e) third-order smoothing filter; f) fourth-order smoothing filter.

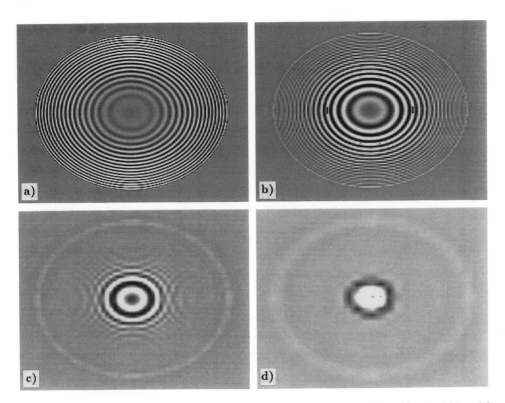

Figure 8.6: Moiré patterns in a Laplace pyramid caused by insufficient smoothing with a 5 × 5 binomial mask.

The formalism becomes easier if we only want to calculate the points on the next finer grid. Then the continuous interpolation kernel reduces to a discrete convolution mask. Since the interpolation kernel (8.19) is separable, we first can interpolate the intermediate points in a row in a horizontal direction before we interpolate the intermediate rows by vertical interpolation. The interpolation kernels are the same in both directions. We need the continuous kernel $h(x)$ at only half integer values for $x/\Delta x$

$$\cdots -5/2 \ -3/2 \ -1/2 \ 1/2 \ 3/2 \ 5/2 \ \cdots \tag{8.21}$$

and obtain the following infinite kernel

$$h = \left[\cdots (-1)^{m-1}\frac{2}{(2m-1)\pi} \cdots \frac{2}{5\pi} -\frac{2}{3\pi}\frac{2}{\pi}\frac{2}{\pi} -\frac{2}{3\pi}\frac{2}{5\pi} \cdots (-1)^{m-1}\frac{2}{(2m-1)\pi}\cdots\right]. \tag{8.22}$$

It is not practicable to use this ideal filter mask. Therefore, we need a useful approximation. The interpolation mask is of even symmetry with an even number of coefficients, since the results are placed halfway between the grid points. Generally, the transfer function of such a filter is given by

$$\hat{h}(\tilde{k}) = \sum_{m=1}^{R} 2a_m \cos \frac{(2m-1)}{2}\pi\tilde{k}. \tag{8.23}$$

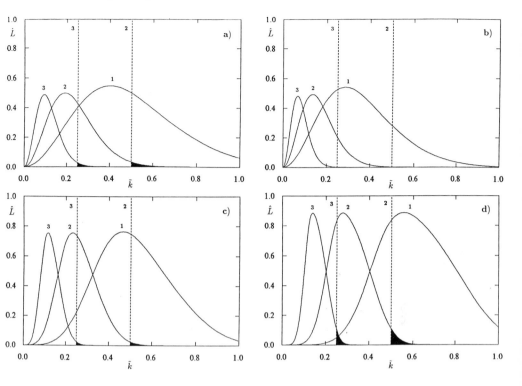

Figure 8.7: Radial cross section through the transfer functions at the levels 1 to 4 of the Laplace pyramid using different smoothing filters: a) $\mathcal{B}^8$; b) $\mathcal{B}^{16}$; c) second-order smoothing filter; d) third-order smoothing filter. The dashed vertical lines mark the maximum wave numbers of the different levels. The parts of the transfer functions which exceed the maximum wave number are shown as black.

The optimization task is to chose the coefficients h_m in such a way that $\hat{h}$ approximates the ideal transfer function (8.20), the box function, in an optimum way using a filter with $2R$ coefficients. We take a similar approach as in section 6.3.4. The cosine functions are expanded in Taylor series. We can then collect all the terms with equal powers in $\tilde{k}$. Our aim is to have a filter with a transfer function which is constant as long as possible. Thus all coefficients of the Taylor expansion, except for the constant term, should vanish and we obtain the linear equation system

$$
\begin{bmatrix}
1 & 1 & 1 & \cdots & 1 \\
1 & 9 & 25 & \cdots & (2R-1)^2 \\
1 & 81 & 625 & \cdots & (2R-1)^4 \\
\vdots & \vdots & \vdots & \ddots & \vdots \\
1^{2R} & 3^{2R} & 5^{2R} & \cdots & (2R-1)^{2R}
\end{bmatrix}
\begin{bmatrix}
a_1 \\
a_2 \\
a_3 \\
\vdots \\
a_r
\end{bmatrix}
=
\begin{bmatrix}
1 \\
0 \\
0 \\
\vdots \\
0
\end{bmatrix}. \tag{8.24}
$$

The simplest interpolation mask is given by $R = 1$. Then we interpolate the intermediate value only from the left and right neighboring pixel. The transfer function reduces to $^{(1)}\hat{h}(\tilde{k}) = \cos(\pi \tilde{k}/2)$ and the filter mask to $1/2\,[1\ 1]$. This convolution operation constitutes a simple *linear interpolation*. In two dimensions, we speak of *bilinear*

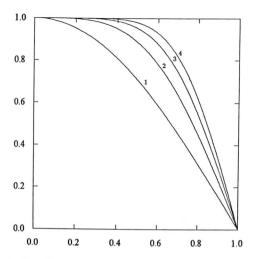

Figure 8.8: Optimal transfer function to interpolate an image to double the size, according to (8.24) for filter sizes R as indicated.

interpolation because we separate the interpolation into a horizontal and a vertical linear interpolation. From the transfer function shown in figure 8.8, it is obvious that linear interpolation is not sufficient. Even periodic structures with intermediate wave numbers are damped significantly, e. g., $\tilde{k} = 1/2$ by 30 %.

For a better interpolation, we need larger filter masks such as

$$
\begin{aligned}
^{(2)}h &= 1/16\,[-1\ 9\ 9\ -1] \\
^{(3)}h &= 1/256\,[3\ -25\ 150\ 150\ -25\ 3] \\
^{(4)}h &= 1/1024\,[-5\ 49\ -245\ 1225\ 1225\ -245\ 49\ -5].
\end{aligned}
\tag{8.25}
$$

With increasing R the transfer function approaches the box function better. However, convergence is slow. For an accurate interpolation, we must either take a large interpolation mask or limit the wave numbers to smaller $\tilde{k}$ by using a larger smoothing mask.

9 Texture

9.1 Introduction

Local orientation (chapter 7) was the first example of a more complex feature describing the structure of the gray values in a local neighborhood. It enabled us to distinguish objects not only because of their gray values but also because of the orientation of the patterns (compare figure 7.1). Real-world objects often carry patterns which differ not only in their orientation, but also in many other parameters. Our visual system is capable of recognizing and distinguishing such patterns with ease, but it is difficult to describe the differences precisely (figure 9.1). Patterns which characterize objects are called *textures* in image processing. Actually, textures demonstrate the difference between an artificial world of objects whose surfaces are only characterized by the color and reflectivity properties to that of real-world imagery. We can see a similar trend in computer graphics. If we place a texture on the surface of objects, a process called *texture mapping*, we obtain much more realistic images (see also plate 3).

In this chapter we systematically investigate operators to analyze and differentiate between textures. These operators are able to describe even complex patterns with few but characteristic figures. We thereby reduce the texture recognition problem to the simple task of distinguishing gray values. To give an overview, we first summarize some simple parameters which might be suitable to describe textures:

- Mean gray value
- Local variance of the gray value
- Local orientation of the gray value structure
- Characteristic scale of the gray value structure
- Variance of local orientation
- Variance of the characteristic scale

This list starts with the trivial feature of the mean gray value. The local variance of the gray value is a simple description of the statistics of the gray values in a small neighborhood (see section 4.2.1). The next two parameters, local orientation and characteristic scale, examine the *spatial structure* of the gray values more closely. The first tells us in which direction the gray values predominantly change and the second with which spatial periodicity. We can regard the first two features, the mean and variance of the gray value, as zero-order spatial features, since they do not depend on the spatial structure at all. The local variance and the characteristic spatial scale give a first-order

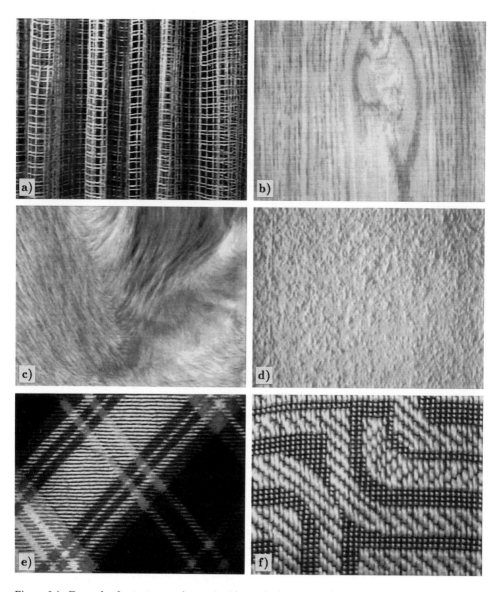

Figure 9.1: Examples for textures: a) curtain; b) wood; c) dog fur; d) woodchip paper; e), f) clothes.

description of the spatial features of a local neighborhood.

At this level we can continue the description with larger neighborhoods. We can calculate the mean and the variance of these features. In this way our attention is again focused on the fact that image processing is a hierarchical process. We just need a small set of elementary operations and can apply them to different levels.

The crucial question is whether this is a valid approach. We may compare it to the Taylor expansion of a function. The more precisely we want to describe the function, the more high order terms we must take into account. However, with several functions we might not be successful. The Taylor expansion may converge too slowly or not at all. Analogously, we are faced with the same problem in texture analysis.

Texture can be regular or random. Most natural textures are random. This means that all the parameters discussed so far may be subject to random fluctuations. Textures may be organized in a *hierarchical* manner, i.e., they may look quite different at different scales. A good example is the curtain shown in figure 9.1a. On the finest scale our attention is focused on the individual thread. Then the characteristic scale is the thickness of the threads. They also have a predominant local orientation. On the next coarser level, we will recognize the meshes of the net. The characteristic scale here shows the diameter of the meshes. At this level, the local orientation is well distributed. Finally, at an even coarser level, we no longer recognize the individual meshes, but observe the folds of the curtain. They are characterized by yet another characteristic scale, showing the period of the folds and their orientation. These considerations emphasize the importance of *multiscale texture analysis*. The descriptions in chapter 8 on multigrid image data structures are essential for texture analysis.

We can separate texture parameters into two classes. Texture parameters may be or may be not rotation and scale invariant. This classification is motivated by the task we have to perform. Imagine a typical industrial or scientific application in which we want to recognize objects which are randomly orientated in the image. We are not interested in the orientation of the objects but in the distinction from others. Therefore texture parameters which depend on the orientation are of no interest. We might still use them but only if the objects have a characteristic shape which then allows us to determine their orientation. We can use similar arguments for scale-invariant features. If the objects of interest are located at different distances from the camera, the texture parameter used to recognize them should also be scale-invariant. Otherwise the recognition of the object will depend on the distance. However, if the texture changes its characteristics with the scale — as in the example of the curtain in figure 9.1a — the scale-invariant texture features may not exist at all. Then the use of textures to characterize objects at different distances becomes a difficult task.

In the examples above, we were interested in the objects themselves but not in their orientation in space. The orientation of surfaces is a key feature for another image processing task, the reconstruction of a three- dimensional scene from a two-dimensional image. If we know the surface of an object shows a uniform texture, we can analyze the orientation and scales of the texture for the orientation of the surface in space. For this, the characteristic scales and orientations of the texture are needed.

9.2   Rotation and Scale Invariant Texture Features

9.2.1   Local Variance

All parameters derived from the statistics of the gray values for individual pixels —
in principle — are independent of the orientation of the objects. In section 4.2.3 we
discussed an estimate of the gray value distribution of a homogeneous random field,
i.e., averaged over the whole image. Besides the mean value, we learnt to characterize
the gray value distribution by the mean, variance and higher moments (section 4.2.1).

To be suitable for texture analysis, the estimate of these parameters has to be
adapted to a local neighborhood. In the simplest case, we can select a window W and
compute the parameters only from the pixels contained in this window. The *variance
operation*, for example, is then given by

$$V_{mn} = \frac{1}{P-1} \sum_{k,l \in W} (G_{m-k,n-l} - \langle G \rangle_{mn})^2 . \tag{9.1}$$

The sum runs over the P image points of the window. The expression $\langle G \rangle_{mn}$ denotes
the mean of the gray values at the point (m,n), computed over the same window W:

$$\langle G \rangle_{mn} = \frac{1}{P} \sum_{k,l \in W} G_{m-k,n-l}. \tag{9.2}$$

It is important to note that the variance operator is nonlinear. However, it resembles the
general form of a neighborhood operation — a convolution. Combining (9.1) and (9.2)
we can show it as a combination of linear convolution and nonlinear point operations

$$V_{mn} = \frac{1}{P-1} \left[\sum_{k,l \in W} G^2_{m-k,n-l} - \left(\frac{1}{P} \sum_{k,l \in W} G_{mn} \right)^2 \right], \tag{9.3}$$

or, in operator notation,

$$\mathcal{V} = \mathcal{R}(\mathcal{I} \cdot \mathcal{I}) - (\mathcal{R} \cdot \mathcal{R}). \tag{9.4}$$

The operator $\mathcal{R}$ denotes a smoothing over all the image points with a box filter of the
size of the window W. The operator $\mathcal{I}$ is the identity operator. Therefore the operator
$\mathcal{I} \cdot \mathcal{I}$ performs a nonlinear point operation, namely the squaring of the gray values at
each pixel. Finally, the variance operator subtracts the square of a smoothed gray value
from the smoothed squared gray values. From discussions on smoothing in section 6.1
we know that a box filter is not an appropriate smoothing filter. Thus we obtain a
better variance operator if we replace the box filter $\mathcal{R}$ with a binomial filter $\mathcal{B}$

$$\mathcal{V} = \mathcal{B}(\mathcal{I} \cdot \mathcal{I}) - (\mathcal{B} \cdot \mathcal{B}). \tag{9.5}$$

We know the variance operator to be isotropic. It is also scale independent if the
window is larger than the largest scales in the textures and if no fine scales of the
texture disappear because the objects are located further away from the camera. This
suggests that a scale invariant texture operator only exists if the texture itself is scale
invariant.

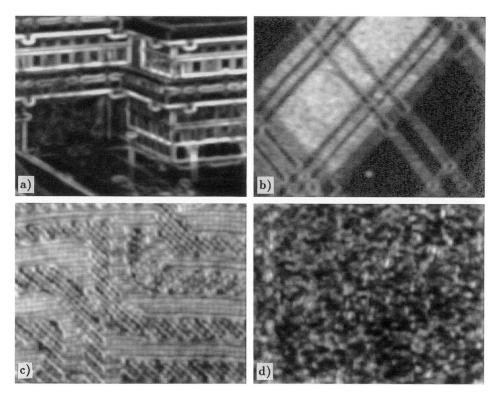

Figure 9.2: Variance operator applied to different images: a) figure 6.6a; b) figure 9.1e; c) figure 9.1f; d) figure 9.1d.

The application of the variance operator (9.5) with $\mathcal{B}^{16}$ to several images is shown in figure 9.2. In figure 9.2a, the variance operator turns out as an isotropic edge detector, since the original image contains areas with more or less uniform gray values. The other three examples in figure 9.2 show variance images from textured surfaces. The variance operator can distinguish the areas with the fine horizontal stripes in figure 9.1e from the more uniform surfaces. They appear as uniform bright areas in the variance image (figure 9.2b). The variance operator cannot distinguish between the two textures in figure 9.2c. The chipwood paper (figure 9.2d) gives no uniform response to the variance operator since the scales are too coarse for the smoothing operator applied.

Besides the variance, we could also use the higher moments of the gray value distribution as defined in section 4.2.1 for a more detailed description. The significance of this approach may be illustrated with examples of two quite different gray value distributions, a normal and a bimodal distribution

$$p(g) = \frac{1}{\sqrt{2\pi}\sigma} \exp\left(-\frac{g - \langle g \rangle}{2\sigma^2}\right), \quad p'(g) = \frac{1}{2}\left(\delta(\langle g \rangle + \sigma) + \delta(\langle g \rangle - \sigma)\right).$$

Both distributions show the same mean and variance but differ in higher-order moments.

9.3   Rotation and Scale Variant Texture Features

9.3.1   Local Orientation

As local orientation has already been discussed in detail in chapter 7, we now only discuss some examples to illustrate the significance of local orientation for texture analysis. The local orientation computed from the texture examples in figure 9.1 is shown in plate 12. In the images of the dog fur (plate 12a and b) and the piece of cloth (plate 12c and d) most areas show well oriented textures. In contrast, plate 12e and f contains patterns with orientations in all directions.

9.3.2   Local Wave Number

Plate 11a shows an image where we have difficulty in recognizing any object at all. Only after comparing the original with the analyzed image (plate 11b), do we discover that the greyhound dogs differ from the background by a finer scale of the random gray value fluctuations. This image is an example where all the texture operators discussed so far will fail. The textures of the object and the background in plate 11 differ only by characteristic scale, so we need a suitable operator which computes the local wave number.

Knutsson [1982] and *Knutsson and Granlund* [1983] suggested an operator which works similar to the operator for local orientation (section 7.2). They use the same type of quadrature filters as for local orientation (7.6):

$$\hat{l}(q) = \exp\left[-\frac{\ln^2(q/q_k)}{(B/2)^2 \log 2}\right]$$

$$\hat{k}_e(\phi) = \cos^{2l}(\phi - \phi_0) \tag{9.6}$$

$$\hat{k}_o(\phi) = i \cos^{2l}(\phi - \phi_0) \, \text{signum}\left[\cos(\phi - \phi_0)\right].$$

This time, however, a set is used in which the directional dependence, i. e., l, is kept constant. The filters differ by the radial maximum q_k. As with local orientation, the filter responses are added vectorially but the angle of the filters now refers to a local wave number instead of a local orientation. *Knutsson* [1982] showed that, with a suitable choice of q_k, an exact determination of the local wave number of a purely periodic structure is possible.

The image shown in plate 11b was filtered with this operator. Areas in which the local wave number exceeds a certain threshold are shown in red.

9.3.3   Pyramidal Texture Analysis

The Laplace pyramid is an alternative to the local wave number operator, since the different scales of the texture are placed at different levels of the Laplace pyramid. This

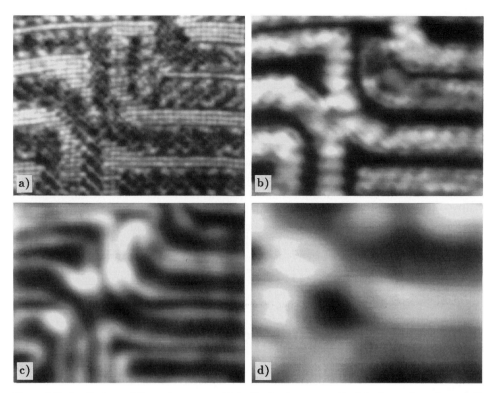

Figure 9.3: Application of the variance operator to the Laplace pyramid of the image from figure 9.1f.

decomposition does not compute a local wave number directly, but we can obtain a series of images which show the different scales of the texture.

The variance operator takes a very simple form with a Laplace pyramid, since the mean gray value — except for the coarsest level — is zero

$$\mathcal{V} = \mathcal{B}(\mathcal{L}^{(p)} \cdot \mathcal{L}^{(p)}). \tag{9.7}$$

Figure 9.3 demonstrates how the different textures from figure 9.1f appear at different levels of the Laplace pyramid. In the finest scale at the zero level of the pyramid (figure 9.3a), the texture with small periodically arranged dots becomes apparent, while the first level (figure 9.3b) shows other areas with vertically oriented threads. The second level of the Laplace pyramid (figure 9.3c) is too coarse to show any textures. The bright areas now mark the edges between the two textures.

Nonlinear operators like the variance operator must be used with caution because of the sampling theorem. Point-wise squaring of the gray values in the spatial domain corresponds to a convolution operation of the image with itself in the wave number space. Consequently, the range of wave numbers doubles. We can illustrate this phenomenon with a periodic structure

$$g(\boldsymbol{x}) = \cos(\boldsymbol{x}\boldsymbol{k}). \tag{9.8}$$

After squaring, we obtain two terms

$$g(\boldsymbol{x}) = \cos^2(\boldsymbol{x}\boldsymbol{k}) = \frac{1}{2} + \frac{1}{2}\cos(\boldsymbol{x}2\boldsymbol{k}), \tag{9.9}$$

one with a double wave number and another with a constant term. As a result, we have to use *supersampled* images in order not to obtain Moiré patterns after squaring. Thus it seems to be advisable to sample each periodic structure with at least four samples per wavelength if we apply a nonlinear operator as the variance operator.

The Laplace pyramid is a very well adapted data structure for the analysis of hierarchically organized textures which may show different characteristics at different scales as in the example of the curtain discussed in section 9.1. In this way we can apply such operators as local variance and local orientation at each level of the pyramid. The simultaneous application of the variance and local orientation operators at multiple scales gives a rich set of features which allows even complex hierarchical organized textures to be distinguished as demonstrated in plate 13. It is important to note that application of these operations on all levels of the pyramid only increases the computation by a factor of $4/3$.

9.4   Fractal Description of Texture

For several years it has been known that many natural patterns can be adequately described using the methods of *fractal geometry* [*Mandelbrot*, 1982]. Fractal objects have found an important place in computer graphics, as they are capable of producing naturally looking objects such as clouds, mountain trains and water surfaces [*Peitgen and Richter*, 1986]. This seems to indicate that fractal geometry could be an appropriate description of textures in images.

The inverse step to find a simple fractal description of a given texture is a much more complex task. A first success was achieved by *Barnsley and Sloan* [1988] and *Barnsley* [1988]. So-called *iterated function systems* (IFS) are used to describe complex patterns with a few figures. This compact code also seems to be suitable to describe and analyze textures.

But more difficult questions need to be solved. We need to analyze how similar patterns are mapped to the IFS code to distinguish between the different textures. Currently, the enormous effort needed to compute the IFS-code from a given pattern is a big obstacle. Even on a fast workstation, it takes hours to compute the code for a single color image. If these problems can be solved exciting new perspectives open up for image processing. We also need to wait for more progress in algorithms and hardware before we arrive at a practical application of fractal texture analysis.

10 Segmentation

10.1 Introduction

All image processing operations discussed so far have helped us to "recognize" objects of interest, i. e., to find suitable local features which allow us to distinguish them from other objects and from the background. The next step is to check each individual pixel whether it belongs to an object of interest or not. This operation is called *segmentation* and produces a *binary image*. A pixel has the value one if it belongs to the object; otherwise it is zero. Segmentation is the operation at the threshold between low-level image processing and the operations which analyze the shape of objects, such as those discussed in chapter 11. In this chapter, we discuss several types of segmentation methods. Basically we can think of three concepts for segmentation. Pixel-based methods only use the gray values of the individual pixels. Edge-based methods detect edges and then try to follow the edges. Finally, region-based methods analyze the gray values in larger areas.

10.2 Pixel-Based Methods

Point-based segmentation only takes the gray value of a pixel in order to decide whether it belongs to the object or not. In order to perform this task, we have to find the gray value range which characterizes the object of interest. In the following we will consider a simple scene with one type of object. If we have found a good feature to separate the object from the background, the histogram of the gray values — or more generally feature values — will show a *bimodal distribution* with two distinct maxima (figure 10.1). Ideally, a zone will exist between the two maxima where no features exist. Then the histogram is zero in this range and we can place a threshold anywhere in this range yielding a perfect separation between object and background.

It is the aim of low-level image processing to achieve this ideal situation. However, we may fall short. It is still quite simple to handle a situation in which a non-zero minimum exists between two well-pronounced maxima. This can occur even when the object and the background have clearly distinct gray values, since intermediate gray values will always occur at the edges of the objects. The probability density functions for the gray

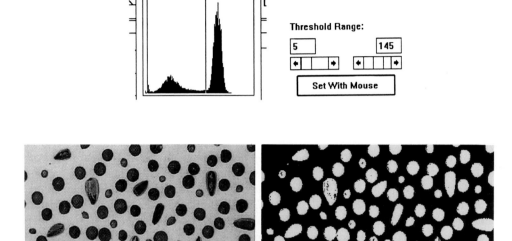

Figure 10.1: Ideal image for segmentation: a) image; b) histogram with bimodal gray value distribution; c) segmented image with the threshold indicated by the vertical line in the histogram; processed using OPTIMAS.

values of the object and the background will overlap. This overlap means that some mis-correspondences could be unavoidable. Some object pixels will be recognized as background and vice versa. If we know the probability distribution for the object and the background pixels, we can use a statistical analysis of the decision process to find an optimum threshold with the minimum number of erroneous correspondences [*Rosenfeld and Kak*, 1982]. The gray value distributions of the object and the background can be estimated by local histograms which only include areas from either the object or the background. These areas must be selected manually.

In less favorable circumstances, the histogram might not show a minimum at all, in which case an adequate threshold does not exist. This situation occurs, for example, in a scene with uneven illumination even if the object clearly juts out of the background (figure 10.2). The literature is full of concepts to handle such cases. We can, for example, compute histograms from smaller areas and use these histograms to find local thresholds.

However, it is much better to solve the problem at its root, i. e., to optimize the illumination of the scene we observe. If this is not possible, we should try to correct for the uneven illumination (as discussed in section 4.3.3) before we apply a complex segmentation procedure.

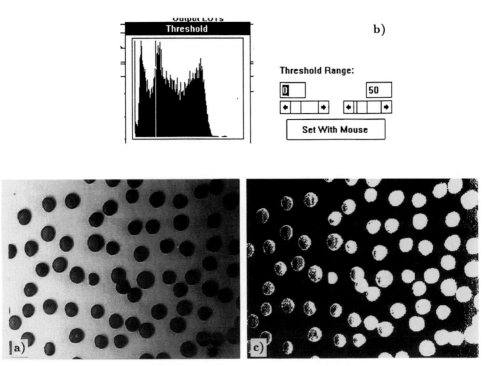

Figure 10.2: Segmentation of an image with uneven illumination: a) image; b) histogram; c) segmented image; processed using OPTIMAS.

10.3 Region-Based Methods

Region-based methods focus our attention on an important aspect of the segmentation process we missed with point-based techniques. There we classified a pixel as an object pixel judging solely on its gray value independent of the context. This means that any isolated points or small areas could be classified as being object pixels, disregarding the fact that an important characteristic of an object is its *connectivity*.

In this section we will not discuss such standard techniques as spilt-and-merge or region-growing techniques. Interested readers are referred to *Rosenfeld and Kak* [1982] or *Jain* [1989]. Here we point out one of the central problems of the segmentation process and discuss the use of pyramids in order to solve it.

If we do not use the original image but a feature image for the segmentation process, the features do not represent a single pixel but a small neighborhood depending on the mask sizes of the operators used. At the edges of the objects, however, where the mask size includes pixels from both the object and the background, any feature that could be useful cannot be computed. The correct procedure would be to limit the mask size at the edge to points of either the object or the background. But how can this be achieved if we can only distinguish the object and the background after computation of the feature? A similar problem occurs later in this book with the computation of displacement vector fields in image sequences (see chapter 16).

Obviously, this problem cannot be solved in one step, but only iteratively using a procedure in which feature computation and segmentation are performed alternately. Principally, we proceed as follows. In the first step, we compute the features disregarding any object boundaries. Then we perform a preliminary segmentation and compute the features again, now using the segmentation results to limit the masks of the neighborhood operations at the object edges to either the object or the background pixels, depending on the location of the center pixel. To improve the results, we can repeat both steps until the procedure converges into a stable result.

Burt [1984] suggested a *pyramid-linking* algorithm as an effective implementation of a combined segmentation feature computation algorithm. We will demonstrate it using the illustrative example of a noisy *step edge* (figure 10.3). In this case, the computed feature is simply the mean gray value. The algorithm includes the following steps:

1. *Computation of the Gaussian pyramid.* As shown in figure 10.3a, the gray values of four neighboring pixels are averaged to form a pixel on the next higher level of the pyramid. This corresponds to a smoothing operation with a box filter.

2. *Segmentation by pyramid-linking.* Since each pixel contributes to two pixels on the higher level, we can now decide to which it most likely belongs. The decision is simply made by comparing the gray values and choosing the pixel. The link is pictured in figure 10.3b by an edge connecting the two pixels. This procedure is repeated through all the levels of the pyramid. As a result, the links on the pyramid constitute a new data structure. Starting from the top of the pyramid one pixel is connected with several pixels on the next lower level. Such a data structure is called a *tree* in computer science. The links are called *edges*, the data points are the gray values of the pixels, and are denoted as *nodes* or *vertices*. The node at the highest level is called the *root* of the tree, the nodes which have no further links are called the *leaves* of the tree. A node linked to a node at a lower level is denoted as the *father node* of this node. Correspondingly, each node linked to a node at a higher level is defined as the *son node* of this node.

3. *Averaging of linked pixels.* Next, the resulting link structure is used to recompute the mean gray values, now using only the linked pixels (figure 10.3c), i. e., the new gray value of each father node is computed as the average gray value of all the son nodes. This procedure starts at the lowest level and is continued through all the levels of the pyramid.

The last two steps are repeated iteratively until we reach a stable result which is shown in figure 10.3d. An analysis of the link-tree shows the result of the segmentation procedure. In figure 10.3d we recognize two *subtrees*, which have their roots in the third level of the pyramid. At the next lower level, four subtrees originate. But the differences in the gray values at this level are significantly smaller. Thus we conclude that the gray value structure is obviously parted into two regions. Then we obtain the final result of the segmentation procedure by transferring the gray values at the roots of the two subtrees to the linked nodes at the lowest level. These values are shown as braced numbers in figure 10.3d.

The application of the pyramid-linking segmentation algorithm to two-dimensional

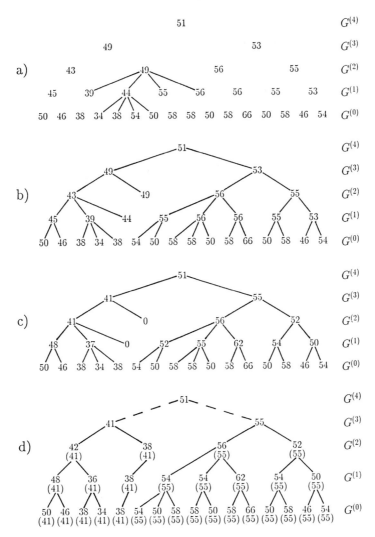

Figure 10.3: Demonstration of the pyramid-linking segmentation procedure with a one-dimensional noisy edge: a) first step: Computation of the Gaussian pyramid; b) second step: node-linking: each node is linked with the father node at the next higher level whose value is closest to the value of the node; c) re-computation of the mean gray values at the father nodes, now only using the linked son nodes; d) final result after several iterations of steps b) and c). The braced values indicate the regional means of the sub-trees with their roots in the third level of the pyramid. At the lowest level, these values represent the estimate of the noisy edge by a step-edge [*Burt*, 1984].

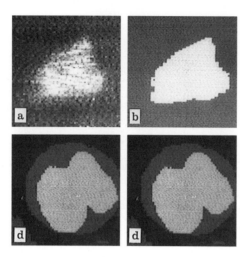

Figure 10.4: Noisy images of a tank (a) and a blood cell (c) segmented with the pyramid-linking algorithm in two and three regions (b) and (d), respectively; after *Burt* [1984].

images is shown in figure 10.4. Both examples point out that even very noisy images can be successfully segmented with this procedure. There is no restriction to the form of the segmented area.

The pyramid-linking procedure merges the segmentation and the computation of mean features for the objects extracted in an efficient way by building a tree on a pyramid. It is also advantageous that we do not need to know the number of segmentation levels beforehand. They are contained in the structure of the tree. The tree also includes the correctly averaged gray or feature values for the segmented areas. Further details of pyramid-linking segmentation are discussed in *Burt et al.* [1981] and *Pietikäinen and Rosenfeld* [1981].

10.4 Edge-Based Methods

Even with a perfect illumination, pixel-based segmentation may easily result in a bias of the size of the segmented object. Figure 10.5 illustrates how the size of the objects depends on the threshold level. The size variation results from the fact that the gray values at the edge of an object change only gradually from the background to the object value. No bias in the size occurs if we take the mean of the object and the background gray values as the threshold. However, this approach is only possible, if all objects show the same gray values. In case of differently bright objects and a black background, a bias in the size of the objects is unavoidable. Darker objects will become too small, brighter objects too large.

An edge-based segmentation approach can be used to avoid a bias in the size of the segmented object. The position of an edge is given by an extremum of the first-order

a)   b)

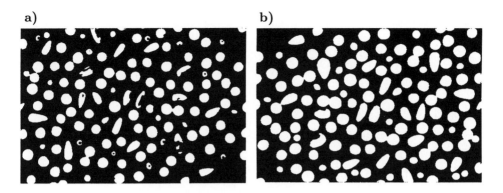

Figure 10.5: Dependence of the size of the segmented objects on the threshold level: a) threshold = 100 bits; b) threshold = 140 bits (original image figure 10.1a)

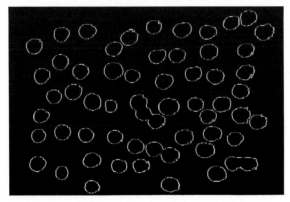

Figure 10.6: Result of edge-based segmentation of the unevenly illuminated image shown in figure 10.2; processed using BioScan OPTIMAS.

derivative or a zero crossing in the second-order derivative (see section 6.2).

Edge-based segmentation is a sequential method. The image is scanned line by line for, e. g., maxima in the gradient. When a maximum is encountered, a *tracing algorithm* tries to follow the maximum of the gradient around the object until it reaches the starting point again. Then the next maximum in the gradient is searched. As region-based segmentation, edge-based segmentation takes into account that an object is characterized by adjacent pixels.

The image processing software OPTIMAS includes a number of different algorithms to trace the boundary of objects. We can trace the maximum of the gradient, an extremum, or a certain luminance level. Although edge-based segmentation is computationally more costly than a simple global threshold approach, superior results are gained. Figure 10.6 illustrates that it also can process unevenly illuminated images successfully. We could not segment this image with a global threshold (figure 10.2b). Contour-following algorithms are discussed in *Jain* [1989].

11 Shape

11.1 Introduction

After the segmentation process, which we discussed in the previous chapter, we know which pixels belong to the object of interest. Now we can perform the next step and analyze the *shape* of the objects. This is the topic of this chapter. First we will discuss a class of neighborhood operations, the morphological operators on binary images, which work on the form of objects. Second, we will consider the question how to represent a segmented object. Third, we will discuss parameters to describe the form of objects.

11.2 Morphological Operators

11.2.1 Neighborhood Operations on Binary Images

In our survey of digital image processing, operators which relate pixels in a small neighborhood have emerged as a versatile and powerful tool for scalar and vectorial images. Consequently, we ask whether they might also be of use for binary images. In sections 5.1.1 and 5.1.3 we discussed the two basic operations to combine neighboring pixels of gray value images: convolution ("weight and sum up") and rank value filtering ("sort and select"). With binary images, we do not have much choice as to which kind of operations to perform. We can combine pixels only with the logical operations of Boolean algebra. We might introduce a *binary convolution* by replacing the multiplication of the image and mask pixels with an *and operation* and the summation by an *or operation*

$$G'_{mn} = \bigvee_{k=-R}^{R} \bigvee_{l=-R}^{R} M_{k,l} \wedge G_{m-k,n-l}. \tag{11.1}$$

The $\wedge$ and $\vee$ denote the logical *and* and *or* operation, respectively. The binary image G is convolved with a symmetric $2R + 1 \times 2R + 1$ mask M.

What does this operation achieve? Let us assume that all the coefficients of the mask are set to 'one'. If one or more object pixels, i.e., 'ones', are within the mask, the result of the operation will be one, otherwise it is zero (figure 11.1). Hence, the object

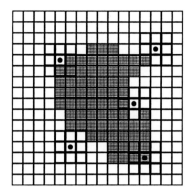
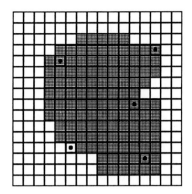

Figure 11.1: Dilation of a binary object with the binary convolution operation as defined in (11.1). Shown is the application of a 3 × 3 mask.

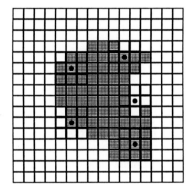
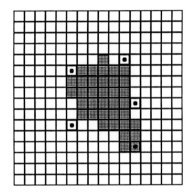

Figure 11.2: Erosion of a binary object with a 3 × 3 mask.

will be dilated. Small holes or cracks will be filled and the contour line will become smoother, as shown in figure 11.3b. The operator defined by (11.1) is known as the *dilation operator*. Interestingly, we can end up with the same effect if we apply *rank value filter* operations (see section 5.13) to binary images. Let us take the *maximum operator*. The maximum will then be one if one or more 'ones' are within the mask, just as with the binary convolution operation in (11.1).

The *minimum operator* has the opposite effect. Now the result is only one if the mask is completely within the object (figure 11.2). In this way the object is eroded. Objects smaller than the mask completely disappear, objects connected only by a small bridge will become disconnected (figure 11.4b). The *erosion* of an object can also be performed using binary convolution. In order to erode the object, we dilate the background:

$$G'_{mn} = \overline{\bigvee_{k=-R}^{R} \bigvee_{l=-R}^{R} M_{k,l} \wedge \overline{G_{m-k,n-l}}}. \tag{11.2}$$

In this equation, the image is negated to convert the background to the object and vice versa. The result must be negated to reverse this negation.

By transferring the concepts of neighborhood operations for gray value images to binary images we have gained an important tool to operate on the form of objects. We have already seen in figures 11.1 and 11.2 that these operations can be used to fill small holes and cracks or to eliminate small objects. The size of the mask governs the effect of the operators, therefore the mask is often called the *structure element*. For example, an erosion operation works like a net which has holes in the shape of the mask. All objects smaller than the hole will slip through and disappear from the image. The operations that work on the form of objects are called *morphological operators*. The name originates from the research area of morphology which describes the form of objects in biology and geosciences.

We used a rather unconventional way to introduce morphological operations. Normally, these operations are defined as operations on sets of pixels. We regard G as the set of all the pixels of the matrix which are not zero. M is the set of the non-zero mask pixels. With M_p we denote the mask shifted with its reference point (generally but not necessarily its center) to the pixel p. Erosion is then defined as

$$G \ominus M = \{p : M_p \subseteq G\} \tag{11.3}$$

and dilation as

$$G \oplus M = \{p : M_p \cap G \neq \emptyset\}. \tag{11.4}$$

These definitions are equivalent to (11.1) and (11.2), respectively, except for the fact that the mask in the convolution operation is rotated by $180°$ (see section 5.1.1). We can now express the erosion of the set of pixels G by the set of pixels M as the set of all the pixels p for which M_p is completely contained in G. In contrast, the dilation of G by M is the set of all the pixels for which the intersection between G and M_p is not an empty set. Since the set theoretical approach leads to more compact and illustrative formulas, we will use it now. Equations (11.1) and (11.2) still constitute the basis from which to implement morphological operations. The erosion and dilation operator can be regarded as elementary morphological operators from which other more complex operators can be built. Their properties are studied in detail in the next section.

11.2.2   General Properties of Morphological Operations

Morphological operators share most of the properties we have discussed in chapter 5.

Shift Invariance
Shift invariance results directly from the definition of the erosion and dilation operator as convolutions with binary data in (11.1) and (11.2). Using the shift operator S as defined in (5.24) and the operator notation, we can write the shift invariance of any morphological operator $\mathcal{M}$ as

$$\mathcal{M}\left({}^{kl}SG\right) = {}^{kl}S\left(\mathcal{M}G\right). \tag{11.5}$$

Principle of Superposition
What does the *superposition principle* for binary data mean? For gray value images it is defined as

$$\mathcal{H}(aG + bG') = a\mathcal{H}G + b\mathcal{H}G'. \tag{11.6}$$

The factors a and b make no sense for binary images; the addition of images corresponds to the union or *logical or* of images. The superposition principle for binary images is given as

$$\mathcal{M}(G \cup G') = (\mathcal{M}G) \cup (\mathcal{M}G') \quad \text{or} \quad \mathcal{M}(G \vee G') = (\mathcal{M}G) \vee (\mathcal{M}G'). \tag{11.7}$$

The operation $G \vee G'$ means a point-wise *logical or* of the elements of the matrices G and G'. Generally, morphological operators are not additive in the sense of (11.7). While the dilation operation meets the superposition principle, the erosion does not. The erosion of the union of two objects is generally a superset of the union of two eroded objects:

$$\begin{aligned}
(G \cup G') \ominus M &\supseteq (G \ominus M) \cup (G' \ominus M) \\
(G \cup G') \oplus M &= (G \oplus M) \cup (G' \oplus M).
\end{aligned} \tag{11.8}$$

Commutativity and Associativity
Also morphological operators are not generally commutative:

$$M_1 \oplus M_2 = M_2 \oplus M_1, \quad \text{but } M_1 \ominus M_2 \neq M_2 \ominus M_1. \tag{11.9}$$

We can see that the erosion is not commutative if we take the special case that $M_1 \supset M_2$. Then the erosion of M_2 by M_1 yields the empty set. However, both erosion and dilation masks consecutively applied in a cascade to the same image G are commutative:

$$\begin{aligned}
(G \ominus M_1) \ominus M_2 &= G \ominus (M_1 \oplus M_2) = (G \ominus M_2) \ominus M_1 \\
(G \oplus M_1) \oplus M_2 &= G \oplus (M_1 \oplus M_2) = (G \oplus M_2) \oplus M_1.
\end{aligned} \tag{11.10}$$

These equations are important for the implementation of morphological operations. Generally, the cascade operation with k structure elements $M_1, M_2, \ldots, M_k$ is equivalent to the operation with the structure element $M = M_1 \oplus M_2 \oplus \ldots \oplus M_k$. In conclusion, we can decompose large structure elements in the very same way as we decomposed linear shift-invariant operators. An important example is the composition of separable structure elements by the horizontal and vertical element $M = M_x \oplus M_y$. Another less trivial example is the build-up of large one-dimensional structure elements by structure elements including many zeros:

$$[1\ 1\ 1\ 1\ 1\ 1\ 1\ 1\ 1] = [1\ 1\ 1] \oplus [1\ 0\ 0\ 1\ 0\ 0\ 1]. \tag{11.11}$$

In this way, we can build up large structure elements with a minimum number of logical operations just as we built up large smoothing masks in section 6.3.3. It is more difficult to obtain isotropic, i.e., circular-shaped, structure elements. The problem is that the dilation of horizontal and vertical structure elements always results in a rectangular-shaped structure element, but not in a circular mask. A circular mask can, however, be approximated with one-dimensional structure elements running in more directions than only along the axes. Again, we can learn how to proceed from kernels for gray value images. If we take component kernels of the same shape, the binary structure element contains all the points where the corresponding kernel coefficients are non-zero. Thus the concepts to construct large binomial kernels discussed in section 6.3.3, especially (6.61), give good approximations to construct large isotropic structure elements efficiently.

Monotony
Erosion and dilation are monotonous operations

$$
\begin{aligned}
G_1 \subseteq G_2 &\rightsquigarrow G_1 \oplus M \subseteq G_2 \oplus M \\
G_1 \subseteq G_2 &\rightsquigarrow G_1 \ominus M \subseteq G_2 \ominus M.
\end{aligned}
\tag{11.12}
$$

The monotony property means that the subset relations are invariant with respect to erosion and dilation.

Distributivity
Linear shift-invariant operators are distributive with regard to addition. The corresponding distributivities for erosion and dilation with respect to the union and intersection of two images G_1 and G_2 are more complex:

$$
\begin{aligned}
(G_1 \cap G_2) \oplus M &\subseteq (G_1 \oplus M) \cap (G_2 \oplus M) \\
(G_1 \cap G_2) \ominus M &= (G_1 \ominus M) \cap (G_2 \ominus M)
\end{aligned}
\tag{11.13}
$$

and

$$
\begin{aligned}
(G_1 \cup G_2) \oplus M &= (G_1 \oplus M) \cup (G_2 \oplus M) \\
(G_1 \cup G_2) \ominus M &\supseteq (G_1 \ominus M) \cup (G_2 \ominus M).
\end{aligned}
\tag{11.14}
$$

Erosion is distributive over the intersection operation, while dilation is distributive over the union operation.

Duality
Erosion and dilation are *dual* operations. By negating the binary image erosion converts to dilation and vice versa:

$$
\begin{aligned}
\overline{G \ominus M} &= \overline{G} \oplus M \\
\overline{G \oplus M} &= \overline{G} \ominus M.
\end{aligned}
\tag{11.15}
$$

In the following we will learn about more dual pairs of morphological operators.

The mathematical foundation of morphological operations including complete proofs for all the properties stated in this section can be found in the classic book by *Serra* [1983].

11.2.3   Further Morphological Operations

Using the elementary erosion and dilation operations we now develop further useful operations to work on the form of objects. While in the previous section 11.2.2 we focused on the general and theoretical aspects of morphological operations, we now concentrate on application.

Opening and Closing
The erosion operation is useful to filter out small objects. According to (11.3) all objects O disappear which meet the condition

$$
O \ominus M = \emptyset \equiv M_p \supset O \; \forall p.
\tag{11.16}
$$

By a proper choice of the structure element, we can eliminate objects with a certain form (figure 11.3a and b). However, the erosion operation shows the disadvantage that

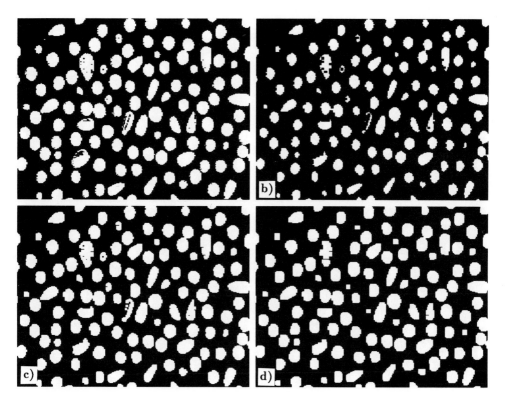

Figure 11.3: Examples of morphological operations: a) original binary image; b) erosion with a 3 × 3 mask; c) opening with a 3 × 3 mask; d) opening with a larger mask.

all the remaining objects shrink in size. We can avoid this effect by dilation of the image after erosion with the same structure element. This combination of operations is called an *opening operation*

$$G \circ M = (G \ominus M) \oplus M. \qquad (11.17)$$

The opening sieves out objects which are smaller than the structure element, but avoids a general shrinking of the size (figure 11.3c, d). It is also an ideal operation to remove lines with a diameter that is smaller than the diameter of the structure element.

In contrast, dilation enlarges objects and closes small holes and cracks. General enlargement of the object by the size of the structure element can be reversed by a following erosion (figure 11.4c, d). This combination of operations is called a *closing operation*

$$G \bullet M = (G \oplus M) \ominus M. \qquad (11.18)$$

The size change of objects with different operations may be summarized by the following relations:

$$G \ominus M \subseteq G \circ M \subseteq G \subseteq G \bullet M \subseteq G \oplus M. \qquad (11.19)$$

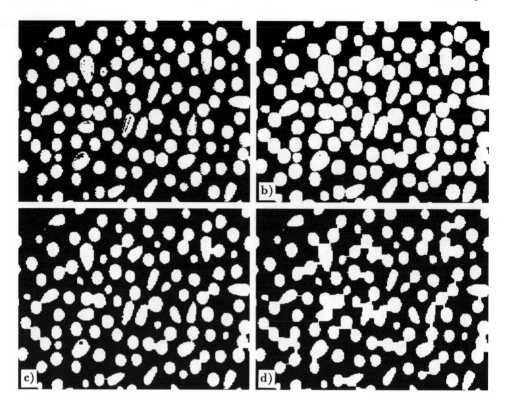

Figure 11.4: Examples of morphological operations: a) original binary image; b) dilation with a 3 × 3 mask; c) closing with a 3 × 3 mask; d) closing with a larger mask.

Opening and closing are idempotent operations

$$\begin{aligned} G \bullet M &= (G \bullet M) \bullet M \\ G \circ M &= (G \circ M) \circ M, \end{aligned} \tag{11.20}$$

i. e., a second application of a closing and opening with the same structure element does not show any further effects.

Object Boundary Extraction; Hit-or-Miss Operator
So far, we only discussed operators which shrink or expand objects. Now we turn to the question how to extract the boundary of an object. Boundary points miss at least one of their neighbors. As we discussed in section 2.3.1, we can define a 4- and 8-neighborhood on a rectangular grid. We can remove the boundary points by eroding the object with a structure element which contains all the possible neighbors of the central pixel

$$M = \begin{bmatrix} 1 & 1 & 1 \\ 1 & 1 & 1 \\ 1 & 1 & 1 \end{bmatrix} \quad \text{and} \quad M = \begin{bmatrix} 0 & 1 & 0 \\ 1 & 1 & 1 \\ 0 & 1 & 0 \end{bmatrix} . \tag{11.21}$$

$$\underbrace{\phantom{\begin{bmatrix} 1 & 1 & 1 \\ 1 & 1 & 1 \\ 1 & 1 & 1 \end{bmatrix}}}_{\text{8-neighborhood}} \qquad \underbrace{\phantom{\begin{bmatrix} 0 & 1 & 0 \\ 1 & 1 & 1 \\ 0 & 1 & 0 \end{bmatrix}}}_{\text{4-neighborhood}}$$

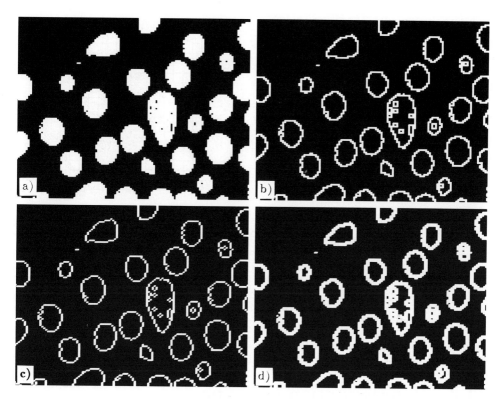

Figure 11.5: Boundary extraction: a) original binary image; b) 4-connected boundary c) 8-connected boundary extracted with the operator (11.22); d) boundary extraction with the hit-or-miss operator.

The boundary is then gained by the set difference (/ operator) between the object and the eroded object

$$B = G/(G \ominus M) = G \cap \overline{(G \ominus M)} = G \cap (\overline{G} \oplus M). \tag{11.22}$$

As shown in the formula, we can also understand the set difference as the intersection of the object with the dilated background. It is important to note that the boundary line shows the dual connectivity to the connectivity of the eroded object. If we erode the object with the 8-neighbor structure element, the boundary is 4-connected, and vice versa. An example for boundary extraction is shown in figure 11.5.

Another useful operator is the *hit-or-miss operator*, yet another combination of the erosion and dilation operator which uses different structure elements for the erosion and dilation operation

$$\begin{aligned}
G \oslash M &= (G \ominus M_1) \cap \overline{(G \oplus M_2)} = (G \ominus M_1) \cap (\overline{G} \ominus M_2) \\
&\text{with } M = M_1 \cup M_2, \quad M_1 \cap M_2 = 0.
\end{aligned} \tag{11.23}$$

After the hit-or-miss operation, the object only includes those pixels p for which $M_{1p} \subseteq G$ and $M_{2p} \subseteq \overline{G}$. From this condition, the requirement that M_1 and M_2 must be disjunct becomes clear. The shape of the borderline extracted depends on the structure elements M_1 and M_2.

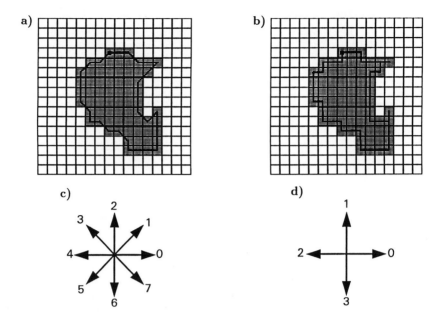

Figure 11.6: Boundary representation with the chain code: a) 8-connected boundary; b) 4-connected boundary; c) direction coding in 8-neighborhood; d) direction coding in 4-neighborhood.

11.3 Representation of Shape

Morphological operations work on binary images represented on a matrix. This means that we still store each pixel of the object and all the background pixels. We realize that all information about binary images can be stored in a much more compact form. For example, all information on the object is contained in its boundary pixels. It is therefore sufficient to store only the boundary pixels of an object. Obviously, this is a much more compact representation of a binary image. It is worthwhile studying whether the extraction of shape parameters or operations modifying the shape of the object can also be performed using this data structure. As an example, we will study the representation of binary objects with *chain codes* and *quad-trees*. This section concludes with some general remarks on the limitations of shape representation on discrete grids and show some alternatives.

11.3.1 Chain Code

The *chain code* is a data structure to represent the boundary of a binary image on a discrete grid in an effective way. Instead of storing the positions of all the boundary pixels, we select a starting pixel and store only its coordinate. If we use an algorithm which scans the image line by line, this will be the uppermost left pixel of the object (figure 11.6a and b). Then we follow the boundary in clockwise direction. In a 4-

a) gray value image

original line (hex): 12 12 12 20 20 20 20 25 27 25 20 20 20 20 20 20

code (hex): 82 **12** 83 **20** 2 **25 27 25** 85 **20**

b) binary image

original line (hex): 1 1 1 1 1 1 0 0 0 1 1 1 0 0 1 0 0 0 0 0 1 1 1 1 1 1 1 1

code (hex): 0 6 3 3 2 1 5 8

Figure 11.7: Demonstration of the run-length code: a) gray value image; b) binary image.

neighborhood there are 4, in an 8-neighborhood there are 8 possible directions to go which we can decode with a 3-bit or 2-bit code as indicated in figure 11.6c and d.

The chain code shows a number of obvious advantages over the matrix representation of a binary object:

- The chain code is a compact representation of a binary object. Let us assume a disk-like object with a diameter of R pixels. In a direct matrix representation we need to store the bounding rectangle of the object, i.e., about R^2 pixels which are stored in R^2 bit. The bounding rectangle is the smallest rectangle enclosing the object. If we use an 8-connected boundary, the disk shows about πR boundary points. The chain code of the πR points can be stored in about $3\pi R$ bit. For objects with a diameter larger than 10, the chain code is a more compact representation.
- The chain code is a *translation invariant* representation of a binary object. This property makes the comparison of objects easier.
- Since the chain code is a complete representation of an object or curve, we can principally compute any shape feature from the chain code. As shown below, we can compute a number of shape parameters — including the perimeter and area — more efficiently using the chain-code representation than in the matrix representation of the binary image.

If the object is not connected or if it has holes, we need more than one chain code to represent it. We must also include the information whether the boundary surrounds an object or a hole. Reconstruction of the binary image from a chain code is an easy procedure. First we might draw the outline of the object and then use a *fill operation* to paint it.

11.3.2   Run-length Code

Another compact representation of a binary image is the *run-length code*. A binary image is scanned line by line. If a line contains a sequence of p equal pixels, we do not store p times the same figure, but store the value of the pixel and indicate that it

a)   b)

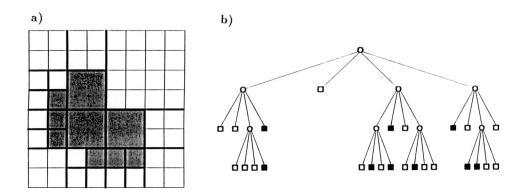

Figure 11.8: Representation of a binary image by a region quadtree: a) successive subdivision of the binary array into quadrants; b) the corresponding region quadtree.

occurs p times (figure 11.7). In this way large uniform line segments can be stored in a very efficient way. For binary images, the code can be especially efficient since we have only the two pixel values zero and one. Since a sequence of zeros is always followed by a sequence of ones, there is no need to store the pixel value. We only need to store the number of times a pixel value occurs (figure 11.7b).

We must be careful, however, at the beginning of a line since it may begin with a one or a zero. This problem can be resolved if we assume a line to begin with zero. If a line should start with a sequence of ones, we start the run-length code with a zero to indicate that the line begins with a sequence of zero zeros (figure 11.7b). Run-length code is suitable for compact storage of images. It has become an integral part of several standard image formats, for example, the TGA or the TIFF formats. Run-length code is, however, not very useful for direct processing of images, because it is not object oriented. As a result, run-length encoding is only useful for compact image storage. Not all types of images can be successfully compressed. Digitized gray-value images, for example, always contain some noise so that the probability for sufficiently long sequences of pixels with the same gray value is very low. High data reduction factors, however, can be achieved with binary images and many types of computer-generated gray-value and color images.

11.3.3   Quadtrees

The run-length and chain codes discussed in the last two sections are line- or boundary-oriented representations of binary images. Thus they decode one-dimensional rather than two-dimensional data. In contrast, *quadtrees* are based on the principle of recursive decomposition of space, as illustrated in figure 11.8.

First, the whole image is decomposed into four equal-sized *quadrants*. If one of the quadrants does not contain a uniform region, i.e., the quadrant is not included entirely in the object or background, it is again subdivided into four subquadrants. The decomposition stops if only uniform quadrants are encountered or if the quadrants contain only one pixel.

The recursive decomposition can be represented in a *tree* (figure 11.8b). At the top level of the tree, known as the *root*, the decomposition starts. The root corresponds to the entire binary image. It is connected via four *edges* to four *son nodes* which represent from left to right the NW, NE, SW, and SE quadrants. If a quadrant needs no further subdivision, it is represented by a *terminal* or *leaf node* in the tree. It is called *black* when the quadrant belongs to an object and *white* otherwise and indicated by a filled and open square, respectively. Nonleaf nodes require further subdivision and are said to be *gray* and are shown as open circles (figure 11.8b).

Quadtrees can be encoded, for example, by a *depth-first traversal* of the tree starting at the root. It is only required to store the type of the node with the symbols b (black), w (white), and g (gray). We start the code with the value of the root node. Then we list the values of the child nodes from left to right. Each time we encounter a gray node, we continue encoding at one level lower in the tree. This rule is applied recursively. This means that we return to a higher level in the tree only after the visited branch is completely encoded down to the lowest level. This is why this encoding is known as depth-first.

The example quadtree shown in figure 11.8b results in the code

$$ggwwgwwwbbwggwbwbbwgwbwwgbwgbbwww.$$

The code becomes more readable if we include a left parenthesis each time we descend one level in the tree and a right parenthesis when we ascend again

$$g(g(wwg(wwwb)b)wg(g(wbwb)bwg(wbww))g(bwg(bbww)w)).$$

However, the code is unique without the parentheses. A quadtree is a compact representation of a binary image if it contains many leaf nodes at high levels. However, in the worst case, for example a regular checkerboard pattern, all leaf nodes are at the lowest level. The quadtree then contains as many leaf nodes as pixels and requires much more bytes of storage space than the direct representation of the binary image as a matrix.

The region quadtree discussed here is only one of the many possibilities for recursive spatial decomposition. An extensive discussion of quadtrees is given by *Samet* [1990a]. Three-dimensional binary images can be recursively decomposed in a similar way. The 3-D image is subdivided into eight equally sized octants. The resulting data structure is called a *region octree*. Quadtrees and octrees have gained significant importance in geographic information systems and computer graphics. An overview of applications is given by *Samet* [1990b].

Quadtrees are a more adequate encoding technique for images than the line-oriented run-length code. However, it is rather difficult to perform shape analysis directly on quadtrees. Without going into further details this can be seen from the simple fact that an object shifted by one pixel in any direction results in a completely different quadtree. From the codes discussed so far, the object-oriented and translation-invariant chain code seems to be best for shape analysis and comparison.

11.4   Shape Parameters

After the discussion of the different possibilities to represent binary objects extracted from image data, we now turn to the question as to how describe the shape of these objects with simple but adequate parameters. This section describes a number of shape parameters from rather trivial ones such as area and perimeter to sophisticated descriptions based on moments or the Fourier transform of object boundaries.

The parameters described in this section are illustrated by BioScan OPTIMAS, a Windows-based PC image processing software which contains a rich collection of shape parameters and a powerful but easy-to-use object data collection tool. OPTIMAS distinguishes three classes of objects: points, lines, and areas. Here we deal only with the latter. After image segmentation, the software can compute object parameters in two different modes. In the single object mode, individual objects can be selected interactively using a pointing device. The parameters selected can then be displayed in so-called view boxes in graphical or numerical form and they can be exported to a data file or via dynamic data exchange (DDE, Microsoft Windows' communication protocol) to other concurrently running programs.

In the multiple object mode, the selected shape parameters are automatically extracted from all objects of an image. In this way, a fully automated object analysis can be performed. In the following, the OPTIMAS names for the different parameters are written in `Courier` letters.

11.4.1   Simple Geometric Parameters

Area (`ArArea`)
The most trivial shape parameter is the *area* A of an object. In a digital binary image the area is given by the number of pixels that belong to the image. In the matrix or pixel list representation of the object, area computing simply means counting the number of pixels.

At first glance, area computation of an object which is described by its chain-code seems to be a complex operation. However, the contrary is true. Computation of the area from the chain code is much faster than counting pixels since the boundary of the object contains only a small fraction of the object's pixels and requires only two additions per boundary pixel.

The algorithm works in a similar way as numerical integration. We assume a horizontal base line drawn at an arbitrary vertical position in the image. Then we start the integration of the area at the uppermost pixel of the object. The distance of this point to the base line is B. We follow the boundary of the object and increment the area of the object according to the figures in table 11.1. If we, for example, move to the right (chain code 0), the area increases by B. If we move upwards to the right (chain code 1), the area also increases by B, but B must be incremented, since the distance between the boundary pixel and the base line has increased. For all movements to the left, the area is decreased by B. In this way, we subtract the area between the lower boundary line of the object and the base line, which was included in the area computation when

Table 11.1: Computation of the area of an object from the contour code. Initially, the area is set to zero. With each step, the area and the parameter B are incremented corresponding to the value of the contour code; after *Zamperoni* [1989].

Contour code	Area increment	Increment of B
0	+B	0
1	+B	1
2	0	1
3	-B	1
4	-B	0
5	-B	-1
6	0	-1
7	+B	-1

moving to the right.

Perimeter (ArPerimeter)

The *perimeter* is another geometrical parameter, which can easily be obtained from the chain code of the object boundary. We just need to count the length of the chain code and take into consideration that steps in diagonal directions are by a factor of $\sqrt{2}$ longer. The perimeter p is then given by an 8-neighborhood chain code:

$$p = n_e + \sqrt{2}n_o, \tag{11.24}$$

where n_e and n_o are the number of even and odd chain code steps, respectively. In contrast to the area, the perimeter is a parameter which is sensitive to the noise level in the image. The more noisy the image, the more rugged and thus longer the boundary of an object will become in the segmentation procedure. This means that care must be taken in comparing perimeters which have been extracted from different images. We must be sure that the smoothness of the boundaries in both images is comparable.

Circularity (ArCircularity)

Area and perimeter are two parameters which describe the size of an object in one or the other way. In order to compare objects which are observed from different distances, it is important to use shape parameters which do not depend on the size of the object on the image plane. The *circularity* c is one of the simplest parameters of this kind. It is defined as

$$c = \frac{p^2}{A}. \tag{11.25}$$

The circularity is a dimensionless number with a minimum value of $4\pi \approx 12.57$ for circles. The circularity is 16 for a square and $12\sqrt{3} \approx 20.8$ for an equilateral triangle. Generally, it shows large values for elongated objects.

Area, perimeter, and circularity are shape parameters which do not depend on the orientation of the objects on the image plane. Thus they are useful to distinguish objects independent of their orientation. We will show an example how to use these simple shape parameters for object classification in section 12.5.

11.4.2 Moment-based Shape Features

Definitions
We could continue to define more parameters like those discussed above, but we will gain more insight into the description of shape by a more systematic approach. In this chapter we will first define *moments* for gray value and binary images and then show how to extract useful shape parameters from this approach. We will discuss Fourier descriptors in a similar manner in the next section.

We have used moments in section 4.2.1 to describe the probability density function for gray values. Here we extend this description to two dimensions and define the moments of the gray value function $g(\boldsymbol{x})$ of an object as

$$m_{p,q} = \int d^2x \ (x_1 - \langle x_1 \rangle)^p (x_2 - \langle x_2 \rangle)^q \ g(\boldsymbol{x}), \qquad (11.26)$$

where

$$\langle x_i \rangle = \int d^2x \ x_i g(\boldsymbol{x}) \Big/ \int d^2x \ g(\boldsymbol{x}). \qquad (11.27)$$

The integration includes the area of the object. Instead of the gray value, we may use more generally any pixel-based feature to compute object moments. The vector $\langle \boldsymbol{x} \rangle = (\langle x_1 \rangle, \langle x_2 \rangle)$ is called the *center of mass* (ArCenterOfMass) of the object in analogy to classical mechanics. (Think of $g(\boldsymbol{x})$ as the density $\rho(\boldsymbol{x})$ of the object; then the zero-order moment $m_{0,0}$ becomes the total mass of the object.)

All the moments defined in (11.26) are related to the center of mass. Therefore they are often denoted as *central moments*. Central moments are invariants under a translation of the coordinates and thus are useful features to describe the shape of objects.

For discrete binary images, the moment calculation reduces to

$$m_{p,q} = \sum (x_1 - \langle x_1 \rangle)^p (x_2 - \langle x_2 \rangle)^q. \qquad (11.28)$$

The summations include all pixels belonging to the object. For the description of object shape we may either use moments based on binary or feature images.

Normalized Moments
Often it is necessary to use shape parameters which do not depend on the size of the object. This is always required if objects must be compared which are observed from different distances. Moments can be normalized in the following way to obtain scale-invariant shape parameters. If we scale an object $g(\boldsymbol{x})$ by a factor of α, $g'(\boldsymbol{x}) = g(\boldsymbol{x}/\alpha)$, its moments are scaled by

$$m'_{p,q} = \alpha^{p+q+2} \ m_{p,q}.$$

We can then normalize the moments with the zero-order moment, $m_{0,0}$, to gain scale-invariant moments

$$\bar{m} = \frac{m_{p,q}}{m_{0,0}^{(p+q+2)/2}}.$$

Since the zero-order moment of a binary object gives the area of the object (11.28), the normalized moments are scaled by the area of the object.

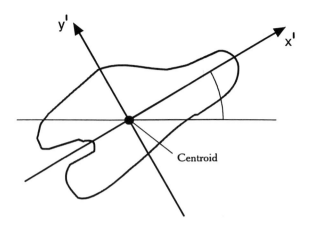

Figure 11.9: Principal axes of the inertia tensor of an object for rotation around the center of mass.

Object Orientation; the Inertia Tensor
Shape analysis starts with the second-order moments. The zero order moment just gives the area or "total mass" of a binary or gray value object, respectively. The first-order central moments are, by definition, zero.

The analogy to mechanics is again helpful to understand the meaning of the second-order moments $m_{2,0}$, $m_{0,2}$, and $m_{1,1}$. They contain terms in which the gray value function, i. e., the density of the object, is multiplied by squared distances from the center of mass. Exactly the same terms are also included in the inertia tensor which has been discussed in section 7.3 (see (7.16) and (7.17)). The three second-order moments form the components of the *inertia tensor* for rotation of the object around its center of mass:

$$J = \begin{bmatrix} m_{0,2} & -m_{1,1} \\ -m_{1,1} & m_{2,0} \end{bmatrix}. \tag{11.29}$$

Because of this analogy, we can transfer all the results from section 7.3 to shape description with second-order moments. The *orientation* of the object is defined as the angle between the x axis and the axis around which the object can be rotated with minimum inertia. The object is most elongated in this direction (figure 11.9). According to (7.24), this angle is given by

$$\phi = \frac{1}{2} \arctan \frac{2m_{1,1}}{m_{2,0} - m_{0,2}}. \tag{11.30}$$

As a measure for the *eccentricity* ε, we can use what we have defined as a coherence measure for local orientation (7.34):

$$\varepsilon = \frac{(m_{2,0} - m_{0,2})^2 + 4m_{1,1}^2}{(m_{2,0} + m_{0,2})^2}. \tag{11.31}$$

The eccentricity ranges from 0 to 1. It is zero for a circular object and one for a line-shaped object. Shape description by second-order moments essentially models the object as an *ellipse*.

Once the orientation of an object is known, we can draw a box around it which is aligned with the principal axes and just large enough to contain all object pixels. This box is known as the *bounding rectangle* of an object. The width and height of the bounding rectangle are two other orientation-independent parameters to describe the shape of an object.

11.4.3 Fourier Descriptors

Cartesian Fourier Descriptors (ArFDCartesian)
The description of the object shape by moments is related to the area because it uses all pixels within the objects. Since the shape of an object is entirely described by its boundary, an alternative possibility for shape analysis, the *Fourier descriptors*, use only the boundary of the object. This approach has the advantage that it requires much less computational effort.

We can consider the boundary as a pair of *cyclic* waveforms, $x(p)$ and $y(p)$, which provides a *parametric* description of the boundary trace. The parameter p is then the path length of the boundary line computed from the starting to the current point. Sampling of $x(p)$ and $y(p)$ results in equidistant points around the area perimeter of the object. The two sampled waveforms $\boldsymbol{x}$ and $\boldsymbol{y}$ are vectors with M samples and can be combined into one complex vector $\boldsymbol{l} = \boldsymbol{x} + \mathrm{i}\boldsymbol{y}$ which gives a complete description of the sampled boundary trace. The coefficients of the discrete Fourier transform of this complex vector,

$$\hat{l}_u = \frac{1}{M} \sum_{m=0}^{M-1} l_m \exp\left(-\frac{2\pi\mathrm{i}\,mu}{M}\right),\tag{11.32}$$

are known as the *Cartesian Fourier descriptors* of the boundary. The first coefficient,

$$\hat{l}_0 = \frac{1}{M} \sum_{m=0}^{M-1} x_m + \mathrm{i}\frac{1}{M} \sum_{m=0}^{M-1} y_m,\tag{11.33}$$

gives the "mean vertex" of the object's boundary, the so-called *centroid* (ArCentroid). With increasing index, i.e., wave number, the Fourier descriptors give more and more fine details of the boundary.

Polar Fourier Descriptors (ArFDPolar)
An alternative approach uses another parameterization of the boundary line. Here the angle θ between the radius drawn from the centroid to a point on the boundary and the x axis is used. This means that we directly describe the *radius* of the object as a function of the angle. Now we need only a real-valued sequence, $\boldsymbol{r}$, with M equiangular samples to describe the boundary. The coefficients of the discrete Fourier transform of this sequence,

$$\hat{r}_u = \frac{1}{M} \sum_{m=0}^{M-1} r_m \exp\left(-\frac{2\pi\mathrm{i}\,mu}{M}\right),\tag{11.34}$$

are known as the *polar Fourier descriptors* of the boundary. Here, the first coefficient, $\hat{r}_0$ is equal to the mean radius. Although conceptually more comprehensive, the polar Fourier descriptors cannot be used for all types of boundaries. The radial boundary parameterization $r(\theta)$ must be single-valued.

Invariants

The Fourier descriptors give a complete and flexible description of the shape of an object which can be made translation, rotation, and scale invariant. Using the basic properties of the discrete Fourier transform (see appendix A.3), we can easily derive invariant descriptions.

All Fourier descriptors, except for $\hat{l}_0$ which gives the centroid of the object, are *translation invariant*. If we scale an object by a factor of α, the Fourier descriptors are multiplied by the same (real-valued) factor. Therefore the ratios of the Fourier descriptors of two similar objects are a real-valued constant which is equal to the size ratio. If an object is rotated by an angle θ, the Fourier descriptors are multiplied by a phase factor. We can recognize a rotated copy of an object from the fact that the ratio of the Fourier descriptors is a complex number with unit magnitude. In other words, their power spectra, $|\hat{l}_u|^2$, are identical.

Symmetry

Fourier descriptors are also well suited to detect symmetries of objects. If an object can be rotated around its centroid by an angle of $2\pi/n$ without changing shape, it is said to have an *n-fold symmetry*. It is *rotational symmetric* if it can be rotated by any angle without changing shape. A rotational symmetric object is a circle. Consequently all polar Fourier descriptors except for $\hat{r}_0$ are equal to zero.

The boundary of an object with n-fold symmetry shows a pattern which repeats n times. Consequently, only the Fourier descriptors with the indices $u = pn$, $p = 1, 2, \ldots$ are unequal to zero. Thus the quantity

$$s_n = \frac{\sum_{u=1}^{U/n} |\hat{r}_{un}|}{\sum_{u=1}^{U} |\hat{r}_u|} \tag{11.35}$$

is a good measure for n-fold symmetry. It is equal to one if the object has n-fold symmetry. As indicated, the sum includes not all M Fourier descriptors but only U since the high-order Fourier descriptors may be corrupted by noise. Figure 11.10 shows several objects and their Fourier descriptors for illustration.

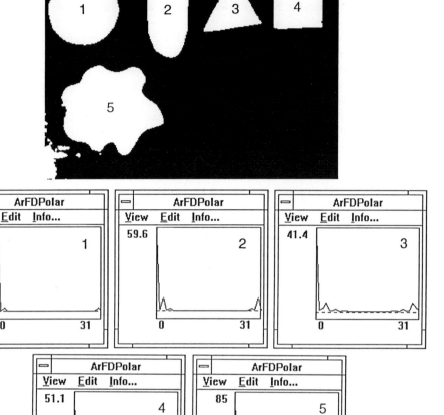

Figure 11.10: Some examples of shape analysis by Fourier descriptors.

12 Classification

12.1 Introduction

When objects are detected with suitable operators and their shape is described (see chapter 11), image processing has reached its goal for some applications. For other applications, further tasks remain to be solved. In this introduction we explore several examples which illustrate how the image processing tasks depend on the questions we pose.

In many image processing applications, the size and shape of particles such as bubbles, dust particles, drops, or cell nuclei must be analyzed. From such images we want to analyze the probability with which those particles occur depending upon their diameter and other external parameters. In this case, the parameters of interest are clearly defined and directly measurable. We determine the area and the position of each particle detected with the methods discussed in section 11.4 (figure 12.1c). Knowing the diameter and position of the bubbles allows all the questions of interest to be answered. From the data collected, we can, for example, compute histograms of the particle area (figure 12.1d). This example is typical for a wide class of scientific applications. Parameters of the objects which can be gained directly and unambiguously from the image data help to answer the scientific questions asked.

However, in many other applications, the relationship between the parameters of interest and the image data is much less evident. Furthermore, we are interested in separating the observed objects into different classes. This is in clear contrast to our previous example, where the diameter of the bubbles showed a continuous parameter space.

"*Waldsterben*" (large-scale forest damage by acid rain and other environmental pollution) is one of the many large problems with which environmental scientists are faced. In remote sensing, the task is to map and classify the extent of the damage in forests from *aerial* and *satellite imagery*. In this example, the relationship between the different classes of damage and features in the images is less evident. Detailed investigations are necessary to reveal these complex relationships. Aerial images must be compared with ground truth data. We can expect to need more than one feature to identify certain classes of forest damage.

There are many similar applications in medical and biological science. One of the standard questions in medicine is to distinguish between "healthy" and "ill". Again, it

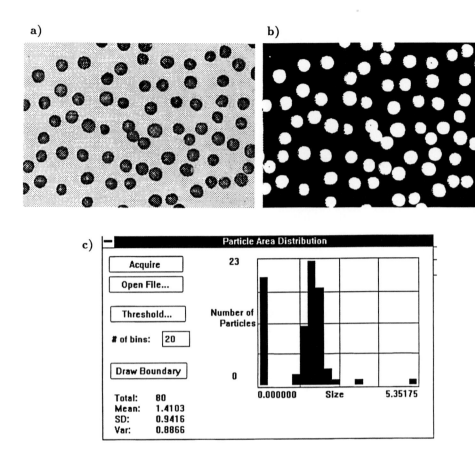

Figure 12.1: Illustration of the steps to analyze the size distribution of particles: a) original image; b) binary image; c) particle area distribution.

is obvious that we cannot expect a simple relationship between these two object classes and features of the observed objects in the images.

Summing up these two examples, we see that two tasks must be performed:

- First, the relation between the image features and the object classes sought must be investigated in as much detail as possible. This topic is partly comprised in the corresponding scientific area and partly in image formation, i. e., optics, as discussed in section 2.2.

- From the multitude of possible image features, we must select an optimal set which allows us to distinguish the different object classes unanimously and with as few errors as possible. This task, known as *classification*, is the topic of this chapter and is incorporated in the more general research area of *pattern recognition*.

Another aspect of classification is of interest to science. Often, the phenomena observed in images are not very well known. Analysis of the features of the observed objects may give some new insight into the phenomena observed. Actually, there are a number of examples where unexpected features were found in satellite or aerial imagery and which led to scientific discoveries. One such example has already been discussed in section 1.2.1 (figure 1.1). Scientists were first puzzled by the strong variations of the radar backscatter in correlation to the bottom topography in the imagery, knowing that microwaves do not penetrate the water surface and thus cannot image the bottom topography directly. It took some time to find out that a complex chain of interactions finally leads to the influence of the bottom topography on the small scale waves on the ocean surface which govern the backscatter of microwaves.

12.2   Feature Space; Clusters

Let us assume a well-defined class of objects. In satellite imagery this might be forests, inshore waters, agricultural or populated areas. Object classes may also be organized in a hierarchical manner. We might denote agricultural areas according to the crop planted and even separate them further by the quality of the crop such as ripeness, damage by parasites, or humidity of the soil.

Furthermore, let us assume that a set of P features has been extracted from the imagery. These features may either be pixel- or object-based. In the pixel-based case, it is often not possible to perform a segmentation with a single feature. Then we need more than one feature for each pixel to separate different classes of objects from each other and from the background. In the object-based classification, the objects could already be separated from the background. Then all the previously pixel-based features such as the mean gray value, local orientation, local wave number, and gray value variance can be averaged over the whole area of the object. Furthermore, we can use all parameters describing the shape of the objects as discussed in section 11.4.

Thus a classification can be performed at two different stages in image processing:
- *Pixel-based classification* in complex cases, where a segmentation of the objects is not possible with a single feature.
- *Object-based classification* to separate objects into different classes.
If at all possible, the latter case is preferable, since much less data must be handled; that is only one set of P features for each object detected.

The set of P features form a P-dimensional space, denoted as the *feature space*. Each pixel or object is represented as a *feature vector* in this space. If the features represent an object class well, all feature vectors of the objects from this class should lie close to each other in the feature space. We regard classification as a statistical process and assign a P-dimensional probability density function to each object class. In this sense, we can estimate this probability function by taking a probe of objects from a given class and increment the point in the discrete feature space in which the feature vector is pointing. This procedure is that of a generalized P-dimensional *histogram* (see section 4.2.3). When an object class shows a narrow probability distribution in the feature space, we speak of a *cluster*. It will be possible to separate the objects into the

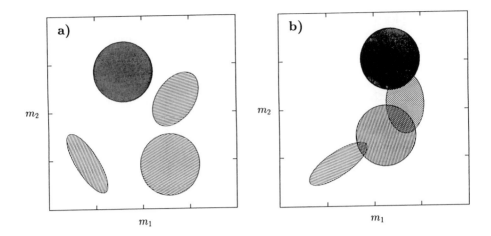

Figure 12.2: Schematic presentation of a two-dimensional feature space with four object classes:
a) well separated object classes; b) overlapping object classes.

given object classes if the clusters for the different object classes are well separated from
each other, as schematically illustrated in figure 12.2a. With less suitable features, the
clusters overlap each other (figure 12.2b). In this case, an error-free classification is not
possible.

We can regard the classification problem as an analysis of the structure of the feature
space. One object is thought of as a *pattern* in the feature space. Generally, we can
distinguish between *supervised* and *unsupervised* classification procedures. Supervision
of a classification procedure means determining the clusters in the feature space with
known objects beforehand. Then we know the number of classes and their location
and extension in the feature space. With unsupervised classification, no knowledge is
presumed about the objects to be classified. We compute the patterns in the feature
space from the objects we want to classify and then perform an analysis of the clusters in
the feature space. In this case, we even do not know the number of classes beforehand.
They result from the number of well-separated clusters in the feature space. Obviously,
this method is more objective, but it may result in a less favorable separation.

Finally, we speak of *learning* methods if the feature space is updated by each new
object which is classified. Learning methods can compensate any temporal trends in
the object features. Such trends may be due to simple reasons such as changes in the
illumination which could easily occur in an industrial environment because of changes
in daylight, ageing or dirtying of the illumination system.

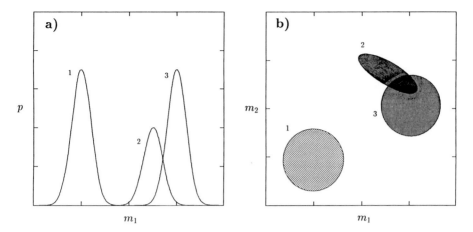

Figure 12.3: a) One-dimensional feature space with three object classes. b) Extension of the feature space with a second feature. The same object classes are shown.

12.3 Feature Selection; Principal-Axes Transform

The quality of the features is critical for a good classification. What does this mean? At first glance, we might think that as many features as possible would be the best solution. Generally, this is not the case. Figure 12.3a shows a one-dimensional feature space with three object classes. The features of the first and second class are separated, while those of the second and third class overlap considerably. A second feature does not necessarily improve the classification, as demonstrated in figure 12.3b. The clusters of the second and third class are still overlaid. A closer examination of the distribution in the feature space explains why: the second feature does not tell us much new. When feature one is low, feature two is low as well. The two features are correlated.

From this observation we draw the conclusion that we must choose the object features very carefully. Each feature should bring in new information which is orthogonal to what we already know about the object classes, i. e., object classes which show a similar distribution in one feature should differ in another feature. In other words, the features should be uncorrelated. The correlation of features can be studied with the statistical methods discussed in section 4.5.2.

The important quantity is the *cross covariance* of two features m_k and m_l (4.34)

$$C_{kl} = \langle (m_k - \langle m_k \rangle)(m_l - \langle m_l \rangle) \rangle . \qquad (12.1)$$

The cross-covariance is zero if both features are uncorrelated. With P features, we can form a symmetric matrix with the coefficients C_{kl}, the *covariance matrix*

$$C = \begin{bmatrix} C_{11} & C_{12} & \cdots & C_{1,P} \\ C_{12} & C_{22} & \cdots & C_{2,P} \\ \vdots & \vdots & \ddots & \vdots \\ C_{1,P} & C_{2,P} & \cdots & C_{P,P} \end{bmatrix} . \qquad (12.2)$$

The diagonal elements of the covariance matrix contain the variances of the P features, while the off-diagonal elements constitute the cross-covariances. As in every symmetric matrix, the covariance matrix can be diagonalized (compare our discussion on the inertia tensor in section 7.3.2). This procedure is called the *principal-axes transform*. It means that we can find a new coordinate system in which all features are uncorrelated. Those new features are linear combinations of the old features and are the eigenvectors of the covariance matrix. The corresponding eigenvalues are the variances. The best features show the largest variance; features with low variances are not of much help in separating different object classes and can be omitted without making the classification significantly worse.

A trivial, but illustrative example is the case when two features are nearly identical. Let us first assume that they are equal. Then the two rows in the covariance matrix are equal. The determinant of the matrix is zero and thus at least one eigenvalue equals zero. The corresponding eigenvector is the difference vector between the two features, since the variance of the difference of two equal features vanishes. In a similar train of thought we can argue for two very similar features. The difference between the two features will show a very small variance. If all other features are more distinct, the difference between the two features will be close to an eigenvector with the smallest eigenvalue (variance).

In this way we can use the principal-axes transform to reduce the dimension of the feature space and find a smaller set of features which does nearly as good a job. To avoid misunderstandings, the principal-axes transform cannot improve the separation quality. If a set of features cannot separate two classes, the same feature set transformed to the principal-axes coordinate system will not do it either. Given a set of features, we can only find an optimal subset and thus reduce the computational costs of classification.

Another principal consideration is worth mentioning. It is often overlooked how many different classes can be separated with a few parameters. Let us assume that one feature can only separate two classes. Then ten features can separate $2^{10} = 1024$ object classes. This simple example illustrates the high separation potential of just a few parameters. The essential problem is the even distribution of the clusters in the feature space. Consequently, it is important to find the right features, i. e., to study the relationship between the features of the objects and those in the images very carefully. The principal-axes transform will be very helpful in removing any unnecessary features.

Even if we take the best features available there may be classes which cannot be separated. In such a case it is always worth reminding ourselves that separating the objects in well-defined classes is only a model of reality. Often the transition from one class to another may not be abrupt but rather gradual. For example, anomalies in a cell may be present to a varying degree, there not being two distinct classes, "normal" and "pathological", but rather a continuous transition between the two. Thus we cannot expect to always find well separated classes in the feature space.

In another important application, *optical character recognition*, or OCR, we do have distinct classes. Each letter is a well-defined class. While it is easy to distinguish most letters, some such as the large 'O' and the figure '0', or the letters 'b' and 'p' are very similar, i. e., lie close to each other in the feature space. Such similar but distinct classes cause serious problems.

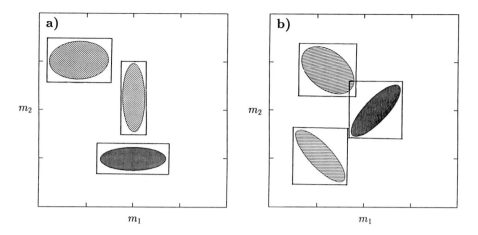

Figure 12.4: Classification according to the box method: a) with orthogonal features; b) with correlated features.

12.4   Classification Techniques

In this section we study the different classification methods. For a more detailed discussion we refer to *Niemann* [1981]. We assume that the classes and their distribution in the feature space are known (supervised classification).

The simplest classification method is the *look-up method*. In this case, we attribute a number indicating the object class to each point in the discrete feature space. This approach is difficult only if the distributions of two classes overlap. In this case we have two choices. First, we could take the class which shows the higher probability at this point. Second, we could argue that an error-free classification is not possible with this feature and give it the attribute zero indicating that we cannot classify an object with this feature. The same attribute is given to all the points in the feature space which do not belong to any object class. After this procedure known as *labeling*, we just have to look up which class a feature vector belongs to. We regard the feature space as a *multidimensional look-up table*. Without doubt, this method is best with respect to the computing time. However, concerning the memory needed to store the feature space it is not so advantageous. A three-dimensional $64 \times 64 \times 64$ feature space already requires 1/4 Mbyte memory. Consequently, the look-up method is only feasible for low-dimensional feature spaces.

All other classification methods model the pattern classes in the feature space to reduce storage requirements. The *box method* approximates a class by a surrounding box. Figure 12.4a illustrates that this approximation works well if the features are orthogonal. The box method results in a poor approximation with correlated features (figure 12.4b). Then the boxes are much larger than the clusters and may overlay each other although the clusters themselves may be very well separated. The box method is also very fast, since only comparison operations with the components of the feature

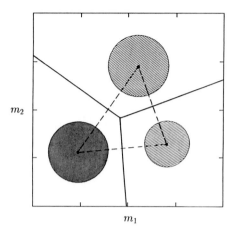

m_2

m_1

Figure 12.5: Classification according to the minimum distance method.

coordinates are necessary to check in which box a feature vector is located. The method also requires that all boxes representing the different classes are disjunct.

If this is not the case, we need to use other methods. An object class in feature space can also be represented by its *center of mass*. If the standard deviations of the clusters are about the same, we can use the *minimum distance method* to determine which class a feature vector belongs to. We compute the distance of the feature vector to all cluster centers and choose the class which has the minimum distance. Geometrically, we part the feature space by hyperplanes which meet the lines connecting the centers of gravity perpendicularly half way (figure 12.5).

Finally, we might approximate each pattern class in the P-dimensional feature space by a P-dimensional normal probability function. For each of the object classes, we then compute the probability that a given feature belongs to it and choose the class which shows the *maximum* probability for this feature. This approach is known as the *maximum probability method*. It also allows us to compute the statistical significances with which we attribute the feature vector to one or another class.

12.5   Application

In conclusion of this chapter, we discuss a realistic classification problem. Figure 12.7a shows the image with three different seeds, namely sunflower seeds, lentils, and peppercorns. This simple example shows many properties which are typical for a classification problem. Although the three classes are well defined, a careful consideration of the features to be used for classification is necessary since it is not immediately evident which parameters can be successfully used to distinguish between the three classes. Furthermore, the shape of the seeds, especially of the sunflower seeds shows

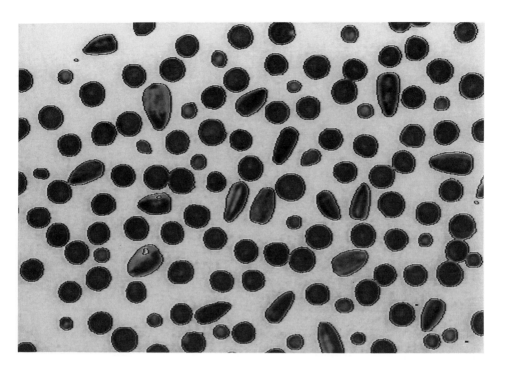

Figure 12.6: A segmented image containing three classes of seeds, lentils, sunflower seeds, and peppercorns. The detected object boundaries based on a simple pixel-based threshold segmentation are marked black. Processed with BioScan OPTIMAS.

Table 12.1: Parameters and results of the simple box classification for the seeds shown in figure 12.7. The corresponding feature space is shown in Figure 12.8.

	Area	Circularity	Number
total	-	-	130
peppercorns	0.1–1.0	< 15.0	23
lentils	1.0–2.0	< 14.6	66
sunflower seeds	> 1.5	14.6-20.0	18
not classified			23

considerable fluctuations.

As a first feature we consider the area. Obviously, the lentils are larger than the peppercorns but comparable in size with the sunflower seeds. Consequently, the area alone is not sufficient to separate the three classes. We arrive at a similar conclusion if we consider the circularity (see section 11.4). We will probably only separate the more elongated sunflower seeds from the circular peppercorns and lentils.

Using both parameters, area and circularity, we can separate all the three classes. We observe two clusters in the lower left of the feature space which correspond to the

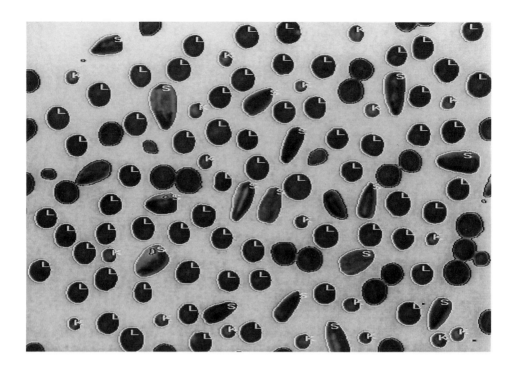

Figure 12.7: Same image as in figure 12.6 after classification. The boundaries of the classified objects are labeled (L: lentils, S: sunflower seeds, and K: peppercorns). Processed with BioScan OPTIMAS.

peppercorns and the lentils (figure 12.8). Because of the larger fluctuations in the shape of the sunflower seeds, we do not recognize a similar cluster for them. A simple box classification is sufficient to separate the three classes. The boxes are marked in figure 12.8. OPTIMAS allows to write down the rules for class membership in a powerful macro language. The conditions for the box classification shown in table 12.1 read as

```
Peppercorns:     ArArea > 0.1 && ArArea < 1.0 && ArCircularity < 15.0
Lentils:         ArArea > 1.0 && ArArea < 2.0 && ArCircularity < 14.6
Sunflower seeds: ArArea > 1.5 && ArCircularity > 14.6 && ArCircularity < 20.0
```

The result of the classification is shown in figure 12.7 and table 12.1. The boundaries of the classified objects are highlighted and the objects are marked with a letter indicating the class membership. From a total of 130 objects, 107 objects could be recognized. Objects which do not belong to any class are shown with a black boundary. They could not be assigned to any of the three classes, because of one of the following reasons:

- Two or more objects were so close to each other that they merged into one object. Then both the area and the circularity show high values.
- The object was located at the edge of the image and thus was only partly visible.
- The object was a small dirt particle or a hole in another object.

Although we chose a simple classification method, the results are satisfying. After

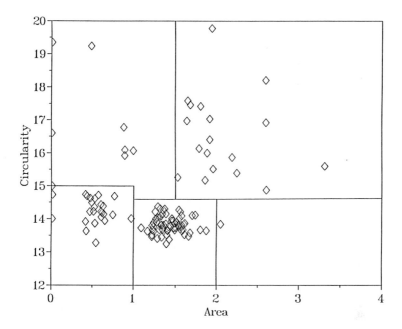

Figure 12.8: Feature space for the classification of the different types of seeds from figure 12.7a. The feature space is spanned by the features area and circularity.

classification, we can interactively select objects to check for their parameters. Figure 12.9 shows a selected object, the merger of two lentils, and the corresponding features area and circularity in view boxes. It has about twice the circularity of a circular object.

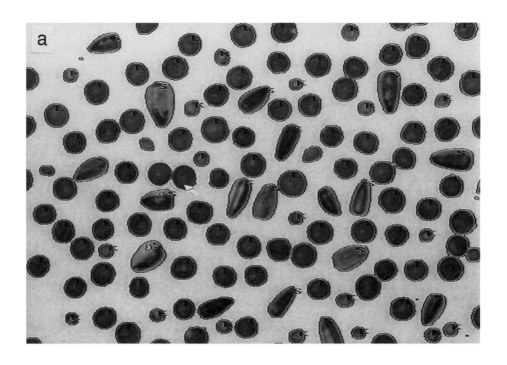

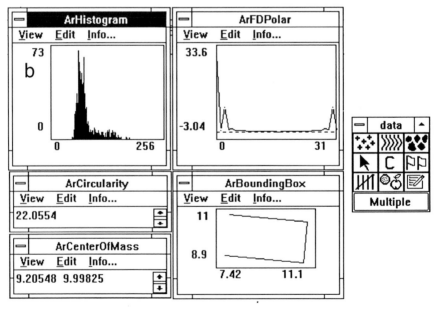

Figure 12.9: Interactive display of the features of a selected object in view boxes: a) selected object; b) viewboxes on the Windows screen. Processed with BioScan OPTIMAS.

13 Reconstruction from Projections

13.1 Introduction

In chapter 2 we discussed in detail how a discrete two-dimensional image is formed from a three-dimensional scene by an optical system. In this chapter we discuss the *inverse* process, the reconstruction of a three-dimensional scene from two-dimensional projections. Reconstruction from only one projection is an *underdetermined inverse problem* which generally shows an infinite number of solutions. As an illustration, figure 13.1 shows the perspective projection of a bar onto an image plane. We will obtain identical projections at the image plane, whenever the endpoints of a bar lie on the same projection beams. Even if the bar shows a curvature in the projection plane, we will still see a straight line at the image plane.

In order to gain the third dimension, we need additional information. In this introduction we will first summarize the many sources from which we can infer depth information. From the research on the reconstruction problem different key areas emerged and are denoted as *structure from ...* paradigms.

Structure from Stereo
The human visual system perceives depth by observation with two eyes. Thus it seems quite natural to imitate this property of the biological visual systems with a stereo

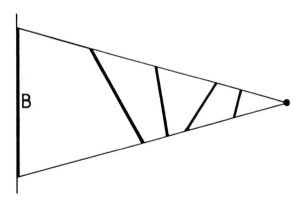

Figure 13.1: Ambiguities of the perspective projection of a bar onto an image plane.

camera setup. As discussed in section 2.2.9, we can infer the depth of an object point from its displacement (parallax) between the two images. This method only works if a *single* opaque surface is projected onto the image plane but no longer if the intensity on the image plane is composed of projections from many transparent objects. Although this is a severe restriction, it does not restrict the reconstruction of natural scenes significantly, since most scenes contain only non-transparent surfaces.

Structure from Projections

Scenes which contain true three-dimensional objects and not just nontransparent surfaces are common in scientific applications. They include tomographic techniques as discussed in section 2.2.10, focus series (section 2.2.5), and series of cross sectional images (section 2.2.8). Common to all these techniques is the fact that they take a large number of images. In tomographic applications, projections are taken from many different directions to reconstruct the three-dimensional structure of the observed object.

Structure from Shape

In section 1.3 we were already faced with the astonishing capability of the human visual system to recognize the three-dimensional shapes (figure 1.5). This approach to the reconstruction problem is called *structure from shape*. It can only be successful if an enormous amount of knowledge about geometrical shapes is available which can be used to evaluate the newly experienced perception.

Structure from Shading

The brightness of a surface depends on its orientation with respect to the illumination and the observer, as discussed in section 2.1. Generally, edges of an object show up as brightness discontinuities. If the illumination of a scene is uniform, constant brightness can be found if the object surfaces are flat. Gradually changing brightness indicates curved surfaces. It is easy to recognize cylindrical and spherical surfaces (see also plates 3 and 6a). So far, the qualitative reasoning sounds promising. A more quantitative analysis, however, is very difficult and depends on a good knowledge of the illumination conditions. Shape analysis also shows ambiguities. A convex-shaped surface illuminated from above shows the same surface shading as a concave-shaped surface illuminated from below.

Structure from Texture

Characteristic scales and orientation of the texture depend on the orientation of the surface. Thus we can infer the orientation of a surface from the orientation of the texture. Moreover, we can infer the depth of the surface from the characteristic scale of the texture. In this sense, texture is a richer feature than the shading of an object. Edges between surfaces can be recognized by discontinuities in the orientation of the texture. Gradual changes give clues on cylindrically and spherically shaped surfaces.

Structure from Motion

The analysis of motion also provides clues as to the depth of a scene. Intuitively, a more distant object will move slower on the image plane. If the camera moves towards a scene, objects which are closer to the camera move faster than more distant objects. Moreover, motion of the camera results in an observation of the scene from a different point of view. Objects which are occluded by observation from one perspective might be visible from another perspective. Since we will discuss motion analysis in detail in chapters 14–17, we will leave the discussion here with these few qualitative remarks.

Summary
Many of the briefly outlined approaches are still at the beginning. All of them are still active areas of research. Interested readers can find a good survey in the "Readings on Computer Vision", edited by *Fischler and Firschein* [1987], the special issue of the journal *Artificial Intelligence* 17, 1–3 [1981] on computer vision, and *Shirai* [1987].

In this chapter we focus on the reconstruction methods which are widely used in scientific applications. Basically, we discuss two different approaches. In our discussion on optical imaging, we concluded that the depth of focus depends to a large extent on the imaging conditions (section 2.2.5), as do three-dimensional imaging and reconstruction methods. In section 13.2 we discuss the reconstruction from focus series. Focus series are taken with microscopes where the depth of focus is very low. Then, in section 13.3, we discuss reconstruction from tomographic images (see section 2.2.10). Tomographic imaging is characterized by a large depth of focus. Absorption or emission of radiation from all depths of the observed objects is superimposed evenly in the observed projections.

Reconstruction of the depth of surfaces from stereo images can be regarded as a special case of motion analysis. A stereo image can be thought as two consecutive images of an image sequence, where the camera moves from the position of the left to the position of the right stereo camera while observing a static scene. Consequently, we discuss stereo image analysis not in a separate section but together with the analysis of motion in chapter 17.

13.2   Focus Series

13.2.1   Reconstruction of Surfaces in Space

Before we discuss the more complex problem of reconstructing a truly three-dimensional object from focus series, we study the simpler case of the reconstruction of a single surface. Surfaces occur in all cases where non-transparent surfaces are observed with microscopes. *Steurer et al.* [1986] developed a simple method to reconstruct a *depth map* from a light microscopic focus series. A depth map is a two-dimensional function which gives the depth of an object point $d(x_1, x_2)$ — relative to a reference plane — as a function of the image coordinates (x_1, x_2). In the literature on artificial intelligence, such a depth map is also called a *2 1/2-D sketch* of the scene.

With the given restrictions, only one depth value for each image point needs to be found. We can make use of the fact that the three-dimensional point spread of optical imaging we discussed in detail in section 2.2.6 has a distinct maximum on the focal plane, because the intensity falls off with the square of the distance from the focal plane. This means that at all points where we get distinct image points, such as edges,

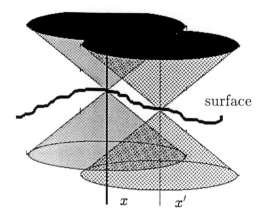

Figure 13.2: Superposition of the point spread function of two neighboring points on a surface.

lines, or local extrema, we will also obtain an extremum in the gray value on the focal plane. Figure 13.2 illustrates that the point spread functions of neighboring image points do not influence each other close to the focal plane.

Steurer's method makes use of the fact that a distinct maximum of the point spread function exists in the focal plane. His algorithm includes the following steps:

1. A focus series of 16 images is taken with constant depth differences. In order to improve the signal-to-noise ratio, several images are digitized and averaged at each depth level.

2. Then the magnitude of the difference between consecutive images is computed. The magnitude of the difference is maximal on the focal plane.

3. Such a maximum only occurs in image regions with gray value changes. Therefore, a Sobel operator is used to filter out such image regions. The highpass filtered images are segmented to obtain a mask for the regions with gray value changes.

4. In the masked regions, we then search the maximal magnitude of the difference in all the images of the focus series. The image in which the maximum occurs gives a depth value for the depth map.

5. Since the depth map will not be dense, an interpolation of the depth map is necessary. Steurer used a region-growing method followed by an adaptive lowpass filtering which is applied only to the interpolated regions, in order not to corrupt the directly computed depth values.

This method was successfully used to determine the surface structure of worked metal pieces by a noninvasive method. Figure 13.3 shows that good results have been achieved. A filing can be seen which sticks out of the surface. Moreover, the surface shows clear traces from the grinding process.

13.2.2 Reconstruction by Inverse Filtering

If true three-dimensional objects and not only surfaces are involved, we need to reconstruct the 3-D object function $g(\boldsymbol{x})$ from the 3-D focus series which is blurred by the

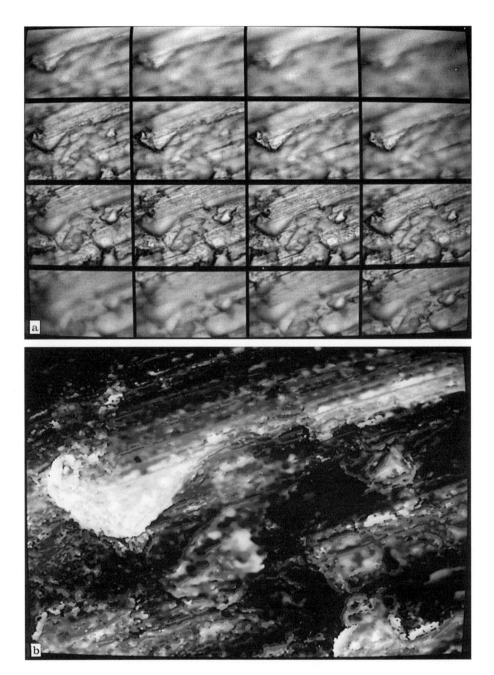

Figure 13.3: a) Focus series with 16 images of a metallic surface taken with depth distances of $2\,\mu$m; the focal plane becomes deeper from the right to the left and from top to bottom. b) Depth map computed from the focus series. Depth is coded by intensity. Objects closer to the observer are shown brighter. From *Steurer et al.* [1986].

3-D point spread function of optical imaging. It is obvious that an exact knowledge of the PSF is essential for a good reconstruction. In section 2.2.6 we computed the 3-D PSF of optical imaging neglecting lens errors and resolution limitation due to diffraction. However, high magnification microscopy images are diffraction-limited. Therefore the simple analysis in section 2.2.6 is not adequate.

The diffraction-limited 3-D PSF was computed by *Erhardt* [1985]. The resolution limit basically changes the double-cone close to the focal plane. At the focal plane it does not reduce to a point but to a diffraction disk. As a result, the OTF drops off to higher wave numbers in the k_x, k_y plane. We can regard the diffraction-limited resolution as an additional lowpass filter by which the OTF for unlimited resolution is multiplied. This filtering produces the effects on the PSF and OTF described above.

If the OTF is known exactly, reconstruction by *inverse filtering* becomes — at least principally — a simple procedure. The distortion of the focus series by the point spread function H must be reversed by application of the *inverse operator* H^{-1}. We can perform this operation either in the Fourier or in the space domain:

$$
\begin{aligned}
G &= \mathcal{F}^{-1}\left(\hat{H}^{-1}\mathcal{F}G'\right) \\
G &= \left(\mathcal{F}^{-1}\hat{H}^{-1}\right) * G'.
\end{aligned}
\tag{13.1}
$$

G' and G denote the measured and original 3-D image, respectively, and $\mathcal{F}$ is the Fourier transform operator. In the Fourier domain, we multiply the Fourier transformed focus series by the inverse OTF $\hat{H}^{-1}$. From the result we compute the inverse Fourier transform and obtain the reconstructed focus series. We can also perform the inverse filter operation in the space domain. First we compute the inverse Fourier transform of the inverse of the OTF $\hat{H}^{-1}$. Then we obtain a convolution kernel which inverses the effect of the PSF.

So far the procedure looks simple and straightforward. The real problems are related to the fact that the OTF shows a wide range in which it vanishes (see figure 2.9 in section 2.2.7).

This means that a whole range of periodic structures is completely lost in the image. Without additional knowledge we cannot reconstruct these components from the focus series. The reconstruction problem becomes even more complicated if the images are corrupted with noise. If a periodic component is attenuated below the noise level, we must multiply the Fourier transformed focus series at the corresponding wave number by a large factor. The periodic component will get back to its original value, but the noise level will increase also. In other words, the signal-to-noise ratio will be left unchanged.

The simplest approach to yield an optimum reconstruction is to limit application of the inverse OTF to the wave number components which are not damped below a critical threshold. This threshold depends on the noise in the images. In this way, the true inverse OTF is replaced by an effective inverse OTF which approaches zero again in the wave number regions which cannot be reconstructed.

The results of such a reconstruction procedure are shown in plate 14. A $64 \times 64 \times 64$ focus series has been taken from the nucleus of a cancerous rat liver cell. The resolution in all directions is $0.22\,\mu\text{m}$. The images clearly verify the theoretical considerations. The reconstruction considerably improves the resolution in the xy image planes, while the resolution in z direction is clearly worse.

Better resolution can only be achieved if additional knowledge is introduced into the reconstruction process. We illustrate the importance of such conditions with a simple example. Let us assume that our image contains only two gray values as, for example, a sheet of paper with letters. Assuming that only two gray values are present in the image and that the PSF of the blurring is even, we know that the edges between the letters and the background are located at the mean between the two gray values. Thus we may suggest a very simple reconstruction process which is just a simple point-based segmentation process with a threshold at that level. Reconstruction methods which impose constraints on the reconstructed images are known as *constrained deconvolution* or *constraint inverse filtering*.

Unconstrained inverse filtering can also be performed in the space domain using an iterative method. Let $\mathcal{H}$ be the blurring operator. We introduce a new operator $\mathcal{H}' = \mathcal{I} - \mathcal{H}$. Then the inverse operator

$$\mathcal{H}^{-1} = \frac{\mathcal{I}}{\mathcal{I} - \mathcal{H}'} \tag{13.2}$$

can be approximated by the Taylor expansion

$$\mathcal{H}^{-1} = \mathcal{I} + \mathcal{H}' + \mathcal{H}'^2 + \mathcal{H}'^3 + \ldots + \mathcal{H}'^k, \tag{13.3}$$

or explicitly written for the OTF in the Fourier domain

$$\hat{H}^{-1} = 1 + \hat{H}' + \hat{H}'^2 + \hat{H}'^3 + \ldots + \hat{H}'^k. \tag{13.4}$$

In order to understand how the iteration works, we consider periodic structures. First, we take one which is only slightly attenuated. This means that $\hat{H}$ is only slightly less than one. Thus $\hat{H}'$ is small and the expansion converges rapidly. The other extreme could be if the periodic structure has nearly vanished. Then $\hat{H}'$ is close to one. Consequently the amplitude of the periodic structure increases by the same amount with each iteration step (linear convergence). This procedure shows the advantage that we can stop the iteration when the noise becomes visible.

Unfortunately it is an exception that constraints lead to such a straightforward reconstruction algorithm as for our simplistic example. Generally, the introduction of constraints poses difficult mathematical problems which are beyond the scope of this book.

13.2.3 Confocal Laser Scanning Microscopy

From the previous section we can conclude that it is not possible to reconstruct three-dimensional images entirely from a focus series obtained with conventional light microscopy. A wide range of wave numbers is lost completely, because of the zeros in the OTF. Generally, the lost structures cannot be recovered. Therefore the question arises, whether it is possible to change the image formation and thus the point spread function so that the optical transfer function no longer vanishes, especially in the z direction.

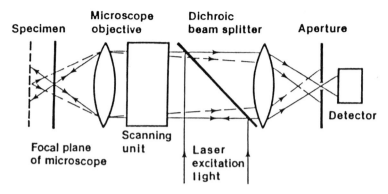

Figure 13.4: Principle of confocal laser scanning microscopy.

One answer to this question is *confocal laser scanning microscopy*. Its basic principle is to illuminate only the points in the focal plane. This is achieved by a laser beam which scans over the image plane and is focused by the optics of the microscope onto the focal plane (figure 13.4). Since the same optics are used for imaging and illumination, the intensity distribution in the object is given approximately by the point spread function of the microscope. (Slight differences occur since the light is coherent.) Only a thin slice close to the focal plane receives a strong illumination. Outside this slice, the illumination falls off with the distance squared from the focal plane. In this way contributions from defocused objects outside the focal plane are strongly suppressed and the distortions decrease. But can we achieve a complete distortion-free reconstruction? We will use two independent trains of thought to answer this question.

Let us first imagine a periodic structure in the z direction. In conventional microscopy, this structure is lost since all depths are illuminated equally. In confocal microscopy, however, we can still observe a periodic variation in the z direction because of the strong decrease of the illumination intensity provided that the wavelength in the z direction is not too small.

The same fact can be illustrated using the PSF. The PSF of confocal microscopy is given as the product of spatial intensity distribution and the PSF of the optical imaging. Since both functions fall off with z^{-2}, the PSF of the confocal microscope falls off with z^{-4}. This much sharper localization of the PSF in the z direction results in a non-zero OTF in the z direction up to the z resolution limit.

The superior 3-D imaging of confocal laser scanning microscopy can be seen in the original images of the focus series (plate 15). Although these images are noisier, they contain more details than seen in plate 14. Furthermore, the resolution in the z direction is much better.

The laser scanning microscope has found widespread application in medical and biological sciences.

13.3   Reconstruction of Tomographic Images

13.3.1   Introduction

Now we turn to the reconstruction of 3-D objects from which projections have been taken with tomographic methods (section 2.2.10). With these techniques, we first slice the object. Then we observe the one-dimensional projections of these slices from all directions, i. e., in an angular range from 0 to π. Therefore, our task is the reconstruction of these slices. The final three-dimensional object is then given by a stack of these slices.

Tomographic methods have gained significant importance in medical diagnostics. Three-dimensional data from within the human body are essential for the exact location of tumors, the planning of complex surgery, and other diagnostic or therapeutic tasks. A wide variety of methods is used to image different properties of the tissue. Basically, we can distinguish three imaging methods: *absorption-*, *emission-* and *time-of-flight* tomography.

The best known example is probably X-ray tomography. The part of the patient's body to be examined is X-rayed from different directions. The intensity variations in the projections are related to a) the path length through the body and b) the absorption coefficient which depends on the nature of the tissue, basically the atomic weight of the elements. Emission tomography can be applied by injection of radioactive substances into the organ to be investigated. A complex form of stimulated emission tomography is *nuclear magnetic resonance tomography* (NMR).

Ultrasonic imaging is another important area. As with X-rays, we can measure the absorption for imaging. Furthermore, the speed of sound depends on the elasticity properties of the medium. The speed of sound can be investigated by measuring the time-of-flight. All this might look very promising, but ultrasonic imaging is made very difficult by the reflection and refraction of rays at interfaces between the layers of different speeds of sound.

Besides medical applications, tomographic methods are used in many other scientific areas. This is not surprising, since many complex phenomena can only be understood adequately if three-dimensional data can be obtained such as acoustic tomography in oceanography [*Knox*, 1989], the study of technical combustion, and three-dimensional imaging of turbulent flows with holographic methods.

Before we can discuss the reconstruction algorithms themselves, we must carefully study the prerequisites necessary to find a solution. If we want to treat the problem with a linear method, it is essential that the objects are linearly superimposed in the projections. This condition is met when the imaged property κ can be integrated along a projection beam.

$$I = \int_{\text{path}} d\boldsymbol{s}\ \kappa(s). \tag{13.5}$$

In emission tomography, the emitted radiation may not be absorbed from other parts of the object. In absorption tomography, the imaged property is the absorption coefficient μ. The differential intensity loss dI along a path element $d\boldsymbol{s}$ is proportional to

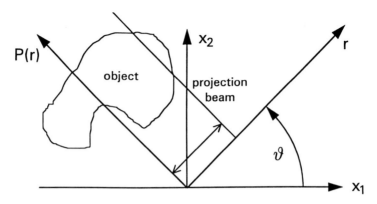

Figure 13.5: Geometry of a projection beam.

the absorption coefficient $\mu(\boldsymbol{x})$, to ds, and to the intensity $I(\boldsymbol{x})$:

$$dI = -\mu(\boldsymbol{x})I(\boldsymbol{x})\,d\boldsymbol{s}. \tag{13.6}$$

Integration yields

$$\ln\frac{I}{I_0} = -\int_{\text{path}} d\boldsymbol{s}\,\mu(\boldsymbol{x}). \tag{13.7}$$

The logarithm of the intensity is the proper quantity to be measured, since it results from a linear superimposition of the absorption coefficient. Generally, the intensity is not suitable, except when the total absorption is low. Then we can approximate $\ln(I/I_0)$ by $I/I_0 - 1$.

Tomographic reconstruction does not work at all if opaque objects are contained in the examined scene. In this case, we get only the shape of the opaque object in the projection, but not any information on the transparent objects which lie before, in, or behind this object.

13.3.2   Radon Transform and Fourier Slice Theorem

In section 2.2.10 we described the parallel projection but only qualitatively. First it is important to note that the projections under all the angles ϑ can be regarded as another two-dimensional representation of the image. One coordinate is the position in the projection profile, r, the other the angle ϑ. Consequently, we can regard the parallel projection as a transformation, which transforms the image into another two-dimensional representation. Reconstruction then just means applying the inverse transformation provided that it exists.

A projection beam is characterized by the angle of the normal to the projection beam, ϑ, and the offset r (figure 13.5). Furthermore, we assume that we slice the three-dimensional object parallel to the x_1x_2 plane. Then the scalar product between a vector $\boldsymbol{x}$ on the projection beam, and a unit vector $\boldsymbol{n}^T = \begin{bmatrix} \cos\vartheta, \sin\vartheta \end{bmatrix}$ normal to the projection beam is constant and equal to the offset r of the beam

$$\boldsymbol{x}^T\boldsymbol{n} - r = x_1\cos\vartheta + x_2\sin\vartheta - r = 0. \tag{13.8}$$

The projected intensity $P(r, \vartheta)$ is given by integration along the projection beam:

$$P(r, \vartheta) = \int_{path} d\boldsymbol{s} \; g(\boldsymbol{x}) = \int_{-\infty}^{\infty} d\boldsymbol{s} \; g(\boldsymbol{x}) \delta(x_1 \cos \vartheta + x_2 \sin \vartheta - r). \qquad (13.9)$$

The projective transformation of a two-dimensional function $g(\boldsymbol{x})$ onto $P(r, \vartheta)$ is named after the mathematician *Radon* as the *Radon transform*. To understand the properties of the Radon transform better, we analyze it in the Fourier space. This is easily done if we rotate the coordinate system so that the direction of a projection beam coincides with the x_1 axis. Then the r coordinate in $P(r, \vartheta)$ also coincides with the x_2 coordinate and we can write the Fourier transform of the projection function in the rotated coordinate systems (x_1', x_2') and (k_1', k_2'), respectively:

$$\hat{P}(k_2', 0) = \int_{-\infty}^{\infty} dx_2' P(x_2', 0) \exp(-ik_2' x_2'). \qquad (13.10)$$

The angle ϑ is zero in the rotated coordinate system. Replacing $P(x_2', 0)$ by the definition of the Radon transform (13.9) we yield

$$\hat{P}(k_2', 0) = \int_{-\infty}^{\infty} dx_2' \left[\int_{-\infty}^{\infty} dx_1' \; g(x_1', x_2') \right] \exp(-ik_2' x_2') = \hat{g}(0, k_2'), \qquad (13.11)$$

or, with regard to the original coordinate system,

$$\hat{P}(r, \vartheta) = \hat{P} \left[|\boldsymbol{k}|, \arctan(k_2/k_1) \right] = \hat{g}(\boldsymbol{k}^T \boldsymbol{n}). \qquad (13.12)$$

The spectrum of the projection is identical to the spectrum of the original object on a beam normal to the direction of the projection beam. This important result is called the *Fourier slice theorem* or *projection theorem*.

We can derive the Fourier slice theorem without any computation if we regard the projection as a linear shift-invariant filter operation. Since the projection adds up all the gray values along the projection beam, the point spread function of the projection operator is a δ line in the direction of the projection beam. In the Fourier domain this convolution operation corresponds to a multiplication with the transfer function, a δ line normal to the δ line in the space domain (see appendix A.2). In this way, the projection operator cuts out a slice of the spectrum in the normal direction to the projection direction.

13.3.3 Filtered Back Projection

Principle

The considerations of the previous section form the base for a reconstruction procedure which is called *filtered back projection*. If the projections include projections from all directions, the obtained slices of the spectrum eventually cover the complete spectrum of the object. Inverse Fourier transform then yields the original object. Filtered back projection uses this approach with a slight modification. If we just added the spectra of the individual projection beams to obtain the complete spectrum of the object, the spectral density for small wave numbers would be too high since the beams are closer to each other for small radii. Thus we must correct the spectrum with a suitable weighting factor. In the continuous case, the geometry is very easy. The density of the projection beams aligns with $|\boldsymbol{k}|^{-1}$. Consequently, the spectra of the projection beams must be multiplied by $|\boldsymbol{k}|$. Thus filtered back projection is a two-step process:

1. *Filtering of the projections*: In this step, we multiply the spectrum of each projection direction by a suitable weighting function $\hat{w}(|\boldsymbol{k}|)$. Of course, this operation can also be performed as a convolution with the inverse Fourier transform of $\hat{w}(|\boldsymbol{k}|)$, $w(r)$. Because of this step, the procedure is called the *filtered* back projection.

2. *Addition of the back projections*: Each projection gives a slice of the spectrum. Adding up all the filtered spectra yields the complete spectrum. Since the Fourier transform is a linear operation, we can add up the filtered projections in the space domain. In the space domain, each filtered projection contains part of the object which is constant in the direction of the projection beam. Thus we can backproject the corresponding gray value of the filtered projection along the direction of the projection beam and add it up to the contributions from the other projection beams.

Continuous Case

After this illustrative description of the principle of the filtered back projection algorithm we derive the method quantitatively. First we restrict to the continuous case. We start with the spectrum of the object and write the inverse transformation in polar coordinates (r, ϑ) in order to make use of the Fourier slice theorem

$$g(\boldsymbol{x}) = \int\limits_0^{2\pi} d\vartheta \int\limits_0^\infty dr\, r\hat{g}(r,\vartheta) \exp[ir(x_1 \cos\vartheta + x_2 \sin\vartheta)]. \qquad (13.13)$$

In this formula, the spectrum is already multiplied by the magnitude of the wave number, r, but the integration boundaries are not yet correct to be applied to the Fourier slice theorem (13.12). r should run from $-\infty$ to ∞ and ϑ only from 0 to π. In (13.13) we integrate only over half beams. We can compose a full beam from two half beams at the angles ϑ and $\vartheta + \pi$. Thus we split the integral in (13.13) into two over the angle ranges $0 - \pi$ and $\pi - 2\pi$ and obtain

$$\begin{aligned} g(\boldsymbol{x}) &= \int\limits_0^\pi d\vartheta \int\limits_0^\infty dr\, r\hat{g}(r,\vartheta) \exp[ir(x_1 \cos\vartheta + x_2 \sin\vartheta)] \\ &+ \int\limits_0^\pi d\vartheta' \int\limits_0^\infty dr\, r\hat{g}(-r,\vartheta') \exp[-ir(x_1 \cos\vartheta' + x_2 \sin\vartheta')]. \qquad (13.14) \end{aligned}$$

We used the following identities: $\vartheta' = \vartheta + \pi$, $\hat{g}(-r,\vartheta) = \hat{g}(r,\vartheta')$, $\cos(\vartheta') = -\cos(\vartheta)$, $\sin(\vartheta') = -\sin(\vartheta)$. Now we can recompose the two integrals again, if we substitute r by $-r$ in the second integral and replace $\hat{g}(r,\vartheta)$ by $\hat{P}(r,\vartheta)$ because of the Fourier slice theorem (13.12):

$$g(\boldsymbol{x}) = \int\limits_0^\pi d\vartheta \int\limits_{-\infty}^\infty dr\, |r|\hat{P}(r,\vartheta) \exp[ir(x_1 \cos\vartheta + x_2 \sin\vartheta)]. \qquad (13.15)$$

With the abbreviation

$$t = x_1 \cos \vartheta + x_2 \sin \vartheta$$

we can reduce the two steps of the filtered back projection algorithm to the following formulas:

1. *Filtering; inner integral in (13.15):*

$$P' = \mathcal{F}^{-1}(|\boldsymbol{k}|\mathcal{F}P). \tag{13.16}$$

$\boldsymbol{F}$ denotes the Fourier transform operator. P' is the projection function P multiplied in the Fourier space by $|k|$. If we perform this operation as a convolution in the space domain, we can formally write

$$P' = [\mathcal{F}^{-1}(|\boldsymbol{k}|)] * P. \tag{13.17}$$

2. *Back projection; outer integral in (13.15):*

$$g(\boldsymbol{x}) = \int_0^\pi P'(r, \vartheta)\, d\vartheta. \tag{13.18}$$

This equation shows how the object is built up by the back projections from all directions.

Discrete Case

There are several details which we have not yet discussed, but which cause serious problems for the reconstruction in the infinite continuous case, especially:

• The inverse Fourier transform of the weighting function $|\boldsymbol{k}|$ does not exist, because this function is not square-integrable.

• It is impossible to reconstruct the mean "gray value" of an object because of the multiplication by $|r| = |\boldsymbol{k}|$ in the Fourier domain (13.15).

   Actually, we never apply the infinite continuous case, but only compute using discrete data. Basically, there are three effects which distinguish the idealized reconstruction from the real-world:

• The object is of limited size. In practice, the size limit is given by the distance between the radiation source and the detector.

• The resolution of the projection profile is limited by the combined effects of the extent of the radiation source and the resolution of the detector array in the projection plane.

• Finally, we can only take a limited number of projections. This corresponds to a sampling of the angle ϑ in the Radon representation of the image.

   In the following we will discuss some of these practical reconstruction problems using illustrative examples.

Projection and Reconstruction of a Point

We can learn a lot about the projection and reconstruction by considering the reconstruction of a simple object, a point. Then the projections from all directions are equal (figure 13.6a) and show a sharp maximum in the projection functions $P(r, \vartheta_i)$. In the first step of the filtered back projection algorithm, P is convolved with the $|k|$ filter.

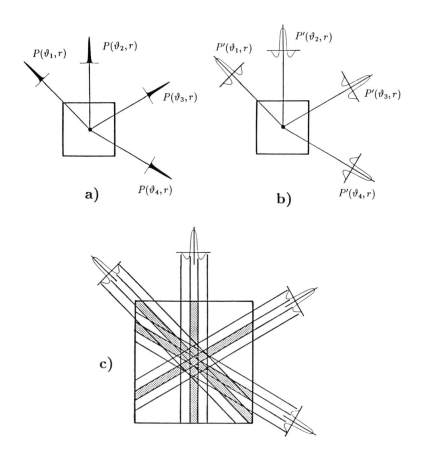

Figure 13.6: Illustration of the filtered back projection algorithm with a point object: a) projections from different directions; b) filtering of the projection functions; c) back projection: adding up the filtered projections.

The result is a modified projection function P' which is identical to the point spread function of the $|k|$ filter (figure 13.6b).

In a second step, the back projections are added up in the image. From figure 13.6c we can see that at the position of the point in the image the peaks from all projections add up. At all other positions in the images, the filtered back projections superimpose each other in a destructive manner, since they show negative and positive values. If the projection directions are sufficiently close to each other, they cancel each other except for the point in the center of the image. Figure 13.6c also demonstrates that an insufficient number of projections leads to star-shaped distortion patterns.

The simple example of the reconstruction of a point from its projections is also useful to show the importance of filtering the projections. Let us imagine what happens when we omit this step. Then we would add up δ lines as back projections which rotate

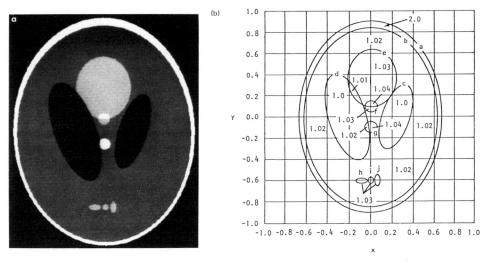

Figure 13.7: The head phantom [*Shepp and Logan*, 1974] is a widely used test object for tomographic reconstruction algorithms. It consists of 10 ellipses, which partly show only faint gray value differences. From *Kak* [1984].

around the position of the point. Consequently, we would not obtain a point but a rotational symmetric function which falls off with $|\boldsymbol{x}|^{-1}$. As a result, the reconstructed objects would be considerably blurred. The point spread function of the blurring is the $|\boldsymbol{x}|^{-1}$ function.

Practical Application of the Filtered Back Projection
The head phantom shown in figure 13.7 is a widely used artificial test object for tomographic reconstruction algorithms. In order to test the resolution limits of the reconstruction, it partly contains only faint gray value differences. Figure 13.12 shows that the filtered back projection algorithm yields an accurate reconstruction even of fine details and small gray value differences. A detailed discussion of the filtered back projection including the practically important reconstruction from fan-beam projections can be found in *Kak* [1984] and *Jain* [1989].

13.3.4 Algebraic Reconstruction

General Approach
In this section we discuss a totally different approach to the reconstruction from projections. It is based on discrete inverse theory and thus constitutes a very general method which is used in many other applications, not only in image processing. The image is regarded as a one-dimensional *image vector*. This mapping is easily performed by renumbering the pixels of the image matrix row by row (figure 13.9). In this way, a

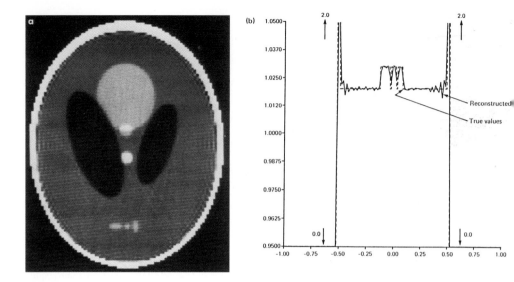

Figure 13.8: Reconstruction of the head phantom (figure 13.7) with the filtered pack projection algorithm. The reconstruction was computed from 100 projection directions with 128 beams: a) reconstructed 128 × 128 image matrix; b) horizontal cross section at $y = -0.605$ at the height of the three small ellipses for a more precise comparison of the reconstructed values with the original values. From *Kak* [1984].

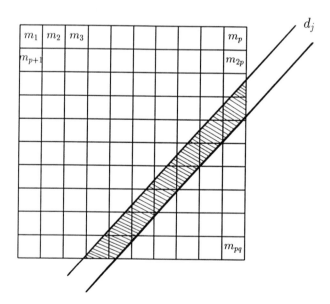

Figure 13.9: Illustration of algebraic reconstruction from projections: A projection beam d_k crosses the image matrix. All pixels which are met by the beam contribute to the projection.

$p \times q$ image matrix is transformed into a column vector with the dimension pq:

$$
\boldsymbol{m} = \begin{bmatrix} m_1 \\ m_2 \\ \vdots \\ m_l \\ \vdots \\ m_{pq} \end{bmatrix}. \tag{13.19}
$$

Now we take a single projection beam which crosses the image matrix (figure 13.9). Then we can attribute a weighting factor to each pixel of the image vector, which represents the contribution of the pixel to the projection beam. We can combine these factors in another $M = pq$ dimensional vector $\boldsymbol{g}_k$:

$$
\boldsymbol{g}_k = \begin{bmatrix} g_{k,1} \\ g_{k,2} \\ \vdots \\ g_{k,l} \\ \vdots \\ g_{k,M} \end{bmatrix}. \tag{13.20}
$$

The total emission or absorption along the kth projection beam d_k can then be expressed as the scalar product of the two vectors $\boldsymbol{g}_k$ and $\boldsymbol{m}$:

$$
d_k = \sum_{l=1}^{M} g_{k,l} m_l = \boldsymbol{g}_k^T \boldsymbol{m}. \tag{13.21}
$$

If N projection beams cross the image matrix, we obtain a linear equation system of N equations and M unknowns:

$$
\underbrace{\boldsymbol{d}}_{N} = \underbrace{\boldsymbol{G}}_{N \times M} \underbrace{\boldsymbol{m}}_{M}. \tag{13.22}
$$

Thus algebraic reconstruction involves solving huge linear equation systems. At this point, it is helpful to illustrate the enormous size of these equation systems. If we only want to reconstruct an image with a coarse resolution, say 64×64 which is crossed by 6000 projection beams, we must solve an equation system with 6000 equations and 4096 unknowns.

Nevertheless, it might be worthwhile carrying this out as the algebraic reconstruction uses a very general and flexible method. It is not limited to parallel projection. The beams can cross the image matrix in any manner and can even be curved. In addition, we obtain a discrete solution. With appropriate weighting factors, we can directly take into account the limited detector resolution and the size of the radiation source.

Since a solution of (13.22) basically involves matrix inversion we speak of a *linear discrete inverse problem*. Problems of this kind are very common in the analysis of experimental data in natural sciences. An experimentalist looks at a discrete inverse problem in the following way: he performs an experiment from which he gains a set of measuring results which are combined in an N dimensional data vector $\boldsymbol{d}$. These data should be compared with a model of the observed process. The parameters of this model are given by an M dimensional model vector $\boldsymbol{m}$. Now we assume that the relationship between the model and the data vector can be described as linear. It can then be expressed by a model matrix $\boldsymbol{G}$ and we obtain (13.22).

In case of the reconstruction problem, the data vector contains the measured projections and the model vector contains the gray values at the pixels of the image matrix. The relationship between these two vectors is given by the model matrix which describes how the projection beams cross the image matrix. It might be instructive to illustrate this with another very familiar problem, the fit of a straight line to a set of experimental data x, y. In this case, our model vector contains only two parameters, the offset and the slope of the straight line $y = a_0 + a_1 x$. The data vector contains all data points y_k, while the model matrix contains the relationship between the data points and model parameters which depends on the x values of the data points. We end up with the linear equation system

$$
\begin{bmatrix} 1 & x_1 \\ 1 & x_2 \\ \vdots & \vdots \\ 1 & x_M \end{bmatrix} \begin{bmatrix} a_0 \\ a_1 \end{bmatrix} = \begin{bmatrix} y_1 \\ y_2 \\ \vdots \\ y_M \end{bmatrix}. \tag{13.23}
$$

If we have only two data points which do not coincide $x_1 \neq x_2$, we get an exact solution of the linear equation system. If more than two data points are available, we have more equations than unknowns. We say that the equation system is *overdetermined*. In this case, it is generally no longer possible to obtain an exact solution. We can only compute an estimate of the model parameters in the sense that the deviation of the data $\boldsymbol{d}$ from the data predicted with the model $\boldsymbol{d}_{\text{pre}} = \boldsymbol{G} \boldsymbol{m}_{\text{est}}$ is minimal. This deviation can be combined into an *error vector* $\boldsymbol{e}$:

$$
\boldsymbol{e} = \boldsymbol{d} - \boldsymbol{d}_{\text{pre}} = \boldsymbol{d} - \boldsymbol{G} \boldsymbol{m}_{\text{est}}. \tag{13.24}
$$

In order to minimize the error vector we need a suitable measure. We may use *norms* which we have already discussed when using inner product vector spaces in section 3.3.1. Generally, the L_n norm of the M dimensional vector $\boldsymbol{e}$ is defined as

$$
||\boldsymbol{e}||_n = \left(\sum_{m=1}^{M} |e_m|^n \right)^{1/n}. \tag{13.25}
$$

A special case is the L_∞ norm

$$
||\boldsymbol{e}||_\infty = \max_m |e_m|. \tag{13.26}
$$

The L_2-Norm is more commonly used; it constitutes the sum of the squared deviations of the error vector elements

$$
||\boldsymbol{e}||_2 = \left(\sum_{m=1}^{M} (d_m - d_{\text{pre},m})^2 \right)^{1/2}. \tag{13.27}
$$

Higher norms rate higher deviations with a more significant weighting. The statistics of the deviations determines which is the correct norm to be taken. It can be proved that

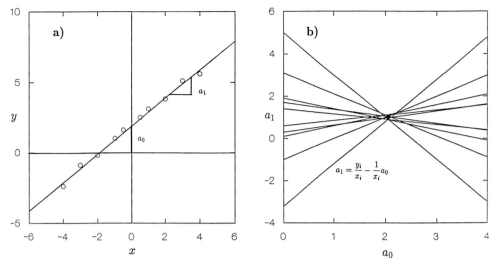

Figure 13.10: Illustration of the Hough transform with the example of a straight-line fit: the Hough transform maps the (x, y) data space onto the (a_0, a_1) model space: a) data space; b) model space.

the L_2 norm corresponds to the normal distribution [*Menke*, 1984]. In appendix A.1 it is shown that the overdetermined linear inverse problem is solved in the sense of a minimum L_2 norm of the error vector by

$$m_{\text{est}} = \left(G^T G\right)^{-1} G^T d. \tag{13.28}$$

Another important point should be mentioned. As all the methods are based on statistics, the solution of the problem also includes an estimate of the errors. The mean deviation between the measured and predicted data points is directly related to the norm of the error vector. The *variance* is

$$\sigma^2 = \frac{1}{N - M} ||e||^2 = \frac{1}{N - M} ||d - G m_{\text{est}}||_2^2. \tag{13.29}$$

In order not to introduce a bias, we only divide by the *degree of freedom* and not by N. (If $M = N$ we obtain an exact solution from which no error estimate is possible.) Besides the variance of the data points, the solution also contains the variances of all the model parameters. If the data are uncorrelated, the matrix $(G^T G)^{-1}$ is identical to the *covariance matrix* except for the factor σ^2. The diagonal of this matrix contains the variances of the model parameters [*Menke*, 1984] (see section 12.3).

Geometrical Illustration of Linear Equation Systems; Hough Transform
Before we study methods to solve such huge linear equation systems, it is helpful to illustrate linear equation systems geometrically.

M model parameters span an M dimensional vector space. Each linear equation of an inverse problem can be regarded as a point in the data space which contains the data itself and the corresponding parameters which are described in the model matrix G. In case of a fit with a straight line a data point contains the x and y value (figure 13.10a). Each linear equation also contains the unknown model parameters and thus a *hyperplane* in the model space is constituted, i. e., a subspace with the dimension $M - 1$ (figure 13.10). This mapping of the data points onto the model space is called the *Hough transform*. M such hyperplanes which are neither parallel nor identical to each other intersect in one point in the model space. This point gives the exact solution of M equations with M unknowns.

In an overdetermined case, more than M hyperplanes are given. Generally they will not intersect each other all in one point, but show a more or less distributed cloud of intersection points of M hyperplanes each (figure 13.10b). We may think of some suitable mean of the set of $(M - N)(M - N - 1)/2$ intersection points as being the optimum solution. The scatter of the intersection points in the directions of the different model parameters is a measure for the standard deviation of the estimates of the corresponding model parameters.

Iterative Methods to Solve Sparse Equation Systems
Now we return to the solution of the algebraic reconstruction problem. Since each projection beam only meets a small fraction of the pixels of the image matrix (figure 13.9), the matrix G contains only a few non-zero weighting factors. Such an equation system is called *sparse*. Most of the projection beams do not even cross each other in the image matrix at all. This means that the corresponding linear equations contain disjunct subsets of model parameters. Geometrically, this means that the corresponding hyperplanes are orthogonal to each other.

The fact that most hyperplanes are orthogonal to each other in sparse equation systems is the base of the following simple iterative solution method of the linear equation system:

$$Gm = d.$$

Without restricting generality, we can modify the equation system so that all row vectors g_k of the matrix G are unit vectors. These vectors are then normal to the hyperplane of the equation they represent. Proof: Any vector which points from the origin to a point of the hyperplane meets the condition $m^T g_k = d$. Any difference vector between two such vectors $m_1 - m_2$ lies on the plane and satisfies $(m_1 - m_2)^T g_k = 0$. Consequently g_k is normal to the hyperplane.

We start the iterative solution with an arbitrary point $m^{(0)}$ and project it onto the first hyperplane. Then we get a new solution which meets the first equation of the linear equation system (figure 13.11):

$$m^{(1)} = m^{(0)} - (g_1 m^{(0)} - d_1)g_1. \tag{13.30}$$

We continue this procedure by projecting the solution of the jth iteration onto the $j + 1$th hyperplane:

$$m^{(j+1)} = m^{(j)} - (g_{j+1} m^{(j)} - d_{j+1})g_{j+1}. \tag{13.31}$$

After we have projected the solution onto all the N hyperplanes, we continue the procedure in a cyclic manner until $m^{(j)}$ has converged sufficiently accurately to give the optimum solution. Figure 13.11 illustrates that the orthogonality of the hyperplanes

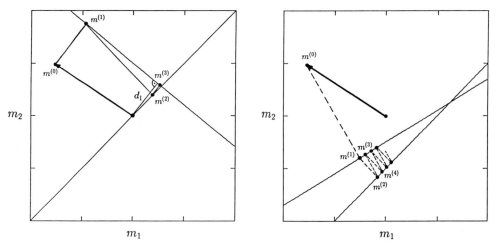

Figure 13.11: Illustration of the iterative solution of a linear equation system by alternating projection onto hyperplanes: a) fast convergence with nearly orthogonal planes; b) slow convergence with nearly parallel hyperplanes.

is the critical parameter for a fast convergence of the iteration. If two hyperplanes meet under an acute angle, iteration is very slow (figure 13.11b).

Intuitively, it is obvious that if all hyperplanes are normal to each other, then an equation system with M equations and M unknowns will converge in exactly M iteration steps.

In this brief overview, we could only scratch the surface of numerical methods to solve large linear equation systems. For a more thorough analysis including detailed algorithms the reader is referred to the excellent survey on matrix computations by *Golub and van Loan* [1989].

Reconstruction from Parallel Projection

Figure 13.12 shows the algebraic reconstruction resulting from an advanced method which is called the *simultaneous algebraic reconstruction technique* [*Andersen and Kak*, 1984]. The reconstruction is considerably worse than those using the filtered back projection algorithm.

What is the reason for this difference? The basic difference between both methods lies in the fact that the filtered back projection technique is closely related to the mathematics of the projection. We may conclude that the reconstruction result should be much more constrained and much less sensitive to noise than the results from the very general concept of algebraic reconstruction.

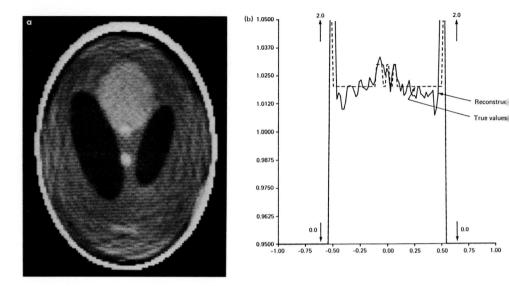

Figure 13.12: a) Reconstruction of the head phantom by algebraic reconstruction from parallel projections under identical conditions as in figure 13.8; b) horizontal cross section through the lower image part where the three small ellipses are located. See figure 13.7 for a more precise comparison of original and reconstructed values; from *Kak* [1984].

14 Motion

14.1 Introduction

In this chapter we extend our considerations from single images to image sequences. We may compare this step with the transition from still photography to motion pictures. Only in image sequences can we recognize and analyze dynamic processes. Thus the analysis of image sequences opens up far-reaching possibilities in science and engineering. A few examples serve as illustration:

- Flow visualization is an old tool in fluid dynamics but has been used for a long time mainly for qualitative description, because manual quantitative evaluation has been prohibitively laborious. Digital image sequence analysis allows area-extended velocity data to be extracted automatically. In section 2.2.8 we discussed an example of flow visualization by particle tracking. Some results are shown in plate 4.
- Satellite image sequences of the sea surface temperature (see section 1.2.1 and plate 1) can be used to determine near-surface ocean currents [*Wahl and Simpson*, 1990].
- In the industrial environment, motion sensors based on image sequence analysis are beginning to play an important role. Their usage covers a wide spectrum starting with remote velocity measurements in industrial processes [*Massen et al.*, 1987] to the control of autonomous vehicles and robots [*Dickmanns*, 1987].

Image sequence analysis is a quite new and complex area of digital image processing. We will approach the problem of motion analysis in four steps which basically follow the historical development:

1. In this chapter we will first become familiar with the problems of image sequence analysis in an intuitive way. Then we will work out the basic knowledge about motion.
2. Historically, image sequence analysis began with the analysis of only two consecutive images. In chapter 15 we discuss different methods to determine the displacement of objects from two images of a sequence with local operations.
3. In chapter 16 we will discuss how we can extend sparse displacement information of local operations in an integral concept to complete displacement information on the whole image plane.
4. In the last chapter of this book we extend the analysis of motion from two to many images of the sequence. We will regard the image sequence as a three-dimensional object with two space and one time coordinates. In this way, a deeper understanding

of motion in image sequences can be worked out. As a result, new algorithms for motion determination are emerging which are superior to the methods using only two images.

14.1.1 Gray Value Changes

Intuitively we associate motion with changes. Thus we start our discussion on motion analysis by observing the differences between two images of a sequence. Figure 14.1a and c show an image pair from a construction area at Heidelberg University. There are differences between the upper and lower image which are, however, not evident from direct comparison. However, if we subtract one image from the other, the differences immediately become visible. In the lower left of the image a truck has moved, while the van and the car just behind it are obviously parked. In the center of the image we discover the outline of a pedestrian which is barely visible in the original images. The bright spots in a row in the top of the image turn out to be bikers moving along a cycle lane. From the displacement of the double contours we can estimate that they move faster than the pedestrian. Even from this qualitative description, it is obvious that motion analysis helps us considerably in understanding such a scene. It would be much harder to detect the cycle lane without observing the moving bikers.

Figure 14.1b and d show the same scene. Now we might even recognize the change in the original images. If we observe the image edges, we notice that the images have shifted slightly in a horizontal direction. What has happened? Obviously, the camera has been panned. In the difference image figure 14.1f all the edges of the objects appear as bright lines. However, the image is dark where the spatial gray value changes are small. Consequently, we can detect motion only in the parts of an image that show gray value changes. This simple observation points out the central role of spatial gray value changes for motion determination.

So far we can sum up our experience with the statement that motion *might* result in temporal gray value changes. Unfortunately, the reverse conclusion that all temporal gray value changes are due to motion is not correct. At first glance, the pair of images in figure 14.2b and d look identical. Yet, the difference image figure 14.2f reveals that the upper image is brighter than the lower. Obviously the illumination has changed. Actually, a lamp outside the image sector shown has been switched off before the image in figure 14.2d was taken. Can we infer where this lamp is located? In the difference image we notice that not all surfaces are equally bright. Surfaces which are oriented towards the camera show about the same brightness in both images, while surfaces oriented towards the left are considerably less bright. Therefore we can conclude that the lamp is located to the left outside the image sector.

Another pair of images (figure 14.2a, c) shows a much more complex scene, although we did not change the illumination. We just closed the door of the lab. Of course, we see strong gray value differences where the door is located. The gray value changes, however, extend to the floor close to the door and to the objects located to the left of the door. As we close the door, we also change the illumination in the proximity of the door since no more light is reflected into this area.

In conclusion, we are faced with the complex problem that motion is inherently

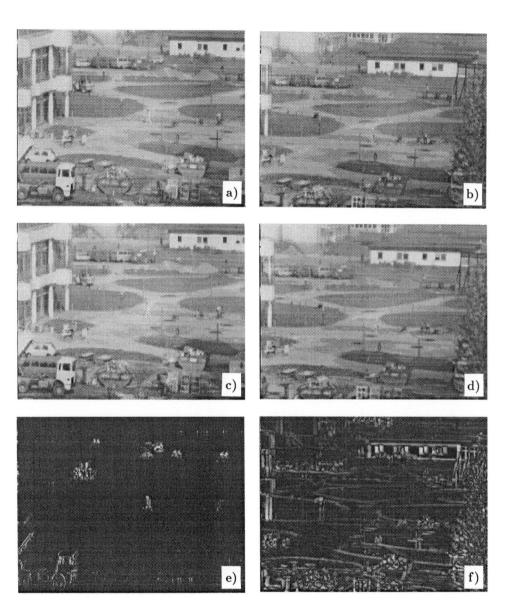

Figure 14.1: a) to d) Two pairs of images from the construction area for the new head clinic at Heidelberg University. What has changed from the upper to the lower image? e) Difference between a) and c); f) difference between b) and d). In both images the magnitude of the difference is shown.

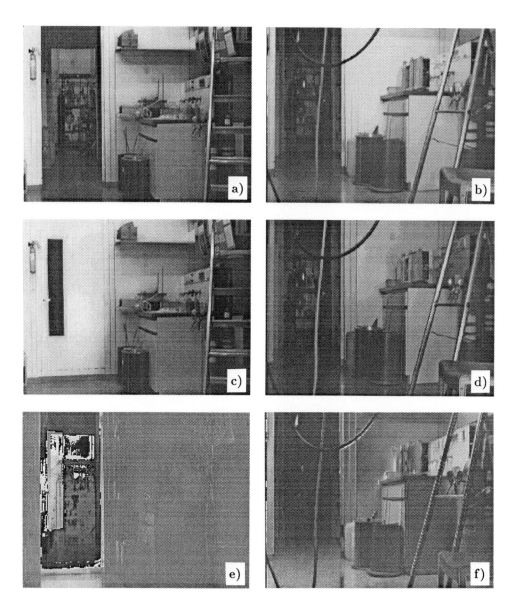

Figure 14.2: a) to d) Two pairs of images from an indoor lab scene. What changes can be seen between the upper and lower image? e) Difference between a) and c); f) difference between b) and d). In both difference images the difference shown is $g^{(2)} - g^{(1)} + 128$.

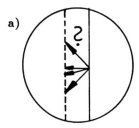
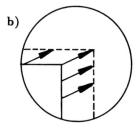

Figure 14.3: Illustration of the aperture problem in motion analysis: a) ambiguity of displacement vectors at an edge; b) unambiguity of the displacement vector at a corner.

coupled with illumination changes in the environment of the moving object (see also section 14.4.2). How can we distinguish gray value changes *directly* caused by motion from those which only result from indirect illumination changes?

14.1.2 The Aperture Problem

So far we learnt that to estimate motion is closely related to spatial and temporal gray value changes. Both quantities can easily be derived with local operators which compute the spatial and temporal derivatives. Such an operator only "sees" a small sector — equal to the size of its mask — of the observed object. We may illustrate this effect by putting a mask or aperture onto the image.

Figure 14.3a shows an edge which moved from the position of the solid line in the first image to the position of the dotted line in the second image. The motion from image one to two can be described by a *displacement vector*, or briefly, DV. In this case, we cannot determine the displacement unambiguously. The displacement vector might go from one point of the edge in the first image to any other point of the edge in the second image (figure 14.3a). We can only determine the component of the DV normal to the edge, while the component parallel to the edge remains unknown. This ambiguity is known as the *aperture problem*.

An unambiguous determination of the DV is only possible if a corner of an object is within the mask of our operator (figure 14.3b). This emphasizes that we can only gain sparse information on motion from local operators.

14.1.3 The Correspondence Problem

The aperture problem is caused by the fact that we cannot find the corresponding point at an edge in the following image of a sequence, because we have no means of distinguishing the different points at an edge. In this sense, we can comprehend the aperture problem only as a special case of a more general problem, the *correspondence problem*. Generally speaking, it means that we are unable to find unambiguous corresponding points in two consecutive images of a sequence. In this section we discuss further examples of the correspondence problem.

Figure 14.4a shows a two-dimensional deformable object — as a blob of paint —

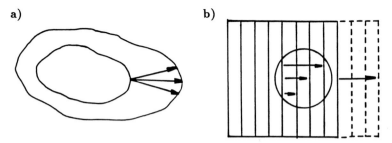

Figure 14.4: Illustration of the correspondence problem with the determination of displacement vectors: a) deformable two-dimensional object; b) regular grid.

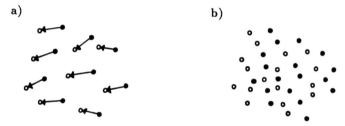

Figure 14.5: Correspondence problem with indistinguishable particles: a) mean particle distance is larger than the mean displacement vector; b) the reverse case. Filled and hollow circles: particles in the first and second image.

which spreads gradually. It is immediately obvious that we cannot obtain any un-ambiguous determination of displacement vectors, even at the edge of the blob. We cannot make any estimate of the displacements in the inner part of the blob, because there are no features visible which we could track. At first glance, we assume that the correspondence problem will not occur with rigid objects which show a lot of gray value variations. The grid as an example of a periodic texture, shown in figure 14.5, demonstrates that this is not the case. As long as we observe the displacement of the grid with a local operator, the displacement is ambiguous concerning the multiples of the grid constant. Only when we observe the whole grid, does the displacement become unambiguous.

Another variation of the correspondence problem occurs if the image includes many objects of the same shape. One typical case is when small particles are put into a flow field in order to measure the velocity field. In such a case the particles are in-distinguishable and we generally cannot tell which particles correspond to each other (figure 14.5b). We can find a solution to this problem if we take the consecutive images at such short time intervals that the mean displacement vector is significantly smaller than the mean particle distance. With this additional knowledge, we can search for the nearest neighbor of a particle in the next image. Such an approach, however, will never be free of errors, because the particle distance is statistically distributed.

These simple examples clearly demonstrate the basic problems of motion analysis. The correspondence problem indicates that the image sequence does not reproduce the reality of the three-dimensional world unambiguously in the two-dimensional image plane. In relation to the problem of corresponding objects we learnt that the *phys-*

ical correspondence, i.e., the real correspondence, may not be identical to the *visual correspondence* in the image. We outline two cases:

1. We can find a visual correspondence without the existence of a physical correspondence, as in case of objects or periodic object textures which are indistinguishable.
2. Despite the existing physical correspondence we might find no visual correspondence. This is the case if the objects show no distinctive marks or if we cannot recognize the visual correspondence because of illumination changes (section 14.1.1).

14.1.4   Motion Analysis and 3-D Reconstruction

The discussion of gray value changes in section 14.1.1 has already shown that we can learn a lot about a scene by means of motion analysis. In this chapter the relationship between the reconstruction of a three-dimensional scene and motion analysis is investigated further.

First, we notice the close relation between image sequence analysis from a pair of images and stereo analysis with two cameras. Let us consider a scene with stationary objects. If we observe the scene with a stereo camera setup, we will get two images which show the scene from two different points of view. We can tell the distance of the objects from the displacement of corresponding points as discussed in section 2.2.9. We will get exactly the same two images if we take only one camera but move it from the position of the left to the position of the right stereo camera [*Nagel*, 1981].

From this close correspondence between stereo and motion analysis we can see that the analysis of stereo images and an image pair from a sequence are identical until we reach the stage where we start interpreting the determined displacements (figure 14.6).

14.2   Motion Kinematics

A well equipped analysis of motion in images requires basic knowledge of motion in the three dimensional world and its projection onto the image plane. Physicists distinguish two types of motion description. *Kinematics* refers to the description of the motion path of the objects. It analyzes which basic or elementary types of motion are possible for a given object. Motion *dynamics* describes how the forces acting on an object change its motion. In this section we will discuss the kinematics of motion in three-dimensional space and its perspective projection onto the image plane.

As in section 2.2, we denote quantities in the three-dimensional world by capital letters and quantities in the image plane by lower-case letters. The *world coordinates* X and their temporal derivatives, the velocity U, are perspectively projected onto the image plane by (2.7)

$$(X_1, X_2, X_3) \mapsto (x_1, x_2)$$
$$(U_1, U_2, U_3) \mapsto (u_1, u_2).$$

In discrete imagery, we do not measure the velocity u but only the displacement s between consecutive images. If Δt is the time interval between two consecutive images,

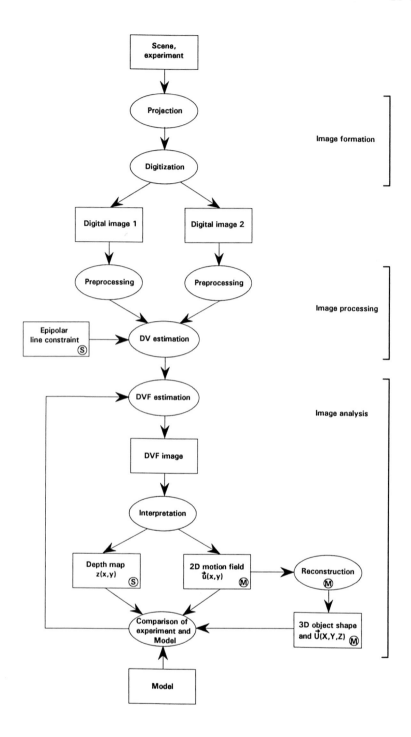

Figure 14.6: Comparative reflection of the analysis of pairs of images from a stereo setup and an image sequence.

an approximation of the velocity is given by dividing the displacement by the time interval:

$$u \approx \frac{s}{\Delta t}. \tag{14.1}$$

Since the velocity and the displacement only differ by a constant factor, we can use both quantities to describe motion in discrete imagery.

14.2.1 Mass points

A *mass point* is the simplest abstraction we can make of an object. The extent of the object is neglected, all mass being concentrated in one point. Translation is the only form of motion for a mass point. Modelling objects as mass points is helpful to discuss some elementary properties of projected motion. From the equation for perspective projection (2.7), the velocity on the image plane can be computed by temporal differentiation

$$x_1 = \frac{X_1}{X_3} \quad \leadsto \quad u_1 = \frac{1}{X_3}(U_1 - x_1 U_3)$$

$$x_2 = \frac{X_2}{X_3} \quad \leadsto \quad u_2 = \frac{1}{X_3}(U_2 - x_2 U_3). \tag{14.2}$$

The motion in the three-dimensional world cannot be inferred unambiguously from the projected velocities. Even if $u = 0$, U is not necessarily zero. Equation (14.2) only results in the constraints

$$\frac{U_1}{U_3} = \frac{X_1}{X_3} \quad \text{and} \quad \frac{U_2}{U_3} = \frac{X_2}{X_3}. \tag{14.3}$$

Geometrically, these constraints mean a motion of the mass point along a projection beam. Thus the velocity vector U, inferred from the projected velocity vector u, contains an unknown additive vector along the projection beam:

$$\left(\alpha \frac{X_1}{X_3}, \alpha \frac{X_2}{X_3}, \alpha \right).$$

The inverse projection problem is underdetermined. This does not mean, however, that we cannot extract useful information on the observed motion from its projections onto the image plane.

As an example, let us consider the very simplest motion problem where the camera is moving with constant velocity $\bar{U}$ relative to a scene at rest.

Focus of Expansion (FOE)
Combining (14.2) and (14.3), we conclude that the velocity field vanishes at the point $\bar{x}$ in the image plane:

$$u_1 = 0 \leadsto \bar{x}_1 = \frac{\bar{U}_1}{\bar{U}_3}$$

$$u_2 = 0 \leadsto \bar{x}_2 = \frac{\bar{U}_2}{\bar{U}_3},$$

provided that $\bar{U}_3 \neq 0$. This point may not lie in the actual field of view of the camera. The velocity vector of the camera motion targets this point on the image plane. Then

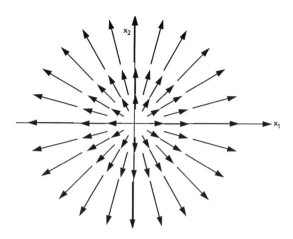

Figure 14.7: Velocity field at the image plane when the camera is moving towards a static scene.

the camera moves towards or away from this point (figure 14.7). Because of the distinct point $\bar{x}$, it is useful to represent the velocity field in a new coordinate system whose origin is located at $\bar{x}$. Using the coordinate transformation $x' = x - \bar{x}$ we yield

$$u_1 = -\frac{\bar{U}_3}{X_3}x_1', \quad u_2 = -\frac{\bar{U}_3}{X_3}x_2',$$

or summarized as a vector equation

$$u = -\frac{\bar{U}_3}{X_3}x' = -\frac{\bar{U}_3}{X_3}(x - \bar{x}). \tag{14.4}$$

All velocity vectors are oriented towards or away from the point $\bar{x}$. If all objects lie at the same distance, the magnitude of the velocity goes with the distance from $\bar{x}$ (figure 14.7). Therefore the point $\bar{x}$ is called the *focus of expansion*, or FOE. If the camera motion is parallel to the image plane ($U_3 = 0$), then the FOE lies in infinity. In this case, the velocity vectors on the image plane and in the three-dimensional world are parallel. The magnitude of the vector is then inversely proportional to the distance of the object from the camera (14.2).

Relative Distance Measurement

From a single image of a three-dimensional scene, we cannot tell the distance of the objects. Likewise, we cannot determine the absolute velocities of the camera in space from the velocity field on the image plane. However, from this velocity field we can determine the relative distance of objects. Let us assume two objects at the distances X_3 and $\tilde{X}_3$, respectively. Then from (14.4) we obtain

$$\frac{\tilde{X}_3}{X_3} = \frac{u_1/x_1'}{\tilde{u}_1/\tilde{x}_1'} \quad \text{and} \quad \frac{\tilde{X}_3}{X_3} = \frac{u_2/x_2'}{\tilde{u}_2/\tilde{x}_2'}. \tag{14.5}$$

This equation is only valid as long as $U_3 \neq 0$, i.e., the FOE does not lie in the infinity. In this case, we get slightly simpler relations which can be derived from (14.2) for $U_3 = 0$:

$$\frac{\tilde{X}_3}{X_3} = \frac{u_1}{\tilde{u}_1} \quad \text{and} \quad \frac{\tilde{X}_3}{X_3} = \frac{u_2}{\tilde{u}_2}. \tag{14.6}$$

Then the apparent velocity of the object is inversely proportional to the distance from the camera.

It is important to note that we can determine the relative distance of the objects without any knowledge about the velocity of the camera. We also do not need to know other parameters of the camera, such as the field of width or the focal length of the camera.

Time to Contact

In robotics and navigational systems, an important issue is the timely detection of potential collision with other objects. One important parameter is the time it takes for the navigated system to collide with one of the objects in its environment. This time can be estimated from the current relative speed of the vehicle towards the object. This quantity is called the *time to contact*, or briefly TTC. An estimate of the TTC is given as the ratio of the distance X_3 and vertical velocity U_3 of the object. Then (14.4) yields

$$\text{TTC} = -\frac{X_3}{U_3} = \frac{x_1'}{u_1} = \frac{x_2'}{u_2}. \tag{14.7}$$

As the relative distance measurement, the TTC determination does not require a calibrated camera system.

14.2.2   Deformable Objects

Modelling an object as a mass point, as in the last section, helped us to gain a first impression of the relationship between motion in the real world and on the image plane. But it is too simplistic an approach to describe the motion of an object adequately. Real world objects do not only translate, but also rotate or might even be deformable. The latter has often been neglected — at least until recently — as the objects were modelled as *rigid bodies* which only underwent translation and rotation.

In this section we explicitly want to include deformation, since we wish to provide a complete description of motion. The kinematics of the motion of deformable objects is a basic problem of classic continuum mechanics. The body is divided into small *volume elements* and we will investigate what happens to the volume element in the course of its motion. The *fundamental theorem of kinematics* states that we can describe the result of motion on the volume elements as a sum of translation, rotation and deformation [*von Helmholtz*, 1858]. This result is so important for motion analysis that we will demonstrate it in this section.

Figure 14.8 shows the motion of a volume element. Within the time interval dt its origin moved from $x(t)$ to $x(t + dt)$. We denote the distance travelled by $s(x)$. During the motion along the infinitesimal path $s(x)$, the volume element has changed its orientation and shape (figure 14.8). We can describe these effects with the three basic vectors which span the volume element and change in both orientation and length. In total, the motion of a deformable volume element has twelve *degrees of freedom*: three in the translation vector and three in each basis vector spanning the volume element. We can also describe the motion of the volume element with the two vectors $s(x)$ and $s(x + dx)$, connecting the origin and the corner opposite. This description enables us

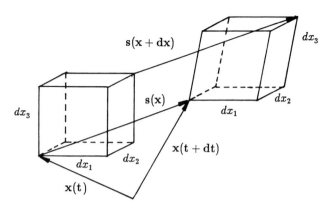

Figure 14.8: Motion of a small volume element of an infinitesimal volume element of a deformable object.

to describe the motion in an easy way. Since only infinitesimal changes are involved, we can expand $\boldsymbol{s}(\boldsymbol{x} + \mathrm{d}\boldsymbol{x})$ in a Taylor series and need only take the first-order terms into account:

$$s_1(\boldsymbol{x} + \mathrm{d}\boldsymbol{x}) = s_1(\boldsymbol{x}) + \frac{\partial s_1}{\partial x_1}\mathrm{d}x_1 + \frac{\partial s_1}{\partial x_2}\mathrm{d}x_2 + \frac{\partial s_1}{\partial x_3}\mathrm{d}x_3$$

$$s_2(\boldsymbol{x} + \mathrm{d}\boldsymbol{x}) = s_2(\boldsymbol{x}) + \frac{\partial s_2}{\partial x_1}\mathrm{d}x_1 + \frac{\partial s_2}{\partial x_2}\mathrm{d}x_2 + \frac{\partial s_2}{\partial x_3}\mathrm{d}x_3$$

$$s_3(\boldsymbol{x} + \mathrm{d}\boldsymbol{x}) = s_3(\boldsymbol{x}) + \frac{\partial s_3}{\partial x_1}\mathrm{d}x_1 + \frac{\partial s_3}{\partial x_2}\mathrm{d}x_2 + \frac{\partial s_3}{\partial x_3}\mathrm{d}x_3.$$

Defining the matrix $\boldsymbol{A}$ with the elements

$$A_{ij} = \frac{\partial s_i}{\partial x_j} \quad (i, j = 1, 2, 3)$$

we can write

$$\boldsymbol{s}(\boldsymbol{x} + \mathrm{d}\boldsymbol{x}) = \boldsymbol{s}(\boldsymbol{x}) + \boldsymbol{A}\,\mathrm{d}\boldsymbol{x}. \tag{14.8}$$

The nine components of the matrix contain all the nine degrees of freedom for the orientation and shape change of the volume element. In order to decompose the motion into the main motion types, we separate the matrix into its symmetric and antisymmetric parts:

$$\begin{aligned} \text{symmetric part:} \quad & \boldsymbol{A}^s = \tfrac{1}{2}(\boldsymbol{A} + \boldsymbol{A}^T) \\ \text{antisymmetric part:} \quad & \boldsymbol{A}^a = \tfrac{1}{2}(\boldsymbol{A} - \boldsymbol{A}^T). \end{aligned}$$

$\boldsymbol{A}^T$ denotes the transpose of the matrix $\boldsymbol{A}$.

The Antisymmetric Matrix (Rotation)
The antisymmetric matrix $\boldsymbol{A}^a$ reads

$$A_{ii}^a = 0$$

$$A_{ij}^a = \frac{1}{2}\left(\frac{\partial s_i}{\partial x_j} - \frac{\partial s_j}{\partial x_i}\right).$$

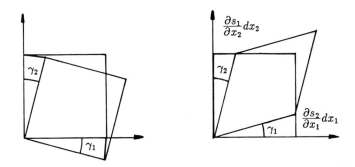

Figure 14.9: Rotation a) versus shearing b) of the surface element of a volume element.

This matrix shows only three degrees of freedom. The off-diagonal terms only contain cross-partial derivatives, i.e., changes perpendicular to the direction of the vector. Such changes typically occur with rotation. Rotation can be expressed by the vector $\boldsymbol{\omega}$

$$\boldsymbol{\omega} = \nabla \times \boldsymbol{s} \quad \text{with} \quad \boldsymbol{\omega} = (\omega_1, \omega_2, \omega_3).$$

The direction of $\boldsymbol{\omega}$ gives the direction of the rotation axis, while the magnitude of $\boldsymbol{\omega}$ denotes the *angular velocity*. Using $\boldsymbol{\omega}$, the antisymmetric matrix $\boldsymbol{A}^a$ reduces to

$$\begin{bmatrix} ds_1^a \\ ds_2^a \\ ds_3^a \end{bmatrix} = \begin{bmatrix} 0 & -\omega_3 & \omega_2 \\ \omega_3 & 0 & -\omega_1 \\ -\omega_2 & \omega_1 & 0 \end{bmatrix} \begin{bmatrix} dx_1 \\ dx_2 \\ dx_3 \end{bmatrix}.$$

For illustration, we consider the ω_3 component in detail (figure 14.9a). The differential displacements $dx_1 \cdot \partial s_2/\partial x_1$ and $dx_2 \cdot \partial s_1/\partial x_2$ cause a rotation of the corresponding edges dx_1 and dx_2 by the angles γ_1 and γ_2. Using these quantities, we can write

$$\omega_3 = -\frac{1}{2}\left(\frac{\partial s_1}{\partial x_2} - \frac{\partial s_2}{\partial x_1}\right) = -\frac{1}{2}\left(\frac{\dfrac{\partial s_1}{\partial x_2}dx_2}{dx_2} - \frac{\dfrac{\partial s_2}{\partial x_1}dx_1}{dx_1}\right) = -\frac{1}{2}\left(-\gamma_2 - \gamma_1\right) = \frac{1}{2}\left(\gamma_1 + \gamma_2\right).$$

Consequently, the mean of the two angles γ_1 and γ_2 denotes the differential rotation of the volume element around the x_3 axis (figure 14.9a). We can distinguish two principal cases:

- $\gamma_1 = \gamma_2$: pure rotation; the shape of the surface element is not changed.
- $\gamma_1 = -\gamma_2$: results in $\omega_3 = 0$, i.e., no rotation. The volume element is rather sheared.

The Symmetric Matrix (Deformation)
The remaining symmetric part, $\boldsymbol{A}^s$, holds the diagonal elements

$$A_{ii}^s = \frac{\partial s_i}{\partial x_i}.$$

They denote the length change of the edges of the volume element. The off-diagonal elements read

$$A_{ij}^s = \frac{1}{2}\left(\frac{\partial s_i}{\partial x_j} + \frac{\partial s_j}{\partial x_i}\right).$$

These elements describe the shearing of the volume elements. Let us discuss an example similar to that of rotation:

$$A^s_{1,2} = \frac{1}{2}\left(\frac{\partial s_1}{\partial x_2} + \frac{\partial s_2}{\partial x_1}\right) = \frac{1}{2}(\gamma_1 - \gamma_2).$$

$A^s_{1,2}$ gives the difference of the two angles γ_1 and γ_2. This angle difference describes the shearing of a surface element (figure 14.9b).

In total, deformation has six degrees of freedom, which we so far have decomposed into the length changes of the three edges of the volume element and the shearing of its three surface elements. Other useful decompositions are also possible. Each symmetric matrix can be diagonalized by a suitable transformation (see section 12.3):

$$A^{s'} = \begin{bmatrix} \dfrac{\partial s'_1}{\partial x'_1} & 0 & 0 \\ 0 & \dfrac{\partial s'_2}{\partial x'_2} & 0 \\ 0 & 0 & \dfrac{\partial s'_3}{\partial x'_3} \end{bmatrix}.$$

x'_1, x'_2, x'_3 denote the coordinates in the principal-axes system.

Volume Dilation

Deformation of the volume elements may result in a volume change of the moving object. The differential volume change is called the *volume dilation* Θ_V and is given by the divergence of the velocity field

$$\Theta_V = \frac{dV' - dV}{dV} = \nabla s = \text{trace}(A^s), \tag{14.9}$$

which is equal to the sum of the diagonal elements or *trace* of the symmetric matrix A^s. The volume dilation is important since a number of moving objects, for example, incompressible flows, do not allow for volume dilations.

Summary

The general motion of an infinitesimal volume element of a deformable object can be divided into three principal components

$$
\begin{array}{ccccccc}
s(x + dx) & = & s(x) & + & \omega \times dx & + & A^s dx \\
\text{Motion} & & \text{Translation} & & \text{Rotation} & & \text{Deformation}
\end{array}
$$

14.2.3   Kinematics of Projected Motion

After the detailed discussion of motion concerning three dimensions, we can move on to the motion of deformable surfaces on the image plane. Now we think of the two-dimensional objects as being composed of infinitesimal surface elements and consider the differential changes which are caused by motion. The motion again is composed of translation, rotation, and deformation. The antisymmetric 2×2 matrix

$$A^a = \frac{1}{2}\begin{bmatrix} 0 & -\omega_3 \\ \omega_3 & 0 \end{bmatrix} \quad \text{with} \quad \omega_3 = \frac{\partial s_2}{\partial x_1} - \frac{\partial s_1}{\partial x_2}$$

contains only one degree of freedom, a rotation of the surface element around an axis normal to the image plane (ω_3). A rotation about any other axis is not possible since it would rotate the surface element out of the image plane. Deformation is described by the symmetric 2×2-matrix

$$
\boldsymbol{A}^s = \frac{1}{2}
\begin{bmatrix}
2\dfrac{\partial s_1}{\partial x_1} & \dfrac{\partial s_1}{\partial x_2} + \dfrac{\partial s_2}{\partial x_1} \\[2ex]
\dfrac{\partial s_1}{\partial x_2} + \dfrac{\partial s_2}{\partial x_1} & 2\dfrac{\partial s_2}{\partial x_2}
\end{bmatrix}.
$$

This matrix has three independent elements, corresponding to three degrees of freedom for deformation. The coefficients of the matrix do not coincide with principal types of deformation. Here we want to show that deformation of a surface element can be divided into surface dilation, area-conserving shearing and change of the aspect ratio.

Surface dilation is given — similar to volume dilation in 3-D — by the divergence of the velocity field. The divergence is equal to the trace of the matrix $\boldsymbol{A}^s$. The trace of the matrix is invariant with respect to coordinate transformations. This corresponds to the fact that the area change must be independent of the coordinate system selected. Since surface dilation describes the area change of the surface element, the two other degrees of freedom for deformation conserve the area. Consequently, the matrices describing them must have the trace zero. This results in the following partition of the matrix:

$$
\begin{aligned}
\boldsymbol{A}^s =\ &
\begin{bmatrix}
\dfrac{1}{2}\left(\dfrac{\partial s_1}{\partial x_1} + \dfrac{\partial s_2}{\partial x_2}\right) & 0 \\[2ex]
0 & \dfrac{1}{2}\left(\dfrac{\partial s_1}{\partial x_1} + \dfrac{\partial s_2}{\partial x_2}\right)
\end{bmatrix} \\[3ex]
+\ &
\begin{bmatrix}
\dfrac{1}{2}\left(\dfrac{\partial s_1}{\partial x_1} - \dfrac{\partial s_2}{\partial x_2}\right) & 0 \\[2ex]
0 & -\dfrac{1}{2}\left(\dfrac{\partial s_1}{\partial x_1} - \dfrac{\partial s_2}{\partial x_2}\right)
\end{bmatrix} \\[3ex]
+\ &
\begin{bmatrix}
0 & \dfrac{1}{2}\left(\dfrac{\partial s_1}{\partial x_2} + \dfrac{\partial s_2}{\partial x_1}\right) \\[2ex]
\dfrac{1}{2}\left(\dfrac{\partial s_1}{\partial x_2} + \dfrac{\partial s_2}{\partial x_1}\right) & 0
\end{bmatrix}.
\end{aligned}
\tag{14.10}
$$

The first matrix describes the area change, the second a form change without changes of the angles. The square is transferred into a rectangle with an equal area. The third matrix finally describes a shearing of the square to a rhombus.

In summary, the velocity field contains six independent infinitesimal changes of the surface element (figure 14.10).

- *Translation*; two degrees of freedom
- *Rotation* around an axis normal to the image plane

$$
\omega_3 = (\nabla \times \boldsymbol{s})_3 = \frac{\partial s_2}{\partial x_1} - \frac{\partial s_1}{\partial x_2} = A_{21} - A_{12}.
$$

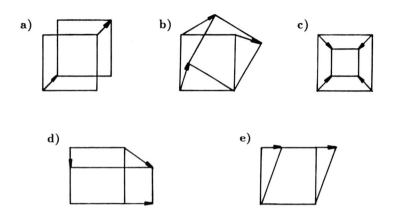

Figure 14.10: Basic types of the motion of a surface element: a) translation; b) rotation; c) surface dilation; c) stretch; d) shearing.

- *Surface dilation*

$$\Theta_S = \nabla s = \frac{\partial s_1}{\partial x_1} + \frac{\partial s_2}{\partial x_2} = A_{11} + A_{22}.$$

- *Stretch* under conservation of angles and area

$$A_{11} - A_{22}.$$

- *Shearing* under conservation of area and edge length

$$A_{12} + A_{21}.$$

14.3   Motion Dynamics

So far we have only analyzed what kind of motions can occur, but not how an object actually moves under the influence of the forces it experiences, i.e., the *dynamics of motion*. The inclusion of the physical laws of motion into image sequence processing cannot be carried out if we only consider two consecutive images of a sequence, as only the momentary state of the velocity field would be obtained. The dynamic laws of motion, however, tell us how the velocity of an object changes under the forces applied to it. The laws of motion, even for complex systems, are all based on Newton's first law which states that the temporal derivative of the velocity of a mass point, the *acceleration* a, is defined as the ratio of the force divided by the mass m

$$a = \frac{F}{m}. \tag{14.11}$$

Thus the dynamics of motion can only be included if we extend the image sequence analysis to more than two images of a sequence. Consequently, the analysis of motion in space-time images, as will be discussed in chapter 17, is not just an improvement, but a qualitative step ahead because:

- Motion dynamics is a powerful tool which allows us to understand motion even if the motion information extracted from the images is sparse. Because of the inertia of the objects, motion only changes gradually, except in extreme cases like collisions between objects.

- The inclusion of motion dynamics adds another level of abstraction to the image sequence analysis. In motion kinematics we would just describe the translation, rotation, and deformation of the observed object. Motion dynamics reveals the underlying laws which govern the motion of objects. We only need to know the initial positions and velocities of the objects and the forces acting between them to be able to compute the motion. In this way, motion dynamics is a powerful tool for prediction.

At this point, it is illustrative to compare image sequence processing and computer animations. In several respects, we have already found that image processing and analysis and computer graphics have much in common. Now analyzing image sequences, we become aware of the fact that they are essentially the same except for the fact that they are working in opposite directions (figure 14.11). In image sequence processing we start with an image sequence from which we want to extract the motion of the objects to understand what is going on in the observed scene. In computer animation, a two-dimensional image sequence is produced which is projected from a three-dimensional model of the scene.

Figure 14.11 shows that the similarities in the approaches both in computer animations and image sequence processing remain down to the finest details. A better understanding of the underlying processes leads to more realistic animations in computer graphics and enhances our ability to extract the motion of objects in image sequence analysis. Despite all these similarities, an integral scientific approach to computer graphics and image processing is still missing. It is encouraging to see, however, that progress in both areas is closely linked. At about the time when motion dynamics were included into image sequence processing, physically based modelling emerged in computer animations.

14.4 Motion Models

In the previous sections of this chapter we discussed the kinematics and dynamics of the motion for two- and three-dimensional motion separately. Now we turn to the question how we can compute the three-dimensional velocity field from the two-dimensional velocity field on the image plane. Generally, this is an underdetermined problem which cannot be solved unambiguously.

However, we can solve it if we add global information. We make use of the fact that all displacement vectors found in a certain area belong to an object, so that the individual points of the objects move in a coherent way consistent to the properties of the object. We will discuss two possible ways of representing the objects. We can either compose them as a collection of points or a collection of planar surface patches.

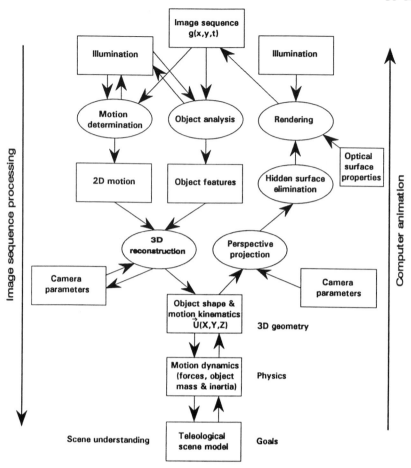

Figure 14.11: Comparison between image sequence processing and computer animation.

14.4.1 Motion of Points

Generally, a description of the motion of a point in 3-D space requires 6 parameters, 3 for the position and 3 for the velocity (table 14.4). On the image plane, we have only 4 parameters, 2 for the position and 2 for the velocity (table 14.4). As a result, for each point we obtain only 4 equations for 6 unknowns. However, if we know that the points belong to an object, we get additional constraints, which — at least in principle — allow us to extract both the position and motion of the object in the three-dimensional space.

As a simple example, we discuss the motion of a rigid body with n points. Instead of $3n$ degrees of freedom for the motion of n disconnected points, we obtain only 6 degrees of freedom, 3 for translation and 3 for rotation, independent of the number of points. Each projected point yields four variables. In conclusion, we obtain $4n$ equations for $6 + 3n$ unknowns. At least 6 points are necessary to determine the motion parameters and the positions of the points in space unambiguously. So far, the problem looks easy. It is not, however, because the equations turn out to be nonlinear. Let us assume that

Table 14.1: Summary of the degrees of freedom for two- and three-dimensional motion with different motion models.

Model	Structure		Motion			Sum
	Position	Orientation	Translation	Rotation	Deformation	
Motion of individual points						
3-D	3	–	3	–	–	$3 + 3 = 6$
2-D	2	–	2	–	–	$2 + 2 = 4$
3-D motion of deformable volume elements						
	3	3	3	3	6	$6 + 12 = 18$
$\nabla \boldsymbol{u} = 0$	3	3	3	3	5	$6 + 11 = 17$
3-D motion of planar surfaces of rigid bodies						
	3	2	3	3	–	$5 + 6 = 11$
Cross section through an incompressible 3-D flow						
	2	–	3	3	5	$2 + 11 = 13$
Motion of deformable surface elements						
	2	–	2	1	3	$2 + 6 = 8$

the origin of the coordinate systems lies in the center of gravity of the object. Then we obtain the velocity field

$$U(\boldsymbol{x}) = \left(\frac{\partial}{\partial t} + \boldsymbol{\Omega} \times\right) \boldsymbol{X} = \boldsymbol{U}_t + \boldsymbol{\Omega} \times \boldsymbol{X}. \tag{14.12}$$

Using (2.7) for the perspective projection, we obtain the two-dimensional velocity field on the image plane

$$
\begin{aligned}
u_1 &= \left(\frac{U_1}{X_3} - x_1 \frac{U_3}{X_3}\right) + \left(-x_1 x_2 \Omega_1 + (1 + x_1^2)\Omega_2 - x_2 \Omega_3\right) \\
u_2 &= \left(\frac{U_2}{X_3} - x_2 \frac{U_3}{X_3}\right) + \left(-(1 + x_2^2)\Omega_1 + x_1 x_2 \Omega_2 + x_1 \Omega_3\right).
\end{aligned}
\tag{14.13}
$$

The projection equations are nonlinear, since the unknown X_3 appears in the denominator. Therefore the solution of an equation system with many of these equations is not straightforward. Many different approaches are discussed in the literature. Summarized discussions can be found in *Nagel* [1981] and *Aggarwal* [1986].

Since the nonlinearity basically results from the missing depth information, it seems reasonable to merge motion analysis and stereo imaging [*Waxman and Duncan*, 1986]. By using stereo images, we directly extract the three-dimensional positions and velocities. At first glance, we might think that it is now simple to extract the motion parameters of the rigid body. Let a rigid body rotate around its center of gravity $\boldsymbol{X}_s$ with the angular velocity $\boldsymbol{\Omega}$. Let the translation of the center of gravity be $\boldsymbol{U}_s$. Then the velocity at an arbitrary point $\boldsymbol{X}$ is given by

$$U(\boldsymbol{X}) = \boldsymbol{U}_s + \boldsymbol{\Omega} \times (\boldsymbol{X} - \boldsymbol{X}_s). \tag{14.14}$$

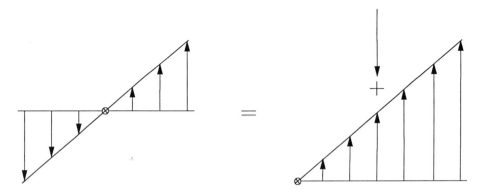

Figure 14.12: Ambiguity of the translation of the center of gravity and the rotation axis: $\boldsymbol{\Omega} \times \boldsymbol{X}$ and $\boldsymbol{\Omega} \times \boldsymbol{X}_s + \boldsymbol{\Omega} \times (\boldsymbol{X} - \boldsymbol{X}_s)$ result in the same 3-D velocity field.

Figure 14.13: Representation of an opaque 3-D object by surface elements.

From this equation, we see that we cannot unambiguously determine the rotational axis and the translation of the center of gravity, because $\boldsymbol{U}_s - \boldsymbol{\Omega} \times \boldsymbol{X}_s$ results in a nondecomposable new constant even if $\boldsymbol{\Omega}$ is known.

The determination of the angular velocity is also not trivial. By subtraction of the velocity of two points

$$\boldsymbol{U}_2 - \boldsymbol{U}_1 = \boldsymbol{\Omega} \times (\boldsymbol{X}_2 - \boldsymbol{X}_1) \qquad (14.15)$$

we can eliminate $\boldsymbol{U}_s$ and $\boldsymbol{X}_s$, but we cannot determine the component of the angular velocity which is parallel to the position difference $\boldsymbol{X}_2 - \boldsymbol{X}_1$, since for this component the vector product vanishes. Thus we need at least three points which may not lie on a line.

14.4.2   Motion of Planar Surfaces

Generally, objects are opaque so that all the points we observe lie on the surface of the object. We can make use of this fact if we approximate the surface of the object by small planar facets. The same technique is used in computer graphics to represent opaque 3-D objects. Each surface element is determined by its position in space and its orientation (unit vector normal to the surface, figure 14.13). If we assume that the object is rigid, the surface elements are not deformed. Thus we need 11 parameters to describe their motion: 3 for position, 2 for orientation, 3 for translation and 3 for rotation (table 14.4). Surface elements are a useful description, since they remain surface elements in the projection. In the projection, however, they may be deformed. Thus we need to consider the most general 2-D motion on the image plane which has 8 degrees of freedom (table 14.4). Thus, even under the constraint of rigid surfaces, the reconstruction problem remains underdetermined for a single surface element.

The most interesting question arising from this approach is how the different types of motion in 3-D (translation and rotation) are mapped onto the types of motion in 2-D (translation, rotation and deformation).

Translation

The translation of the surface element is directly given by (14.13). No easy interpretation is possible. The u_1 and u_2 components of the 2-D velocity field include $U_1, U_3, \Omega_1, \Omega_2, \Omega_3$ and $U_2, U_3, \Omega_1, \Omega_2, \Omega_3$, respectively.

Rotation

For 2-D rotation, we only can compute the component ω_3 from (14.13):

$$\omega_3 = \frac{U_3}{2X_3^2}\left(x_1'\frac{\partial X_3}{\partial x_2} - x_2'\frac{\partial X_3}{\partial x_1}\right) + \frac{1}{2}(x_1\Omega_1 + x_2\Omega_2) + \Omega_3. \tag{14.16}$$

In this formula we partly used x_1', x_2' coordinates, where the origin coincides with the focus of expansion (see section 14.2.1). Rotation around an axis normal to the image plane (Ω_3) is directly mapped onto the corresponding rotation in the projection (ω_3). There are, however, two additional terms which result in a complex rotation field:

- Rotation around an axis parallel to the image plane results in a term which is proportional to the distance from the rotation axis. This term is small or even negligible for small fields of view ($x_{1,2} \ll 1$).
- As soon as the surface elements are sloped and $U_3 \neq 0$, a local rotation appears which is proportional to the distance from the focus of expansion and the slope of the surface elements.

Surface Dilation

$$\Theta_s = \nabla u = -\frac{2U_3}{X_3} + \frac{U_3}{X_3^2}\left(x_1'\frac{\partial X_3}{\partial x_1} + x_2'\frac{\partial X_3}{\partial x_2}\right) + 3(x_1\Omega_2 - x_2\Omega_1) \tag{14.17}$$

Surface dilation is composed of the following terms:

- A constant term caused by the translation normal to the image plane.
- A term which results from the rotation around the axis parallel to the image plane. As for ω_3 this term is proportional to the distance from the rotation axis.
- Another term which depends on the slope of the surface elements with respect to the image plane, the velocity normal to the image plane, U_3, and the distance to the focus of extension.

Area-Conserving Deformation

Shearing and stretching of the surface elements are given by

$$\frac{1}{2}\left(\frac{\partial u_1}{\partial x_1} - \frac{\partial u_2}{\partial x_2}\right) = \frac{U_3}{2X_3^2}\left(x_1'\frac{\partial X_3}{\partial x_1} - x_2'\frac{\partial X_3}{\partial x_2}\right) + \frac{1}{2}(x_1\Omega_1 - x_2\Omega_2) \tag{14.18}$$

$$\frac{1}{2}\left(\frac{\partial u_2}{\partial x_1} + \frac{\partial u_1}{\partial x_2}\right) = \frac{U_3}{2X_3^2}\left(x_2'\frac{\partial X_3}{\partial x_1} + x_1'\frac{\partial X_3}{\partial x_2}\right) - \frac{1}{2}(x_1\Omega_1 - x_2\Omega_2). \tag{14.19}$$

These two deformation terms result from the translation normal to the image plane and from the rotation about an axis parallel to the image plane.

Concluding Remarks

The first order terms of the 3-D velocity field (rotation and deformation) map onto the corresponding terms of the two-dimensional velocity field on the image plane in a complex manner. Nevertheless, we can draw some useful conclusions. The relations become much simpler, when $x_{1,2} \ll 1$, i.e., if we use a camera with a narrow field of view. Within the limit of $x_{1,2} \to 0$, the perspective projection becomes an orthoscopic projection.

14.4.3   Motion in Cross-Sectional Images

Motion analysis becomes a very complex issue if the objects in 3-D space are transparent. At one point on the image plane, projections of motions from different depths are superimposed. As we discussed in section 13.3, in such a case it is not possible to reconstruct the 3-D object from a single projection. Likewise, we cannot reconstruct the 3-D velocity field.

For these cases, we can use techniques to obtain *cross-sectional images* by illuminating only a thin sheet normal to the optical axis of the camera. This technique is widely applied in flow visualization (see sections 1.4 and 2.2.8). With cross-sectional images we do obtain velocity information, but as a result a) the velocity component normal to the image plane is lost and b) the velocity field is limited to a certain depth. Therefore, we need to be very careful in interpreting the results.

15 Displacement Vectors

15.1 Introduction

In the last chapter we worked out the basic knowledge which is necessary for a successful motion analysis. Depending on the motion model used, we either need to determine the displacement vectors (DV) at single points, or the displacement vector field (DVF) in order to compute the first-order spatial derivatives (rotation and deformation terms).

In this chapter we discuss the determination of individual DVs, while we turn in chapter 16 to the determination of continuous DVFs. This separation is logical, since it is obvious, from our considerations in section 14.1, that we cannot determine displacement vectors all over the image. Thus the determination of a continuous DVF is a complex task. We need to interpolate a velocity field from individual DVs that are incompletely determined.

In this chapter we discuss the two basic approaches to compute displacement vectors from two consecutive images.

1. *Differential Approaches*: Differential methods start from the basic fact that motion involves gray value changes. These methods try to estimate the displacement vector directly from the gray value images. This approach attempts to gain as much information on the velocity field as possible.
2. *Correlation Approaches*: In contrast to the differential approach, we first select features from which we could expect an unambiguous determination of the displacement vector. This approach omits all questionable image regions from the beginning. In a second step, we try to find the corresponding selected features in both images. The flexibility and success of this approach lies in adequate selection of the correct features. If these do not depend on the illumination, we should get a robust estimate of the displacement vector. We need to analyze carefully how much motion-relevant information is discarded this way. It is crucial to ensure that no essential information is eliminated.

At first glance both methods look very different, and we can understand why the two different approaches are criticized. Our discussions in this chapter will show that both methods have significant deficits and are not as different as they may appear at first glance. They look at the problem of motion analysis from different points of view, but neither of them adequately handles the whole complexity of the problem.

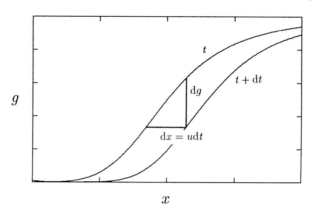

Figure 15.1: Illustration of the differential method to determine motion in the one-dimensional case.

15.2   Differential Methods

15.2.1   Optical Flux

The differential method is based on the continuity of the so-called *optical flux*. This concept has been formulated in a similar manner as in *fluid dynamics*. In case of images, motion causes gray values, i. e., an optical signal, to "flow" over the image plane, just as volume elements flow in liquids and gases. In fluid dynamics the continuity equation plays an important role. It expresses the fact that mass is conserved in a flow. Can we formulate a similar continuity equation for gray values? Are they conserved, or more precisely, under which conditions are they conserved?

In fluid dynamics, the *continuity equation* for the density ϱ of the fluid is given by

$$\frac{\partial \varrho}{\partial t} + \nabla(\boldsymbol{u}\varrho) = \frac{\partial \varrho}{\partial t} + \boldsymbol{u}\nabla\varrho + \varrho\nabla\boldsymbol{u} = 0. \tag{15.1}$$

This equation is valid for two and three dimensional flows. It states the conservation of mass in a fluid in a differential form. The temporal change in the density is balanced by the divergence of the flux density $\boldsymbol{u}\varrho$. By integrating the continuity equation over an arbitrary volume element, we can write the equation in an integral form

$$\int_V \mathrm{d}V \left(\frac{\partial \varrho}{\partial t} + \nabla(\boldsymbol{u}\varrho) \right) = \frac{\partial}{\partial t} \int_V \mathrm{d}V \, \varrho + \oint_A \mathrm{d}\boldsymbol{a} \, \varrho\boldsymbol{u} = 0. \tag{15.2}$$

The volume integral has been converted into a surface integral around the volume using the Gauss integral theorem. $\mathrm{d}\boldsymbol{a}$ is a vector normal to a surface element $\mathrm{d}A$. The integral form of the continuity equation clearly states that the temporal change of the mass is caused by the net flux into the volume integrated over the whole surface of the volume.

How can we draft a similar continuity equation for the optical flux? We may just replace the density ϱ by the gray value g. However, we should be careful and examine the terms in (15.1) more closely. The left divergence term $\boldsymbol{u}\nabla g$ is correct. It describes the temporal change of the gray value by a moving gray value gradient. The second

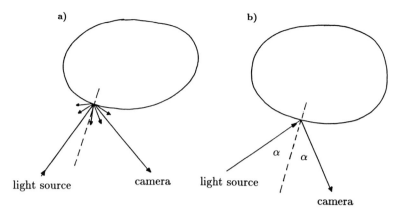

Figure 15.2: a) Backscatter of light from a diffusive reflecting surface element; b) same but for a mirror surface.

term with the divergence of the velocity field $\varrho\nabla\boldsymbol{u}$ seems questionable. It would cause a temporal change even in a region with a constant gray value if the divergence of the flow field is unequal to zero. However, gray values do not accumulate as the mass in a flow. Thus we omit the last term in the continuity equation for the optical term and obtain

$$\frac{\partial g}{\partial t} + \boldsymbol{u}\nabla g = 0. \tag{15.3}$$

In the one-dimensional case, the continuity of the optical flow takes the simple form

$$\frac{\partial g}{\partial t} + u\frac{\partial g}{\partial x} = 0, \tag{15.4}$$

from which we can directly determine the one-dimensional velocity

$$u = -\frac{\partial g}{\partial t} \Bigg/ \frac{\partial g}{\partial x}, \tag{15.5}$$

provided that the spatial derivative does not vanish. The velocity is given as the ratio of the temporal and spatial derivatives. This basic relation can also be derived geometrically, as illustrated in figure 15.1. In the time interval dt a gray value is shifted the distance $dx = u\,dt$ causing the gray value to change by $g(t) - g(t+dt)$. The gray value change can also be expressed as the slope of the gray value edge,

$$g(t) - g(t+dt) = \frac{\partial g}{\partial x}dx = \frac{\partial g}{\partial x}u\,dt, \tag{15.6}$$

from which we readily obtain the continuity of the optical flux (15.4).

Before we turn to the two-dimensional case, we discuss under which conditions the continuity of the optical flow is met. From our discussion on gray value changes in section 14.1.1, we are aware of the many effects which may cause gray value changes in images. With four examples, we will illustrate the complexity of the problem.

Diffusive Reflecting Objects in Parallel Light
We assume that a scene is illuminated with parallel light, for example, direct sunlight in an outdoor scene. Then the illumination of an object neither changes with its distance from the light source nor with the distance from the camera. We further presume that the surfaces of the objects are Lambertian reflectors, i.e., that the surface brightness does not depend on the angle of view (see section 2.1.5). Even under these straightforward illumination conditions, we run into problems with the continuity of the optical flux, since the surface brightness depends on the angle ϵ between the surface normal and the light beam (figure 15.2a):

$$g = g_0 \cos \epsilon. \tag{15.7}$$

Consequently, a rotation of the surface element will change its brightness:

$$\frac{\partial g}{\partial t} = -g_0 \sin \epsilon \frac{\partial \epsilon}{\partial t}. \tag{15.8}$$

These effects are only small if the surface elements are oriented towards the camera.

Diffusive Reflecting Objects in Divergent Light
In divergent light, e.g., the illumination of the scene by a point source, the brightness of the objects depends on their distance from the light source. Let us assume that the lamp is located in the origin of the camera coordinate system. Then the surface brightness of the object is given by

$$g = g_0 \cos \epsilon \frac{\tilde{X}_3^2}{X_3^2}. \tag{15.9}$$

With $\tilde{X}_3$ we denote a reference distance at which the object shows the brightness g_0. Since the brightness depends on X_3, motion normal to the image plane results in a change of the brightness

$$\frac{\partial g}{\partial t} = -2g \frac{U_3}{X_3}. \tag{15.10}$$

Light Emitting Surfaces
A light emitting surface does not incur any additional term in the continuity equation as long as it emits the light isotropically and its image is larger than one pixel. If the latter condition is not met, the brightness of the object will decrease with the distance squared and a term similar to that in (15.9) must be considered. Isotropically emitting surfaces occur in thermal imaging, where surface temperatures are measured by the radiation emitted in the far infrared (3–$20\,\mu$m wavelength; see section 1.2.1 and figure 4.2).

Specular Reflexes
Things become even more complex if the objects reflect like mirrors. Then we see bright spots, so-called *specular reflexes* at those positions of the object where the surface normal halves the angle between the light beam from the light source to the object point and the light beam back to the camera (figure 15.2b).

A small rotation of the object surface with a low curvature causes the specular reflexes to move to another position on the object. It is also possible that the specular reflex remains stationary although the object is moving. This is the case, for example, if a cylindric object is spinning around its symmetry axis.

Consequently, specular reflexes do not move with the object. Rather their position is determined by the inclination of the surface element with regard to the light sources and the camera (figure 15.2b). Specular reflexes distort motion determination significantly. Therefore it is necessary either to avoid or to detect them and to exclude the image regions affected from being interpreted as the motion of the object.

For the continuity of the optical flow, specular reflexes appear only as a disturbing element. Nevertheless, they carry important information, namely the inclination of the reflecting surface element. In this way, *Cox and Munk* [1954] determined the slope statistics of the ocean surface from sun glitter images taken from an airplane. More recently, *Jähne and Waas* [1989] deviced a stereo imaging system to perform combined slope-height measurements of the sea surface roughness using specular reflexes (see also plate 6b).

Concluding Remarks

The four examples discussed substantiate the fact that the continuity of the optical flux depends to a great extent on the illumination conditions and the reflection properties of the objects observed. We cannot establish a generally valid continuity equation. Only in very restricted cases, such as isotropically emitting objects, is the simple continuity equation (15.3) valid. In case of Lambertian surfaces and a point source in the origin of the camera coordinate system, the following continuity equation is valid:

$$\frac{\partial g}{\partial t} + \boldsymbol{u}\nabla g + g_0 \sin \epsilon \, \frac{\partial \epsilon}{\partial t} + 2g\frac{U_3}{X_3} = 0. \qquad (15.11)$$

If the gray value gradient is large, the influence of the two additional terms is small. Thus we can conclude that the determination of the velocity is most reliable for steep gray value edges while it may be significantly distorted in regions with only small gray value gradients.

For scientific applications of image sequence processing which require accurate velocity measurements a proper illumination of the experimental setup is important. In many cases we can arrange the illumination in such a way that the simple continuity equation (15.3) for the optical flux is met. In section 1.4 we discussed the imaging of water surface waves. In this case, the illumination could be set up in such a way that the intensity is proportional to the wave slope [*Jähne and Riemer*, 1990]. Thus the measured gray values directly represent a physical property and are not sensitive to secondary effects in the illumination of the scene.

In the following we will use the simple continuity equation exclusively. Thus we should keep in mind that the inferred results are only valid if the continuity of the optical flux is preserved in this form.

15.2.2 Least Squares Solution of the Aperture Problem

The continuity equation for the optical flux in the n-dimensional space contains n unknowns in a scalar equation. Thus we cannot determine the velocity unambiguously. The scalar product $\boldsymbol{u}\nabla g$ is equal to the magnitude of the gray value gradient multiplied by the velocity component in the direction of the gradient, i. e., normal to the local gray value edge

$$\boldsymbol{u}\nabla g = u_\perp |\nabla g|.$$

This is the quantitative formulation of the *aperture problem* which we already discussed in section 14.1.2. Then we stated that we can only determine the velocity component normal to the edge. From the continuity of the optical flow we obtain

$$u_\perp = -\frac{\partial g}{\partial t} / |\nabla g|. \tag{15.12}$$

With this approach it is not possible to determine the complete velocity vector. In order to do so, we need a larger neighborhood in which the gray value gradient is directed in different directions. We assume that we pick out N points from a two-dimensional neighborhood M in which the velocity does not change significantly. Then we obtain N continuity equations for the N points in the neighborhood M:

$$g_t(k,l) + u_1 g_{x_1}(k,l) + u_2 g_{x_2}(k,l) = 0 \quad \forall \, (k,l) \in M. \tag{15.13}$$

For compact equations, we abbreviate the partial derivatives with an index denoting the derivator. The indices (k, l) denote the spatial position in the mask. In this way, we obtain N equations for the two unknowns (u_1, u_2). In matrix representation, the linear equation system reads

$$\begin{bmatrix} g_{x_1}(1) & g_{x_2}(1) \\ g_{x_1}(2) & g_{x_2}(2) \\ \vdots & \vdots \\ g_{x_1}(N) & g_{x_2}(N) \end{bmatrix} \begin{bmatrix} u_1 \\ u_2 \end{bmatrix} = - \begin{bmatrix} g_t(1) \\ g_t(2) \\ \vdots \\ g_t(N) \end{bmatrix}. \tag{15.14}$$

The points in the mask are counted linearly from 1 to N in this equation.

The Exact Linear Equation System

First we discuss the exactly soluble equation system when we take only two points $(N = 2)$:

$$\begin{bmatrix} g_{x_1}(1) & g_{x_2}(1) \\ g_{x_1}(2) & g_{x_2}(2) \end{bmatrix} \begin{bmatrix} u_1 \\ u_2 \end{bmatrix} = - \begin{bmatrix} g_t(1) \\ g_t(2) \end{bmatrix}. \tag{15.15}$$

Formally, we obtain a solution of the equation by inverting the matrix which contains the partial derivatives

$$\begin{bmatrix} u_1 \\ u_2 \end{bmatrix} = - \begin{bmatrix} g_{x_1}(1) & g_{x_2}(1) \\ g_{x_1}(2) & g_{x_2}(2) \end{bmatrix}^{-1} \begin{bmatrix} g_t(1) \\ g_t(2) \end{bmatrix}. \tag{15.16}$$

The inverse of the matrix exists if and only if its determinant does not vanish:

$$\begin{vmatrix} g_{x_1}(1) & g_{x_2}(1) \\ g_{x_1}(2) & g_{x_2}(2) \end{vmatrix} \neq 0 \quad \rightsquigarrow$$

$$g_{x_1}(1)g_{x_2}(2) \neq g_{x_2}(1)g_{x_1}(2) \quad \text{or} \quad \frac{g_{x_2}(1)}{g_{x_1}(1)} \neq \frac{g_{x_2}(2)}{g_{x_1}(2)}. \tag{15.17}$$

From these condition we conclude that we can solve the equation system provided
• the magnitudes of both gradients do not vanish and
• the gradients are not oriented in the same direction.
Geometrically, this means that a curved edge must cross the neighborhood.

The Overdetermined Equation System
The exact equation system shows the disadvantage that we cannot perform any error analysis. This is a significant drawback since the real gray values contain always a certain level of noise. For further analysis of the estimated velocities, it is also important to know the certainties of the estimated velocities. An overdetermined linear equation system allows such an error analysis. This problem is mathematically similar to the algebraic reconstruction from projections discussed in section 13.3.4. In matrix notation, the linear equation system reduces to

$$\underset{N \times 2}{G} \quad \underset{2}{\tilde{u}} \quad = \quad \underset{N}{-g_t} \ .$$

In the equation the dimensions are marked. With an overdetermined equation system, we cannot compute an exact solution, but only an optimal solution $\tilde{u}$ which minimizes the norm of an error vector e. As in section 13.3.4, we use the method of the least squares

$$\|e\|_2 = \| - g_t - G\tilde{u}\|_2 \rightarrow \text{Minimum}. \tag{15.18}$$

The solution of this inverse problem is given by (section 13.3.4 and appendix A.1):

$$\tilde{u} = -G^{-g}g_t \tag{15.19}$$

with the pseudo inverse

$$G^{-g} = (G^T G)^{-1}G^T. \tag{15.20}$$

We obtain a solution if we can invert the 2×2-matrix $G^T G$. This matrix is given by

$$
G^T G = \begin{bmatrix} g_{x_1}(1) & g_{x_1}(2) & \cdots & g_{x_1}(N) \\ g_{x_2}(1) & g_{x_2}(2) & \cdots & g_{x_2}(N) \end{bmatrix} \begin{bmatrix} g_{x_1}(1) & g_{x_2}(1) \\ g_{x_1}(2) & g_{x_2}(2) \\ \vdots & \vdots \\ g_{x_1}(N) & g_{x_2}(N) \end{bmatrix}
$$

$$
= \begin{bmatrix} \sum_{k=1}^{N} g_{x_1}^2(k) & \sum_{k=1}^{N} g_{x_1}(k)g_{x_2}(k) \\ \sum_{k=1}^{N} g_{x_1}(k)g_{x_2}(k) & \sum_{k=1}^{N} g_{x_2}^2(k) \end{bmatrix}. \tag{15.21}
$$

This matrix can be inverted if

$$|G^T G| = \sum_{k=1}^{N} g_{x_1}^2(k) \sum_{k=1}^{N} g_{x_2}^2(k) - \left(\sum_{k=1}^{N} g_{x_1}(k)g_{x_2}(k) \right)^2 \neq 0. \tag{15.22}$$

From this equation, we can deduce two conditions which must be met:
- Not all partial derivatives g_{x_1} and g_{x_2} must be zero. In other words, the neighborhood may not consist of an area with constant gray values.
- The gradients must not point in the same direction. If this were the case, we could express g_{x_2} by g_{x_1} except for a constant factor and the determinant of $G^T G$ (15.22) would vanish.

In order to simplify the equations further, we introduce the following abbreviation

$$G_{pq} = \sum_{k=1}^{N} g_p(k)g_q(k), \tag{15.23}$$

where g_p and g_q stand for any partial derivative of g. With these abbreviations, the inverse of $G^T G$ reduces to

$$(G^T G)^{-1} = \frac{1}{G_{x_1 x_1} G_{x_2 x_2} - G^2_{x_1 x_2}} \begin{bmatrix} G_{x_2 x_2} & -G_{x_1 x_2} \\ -G_{x_1 x_2} & G_{x_1 x_1} \end{bmatrix}. \tag{15.24}$$

Using (15.19) and (15.20) $\tilde{u}$ reads

$$\tilde{u} = -(G^T G)^{-1} G^T g_t. \tag{15.25}$$

In order to obtain the final estimate, we first multiply the matrix G with the vector g containing the temporal derivatives

$$G^T g_t = \begin{bmatrix} g_{x_1}(1) & g_{x_1}(2) & \cdots & g_{x_1}(N) \\ g_{x_2}(1) & g_{x_2}(2) & \cdots & g_{x_2}(N) \end{bmatrix} \begin{bmatrix} g_t(1) \\ g_t(2) \\ \vdots \\ g_t(N) \end{bmatrix} = \begin{bmatrix} G_{x_1 t} \\ G_{x_2 t} \end{bmatrix}. \tag{15.26}$$

Then we multiply the matrix $(G^T G)^{-1}$ with this vector and obtain

$$\begin{bmatrix} \tilde{u}_1 \\ \tilde{u}_2 \end{bmatrix} = - \begin{bmatrix} \dfrac{G_{x_1 t} G_{x_2 x_2} - G_{x_2 t} G_{x_1 x_2}}{G_{x_1 x_1} G_{x_2 x_2} - G^2_{x_1 x_2}} \\ \dfrac{G_{x_2 t} G_{x_1 x_1} - G_{x_1 t} G_{x_1 x_2}}{G_{x_1 x_1} G_{x_2 x_2} - G^2_{x_1 x_2}} \end{bmatrix}. \tag{15.27}$$

The error of the estimated velocity vector can be computed easily. The diagonal elements of $(G^T G)^{-1}$ contain the variance of the corresponding model parameters except for one factor, the variance of the data

$$\begin{bmatrix} \sigma^2_{u_1} \\ \sigma^2_{u_2} \end{bmatrix} = \begin{bmatrix} \dfrac{\sigma^2 G_{x_2 x_2}}{G_{x_1 x_1} G_{x_2 x_2} - G^2_{x_1 x_2}} \\ \dfrac{\sigma^2 G_{x_1 x_1}}{G_{x_1 x_1} G_{x_2 x_2} - G^2_{x_1 x_2}} \end{bmatrix}. \tag{15.28}$$

The variance of the data can be estimated from the error vector

$$\sigma^2 = \frac{1}{N-2} \|e\|^2_2 = \frac{1}{N-2} \| - g_t - G\tilde{u}\|^2_2. \tag{15.29}$$

The computations performed allow a detailed analysis of the least squares approach. The critical parameter is the determinant of the matrix $G^T G$. As long as the determinant does not vanish, we can compute both components of the velocity vector. If the determinant is close to zero, i.e., the matrix is close to being singular, the errors in $\tilde{u}$ are large (15.28). The error will be minimal if the cross correlation terms $G_{x_1 x_2}$ vanish. This is the case, when the gray value gradients are equally distributed in all directions.

Since the matrix $(G^T G)^{-1}$ is symmetric, we can diagonalize it by a suitable coordinate transformation (see section 12.3). The axes of the principal coordinate system are oriented along the directions of the maximum and minimum sum of squared spatial derivatives. In this coordinate system, the equations for $\tilde{u}$ (15.27) and its variance (15.28) reduce to

$$
\begin{bmatrix} \tilde{u}_1' \\ \tilde{u}_2' \end{bmatrix} = - \begin{bmatrix} \dfrac{G_{x_1' t}}{G_{x_1' x_1'}} \\ \dfrac{G_{x_2' t}}{G_{x_2' x_2'}} \end{bmatrix},
\tag{15.30}
$$

$$
\begin{bmatrix} \sigma_{u_1'}^2 \\ \sigma_{u_2'}^2 \end{bmatrix} = \begin{bmatrix} \dfrac{\sigma^2}{G_{x_1' x_1'}} \\ \dfrac{\sigma^2}{G_{x_2' x_2'}} \end{bmatrix}.
\tag{15.31}
$$

These equations are very similar to the simple solution for velocity in the one-dimensional case (15.5) and the one-point solution for the velocity component in the direction of the gray value gradient (15.12). We can see this as being even more pronounced if we slightly rewrite (15.30)

$$
\begin{bmatrix} \tilde{u}_1' \\ \tilde{u}_2' \end{bmatrix} = - \begin{bmatrix} \dfrac{\sum_{k=1}^{N} g_{x_1'}^2(k)(g_t(k)/g_{x_1'}(k))}{\sum_{k=1}^{N} g_{x_1'}^2(k)} \\ \dfrac{\sum_{k=1}^{N} g_{x_2'}^2(k)(g_t(k)/g_{x_2'}(k))}{\sum_{k=1}^{N} g_{x_2'}^2(k)} \end{bmatrix}.
\tag{15.32}
$$

The velocity results from the ratio of the temporal to the corresponding spatial derivatives. The contribution at each point k in the neighborhood, $g_t(k)/g_{x_1'}(k)$ (compare (15.5)), is weighted by the square of the partial derivative. Such a weighting makes sense, since we can detect displacement more accurately if the gray value gradient is steeper. The averaging in (15.32) is equivalent to averaging a set of data points with individual errors. The weighting factor $w(k)$, which in (15.32) is $g_{x_1'}^2$, is generally equal to the inverse of the variance of the data points.

These equations allow us to analyze the accuracy of the velocity estimate. The error will be small if

- the gray value gradients are equally distributed in all directions (in other words, the neighborhood must not be locally oriented; see chapter 7),
- the mean squared gray value gradient is large,
- the neighborhood is large, and
- the data variance is small.

The data variance is composed of two terms of completely different nature. The first is related to the noise in the gray values which may be caused either by sensor noise or by quantization. The second term mirrors how well the given gray value distribution in the two images coincides with the presumptions.

At this point we should remind ourselves that all our considerations are based on the assumption that the velocity field is constant within the chosen mask size. If this condition is met, the estimated data variance according to (15.29) should be comparable to the noise variance in the image. Thus a significantly larger variance is a clear indicator that the velocity field is not constant because the neighborhood contains, for example, a discontinuity in the velocity field. Such discontinuities occur at the edges of objects. Then a neighborhood contains two regions which move with different velocities. These considerations emphasize the importance of error estimates. They allow us to check our model assumptions. Here we assumed that the velocity field is constant in a local neighborhood.

We conclude our considerations about the least-squares method with some general remarks. The solubility of the linear equation system depends only on the invertibility of the matrix $G^T G$. In this matrix only spatial but not temporal derivatives occur. This means that the spatial derivatives entirely determine whether and how accurately the velocity can be estimated.

The least-squares method is very flexible. We can use any linear model of the velocity field in the local neighborhood to be investigated. So far, we have used the simplest model we can think of: a constant velocity field. As a second example, we consider how we can integrate our considerations on the kinematics of the two-dimensional velocity field (section 14.2.3) into the least-squares approach. Our model of the velocity field then incorporates a first order Taylor expansion with linear variations in the distance from the center of the neighborhood

$$\boldsymbol{u} = \bar{\boldsymbol{u}} + \boldsymbol{A}\Delta\boldsymbol{x},$$

where the matrix $\boldsymbol{A}$ includes all possible types of motion as discussed in section 14.2.3. $\Delta\mathbf{x}$ denotes the distance from the center of the neighborhood. Instead of two, we now have six unknowns. The continuity equation for the optical flux at the point k is given by

$$(\bar{\boldsymbol{u}} + \boldsymbol{A}\Delta\boldsymbol{x}(k))\nabla g(k) = -g_t(k).$$

For N points we obtain the following linear equation system:

$$
\begin{bmatrix}
g_x(1) & g_y(1) & \Delta x(1)g_x(1) & \Delta y(1)g_x(1) & \Delta x(1)g_y(1) & \Delta y(1)g_y(1) \\
g_x(2) & g_y(2) & \Delta x(2)g_x(2) & \Delta y(2)g_x(2) & \Delta x(2)g_y(2) & \Delta y(2)g_y(2) \\
\vdots & \vdots & \vdots & \vdots & \vdots & \vdots \\
g_x(N) & g_y(N) & \Delta x(N)g_x(N) & \Delta y(N)g_x(N) & \Delta x(N)g_y(N) & \Delta y(N)g_y(N)
\end{bmatrix}
\begin{bmatrix}
\bar{u}_1 \\
\bar{u}_2 \\
a_{11} \\
a_{12} \\
a_{21} \\
a_{22}
\end{bmatrix}
= -
\begin{bmatrix}
g_t(1) \\
g_t(2) \\
\vdots \\
g_t(N)
\end{bmatrix}.
$$

For the sake of simplicity, we replaced x_1 and x_2 by x and y, respectively. The structure of this more complex linear equation system is very similar to the equation system for the simple model with a constant velocity field (15.14). Again, the solubility only depends on the invertibility of the matrix $\boldsymbol{G}$. This time, the invertibility not only depends on the spatial structure of the gray values but also on the selection of the

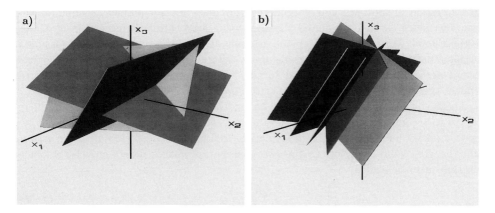

Figure 15.3: Geometric illustration of the solution of a linear equation system with three unknowns using the Hough transform: a) exact soluble equation system; b) singular overdetermined equation system with a matrix of rank two.

points. If all the points selected in the neighborhood lie on a line parallel to the x_1 axis, we cannot determine the spatial change of the velocity field in the x_2 direction.

An approach of this kind which includes planar rotation and surface dilation, i.e., only two of the four terms of the matrix A, has been described by *Schalkoff and McVey* [1982] and *Schalkoff and Labuz* [1984]. The more parameters are contained in a model, the more likely the model matrix will become singular. This will already be the case if only *one* parameter or a certain linear combination of parameters cannot be determined — as in case of the aperture problem where the velocity component is along the edge.

We can illustrate this problem using the *Hough transform* (see section 13.3.4). In case of a three-dimensional model, each equation of the linear equation system can be regarded as a plane in the three-dimensional parameter space. If the matrix is invertible, the three planes will intersect at a point (figure 15.3a). The coordinates of this point are the solution of the linear equation system.

Even in an overdetermined case, the solution needs not necessarily be unique. As illustrated in figure 15.3b, all planes may intersect at a common line. Then the solution is not restricted to a unique point, but only to a line. If this line is oriented along one of the axes, this parameter may take any value; the other two parameters, however, are fixed. In case of an arbitrary orientation of the line, things are more complex. Then the parameter combinations normal to the line are fixed, the parameter combination represented by a vector in the direction of the line is not. Using the *singular value decomposition* [*Press et al.*, 1988 and *Golub and van Loan*, 1989] we can solve singular linear equation systems and separate the solvable and unsolvable parameter combinations.

15.2.3   Differential Geometric Modeling

In the last section we learnt that the spatial structure of the gray values governs the determination of motion. Our approach so far does not adequately account for this basic fact since we just computed the gray value gradients at some points of a local neighborhood. We found that a unique determination of the velocity is only possible if the local neighborhood contains gradients in different directions. If gradients change, second derivatives must be unequal to zero. This being so, the second derivatives connect the isolated points.

These considerations pave the way for another approach to the motion problem. We try to account for the spatial gray value structure as necessary. In other words, we try to model it adequately. Our mathematical tool is *differential geometry*. We assume that the gray value structure in the two consecutive images differs only by a locally constant displacement s:

$$g\left(x - \frac{1}{2}s, t_1\right) = g\left(x + \frac{1}{2}s, t_2\right). \tag{15.33}$$

This approach assumes only a translation of the image and neglects any rotation or deformation of surface elements. We simply assume that the velocity field is locally constant. For the sake of symmetry, we divided the displacement evenly among the two images. With the assumption that the displacement vector s and the size of the surface element are small, we can expand the gray value in both images at the point $x = 0$ in a Taylor expansion. First we consider a first-order expansion, i.e., we approximate the gray value distribution by a *plane*

$$g\left(x \pm \frac{1}{2}s\right) = g_0 + \nabla g\left(x \pm \frac{1}{2}s\right). \tag{15.34}$$

The planes in both images must be identical except for the displacement s. We sort the term in (15.33) in increasing powers of x in order to be able to perform a coefficient comparison

$$g\left(x \pm \frac{1}{2}s\right) = \underbrace{g_0 \pm \frac{1}{2}\nabla g\, s}_{\text{offset}} + \underbrace{\nabla g}_{\text{slope}}\, x. \tag{15.35}$$

The first and second term contain the offset and slope of the plane, respectively. We can now estimate the displacement s from the condition that both planes must be identical. Consequently, the two coefficients must be identical and we obtain two equations:

$$\begin{aligned}
g_0(t_1) - g_0(t_2) &= \tfrac{1}{2}\left(\nabla g(t_1) + \nabla g(t_2)\right) s, \\
\nabla g(t_1) &= \nabla g(t_2).
\end{aligned} \tag{15.36}$$

The second equation states that the gradient must be equal in both images. Otherwise, a plane fit of the spatial gray value does not seem to be a useful representation. The first equation corresponds to the continuity of the optical flux (15.3). In (15.35) only the temporal derivative is already expressed in a discrete manner as the difference of the mean gray values in both images. Another refinement is also due to the digitization of time. The gradient is replaced by the mean gradient of both images. Moreover, we use the displacement vector s instead of the velocity u. As expected, a plane fit of the gray value distribution does not yield anything new. We are still only able to estimate the velocity component in the direction of the gray value gradient.

Therefore we perform a second-order Taylor expansion

$$
\begin{aligned}
g\left(x \pm \tfrac{1}{2}s\right) \; = \; & g_0 \\[4pt]
+ \; & g_{x_1}\left(x_1 \pm \tfrac{1}{2}s_1\right) + g_{x_2}\left(x_2 \pm \tfrac{1}{2}s_2\right) \\[4pt]
+ \; & \tfrac{1}{2}g_{x_1x_1}\left(x_1 \pm \tfrac{1}{2}s_1\right)^2 + \tfrac{1}{2}g_{x_2x_2}\left(x_2 \pm \tfrac{1}{2}s_2\right)^2 \\[4pt]
+ \; & g_{x_1x_2}\left(x_1 \pm \tfrac{1}{2}s_1\right)\left(x_2 \pm \tfrac{1}{2}s_2\right).
\end{aligned}
\tag{15.37}
$$

A comparison of the coefficients of the second-order fit yields six equations in total. The quadratic terms yield three equations which state that all second-order spatial derivatives must coincide in both images:

$$
\begin{aligned}
g_{x_1x_1}(t_1) &= g_{x_1x_1}(t_2), \\
g_{x_2x_2}(t_1) &= g_{x_2x_2}(t_2), \\
g_{x_1x_2}(t_1) &= g_{x_1x_2}(t_2).
\end{aligned}
$$

If this is not the case, the second-order fit to the gray value distribution either does not adequately fit the gray value distribution or the presumption of a constant displacement in the neighborhood is not valid. The coefficient comparison of the zero- and first-order terms results in the following three equations:

$$
\begin{aligned}
-(g_0(t_2) - g_0(t_1)) &= \tfrac{1}{2}\left(g_{x_1}(t_1) + g_{x_1}(t_2)\right)s_1 + \tfrac{1}{2}\left(g_{x_2}(t_1) + g_{x_2}(t_2)\right)s_2, \\[4pt]
g_{x_1}(t_1) - \tfrac{1}{2}g_{x_1x_1}s_1 - \tfrac{1}{2}g_{x_1x_2}s_2 &= g_{x_1}(t_2) + \tfrac{1}{2}g_{x_1x_1}s_1 + \tfrac{1}{2}g_{x_1x_2}s_2, \\[4pt]
g_{x_2}(t_1) - \tfrac{1}{2}g_{x_2x_2}s_2 - \tfrac{1}{2}g_{x_1x_2}s_1 &= g_{x_2}(t_2) + \tfrac{1}{2}g_{x_2x_2}s_2 + \tfrac{1}{2}g_{x_1x_2}s_1.
\end{aligned}
\tag{15.38}
$$

Surprisingly, the coefficient comparison for the zero-order term (offset) yields the same result as the plane fit (15.35). This means that the displacement vector is computed correctly by a simple plane fit, even if the gray value distribution is not longer adequately fitted by a plane but by a second-order polynomial.

The two other equations can be composed into a simple linear equation system with two unknowns

$$
\begin{bmatrix} g_{x_1x_1} & g_{x_1x_2} \\ g_{x_1x_2} & g_{x_2x_2} \end{bmatrix}
\begin{bmatrix} s_1 \\ s_2 \end{bmatrix}
= -\begin{bmatrix} g_{x_1}(t_2) - g_{x_1}(t_1) \\ g_{x_2}(t_2) - g_{x_2}(t_1) \end{bmatrix}.
\tag{15.39}
$$

We can easily invert the 2×2 matrix similar to the inversion of the matrix (G^TG) in (15.21) and (15.24), provided $g_{x_1x_1}g_{x_2x_2} - g_{x_1x_2}^2$ does not vanish

$$
\begin{bmatrix} g_{x_1x_1} & g_{x_1x_2} \\ g_{x_1x_2} & g_{x_2x_2} \end{bmatrix}^{-1}
= \frac{1}{g_{x_1x_1}g_{x_2x_2} - g_{x_1x_2}^2}
\begin{bmatrix} g_{x_2x_2} & -g_{x_1x_2} \\ -g_{x_1x_2} & g_{x_1x_1} \end{bmatrix}
\tag{15.40}
$$

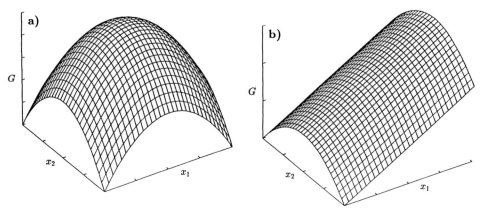

Figure 15.4: a) Sketch of a gray value extremum: the first-order spatial derivatives are zero while the second-order derivatives do not vanish. b) gray value corner; the local coordinate system is oriented in such a way that the x_1 axis coincides with the direction of the steepest gray value ascent (gradient); after *Nagel* [1983].

and obtain the following solution for s

$$\begin{bmatrix} s_1 \\ s_2 \end{bmatrix} = -\frac{1}{g_{x_1 x_1} g_{x_2 x_2} - g_{x_1 x_2}^2} \begin{bmatrix} g_{x_2 x_2} & -g_{x_1 x_2} \\ -g_{x_1 x_2} & g_{x_1 x_1} \end{bmatrix} \begin{bmatrix} g_{x_1}(t_2) - g_{x_1}(t_1) \\ g_{x_2}(t_2) - g_{x_2}(t_1) \end{bmatrix}. \qquad (15.41)$$

Therefore it is possible to estimate the displacement between two images from a local neighborhood if we take into account the *curvatures* of the gray value distribution. We have not yet discussed the conditions the gray value distribution must meet, so that we can invert (15.39). In this way we will relate the determination of the displacement vector to the differential geometry of a local neighborhood. We investigate two typical gray value structures, a *gray value extremum* and a *gray value corner*. Both terms have been coined by *Nagel* [1983].

Gray Value Extremum
A *gray value extremum* is a point at which the first-order spatial derivatives vanish, but the second-order derivatives do not (figure 15.4a). Thus a simple model for the gray value is given by the polynomial

$$g(x) = g_0 - bx_1^2 - cx_2^2.$$

We set the extremum in the first image at $x = 0$; thus in the second image it is shifted by s. We yield the following values for the spatial derivatives in both images

$$\begin{aligned} g_{x_1}(t_1) = g_{x_2}(t_1) &= 0 \\ g_{x_1}(t_2) = -2bs_1 &\neq 0 \\ g_{x_2}(t_2) = -2cs_2 &\neq 0 \\ g_{x_1 x_1}(t_1) = g_{x_1 x_1}(t_2) = -2b &\neq 0 \\ g_{x_2 x_2}(t_1) = g_{x_2 x_2}(t_2) = -2c &\neq 0 \\ g_{x_1 x_2}(t_1) = g_{x_1 x_2}(t_2) &= 0. \end{aligned}$$

Since the matrix in (15.38) is already diagonal $(g_{x_1x_2}(t_1) = g_{x_1x_2}(t_2) = 0)$, the displacement vector $\boldsymbol{s}$ reduces to

$$\begin{bmatrix} s_1 \\ s_2 \end{bmatrix} = - \begin{bmatrix} \dfrac{g_{x_1}(t_2) - g_{x_1}(t_1)}{g_{x_1x_1}} \\[2ex] \dfrac{g_{x_2}(t_2) - g_{x_2}(t_1)}{g_{x_2x_2}} \end{bmatrix}. \tag{15.42}$$

We would obtain no solution, if one of the curvatures is zero. In this case the gray value structure is a valley or a ridge. We would only yield the component of the displacement normal to the ridge. In the other direction we can shift by an arbitrary distance and still match the gray value structures in the two images.

Gray Value Corner
The missing component can be computed if the valley or ridge is inclined. Geometrically, such a structure forms a *gray value corner* (figure 15.4b). We saw in our introductionary discussion on motion analysis (section 14.1.2) that we can estimate the displacement vector completely at a gray value corner. We orient the coordinate system in such a way that the steepest ascent is oriented in the x_1 direction. Then we can model a gray value corner by

$$g(\boldsymbol{x}) = g_0 + bx_1 + cx_2^2.$$

The first- and second-order spatial derivatives in the first and second image meet the following conditions:

$$\begin{aligned} g_{x_1}(t_1) = g_{x_1}(t_2) &= b \neq 0 \\ g_{x_2}(t_1) &= 0 \\ g_{x_2}(t_2) &= -2cs_2 \neq 0 \\ g_{x_1x_1}(t_1) = g_{x_1x_1}(t_2) &= 0 \\ g_{x_2x_2}(t_1) = g_{x_2x_2}(t_2) &= -2c \neq 0 \\ g_{x_1x_2}(t_1) = g_{x_1x_2}(t_2) &= 0. \end{aligned}$$

From the linear equation system (15.38), we only obtain the s_2 component of the displacement vector, while the s_1 component can be computed from the first equation in (15.37):

$$\begin{bmatrix} s_1 \\ s_2 \end{bmatrix} = - \begin{bmatrix} \dfrac{g_0(t_2) - g_0(t_1)}{g_{x_1}} \\[2ex] \dfrac{g_{x_2}(t_2) - g_{x_2}(t_1)}{g_{x_2x_2}} \end{bmatrix}. \tag{15.43}$$

15.3 Correlation Methods

So far, we estimated motion using methods which are based on the continuity of the optical flux. From our considerations in section 15.2.1, however, we know that the continuity of the optical flux in the simple form presented in (15.3) is only valid in very restricted cases. It turned out that we can expect negligible deviations from the continuity only with significant gray value changes, e.g., steep edges (see (15.11)). Consequently, critics of the optical flux method argue that image regions should be picked out where we can expect to estimate the displacement successfully.

Such an approach consists of two steps. First we pick out suitable features. These features should be insensitive to changes in the illumination, i.e., such distortions of the continuity of the optical flux as discussed in sections 14.1.1 and 15.2.1. In the second step, we search the corresponding points in the two images to determine the displacement. First, we discuss this second step, i.e., the general principle of the correlation approach and compare it with the optical flow approach. Then we discuss two types of features which have recently been used for image sequence processing from different authors.

15.3.1 Principle

We assume that we have already found suitable features, i.e., that the gray value image has been converted into a feature image. To find a characteristic feature from the first image in the second, we take a small sector W from the first image $g(t_1)$ and compare it with equal-sized sectors from the second image $g(t_2)$ within a certain search range. In this range we search for the position of the optimum similarity between the two sectors. When do we regard two features as being similar? The similarity measure should be robust against changes in the illumination. Thus we regard two spatial feature patterns as equal if they differ only by a constant factor α which reflects the difference in illumination. In the language of inner product vector spaces (see section 3.3.1 and appendix A.1), this means that the two feature vectors $g(t_1)$ and $g(t_2)$ are parallel. This can be the case if and only if an equality occurs in *Cauchy-Schwarz inequality*

$$\int\limits_W \mathrm{d}^2x \, g(\boldsymbol{x}, t_1) g(\boldsymbol{x} + \boldsymbol{s}, t_2) \leq \left(\int\limits_W \mathrm{d}^2x \, g^2(\boldsymbol{x}, t_1) \int\limits_W \mathrm{d}^2x \, g^2(\boldsymbol{x} + \boldsymbol{s}, t_2) \right)^{1/2}. \qquad (15.44)$$

In other words, we need to maximize the *cross-correlation coefficient*

$$r(\boldsymbol{s}) = \frac{\int\limits_W \mathrm{d}^2x \, g(\boldsymbol{x}, t_1) g(\boldsymbol{x} + \boldsymbol{s}, t_2)}{\left(\int\limits_W \mathrm{d}^2x \, g^2(\boldsymbol{x}, t_1) \int\limits_W \mathrm{d}^2x \, g^2(\boldsymbol{x} + \boldsymbol{s}, t_2) \right)^{1/2}}. \qquad (15.45)$$

The cross-correlation coefficient is a useful similarity measure. It is zero for totally dissimilar (orthogonal) patterns, and reaches a maximum of one for similar features.

In contrast to the differential methods which are based on the continuity of the optical flux, the correlation approach allows for intensity changes between the two images in the sense that within the window chosen the illumination might be different globally. Hence, we can simply also take the cross-correlation technique for gray value images and do not need to extract special illumination insensitive features. This makes correlation-based techniques very useful for stereo-image processing where slight intensity variations always occur between the left and right image because of the two different cameras used.

15.3.2   Fast Implementation

Correlation-based techniques imply large computational costs. For discrete images, (15.44) reads

$$
r^2_{mn;kl} = \frac{\left(\displaystyle\sum_{p,q \in \text{window}} g_{m+p,n+q}(t_1) g_{m+p+k,n+q+l}(t_2) \right)^2}{\displaystyle\sum_{p,q \in \text{window}} g_{m+p,n+q}(t_1) g_{m+p,n+q}(t_1) \; \sum_{p,q \in \text{window}} g_{m+p+k,n+q+l}(t_2) g_{m+p+k,n+q+l}(t_2)}.
$$

$$(15.46)$$

The indices m and n indicate the position of the window in the image, while k and l run over the search range for the maximum cross-correlation coefficient at the position (m, n). Thus the number of arithmetic operations goes with the mask size PQ and the search range KL. If we assume a mask size of 15×15 and a search range of 15×15, $15^4 = 50625$ operations are necessary to find a single feature in the image.

Consequently, a fast implementation of the cross-correlation technique is necessary. In this section we show a two-step approach. First, we discuss a method for a direct determination of the maximum of the cross-correlation coefficient. Second, we discuss how the search can be speeded up by a coarse-to-fine strategy on a pyramid.

Direct Maximum Search

A fast determination of the maximum of the cross-correlation coefficient is based on the fact that we do not actually need to know the whole correlation coefficient within the search range but only enough information to find the maximum. If we assume that we are sufficiently close to the maximum, we can approximate the cross-correlation coefficient by a parabola. Let us first consider a one-dimensional example:

$$
r(s) \approx r_0 - \frac{r_2}{2}(s - \tilde{s})^2. \tag{15.47}
$$

The maximum r_0 occurs at $\tilde{s}$. We can determine $\tilde{s}$ by determining the first- and second-order spatial derivatives without a shift $s = 0$:

$$
\left. \frac{\partial r}{\partial s} \right|_0 \approx r_2 \tilde{s}, \qquad \left. \frac{\partial^2 r}{\partial s^2} \right|_0 \approx -r_2. \tag{15.48}
$$

Then $\tilde{s}$ is estimated by

$$
\tilde{s} \approx - \left. \frac{\partial r}{\partial s} \right|_0 \bigg/ \left. \frac{\partial^2 r}{\partial s^2} \right|_0 . \tag{15.49}
$$

In two dimensions, we can take a similar approach. We expand the cross-correlation coefficient in a second-order Taylor expansion

$$
r(\boldsymbol{s}) \approx r(\tilde{\boldsymbol{s}}) + \frac{1}{2} \left. \frac{\partial^2 r}{\partial s_1^2} \right|_{\tilde{s}} (s_1 - \tilde{s}_1)^2 + \frac{1}{2} \left. \frac{\partial^2 r}{\partial s_2^2} \right|_{\tilde{s}} (s_2 - \tilde{s}_2)^2 + \left. \frac{\partial^2 r}{\partial s_1 s_2} \right|_{\tilde{s}} (s_1 - \tilde{s}_1)(s_2 - \tilde{s}_2). \tag{15.50}
$$

From this expansion, we can compute the first-order derivatives at $\boldsymbol{s} = 0$

$$
\left. \frac{\partial r}{\partial s_1} \right|_0 = - \left. \frac{\partial^2 r}{\partial s_1^2} \right|_{\tilde{s}} \tilde{s}_1 - \left. \frac{\partial^2 r}{\partial s_1 s_2} \right|_{\tilde{s}} \tilde{s}_2
$$

$$\left.\frac{\partial r}{\partial s_2}\right|_0 = -\left.\frac{\partial^2 r}{\partial s_2^2}\right|_{\tilde{s}} \tilde{s}_2 - \left.\frac{\partial^2 r}{\partial s_1 s_2}\right|_{\tilde{s}} \tilde{s}_1. \tag{15.51}$$

If we assume that the second-order derivatives do not change from zero shift to $\tilde{s}$, i. e., the second-order polynomial expansion is correct in this range, we can replace the second-order derivatives at $s = \tilde{s}$ by those at 0 and obtain the following linear equation system for $\tilde{s}$

$$\begin{bmatrix} r_{s_1 s_1} & r_{s_1 s_2} \\ r_{s_1 s_2} & r_{s_2 s_2} \end{bmatrix} \begin{bmatrix} \tilde{s}_1 \\ \tilde{s}_2 \end{bmatrix} \approx - \begin{bmatrix} r_{s_1} \\ r_{s_2} \end{bmatrix}. \tag{15.52}$$

In this equation, we use the abbreviations for derivatives introduced in section 15.2.2. The linear equation system for the correlation approach has a similar form as (15.40) which has been derived by fitting the gray value surface by a second-order polynomial. The gray value function g is replaced by the cross-correlation coefficient r. Furthermore, no temporal derivatives occur.

In discrete images, the partial derivatives are computed from discrete derivative operators. If we use the simple masks $D_x = 1/2 \begin{bmatrix} 1 & 0 & -1 \end{bmatrix}$ and $D_x^2 = \begin{bmatrix} 1 & -2 & 1 \end{bmatrix}$, we obtain, for example, in the one-dimensional case (15.48)

$$\tilde{s}_m \approx \frac{(r_{m;1} - r_{m;-1})/2}{2r_{m;0} - r_{m;1} - r_{m;-1}}. \tag{15.53}$$

The second index indicates the shift between the two images for which the cross-correlation coefficient is computed.

Coarse-to-Fine Strategy

The maximum can only be found with the fast techniques discussed above if the displacements are small enough so that approximation of the cross-correlation function by a polynomial of second order around the maximum is still valid. This requirement is not met in most cases.

This problem can be overcome using a coarse-to-fine strategy on a pyramidal image. On a Gauss or Laplace pyramid, the size of the images shrinks by a factor of two from level to level. Correspondingly, the pixel distances grow by the same factor. On the coarsest level of a 6-level pyramid, the pixel distance is 32 times larger than in the original image. Consequently, we can handle 32 times larger displacements at this level. The cross-correlation is computed using the following operations:

1. *Pointwise multiplication and smoothing*

$$\begin{aligned} R_{1,1;0,0} &= \mathcal{B}\left[G(t_1) \cdot G(t_1)\right] \\ R_{2,2;0,0} &= \mathcal{B}\left[G(t_2) \cdot G(t_2)\right] \\ R_{1,2;k,l} &= \mathcal{B}\left[G(t_1) \cdot {}^{kl}\mathcal{S}G(t_2)\right] \\ r_{1,2;k,l}^2 &= \frac{R_{1,2;k,l}^2}{R_{1,1}{}^{kl}\mathcal{S}R_{2,2}}. \end{aligned} \tag{15.54}$$

As a result, we obtain a number of images $r_{12;kl}$ which contain the cross-correlation coefficient between the two images determined for each pixel in the image. The indices k and l denote the shift in a horizontal and vertical direction, respectively. In order to compute the first and second derivatives, we need to compute nine cross-correlation coefficients within an 8-neighborhood. The smoothing with the binomial operator $\mathcal{B}$ determines the size of the features used for correlation. In contrast to (15.45), this kind of summation does not result in a box-shaped window, but in a gradual decrease of the influence towards the edge of the mask. In our discussion on smoothing filters in section 6.1 we learnt that this approach is much more advantageous.

2. *Computation of Derivatives*

In a second step, we compute the various first- and second-order derivatives of the cross-correlation coefficient, i. e.,

$$
\begin{array}{lll}
\mathcal{D}_x : & (r_{1,2;1,0} - r_{1,2;-1,0})/2 & \\
\mathcal{D}_y : & (r_{1,2;0,1} - r_{1,2;0,-1})/2 & \\
\mathcal{D}_x^2 : & r_{1,2;1,0} - 2r_{1,2;0,0} + r_{1,2;-1,0} & (15.55) \\
\mathcal{D}_y^2 : & r_{1,2;0,1} - 2r_{1,2;0,0} + r_{1,2;0,-1} & \\
\mathcal{D}_{xy} : & r_{1,2;1,-1} + r_{1,2;-1,1} - r_{1,2;1,1} - r_{1,2;-1,-1}.
\end{array}
$$

3. *Estimate of Displacement*

With the derivations above, we have obtained all coefficients of the matrix and vector in (15.51) to determine the displacement vector $\boldsymbol{s}^{(P)}$ on the level P of the pyramid. We will obtain useful estimates at the pixels in which the matrix can be inverted.

Although this estimate of $\boldsymbol{s}^{(P)}$ is only a rough one, it is sufficiently accurate to be used as a starting displacement on the next finer level. Here the pointwise multiplication and smoothing takes into account the first estimate obtained on the level P, i. e., we perform the same operations as in (15.53) but first shift the second image by doubling the estimated displacement

$$
G(t_2)^{(P-1)'} = \mathcal{S}_{-2\boldsymbol{s}^{(P)}} G(t_2)^{(P-1)} \tag{15.56}
$$

where $\mathcal{S}_{-2\boldsymbol{s}^{(P)}}$ denotes the operator which shifts the image by the distance $-2\boldsymbol{s}$. Since the displacement is estimated with subpixel accuracy, this step involves interpolation of the gray values of the second image. In this way, we can proceed through the whole image until we reach the original level.

So far, we have still used gray value images to compute the displacements and tried to compute the displacement at every pixel. In the following two sections we discuss two methods which first select suitable simple features and then perform the correlation analysis but only at the points with useful features. In this way, the computational burden can be decreased significantly.

15.3.3 Monotony Operator

Kories and Zimmermann [1986] suggested using the *monotony operator* to select features for motion and stereo image analysis which are nearly independent of the illumination, but classify the spatial gray value structure simply. The monotony operator is computed in the following way: first we set all the pixels of the mask of the operator to one if their gray value is equal or less than that of the central pixel. Otherwise, the pixels are set to zero. The monotony operator then counts the ones:

$$\epsilon(k,l) = \begin{cases} 1 & g(m,n) > g(m+k,n+l) \\ 0 & \text{else} \end{cases} \quad \forall (k,l) \in \text{mask}$$

$$M(m,n) = \sum_{kl} \epsilon(k,l). \tag{15.57}$$

With a 3×3 mask, the monotony operator maps the local gray value structure onto integers between 0 and 8. The figures represent characteristic gray value structures as shown by the following examples:

$$
\text{Point}: \quad
\begin{matrix}
0 & 0 & 0 & 0 & 0 \\
0 & 0 & 0 & 0 & 0 \\
0 & 0 & 20 & 0 & 0 \\
0 & 0 & 0 & 0 & 0 \\
0 & 0 & 0 & 0 & 0
\end{matrix}
\quad \overset{M}{\mapsto} \quad
\begin{matrix}
0 & 0 & 0 & 0 & 0 \\
0 & 0 & 0 & 0 & 0 \\
0 & 0 & 8 & 0 & 0 \\
0 & 0 & 0 & 0 & 0 \\
0 & 0 & 0 & 0 & 0
\end{matrix} \; ,
$$

$$
\text{Line}: \quad
\begin{matrix}
0 & 0 & 10 & 0 & 0 \\
0 & 0 & 10 & 0 & 0 \\
0 & 0 & 10 & 0 & 0 \\
0 & 0 & 10 & 0 & 0 \\
0 & 0 & 10 & 0 & 0
\end{matrix}
\quad \overset{M}{\mapsto} \quad
\begin{matrix}
0 & 0 & 6 & 0 & 0 \\
0 & 0 & 6 & 0 & 0 \\
0 & 0 & 6 & 0 & 0 \\
0 & 0 & 6 & 0 & 0 \\
0 & 0 & 6 & 0 & 0
\end{matrix} \; ,
$$

$$
\text{Edge}: \quad
\begin{matrix}
0 & 0 & 10 & 10 & 10 \\
0 & 0 & 10 & 10 & 10 \\
0 & 0 & 10 & 10 & 10 \\
0 & 0 & 10 & 10 & 10 \\
0 & 0 & 10 & 10 & 10
\end{matrix}
\quad \overset{M}{\mapsto} \quad
\begin{matrix}
0 & 0 & 3 & 0 & 0 \\
0 & 0 & 3 & 0 & 0 \\
0 & 0 & 3 & 0 & 0 \\
0 & 0 & 3 & 0 & 0 \\
0 & 0 & 3 & 0 & 0
\end{matrix} \; ,
$$

$$
\text{Corner}: \quad
\begin{matrix}
0 & 0 & 0 & 0 & 0 \\
0 & 0 & 0 & 0 & 0 \\
0 & 0 & 10 & 10 & 10 \\
0 & 0 & 10 & 10 & 10 \\
0 & 0 & 10 & 10 & 10
\end{matrix}
\quad \overset{M}{\mapsto} \quad
\begin{matrix}
0 & 0 & 0 & 0 & 0 \\
0 & 0 & 0 & 0 & 0 \\
0 & 0 & 5 & 3 & 3 \\
0 & 0 & 3 & 0 & 0 \\
0 & 0 & 3 & 0 & 0
\end{matrix} \; .
$$

From these examples we see that the monotony operator maps local maxima, lines, corners and edges onto the figures 8, 6, 5, and 3, respectively.

The monotony operator shows several advantages:

- The computational costs are low. Only comparison operations need to be computed.
- The results do not depend on the absolute gray values and the contrast. The result of the operator does not change if the gray values are transformed by an operation which preserves the monotony of the gray values.
- The monotony operator results in a classification which essentially reproduces the topology of the gray value structure. However, this mapping is ambiguous, since permutations of the pixels within the mask — except for the center pixel — do not change the result. Another drawback is that the monotony operator in the form given by (15.56) does not distinguish between local minima, areas with constant gray values,

 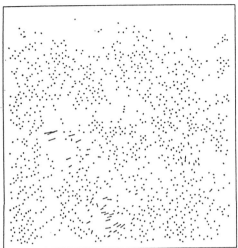

 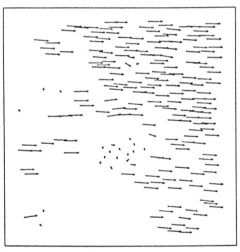

Figure 15.5: Two examples of displacement vector fields determined with the monotony operator: from *Kories and Zimmermann* [1986]. On the left one image of the sequence is shown, on the right the corresponding displacement vectors. Top: scene with an industrial robot, taken from above with a camera at rest. Bottom: detection of a moving car tracked with the camera.

and gray value valleys. All three gray value structures vanish under the monotony operation. Thus the simple form of the monotony operator (15.56) discards velocity relevant gray value features.

- A classification of features, as provided by the monotony operator, facilitates the correspondence algorithm considerably, since only features of the same class must be searched.

Figure 15.5 shows two examples of displacement vectors computed by *Kories and Zimmermann* [1986]. In the robot scene (top image), the moving arm in the lower left of the image and the person moving close to the right edge of the image are clearly detected. In the parking lot scene (lower image), a camera tracked a moving car. Thus this car appears as an object at rest, while all other objects move to the right with the same speed. The image also shows that no displacement could be computed in the areas with constant gray values, especially in the lower left part of the image.

15.3.4   Signum of the Laplace Operator

In section 6.2.2, the Laplace operator proved to be a useful edge detector. Edges are shown as zero crossings bordered by larger areas with positive and negative values. If we only take the signum of the Laplace-filtered image, we have a binary image, which clearly shows the edges of the images (see figure 6.14f). Thus the signum of the Laplace operator seems to be a useful binary feature for displacement determination.

A correlation method using a binary feature shows the significant advantage of computational efficiency. Multiplication is replaced by a logical operation. If we map a negative sign to 0 and a positive sign to 1, the multiplication corresponds to the logical equivalence operation as can be seen from the truth table

$$
\begin{array}{ccc|ccc}
\multicolumn{3}{c|}{\text{Multiplication}} & \multicolumn{3}{c}{\text{Equivalence}} \\
\hline
A & B & AB & A & B & A \leftrightarrow B \\
\hline
+1 & +1 & +1 & 1 & 1 & 1 \\
-1 & +1 & -1 & 0 & 1 & 0 \\
+1 & -1 & -1 & 1 & 0 & 0 \\
-1 & -1 & +1 & 0 & 0 & 1 \\
\end{array}
\tag{15.58}
$$

Cross-correlation is given by

$$
R(p,q) = \sum_{(k,l)\in\text{mask}} B(m+k, n+l, t) \leftrightarrow B(m+k+p, n+l+q, t+1). \tag{15.59}
$$

The equivalence operation between two Boolean variables A and B can be performed by

$$
A \leftrightarrow B = (A \wedge B) \vee (\bar{A} \wedge \bar{B}) = \overline{A \text{ xor } B}. \tag{15.60}
$$

$\wedge$ and $\vee$ denote the logical *and* and *or* operation, respectively, the bar denotes logical negation. A correlation of binary signals does not show a parabolic form around the maximum as with continuous signals, but rather a sharp peak with linearly decreasing values. *Dengler* [1985] showed that the normalized cross-correlation signal can be approximated by

$$
R(s) = 1 - \left[a(s_1 - \tilde{s}_1)^2 + b(s_2 - \tilde{s}_2)^2 + c(s_1 - \tilde{s}_1)(s_2 - \tilde{s}_2) \right]^{1/2}. \tag{15.61}
$$

Then we can approximate the function $(1-R)^2$ by a second-order polynomial and apply the same method for the direct search of the maximum as discussed in section 15.3.2.

16 Displacement Vector Fields

16.1 Introduction

So far we have discussed the problem how displacement vectors (DV) can be determined at single points in the image. Now we turn to the question how a continuous *displacement vector field* (DVF) can be estimated. The idea is to collect the sparse velocity information obtained with the local operations discussed in the last chapter and to compose it into a consistent picture of the motion in the scene observed.

Let us first look at the methods to determine single displacement vectors from this point of view. We then realize that the correlation method yields displacement vectors only at points with certain features. We know nothing about motion at the points in between nor which points belong to the same object, i.e., which show a continuous DVF. The situation is not much better using the differential method (optical flow). Now we attempt to determine a displacement vector at each point, though we know that this will be successful only if certain conditions are met. However, we have made some progress since we know the certainty of each displacement vector.

In this chapter we turn to the question of how a continuous displacement vector field can be obtained. In section 2.3 we have already discussed how much we can conclude from this about the motion in 2-D or 3-D space.

The whole area of motion determination and analysis is one of the actual research topics in image processing. Considerable progress has recently been achieved. A transition is taking place from using *empirical* approaches to approaches being based on the fundamental physical laws of motion and optics. Consequently, from the many confusing approaches basic concepts are gradually emerging. This is the topic of this chapter. Results from some recent publications will also be presented and compared with each other in order to extract the different principles.

Determination of the DVF from a single DV is not a simple interpolation problem, as we might think at first glance.

- Generally, at a single point only *one* component of the DV can be determined, since edges are much more common than corners or local extrema.
- Generally, a scene contains more than one moving object. The velocity field is then discontinuous at the edges of these objects. Since large gray value differences commonly occur at object edges, we often obtain a good estimate of the DVs but unfortunately cannot assume that the DVF extends continuously to *both* sides of the edges.

The many possibilities to determine a DVF will be considered from a unified point of view. Two opposing requirements have to be balanced in an optimal way: Firstly, the DVF should conform as closely as possible to the DV at that points, where they can be determined with sufficient certainty. Secondly, conditions shall be met resulting from the kinematics and dynamics of the motion.

The mathematical tool with which such problems can be handled is *variational calculus*. Before we formulate the problem, the basic elements of variational calculus are compiled.

16.2 Determination of DVF by Variational Calculus

16.2.1 General Approach

Variational calculus is a powerful tool which has found widespread application throughout all the natural sciences. It is especially well known in physics. All basic concepts of theoretical physics can be formulated as extremum principles. Probably the best known is *Hamilton's principle* which leads to the Lagrange equation in *theoretical mechanics* [*Goldstein*, 1980].

Hamilton's principle says that a motion follows a path for which the integral over the *Lagrange function L* is an extremum. For the simple system of one mass point this means:

$$\int_{t_1}^{t_2} dt \ L(x, \dot{x}, t) \rightarrow \text{extremum}. \tag{16.1}$$

The Lagrange function is given as the difference between the kinetic energy T of the mass point and the potential energy V,

$$L(x, \dot{x}, t) = T - V = \frac{1}{2}mu^2 - V(x). \tag{16.2}$$

In this case the path $x(t)$ of the mass point is varied in order to gain an extremum for the integral in (16.1). The above integral equation is solved by the *Euler-Lagrange differential equation*

$$\frac{d}{dt}\frac{\partial L}{\partial \dot{x}} - \frac{\partial L}{\partial x} = 0. \tag{16.3}$$

Now we ask how we can formulate the determination of the DVF as a variation problem. The path of the mass point $x(t)$, a scalar function, has to be replaced by the displacement vector field $\boldsymbol{u}(\boldsymbol{x})$, i.e., by a two-dimensional vector function of a two-dimensional vector variable. Consequently, the Lagrange function now depends on the vector variable $\boldsymbol{x}$. Furthermore, it will not only be a function of the DVF $\boldsymbol{u}(\boldsymbol{x})$ and $\boldsymbol{x}$ explicitly. There will be additional terms depending on the spatial partial derivatives of the DVF. They are required as soon as we demand that the DVF at a point should be dependent on the DVF in the neighborhood. In conclusion, the general formulation of the variation integral for the DVF reads as

$$\int_{sector} d^2x \, L\left(\boldsymbol{u}, \frac{\partial u_i}{\partial x_j}, \boldsymbol{x}\right) \rightarrow \text{minimum.} \tag{16.4}$$

The area integral is calculated over a certain sector of the image. Equation (16.4) already contains the knowledge that the extremum is a minimum. This results from the fact that the DVF should show a minimum deviation from the given DV at certain points with additional constraints. The corresponding Euler-Lagrange equations are ($\boldsymbol{u} = (u_1, u_2) = (u, v)$ and $\boldsymbol{x} = (x_1, x_2) = (x, y)$):

$$\begin{aligned}
\frac{\partial L}{\partial u} - \frac{\partial}{\partial x}\frac{\partial L}{\partial u_x} - \frac{\partial}{\partial y}\frac{\partial L}{\partial u_y} &= 0 \\
\frac{\partial L}{\partial v} - \frac{\partial}{\partial x}\frac{\partial L}{\partial v_x} - \frac{\partial}{\partial y}\frac{\partial L}{\partial v_y} &= 0.
\end{aligned} \tag{16.5}$$

16.2.2 Differential Method as a Minimal Problem

In order to become familiar with variation calculus, we first try to formulate the differential method to obtain DVs (section 15.2.1) as a continuous minimal problem. There we found

$$\sum_{j \in window} [\nabla g(j)\boldsymbol{u} + g_t(j)]^2 \rightarrow \text{minimum.} \tag{16.6}$$

This is a *discrete* formulation of a minimal problem. We pick out certain points in a small sector of the image and demand that continuity of optical flow should be preserved in the sense of a minimum quadratic deviation (L_2-norm $\| \cdot \|_2$). Implicitly, we make use of the constraint that the displacement is constant in the sector considered.

This minimal problem can similarly be written in a continuous space. Then the sum changes to an integral and we obtain

$$\int_{sector} d^2x \left(\nabla g \, \boldsymbol{u} + \frac{\partial g}{\partial t}\right)^2 \rightarrow \text{minimum.} \tag{16.7}$$

In this case, we have a very simple Lagrange function depending only on the DVF $\boldsymbol{u}$ itself

$$L(\boldsymbol{u}) = \left(\nabla g \, \boldsymbol{u} + \frac{\partial g(\boldsymbol{x})}{\partial t}\right)^2. \tag{16.8}$$

Inserting this Lagrange function into the Euler-Lagrange equation (16.5) yields

$$\begin{aligned}
\left(\nabla g \, \boldsymbol{u} + \frac{\partial g}{\partial t}\right)\frac{\partial g}{\partial x_1} &= 0 \\
\left(\nabla g \, \boldsymbol{u} + \frac{\partial g}{\partial t}\right)\frac{\partial g}{\partial x_2} &= 0,
\end{aligned} \tag{16.9}$$

or written as a vector equation

$$\left(\nabla g\, \boldsymbol{u} + \frac{\partial g}{\partial t}\right)\nabla g = \boldsymbol{0}. \tag{16.10}$$

These equations tell us that the DVF cannot be determined when the spatial gradient of ∇g is a zero vector. Otherwise we yield no more constraints than the continuity of the optical flow. Thus we can only determine the component of the velocity in the direction of the gray value gradient.

16.3   Smooth Displacement Vector Fields

16.3.1   Smoothness Constraints

Surprisingly, the continuous minimal problem only yields *isolated local* solutions without any constraints for the spatial variation of the DVF. This results from the fact that formulation of the problem does not include any terms connecting neighboring displacement vectors. The inclusion of such constraints will be dealt with in this chapter, bearing in mind the basic facts about the kinematics of motion as discussed in section 14.2. There we learnt that the velocity field within a single moving object is continuous. Furthermore, it only changes slowly. Therefore we have to introduce restrictions forcing the spatial derivatives to be as small as possible. Such restrictions are called *smoothness constraints*.

In section 15.2.2 we discussed the least squares solution of the aperture problem. This approach implicitly contained a strong smoothness constraint. We assumed that the DVF is constant in a local neighborhood. Obviously, such a constraint is too strong and not flexible enough. Therefore we look for a suitable term to be added to the Lagrange function taking the smoothness constraint into account.

Such a term requires spatial partial derivatives. Therefore we can try the following most simple term containing only first-order derivatives:

$$L = \underbrace{\left(\nabla g\, \boldsymbol{u} + \frac{\partial g}{\partial t}\right)^2}_{\text{similarity term}} + \alpha^2 \underbrace{\left[\left(\frac{\partial u_1}{\partial x_1}\right)^2 + \left(\frac{\partial u_1}{\partial x_2}\right)^2 + \left(\frac{\partial u_2}{\partial x_1}\right)^2 + \left(\frac{\partial u_2}{\partial x_2}\right)^2\right]}_{\text{smoothness term}}. \tag{16.11}$$

In this additional term the partial derivatives come up as a sum of squares. This means that we evaluate the smoothness term with the same norm (L_2-norm, sum of least squares) as the first term. Moreover, in this formulation all partial derivatives are weighted equally. We call the first term containing the optical flow a *similarity term* because this term tends to minimize the difference between the continuous DVF and the individual DV as far as they can by calculated from the optical flow. The factor α^2 indicates the relative weight of the smoothness term compared to the similarity term.

Inserting the Lagrange function (16.11) into the Euler-Lagrange differential equation (16.5) yields the following differential equation:

$$\left(\nabla g \, \boldsymbol{u} + \frac{\partial g}{\partial t}\right)\frac{\partial g}{\partial x_1} - \alpha^2 \left(\frac{\partial^2 u_1}{\partial x_1^2} + \frac{\partial^2 u_1}{\partial x_2^2}\right) = 0$$

$$\left(\nabla g \, \boldsymbol{u} + \frac{\partial g}{\partial t}\right)\frac{\partial g}{\partial x_2} - \alpha^2 \left(\frac{\partial^2 u_2}{\partial x_1^2} + \frac{\partial^2 u_2}{\partial x_2^2}\right) = 0,$$

(16.12)

or summarized in a vector equation:

$$\underbrace{\left(\nabla g \, \boldsymbol{u} + \frac{\partial g}{\partial t}\right)\nabla g}_{\text{similarity term}} - \underbrace{\alpha^2 \Delta \boldsymbol{u}}_{\text{smoothness term}} = \boldsymbol{0}. \qquad (16.13)$$

It is easy to grasp how the DVF results from this formula. First, imagine that the intensity is changing strongly in a certain direction. The similarity term then becomes dominant over the smoothness term and the velocity will be calculated according to the local optical flow. In contrast, if the intensity change is small, the smoothness term becomes dominant. The local velocity will be calculated in such a manner that it is as close as possible to the velocity in the neighborhood. In other words, the DVF is interpolated from surrounding DVs.

This process may be illustrated further by an extreme example. Let us consider an object with a constant intensity moving against a black background. Then the similarity term vanishes completely inside the object, while at the border the velocity perpendicular to the border can be calculated just from this term. This is an old and well known problem in physics: the problem of how to calculate the potential function (without sinks and sources) with given boundary conditions at the edge of the object

$$\Delta \boldsymbol{u} = \boldsymbol{0} \quad \text{Laplace equation.}$$

The smoothness term discussed so far was introduced by *Horn and Schunk* [1981]. Clearly, this is only one of many possibilities to set up such a term. Therefore we have to examine it taking into account what we know about the kinematics of motion. These considerations are not trivial, since even the constant motion of rigid objects does not necessarily result in a constant velocity field in the image plane.

We will use moving planar surface elements as discussed in section 14.2 to examine this question in more detail. For each of the basic forms of motion, we calculate $\Delta \boldsymbol{u}$:

- *Translation parallel to the image plane*: This is the only mode of motion resulting in a constant DVF

$$\boldsymbol{u} = \boldsymbol{u}_0 \rightsquigarrow \Delta \boldsymbol{u} = \boldsymbol{0}$$

- *Translation perpendicular to the image plane*: The DVF has a constant divergence (surface dilation)

$$\boldsymbol{u} = c\boldsymbol{x} \rightsquigarrow \Delta \boldsymbol{u} = \boldsymbol{0}$$

- *Rotation around an axis perpendicular to the image plane*

$$\begin{bmatrix} u_1 \\ u_2 \end{bmatrix} = \begin{bmatrix} -\Omega_3 x_2 \\ \Omega_3 x_1 \end{bmatrix} \rightsquigarrow \Delta \boldsymbol{u} = \boldsymbol{0}$$

- *Rotation around an axis in the image plane* (here: x_2 axis)

$$\begin{bmatrix} u_1 \\ u_2 \end{bmatrix} = \begin{bmatrix} (\tan \varphi x_1 + x_1^2)\Omega_2 \\ x_1 x_2 \Omega_2 \end{bmatrix} \rightsquigarrow \Delta \boldsymbol{u} = \begin{bmatrix} \Omega_2 \\ 0 \end{bmatrix}$$

- *Shear*

$$\begin{bmatrix} u_1 \\ u_2 \end{bmatrix} = \begin{bmatrix} 0 \\ c x_1 x_2 \end{bmatrix} \rightsquigarrow \Delta \boldsymbol{u} = \boldsymbol{0}$$

This is a remarkable result: all basic types of motions of planar surface elements except for rotation around an axis parallel to the image plane result in a vanishing $\Delta \boldsymbol{u}$. This effect is caused by the fact that the DVF is linear in space coordinates in every case. Second-order derivatives only appear if the orientation of the planar surface elements changes or if curved surface elements are considered. A rotation around an axis parallel to the image plane is the only type of motion which changes the orientation of surface elements. This simple consideration shows that the smoothness term was well chosen: as all modes of motion are treated equally, the moving planar surfaces not only minimize the smoothness term optimally, they zero it.

16.3.2   Elasticity Models

The previous considerations will now be illustrated by a physical model. This approach was firstly reported by *Broit* [1981], who applied it in computer tomography. Later it has been used and extended by *Dengler* [1985] for image sequence processing. Nowadays, it is a widely used tool in quite different topics in image processing [*Kass et al.*, 1987; *Terzopoulos et al.*, 1987].

Nonuniform motion causes a slight distortion from one image to the next in a sequence. The same distortions can occur if the image is regarded as an *elastic membrane* which is slightly deformed from image to image. At any point where a DV can be calculated, an *external force* tries to pull the membrane towards the corresponding DV. The *inner elastic forces* distribute these deformations continuously over the image sector.

Let us first consider the external forces in more detail. It does not make much sense to set the deformations at those points where we know the DV to the estimated displacement to be without any flexibility. Rather we allow deviations from the expected displacements which may be larger the more uncertain the determination. Physically this is similar to a small spring whose spring constant is proportional to the certainty with which the displacement can be calculated.

The external spring forces are balanced by the inner elastic forces trying to even out the different deformations. Now let us look again at the Euler-Lagrange equation of the DVF (16.13) from this point of view. We can now understand this equation in the following way:

$$\underbrace{\left(\nabla g \, \boldsymbol{u} + \frac{\partial g}{\partial t} \right) \nabla g}_{\text{external force}} - \underbrace{\alpha^2 \Delta \boldsymbol{u}}_{\text{internal force}} = \boldsymbol{0}, \tag{16.14}$$

where α^2 is an *elasticity constant*. In the expression for the internal forces only second derivatives appear, because a constant gradient of the DVF does not result in net inner forces.

The elasticity features of the membrane are expressed in a single constant. A deeper insight into the inner structure of the membrane is given by the Lagrange function (16.11)

$$L = \alpha^2 \underbrace{\left[\left(\frac{\partial u_1}{\partial x_1} \right)^2 + \left(\frac{\partial u_1}{\partial x_2} \right)^2 + \left(\frac{\partial u_2}{\partial x_1} \right)^2 + \left(\frac{\partial u_2}{\partial x_2} \right)^2 \right]}_{T = \text{deformation energy}} + \underbrace{\left(\nabla g\ u + \frac{\partial g}{\partial t} \right)^2}_{-V = \text{potential}}. \qquad (16.15)$$

The Lagrange function is composed of the *potential* of the external force as it results from the continuity of the optical flow and an energy term related to the inner forces. This term is thus called *deformation energy*. This energy appears in place of the kinetic energy in the classical example of the Lagrange function for a mass point, since the minimum is not sought in time but in space.

The deformation energy may be split up into several terms which are closely related to the different modes of deformation:

$$T = \frac{1}{2} \left[\underbrace{\left(\frac{\partial u_1}{\partial x_1} + \frac{\partial u_2}{\partial x_2} \right)^2}_{\text{dilation}} + \underbrace{\left(\frac{\partial u_1}{\partial x_1} - \frac{\partial u_2}{\partial x_2} \right)^2 + \left(\frac{\partial u_1}{\partial x_2} + \frac{\partial u_2}{\partial x_1} \right)^2}_{\text{shear}} + \underbrace{\left(\frac{\partial u_1}{\partial x_2} - \frac{\partial u_2}{\partial x_1} \right)^2}_{\text{rotation}} \right].$$

$$(16.16)$$

Clearly, the elasticity features of the membrane match the kinematics of motion optimally. Each possible deformation, which may occur because of the different modes of 2-D motion on the image plane, are equally weighted.

Physically, such a membrane makes no sense. The differential equation for a real physical membrane looks altogether different [*Feynman*, 1964].

$$f - (\lambda + \mu)\nabla(\nabla u) - \mu \Delta u = 0. \qquad (16.17)$$

The elasticity of a physical membrane is described by the two constants λ and μ. $\lambda = -\mu$ is not possible; as a result, the additional term (in comparison to the model membrane for the DVF) never vanishes. If there is no cross contraction, only λ can be zero.

With the membrane model, only the elongation is continuous, but not the first-order derivative. Discontinuities occur exactly at the points where external forces are applied to the membrane. We can see this result directly from (16.13). A locally applied external force corresponds to a δ function in the similarity term. Integrating (16.13) we obtain a discontinuity in the first-order derivatives.

These considerations question the smoothness constraints considered so far. We know that the motion of planar surface elements does not result in such discontinuities. A smoothness of the first-order derivatives can be forced if we include second-order derivatives in the smoothness (16.13) or the deformation energy (16.11) term. Physically, such a model is similar to a thin *elastic plate* which cannot be folded like a membrane.

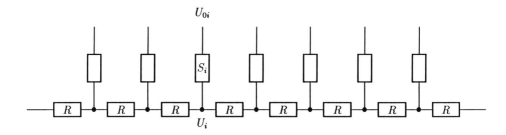

Figure 16.1: Simple one-dimensional network for a one-dimensional smooth DVF; after *Harris* [1987].

16.3.3   Network Models

Elasticity models are only one possibility to illustrate the computation of displacement vector fields. In this section we discuss another which emerged from electrical engineering, the *network model*. Compared to the elasticity models, the network model has the advantage of being a discrete model which directly corresponds to discrete imagery. We can, however, also formulate discrete elasticity models by replacing the continuous elastic material by a network of springs. This section follows the work of *Harris* [1986; 1987]. The study of network models has become popular since network structures can be implemented directly on such massive parallel computer systems as the Connection Machine of Massachusetts Institute of Technology (MIT) [*Harris*, 1987].

One-dimensional Networks
First, we consider the simple one-dimensional case. The displacement is similar to an electric tension. Continuity is forced by interconnecting neighboring pixels with electrical resistors. In this way, we build up a linear resistor chain as shown in figure 16.1. We can force the displacement at a pixel to a certain value by applying a potential at the corresponding pixel. If only one voltage source exists in the resistor chain, the whole network is put to the same constant voltage. If another potential is applied to a second node of the network and all interconnecting resistors are equal, we obtain a linear voltage change between the two points. In summary, the network of resistors forces continuity in the voltage, while application of a voltage at a certain node forces similarity.

There are different types of boundary conditions. On the one hand, we can apply a certain voltage to the edge of the resistor chain and thus force a certain value of the displacement vector at the edge of the image. On the other hand, we can make no connection. This is equivalent to setting the first-order spatial derivative to zero at the edge. The voltage at the edge is then equal to the voltage at the next connection to a voltage source.

In the elasticity models we did not set the displacements to the value resulting from the similarity constraint directly, but allowed for some flexibility by applying the displacement via a spring. In a similar manner we do not apply the voltage to the node

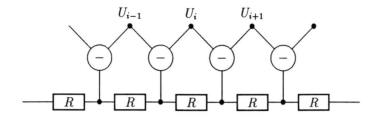

Figure 16.2: Discrete network model for a one-dimensional displacement vector field with smooth first-order derivatives; after *Harris* [1987].

I, U_{0i}, directly but via the resistor S_i (figure 16.1). We set the resistance proportional to the uncertainty of the displacement vector.

The difference equation for the network model is given by the rule that the sum of all currents must cancel each other at every node of the network. Using the definitions given in figure 16.1, we obtain

$$\frac{U_i - U_{0i}}{S_i} + \frac{U_i - U_{i-1}}{R} + \frac{U_i - U_{i+1}}{R} = 0. \tag{16.18}$$

The two fractions on the right side constitute the second-order discrete differentiation operator $\mathcal{D}_x^2$ (see section 6.2.2). Thus (16.18) results in

$$(U - U_0)\frac{R}{S} - \frac{\partial^2 U}{\partial x^2} = 0. \tag{16.19}$$

This equation is the one-dimensional discrete form of (16.13). For a better comparison, we rewrite this equation in a slightly modified version:

$$\left(u + \frac{g_t}{g_x}\right)\frac{g_x^2}{\alpha^2} - \Delta u = 0. \tag{16.20}$$

Now we can quantify the analogy between the displacement vectors and the network model. The resistor ratio R/S is proportional to the square of the spatial derivative. Both quantities express an error estimate for the displacement U_0 determined from the continuity of the optical flux.

Generalized Networks

Now we turn to the question how to integrate the continuity of first-order derivatives into the network model. *Harris* [1986] used an active subtraction module which computes the difference of two signals. All three connections of the element are in- and outputs simultaneously. At two arbitrary inputs we apply a voltage and obtain the corresponding output voltage at the third connection. Such a module requires active electronic components [*Harris*, 1986]. Figure 16.2 shows the integration of this subtraction

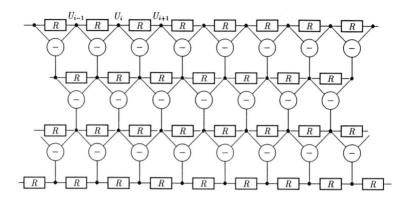

Figure 16.3: Generalized network for a one-dimensional DVF, which keeps higher-order derivatives smooth; after *Harris* [1987].

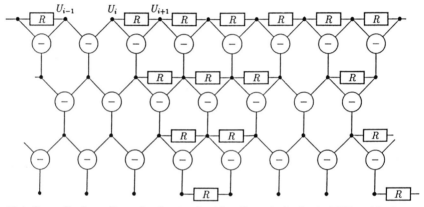

Figure 16.4: Generalized one-dimensional network with a discontinuity in the DVF and its first spatial derivative as indicated.

module into the network. It computes the difference voltage between two neighboring nodes. These differences — and not the voltages themselves — are put into the resistor network. In this way we obtain a network which keeps the first derivative continuous. We can generalize this approach to obtain networks which keep higher-order derivatives continuous by adding several layers with subtraction modules (figure 16.3).

Discontinuities

Displacement vector fields show discontinuities at the edges of moving objects. Discontinuities can easily be implemented into the network model. In the simple network with zero-order continuity (figure 16.1), we just remove the connecting resistor between two neighboring pixels to produce a voltage discontinuity at this point. We can also think of a nonlinear network model with voltage-dependent resistors. We might suspect discontinuities at steep gradients in the velocity field. If the resistance increases with the voltage, we have a mechanism to produce implied discontinuities. These few considerations prove how flexible and illustrative network models are.

Integration of discontinuities is more complex in a generalized network. Here we

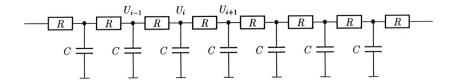

Figure 16.5: One-dimensional network with capacitors to simulate the convergency of iterative solutions.

may place discontinuities at each level of the network, i.e., we may make either the DVF or any of its derivatives discontinuous by removing a resistor at the corresponding level. We need to remove all resistors of deeper lying nodes which are connected to the point of discontinuity (figure 16.4). Otherwise, the higher-order derivatives stay continuous and cause the lower-order derivatives to become continuous.

Two-dimensional Networks
The network model can also be used for higher-dimensional problems. For a two-dimensional network model with zero-order continuity, we build up a two-dimensional mesh of resistors. The setup of two-dimensional generalized network models with higher-order continuity constraints is more complex. In each level we must consider the continuity of several partial derivatives. There are two first-order spatial derivatives, a horizontal and a vertical one. For each of them, we need to build up a separate layer with subtraction modules as shown in figure 16.2, in order to achieve the smoothness constraint. Further details can be found in *Harris* [1987].

Multigrid Networks
One of the most important practical issues is the rate of convergence of iterative methods to solve large equation systems in order to model them with networks. Thus the question arises whether it is also possible to integrate this important aspect into the network model. Iteration introduces a time-dependency into the system, which can be modelled by adding capacitors into the network (figure 16.5). The capacitors do not change at all the *static* properties of the network.

When we start the iteration, we know the displacement vectors only at some isolated points. Therefore we want to know how many iterations it takes to carry this information to distant points where we do not have any displacement information. In order to answer this question, we derive the difference equation for the resistor-capacitor chain as shown in figure 16.5. It is given by the rule that the sum of all currents flowing into one node must cancel each other. In addition, we need to know that the current flowing into a capacitor is proportional to its capacity C and the temporal derivative of the voltage $\partial U / \partial t$:

$$\frac{U_{i-1} - U_i}{R} + \frac{U_{i+1} - U_i}{R} - C\frac{\partial U_i}{\partial t} = 0 \tag{16.21}$$

or

$$\tau\frac{\partial U_i}{\partial t} = (\Delta x)^2\frac{\partial^2 U_i}{\partial x^2}. \tag{16.22}$$

In the second equation, we introduced Δx as the spatial distance between neighboring nodes in order to formulate a spatial derivative, and $\tau = RC$, the time constant of an individual resistor-capacitor circuit. Equation (16.22) is the discrete one-dimensional formulation of one of the most important equations in natural sciences, the *transport* or *diffusion* equation, better known in its multidimensional continuous form [*Jost*, 1960]

$$\frac{\partial c}{\partial t} = D\Delta c, \tag{16.23}$$

where D is the diffusion coefficient and c the concentration of the substance transported. Without explicitly solving (16.22), we can answer the question as to the time constant needed to smooth the displacement vector field over a certain space scale. Let us assume a periodically varying displacement vector field with a wavelength λ. This periodic structure will decay exponentially with a time constant τ_λ which depends on the wavelength λ.

$$U_i = U_{0i}\exp(-t/\tau)\exp(ikx). \tag{16.24}$$

Introducing this formula into (16.22), we obtain

$$\tau_\lambda = \frac{\tau}{(\Delta x\,k)^2} = \frac{\tau}{4\pi^2(\Delta x)^2}\lambda^2. \tag{16.25}$$

With this result, we can answer the question as to convergence time of the iteration. The convergence time goes with the square of the wavelength of the structure. Consequently, it takes four times longer to get gray values at double the distance into equilibrium. Let us arbitrarily assume that we need one iteration step to bring neighboring nodes into equilibrium. We then need 100 iteration steps to equilibrate nodes which are 10 pixels distant. If only isolated displacement vectors are known, this approach is by far too slow to gain a continuous displacement vector field.

Multigrid data structures, which we discussed in chapter 8, are an efficient tool to accelerate the convergence of the iteration. At the coarser levels of the pyramid, distant points come much closer together. In a pyramid with only six levels, the distances shrink by a factor of 32. Thus we can compute the large-scale structures of the DVF with a convergence rate which is about 1000 times faster than on the original image. We do not obtain any small-scale variations of the DVF, but can use the coarse structure of the displacement vector field as the starting point for the iteration at the next level.

In this way, we can refine the DVF from level to level and end up with a full-resolution DVF at the lowest level of the pyramid. The computations at all the higher levels of the pyramid do not add a significant overhead, since the number of pixels at all levels of the pyramid is only one third more than at the lowest level.

16.3.4 Diffusion Models

In our discussion of the network model, we already indicated that the network model including capacitors leads to the general transport or diffusion equation.

Thus we can compare the computation of smooth displacement vector fields with a diffusion process. A component of the displacement vector corresponds to the concentration of diffusing species. Each pixel corresponds to a small cell which is in diffusive

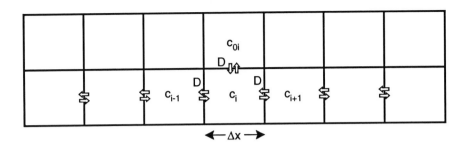

Figure 16.6: The diffusion model to determine smooth displacement vector fields.

contact with the neighboring cells. The flux density between neighboring cells is proportional to the concentration difference and the *diffusion coefficient D* according to Fick's first law [*Jost*, 1960]

$$j = -D \frac{\Delta c}{\Delta x}. \tag{16.26}$$

The similarity constraint inferred from the continuity of the optical flux corresponds to a connection to another cell with a constant concentration c_0 and a diffusion coefficient D'. In steady state, the fluxes into one cell must cancel each other and we obtain

$$(c - c_0) \frac{D'}{D(\Delta x)^2} - \frac{\partial^2 c}{\partial x^2} = 0, \tag{16.27}$$

in a similar way as in (16.19).

We have discussed the analogies to the determination of smooth displacement vector fields in detail to point out the similarities of the approaches in very different areas throughout the natural sciences. This kind of approach will make it much easier to grasp the complex problems discussed in this chapter.

16.4 Controlling Smoothness

After the discussion about the basic properties of smooth DVFs two important questions remain to be answered:

1. How can the complex equations as in (16.13) be solved numerically? Because images are large matrices huge equation systems occur. This question is by no means trivial, as already discussed in section 13.3.4 when dealing with algebraic reconstruction methods.

2. How can we adequately treat discontinuities in the DVF as they occur at object boundaries? In other words, the method to determine DVFs must include a possibility to detect and allow for discontinuities in the DVF.

Let us first discuss the *principal* possibilities to vary the minimal problem within the chosen frame. To do that we rewrite the integral equation for the minimal problem (16.4) using the knowledge about the meaning of the Lagrange function obtained in the last section:

$$\int_{sector} \underbrace{T(\frac{\partial u_i}{\partial x_j})}_{deformation\ energy} - \underbrace{V(\boldsymbol{u})}_{potential}\ \mathrm{d}^2 x \rightarrow \text{minimum}. \tag{16.28}$$

Summing up, we may describe the effect of both terms in the following way:

- The *potential function* $V(\boldsymbol{u})$ forces *similarity* between the two images. Deviations from *locally* calculated displacements result in an increased potential energy. The strength of the potential is proportional to the certainty of this determination. Where no displacement can be calculated the potential function is zero.
- The *deformation energy* causes smoothness of the DVF, since steep changes in the DVF mean a large inner deformation energy. The DVF actually calculated is given in such a way that the sum of both terms over a certain image sector is a minimum.

  It is possible to vary three quantities with this approach:

1. *Integration area.* The integration area is one of the ways that the problem of discontinuities in the DVF may be solved. If the integration area includes discontinuities wrong DVFs are obtained. So algorithms must be found which try to detect edges in the DVF and, as a consequence, restrict the integration area to the segmented areas. Obviously, this is a difficult iterative procedure. First, the edges in the image itself do not necessarily coincide with the edges in the DVF. Second, before calculating the DVF only sparse information is available.
2. *Smoothness.* Modification of the smoothness term is another way to solve the discontinuity problem. At points where a discontinuity is suspected the smoothness constraint may be weakened or even vanished. This allows discontinuities. Again this is an iterative algorithm. The smoothness term must include a control function which switches off the smoothness constraint in appropriate conditions. This property is called *controlled smoothness* [*Terzopoulos*, 1986].
3. *Similarity.* Modifications of the similarity term or deformation energy include all the possibilities available to estimate local DV (discussed in chapter 15). Here the basic question is: how can we safely progress from visual to physical correspondence? We remember that both may not coincide because of changes in the illumination or because of occlusions.

After this compilation of all the possibilities we are well prepared for the following discussion on recent approaches. We will discuss and compare them to see how the complicated and large equation systems can be solved. Since results of recent publications are included and as we are dealing with an area of active research, no final judgement of the different approaches is given. The purpose of the rest of this chapter is to outline the state of the art and the unsolved problems.

16.4.1   Smooth Displacement Vector Fields

Global smoothness as shown in (16.13) was first introduced by *Horn and Schunk* [1981]. Here we now discuss how to solve this equation numerically. *Horn and Schunk* used the

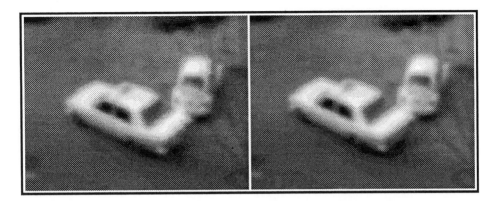

Figure 16.7: Two consecutive images from the Hamburg taxi scene. This scene has been taken in the Computer Science Department at Hamburg University and since then has been used as a test sequence for image sequence processing. The copy shown here was kindly provided by *J. Dengler* and *M. Schmidt*, German Cancer Research Center, Heidelberg.

following approximation for the Laplace operator:

$$\Delta \boldsymbol{u} \approx \overline{\boldsymbol{u}} - \boldsymbol{u}.$$

With $\overline{\boldsymbol{u}}$ we denote a local mean of the DVF $\boldsymbol{u}$. Thus the Laplacian is built by subtracting a mean value from the unfiltered velocity field. We used the same approach in one formulation of the discrete Laplacian operator in section 6.2.2 (6.43) and in building the Laplacian pyramid (section 8.2.2). Using this approach, *Horn and Schunk* found a simple iterative solution based on a simple gradient method:

$$\boldsymbol{u}^{(j+1)} = \overline{\boldsymbol{u}^{(j)}} - \nabla g \frac{\nabla g \, \overline{\boldsymbol{u}^{(j)}} + g_t}{|\nabla g|^2 + \alpha^2}. \tag{16.29}$$

As long as the gray value gradient is small, the local value of the displacement vector is taken from the mean of the neighborhood. In this way, the displacement vector is spread into regions where we cannot determine a displacement vector. If the gray value is large, the displacement vector is corrected by the second term in (16.29), provided that the continuity equation is not yet met by $\boldsymbol{u}^{(j)}$.

Dengler [1985] proposed a modified solution. In his studies he worked with the well-known taxi sequence, in which a taxi turns to the right at a crossing. Two consecutive images of these sequence are shown in figure 16.7. *Dengler's* approach basically shows two modifications.

- First, and most important, he uses a multigrid approach. As discussed in section 16.3.3, multigrid methods are an efficient way to accelerate the convergence of iterative methods.

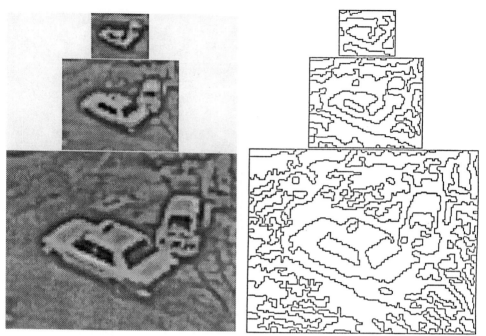

Figure 16.8: a) Three levels of the Laplace pyramid computed from the taxi scene (figure 16.7): a) pseudo-logarithmically filtered gray values; b) zero crossings at the same levels; kindly provided by *M. Schmidt* and *J. Dengler*, German Cancer Research Center, Heidelberg.

- Second, he does not use the gray values in the similarity term directly. Since the image is decomposed into a Laplace pyramid anyway, the *signum of the Laplace operator* at each level seems to be a proper choice for a simple binary feature. Using a binary feature in the similarity term, we can evaluate the displacement vectors with a fast correlation method as discussed in section 15.3.4.

Later *Schmidt* [1988] improved the method even further. Although the signum of the Laplace operator turned out to be a robust feature for the determination of displacement vectors, the accuracy of the estimated displacement vector is limited because a binary feature contains zero crossings only with an accuracy of $\pm 1/2$ pixels.

A *pseudo-logarithmic transformation* of the gray values in the Laplace pyramid

$$g'(x) = \text{sign}(g(x)) \ln(1 + |g(x)|) \tag{16.30}$$

turns out to be a good compromise. It is a more detailed feature but not as sensitive to illumination variations as the gray value. The pseudo-logarithmic transformation adapts well to the gray value histogram in Laplace pyramids. The histograms typically show a sharp peak around the gray value zero and long ridges for high positive and negative gray values. They are caused by the relatively seldom occurrence of edges. The pseudo-logarithmic transformation compresses the gray values with large magnitudes and thus leads to a more even distribution of the features.

Three levels of the pseudo logarithmic filtered Laplace pyramid are shown in figure 16.8a, the computed displacement vector field at the same levels is shown in figures 16.9a–c. From the coarsest to the finest level, the moving car can be recognized

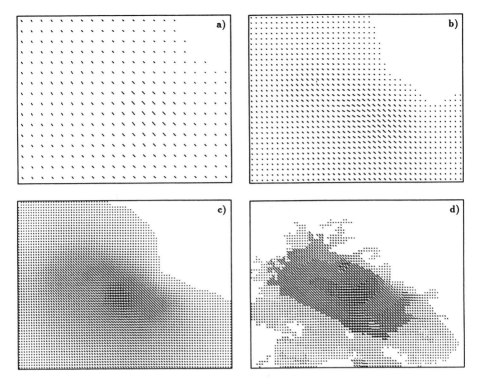

Figure 16.9: Determination of the DVF in the taxi scene (figure 16.7) using the method of the dynamic pyramid: a) through c) three levels of the DVF corresponding to the levels shown in figure 16.8a using a global smoothness constraint; d) final result of the DVF using a region-oriented smoothness constraint; the regions were determined from the zero crossings in figure 16.8b; kindly provided by *M. Schmidt* and *J. Dengler*, German Cancer Research Center, Heidelberg.

from the DVF more and more precisely. However, we also discover some significant errors. Because of the global smoothness constraint, the displacement vector field shows no discontinuities at the edges of the car but rather a gradual decrease towards zero. Furthermore, the DVF extends considerably past the edges of the taxi, especially to the lower right. The shadow of the car is located in this part of the image. Since it moves with the car, it produces an apparent displacement.

16.4.2 Edge-oriented Smoothness

Like *Dengler*, *Hildreth* [1984] uses the Laplace filtered image, any further computations she makes being limited to the zero crossings. The approach is motivated by the fact that zero crossings mark the gray value edges (section 6.2), i. e., the features at which we can compute the velocity component normal to the edge. The big advantage of this approach is that the preselection of promising features considerably decreases any computation required.

By selecting the zero-crossings, the smoothness constraint is limited to a certain

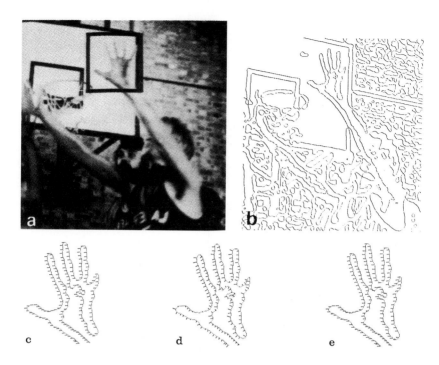

Figure 16.10: Computation of the DVF along zero crossings in a Laplace filtered image: a) original with a marked sector; b) zero crossings of the Laplace filtered image; c) true DVF (pure translation); d) locally computed velocity components normal to the zero-crossings; e) VVF, computed using a smoothness constraint along zero crossings; from *Hildreth* [1984].

edge. This seems useful, since a zero crossing most likely belongs to an object but does not cross the object boundaries. However, this is not necessarily the case (figure 16.8b). If a zero crossing is contained within an object, the velocity along the contour should show no discontinuities. By selecting a line instead of an area for the smoothness constraint, the integration region changes from an area to the line integral

$$\oint ds \left\{ (\boldsymbol{n}\boldsymbol{u} - u_\perp)^2 + \alpha^2 \left[\left(\frac{\partial u_1}{\partial s} \right)^2 + \left(\frac{\partial u_2}{\partial s} \right)^2 \right] \right\} \rightarrow \text{minimum.} \qquad (16.31)$$

$\boldsymbol{n}$ is a unit vector normal to the edge and $u_\perp$ the velocity normal to the edge. The derivatives of the velocities are computed in the direction of the edge. The component normal to the edge is directly given by the similarity term, while the velocity term parallel to the edge must be inferred from the smoothness constraint all along the edge. The solution of the linear equation system resulting from (16.31) is computed iteratively using the method of the conjugate gradients. Figures 16.10c, d show that the method works well. The computed DVF along the zero crossings coincides well with the true DVF.

16.4.3 Region-limited Smoothness

The edge-oriented method shows several significant disadvantages. One has already been pointed out: it is not sure that a zero crossing is contained within an object (see figure 16.8b). Thus we cannot assume that the DVF is continuous along the zero crossing. Since only edges are used to compute the DVF, only one component of the displacement vector can be computed locally. In this way, all features either as gray value maxima or gray value corners which allow an unambiguous local determination of a displacement vector are disregarded.

A region-oriented approach does not omit such points, but still tries to limit the smoothness within objects. Again zero-crossings are used to separate the image into regions. Region-limited smoothness just drops the continuity constraint at the boundaries of the region. The simplest approach to this form of constraint is to limit the integration areas to the different regions and to evaluate them separately.

As expected, a region-limited smoothness constraint results in a DVF with discontinuities at the region's boundaries (figure 16.9d) which is in clear contrast to the globally smooth DVF in figure 16.9c. We immediately recognize the taxi by the boundaries of the DVF. We also observe, however, that the car is segmented further into regions with different DVFs, as shown in the taxi plate on the roof of the car and the back and side windows. The small regions especially show a DVF which is significantly different from that in larger regions. Thus a simple region-limited smoothness constraint does not reflect the fact that there might be separated regions within objects. The DVF may well be smooth across these boundaries.

16.4.4 Oriented Smoothness

The approach of *Nagel* [1986] shows another way to allow for discontinuities in the DVF. *Nagel's* constraint is not as restrictive as that just discussed for region-limited smoothness. He modifies the smoothness constraint in such a way that at steep edges smoothness is only preserved along edges but not across edges. Again this approach is motivated by the fact that gray value edges may also be edges of moving objects. In contrast to the methods previously discussed, the continuity is not completely cut off at a certain threshold but depends on the steepness of the edges. This approach results in a complex smoothness term (the deformation energy T):

$$
\begin{aligned}
T = \frac{\alpha^2}{g_{x_1}^2 + g_{x_2}^2 + 2\gamma} & \left\{ \left(g_{x_1}^2 + g_{x_2}^2 \right) \left[(\nabla u_1 \mathbf{t}_g)^2 + (\nabla u_2 \mathbf{t}_g)^2 \right] \right. \\
+ \ \gamma & \left. \left[\left(\frac{\partial u_1}{\partial x_1} \right)^2 + \left(\frac{\partial u_1}{\partial x_2} \right)^2 + \left(\frac{\partial u_2}{\partial x_1} \right)^2 + \left(\frac{\partial u_2}{\partial x_2} \right)^2 \right] \right\}.
\end{aligned}
\tag{16.32}
$$

For a clear representation of this complex equation different notations for partial derivatives have been used. The vector $\mathbf{t}_g$ is a unit vector parallel to the gray value gradient

$$
\mathbf{t}_g = \left(g_{x_1}^2 + g_{x_2}^2 \right)^{-1/2} \begin{bmatrix} g_{x_2} \\ -g_{x_1} \end{bmatrix}.
$$

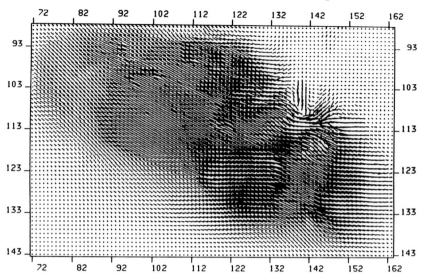

Figure 16.11: DVF for the taxi scene (figure 16.7) as determined with the oriented smoothness constraint by *Enkelmann* [1986].

Equation (16.32) basically contains two terms. The first contains the oriented smoothness constraint which only works along gray value edges, since the velocity gradients are projected onto this direction. The second term contains the well-known homogeneous smoothness constraint.

As long as no significant gray value gradients exist $(g_{x_1}^2 + g_{x_2}^2 \ll 2\gamma)$, the oriented smoothness constraint plays no role. Thus (16.32) reduces the normal homogeneous smoothness constraint. At prominent gray value edges $g_{x_1}^2 + g_{x_2}^2 \gg 2\gamma$, however, the oriented smoothness constraint becomes dominant.

Enkelmann [1986] also applies a multigrid approach to compute the DVF using this smoothness constraint. The final result of the oriented smoothness method applied to the taxi scene is shown in figure 16.11. Despite the detailed smoothness constraint, the computed DVF does not seem to be superior to the results of the other methods (figure 16.9c and d). The erroneous displacement vectors at the upper right edge of the car and the significant variations of the DVF within the taxi are surprising. Qualitatively, we have the impression that the DVF computed using the oriented smoothness constraint lies between the results of the global and region-limited smoothness constraints, as we would expect.

16.5   Summary

The examples discussed in this section demonstrate that significant progress could be achieved in computing DVF. However, the current stage is still not satisfying.

- Unfortunately in nearly all the studies on motion analysis performed so far, image sequences have been used where the true DVF is not known. This is a serious drawback. Only if the true DVF is known, is a quantitative analysis of the accuracy and an objective comparison of different methods possible.

- A convincing solution to incorporate discontinuities into the DVF in an adequate manner still does not seem to exist. Without doubt this is a difficult question. Object edges at which we can determine the displacement vector accurately are simultaneously discontinuities in the DVF. We can neither smooth over these discontinuities as a global smoothness constraint does, nor can we simply cut it off, as other constraints do. We need an object-oriented approach which allows us to determine to which object these velocity vectors belong. *Schmidt* [1988] was the first to consider these facts.

- Bearing in mind all the difficulties in determining displacement vector fields, we might ask the broad question whether it makes sense to compute a DVF and to extrapolate it into regions where we could not determine velocity information. It might be more appropriate, instead of computing a DFV at this early stage of motion analysis, to wait until we have more information to separate the scene into individual objects.

17 Space-Time Images

17.1 Motion is Orientation

So far, we have analyzed motion from only two consecutive images of a sequence, but did not consider the whole sequence. This stemmed from a limited capacity to handle image sequence data. Nowadays, video and computer hardware can record, store, and evaluate long image sequences (see section 1.2.2 and appendix B). It is much more important, however, to recognize that there is no *principal* reason to limit image sequence processing to an image pair. On the contrary, it seems to be an unjustified restriction. That is certainly true for the concepts developed so far. In the differential approach (section 15.2) temporal derivatives play an essential role (see (15.5), (15.12), and (15.27)). With only two consecutive images of a sequence, we can approximate the temporal derivative just by the difference between the two images. This may be the simplest approximation, but not necessarily the best (see section 6.3.5).

In this section, we consider image sequence analysis in a multi-dimensional space spanned by one to three space and one time coordinates. Consequently, we speak of *space-time images* or the xt space. Even a superficial analysis shows the significant advantages of this new approach:

- Motion can also be analyzed in the Fourier domain. The Fourier space corresponding to the xt space is spanned by one to three wave number and one frequency coordinates, and is denoted as the $k\omega$ space.
- The concepts of two-dimensional image processing as local neighborhood operations (chapter 5) and local orientation (chapter 7) can also be used in space-time imagery.
- We can analyze the temporal change of motion. This allows a much better modelling of the displacement vector field. We can include more powerful constraints implied by the dynamics of motion (see section 14.3).
- Using more than two images, we can expect a more robust and accurate determination of motion. This is a crucial issue for scientific applications.

In this introductory section, we show that motion can be regarded as orientation in the xt space. Let us consider a space-time image as shown in figure 17.1. We can think of a three-dimensional space-time image as a stack of consecutive images put one on top of the other, a so-called *image stack* (figure 17.1). An image sequence may also be represented as an *image cube* as shown in figure 1.8. At each visible face of the cube we map a cross section in the corresponding direction. Both representations cannot show

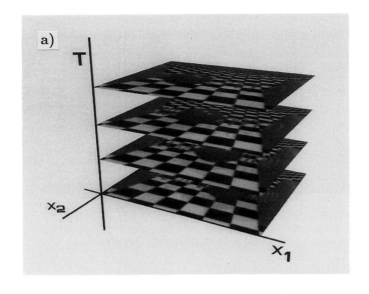

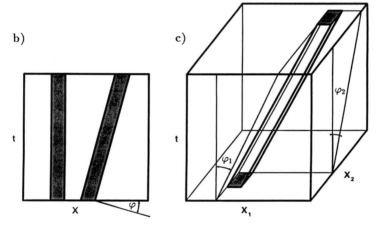

Figure 17.1: Space-time images: a) representation as a stack of images; b) two-dimensional space-time image with one space and one time coordinate; c) three-dimensional space-time image.

the whole sequence at once. In a space-time image a pixel extends to a *voxel*, i.e., it represents a gray value in a small volume element with the extensions Δx_1, Δx_2, and Δt.

To analyze motion in space-time images, we first consider a simple example with one space and one time coordinate (figure 17.1b). A non-moving 1-D object shows vertically orientated gray value structures. If an object is moving, it is shifted from image to image and thus shows up as an inclined gray value structure. Generally, it is obvious that the velocity is directly linked to the orientation in space-time images. In the simple case of a 2-D space-time image, the velocity is given by

$$u = -\tan\varphi,\tag{17.1}$$

Figure 17.2: x_1t-cross sections through an image sequence showing small-scale water surface propagating on the water surface: a) 4 m/s wind speed and 6.2 m fetch; b) 6 m/s wind speed and 21.3 m fetch; unpublished data taken by the author in the Marseille wind/wave facilty.

where φ is the angle between the x axis and the normal to the lines of constant gray values. The extension to two dimensions in space is straightforward and illustrated in figure 17.1c:

$$\boldsymbol{u} = - \begin{bmatrix} \tan \varphi_1 \\ \tan \varphi_2 \end{bmatrix}. \tag{17.2}$$

The angles φ_1 and φ_2 are defined analogously as the angle between the plane normal to the lines of constant gray values and the x_1 and x_2 axes.

Figure 17.2 shows x_1t-cross sections through an image sequence of the water surface waves (see section 1.4 and figure 1.8). We can immediately recognize the different forms of wave motion in the two images. In figure 17.2a, small- and large-scale waves move with the same speed. Motion is much more complex in figure 17.2b. A large-scale wave is rapidly moving through the image with constant speed. The S-shaped lines of constant gray values of the smaller scale waves indicate that the propagation of these waves is modulated by the large scale wave. It is very encouraging that we can recognize such complex superimposing motions in the $\boldsymbol{x}t$ space. May be the transition of motion analysis from image pairs to whole sequences in the $\boldsymbol{x}t$ space is not just an improvement but a qualitatively new approach.

In summary, we come to the important conclusion: *Motion appears as orientation in space-time images.* Consequently, we can extend the concepts of orientation analysis, developed in chapter 7, to the motion problem.

This approach to motion analysis has much in common with the problem of reconstruction of 3-D images from projections. Actually, we can think of a geometrical determination of the velocity by observing the transparent three-dimensional space-time image from different points of view. At the right observation angle, we look along the edges of the moving object and obtain the velocity from the angle between the observation direction and the time axis. If we observe only the edge of an object, we cannot find such an observation angle unambiguously. We can change the component of the angle along the edge arbitrarily and still look along the edge. In this way, we discover the *aperture problem*, discussed in section 14.1.2, from a different point of view.

Starting from the basic fact that motion is equivalent to orientation in the xt space, we come to the final chapter of this book. First we will extend our understanding by analyzing motion in the $k\omega$ space. Then we will revise the corresponding problem and discuss velocity filtering. Finally, we discuss several concepts of analyzing motion in the xt space.

17.2 Motion in Fourier Domain

Introducing the xt space, we gain the significant advantage that we can also analyze motion in the corresponding Fourier domain, the $k\omega$ space. This simple fact opens up a new approach to image sequence analysis. First we consider the example of an image sequence in which all the objects are moving with constant velocity. Such a sequence $g(\boldsymbol{x}, t)$ can be described by

$$g(\boldsymbol{x}, t) = g(\boldsymbol{x} - \boldsymbol{u}t). \tag{17.3}$$

This equation is known as the general solution for the differential equation for dispersion-free propagation of waves. The Fourier transform of this sequence reads

$$\hat{g}(\boldsymbol{k}, \omega) = \frac{1}{(2\pi)^3} \int_t \mathrm{d}t \int_x \mathrm{d}^2 x \, g(\boldsymbol{x} - \boldsymbol{u}t) \exp[-\mathrm{i}(\boldsymbol{k}\boldsymbol{x} - \omega t)]. \tag{17.4}$$

Substituting

$$\boldsymbol{x}' = \boldsymbol{x} - \boldsymbol{u}t$$

we obtain

$$\hat{g}(\boldsymbol{k}, \omega) = \frac{1}{(2\pi)^3} \int_t \mathrm{d}t \left[\int_{x'} \mathrm{d}^2 x' \, g(\boldsymbol{x}') \exp(-\mathrm{i}\boldsymbol{k}\boldsymbol{x}') \right] \exp(-\mathrm{i}\boldsymbol{k}\boldsymbol{u}t) \exp(\mathrm{i}\omega t).$$

The inner integral covers the spatial coordinates and results in the spatial Fourier transform of the image $g(\boldsymbol{x})$, $\hat{g}(\boldsymbol{k})$. The outer integral over the time coordinate reduces to a δ function

$$\hat{g}(\boldsymbol{k}, \omega) = \hat{g}(\boldsymbol{k})\delta(\boldsymbol{k}\boldsymbol{u} - \omega). \tag{17.5}$$

This equation states that an object moving with the velocity $\boldsymbol{u}$ occupies only a subspace in the $k\omega$ space. In the two- and three-dimensional xt space, it is a line and a plane, respectively. The equation for the plane is directly given by the argument of the δ function in (17.5):

$$\omega = \boldsymbol{k}^T \boldsymbol{u}. \tag{17.6}$$

This plane intersects the $k_1 k_2$ plane normal to the direction of the velocity since in this direction the inner product $\boldsymbol{k}\boldsymbol{u}$ vanishes. The slope of the plane, a two-component vector, yields the velocity

$$\nabla_k \omega = \nabla_k (\boldsymbol{k}\boldsymbol{u}) = \boldsymbol{u}.$$

The index k in the gradient operator denotes that the partial derivations are computed with respect to k.

From these considerations, it is obvious — at least in principal — how we can determine the velocity in an image sequence showing a constant velocity. We compute the Fourier transform of the sequence and then determine the slope of the plane on which the spectrum of the sequence is located. We can do this best if the scene contains small-scale structures, i. e., high wave numbers which are distributed in many directions. We cannot determine the slope of the plane unambiguously if the spectrum lies on a line instead of a plane. This is the case when the spatial structure of the gray values is oriented locally. From the line in Fourier space we only obtain the component of the plane slope in the direction of the spatial local orientation. In this way, we encounter the *aperture problem* in the $k\omega$ space.

The introduction of the $k\omega$ space also allows the central problem of image sequence analysis, the *correspondence problem*, to be tackled from a new point of view. The correspondence problem, as discussed in section 14.1.3, states that, under most circumstances, we cannot unambiguously find corresponding features in consecutive images of a sequence.

As an example, we reconsider a periodic gray value structure with the wavelength λ_0, moving with the velocity u_0. Physically speaking, such an object is a planar wave

$$g(\boldsymbol{x}, t) = g_0 \exp[-i(\boldsymbol{k}_0 \boldsymbol{x} - \boldsymbol{u}_0 \boldsymbol{k}_0 t)].$$

Let us imagine that we have taken images at temporal distances Δt. Because of the motion, the phase of the planar wave changes from image to image. The inter-image phase shift is given by

$$\Delta \phi = \boldsymbol{k}_0 \boldsymbol{u}_0 \Delta t. \tag{17.7}$$

Displacements and thus velocities cannot be determined unambiguously from phase shifts, since we cannot distinguish what multiples of a wavelength a wave actually moves. The inter-image displacement is only unambiguous if the magnitude of the displacement is smaller than half a wavelength. This means that the magnitude of the phase shift must be smaller than π:

$$|\Delta \phi| < \pi.$$

Together with (17.7) we yield a condition for the temporal sampling of the image sequence

$$\Delta t < \frac{\pi}{u_0 k_0} = \frac{\pi}{\omega_0} = \frac{T_0}{2}. \tag{17.8}$$

This condition sounds very familiar. It says that we must sample each temporal pattern at least two times per period T_0. This is nothing else but the *temporal sampling theorem*. The correspondence problem arose only because the image pair was an inadequate discrete representation of the temporal properties of the image sequence. In this respect, we can consider the correspondence problem as a temporal *aliasing* problem. If the temporal sampling theorem is not met, we cannot unambiguously determine the frequency and thus the velocity. In other words, the correspondence problem can be entirely avoided if we take images in temporal distances which are short enough to meet (17.8). Because of the importance of the correct temporal sampling, we state the sampling theorem for image sequences in a more formal way, similar to the sampling theorem in section 2.3.3:

If the spectrum $\hat{g}(\mathbf{k})$ of a continuous image sequence $g(\mathbf{x}, t)$ is bandlimited, i. e., $\hat{g}(\mathbf{k}, \omega) = 0 \ \forall |k_i| \geq {}^P k_i / 2$ and $\omega \geq {}^P \omega / 2$, then it can be reconstructed exactly from samples with a distance $\Delta x_i = 2\pi / {}^P k_i$ and $\Delta t = 2\pi / {}^P \omega$.

Let us consider in more detail what the sampling theorem means practically. We assume that an image sequence has been sampled according to the sampling theorem. Then the smallest wavelength is the distance of two pixels. Since the maximum shift from image to image may not exceed half a wavelength it must not be larger than one pixel. At first glance, we might expect that we cannot determine accurate velocities at all from such small shifts. As we will show later in this chapter (section 17.4.5), these small shifts constitute no real problem, since the velocities are not extracted from just two consecutive images.

The larger problem is that image sequences generally do not meet the temporal sampling condition. In this respect it is important to note that the standard sampling, i. e., taking the mean gray value over the elapsed time interval, is not sufficient to avoid temporal aliasing as shown in section 2.3.5. The problem is even more pronounced if we take sequences with short exposure times, e. g., video image sequences with 30 frames/s and exposure times less than 33 ms.

Under certain circumstances, we still can solve the correspondence problem. If our scene contains only rigid objects, then all spatial structures in which we can decompose the object by computing the Fourier transform, move with the same speed. In this case we can apply a *coarse-to-fine strategy* if the object contains wave numbers over a wide range. A classical example is an edge. The bandpass decomposition of the edge with the Laplace pyramid shows that all levels of the pyramid contain a signal (figure 17.3). On the coarsest level of the pyramid, the shift is smaller than half the dominant wavelength at this level. In this case we can determine the displacement unambiguously. Because of the low resolution it will be only a crude estimate, but it is sufficient to shift one of the two images with the displacement that has been determined. At the next level, we only need to compute a correction, which will certainly be smaller than half a wavelength. In this way we can continue iteratively until we reach the bottom of the pyramid.

In this way our considerations about the correspondence problem lead on to a multi-grid algorithm on a pyramidal image data structure. We should bear in mind, however, that the proposed coarse-to-fine strategy is not a generally valid approach. In other cases, for example, an image sequence with waves where each wave component is travelling with a different speed depending on its wave number, the coarse-to-fine strategy is not adequate.

17.3 Velocity Filtering

All objects moving with a given velocity $\mathbf{u}_0$ lie on a plane in the $\mathbf{k}\omega$ space which is described by (17.5). Therefore we can use linear filter operations to select objects which

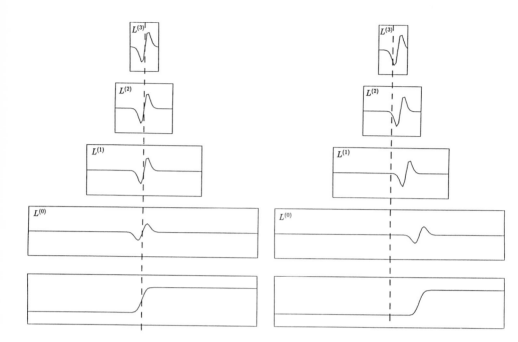

Figure 17.3: Illustration of the correspondence problem with an edge decomposed by a Laplace pyramid.

are moving in a certain velocity range. We are familiar with such linear filter operations from chapters 5–7. We just need to extend these concepts from two to three dimensions. New, and possibly confusing at the beginning is the fact that one of the coordinates is the time coordinate.

17.3.1 Projection Filters

First we discuss the selection of objects which move precisely with the velocity u. The transfer function of a filter, $\hat{h}_u$, that selects the objects with exactly this property is a plane

$$\hat{h}_u = \delta(uk - \omega). \qquad (17.9)$$

The corresponding convolution mask in the xt space is a δ line normal to the plane in the $k\omega$ space.

$$h_u = \delta(x - ut). \qquad (17.10)$$

Thus the selection of objects in the xt space moving with the velocity u is obtained by convolution with a δ line. This convolution is nothing else but a *projection operation* which adds up image by image with the corresponding shift due to the slope of the δ line. We obtain objects with no motion, e.g., by simple adding up all the images of the image sequence

$$g(\boldsymbol{x}; \boldsymbol{u} = 0) = \delta(\boldsymbol{x}) * g(\boldsymbol{x}, t) = \int_t \mathrm{d}t \int_{x'} \mathrm{d}^2 x' \; \delta(\boldsymbol{x} - \boldsymbol{x}') g(\boldsymbol{x}', t) = \int_t \mathrm{d}t \; g(\boldsymbol{x}, t). \qquad (17.11)$$

The selection of objects moving with the velocity $\boldsymbol{u}_0$ is given correspondingly as

$$g(\boldsymbol{x}; \boldsymbol{u} = \boldsymbol{u}_0) = \delta(\boldsymbol{x} - \boldsymbol{u}_0 t) * g(\boldsymbol{x}, t) = \int_t \mathrm{d}t \; g(\boldsymbol{x} - \boldsymbol{u}_0 t, t). \qquad (17.12)$$

At this point it is important to note the close connection between the projection of a three-dimensional image onto a two-dimensional image plane via a parallel projection (section 13.3.2) and the selection of a velocity component in the three-dimensional $\boldsymbol{x}t$ space. Both operations are mathematically identical and are described by the same projection operator $h_{\boldsymbol{u}}$. Through this analogy, the *Radon transform* (section 13.3.2) has a new meaning. We can regard the Radon transform in a slightly modified form as the decomposition of the velocity components of an image sequence.

So far we have discussed projection filters only using the infinite, continuous space. For practical applications, it is very important to consider the influence of both spatial and temporal limitation in the real-world images. Any limitation of an image sequence means multiplication of the image sequence by a corresponding window function. As a *window function* we take a three-dimensional Gaussian function of the form

$$w(\boldsymbol{x}, t) = \exp\left(-\frac{\boldsymbol{x}^2}{2\sigma_x^2}\right) \exp\left(-\frac{t^2}{2\sigma_t^2}\right), \qquad (17.13)$$

which shows the same shape in the Fourier domain

$$\hat{w}(\boldsymbol{k}, \omega) = \exp\left(-\frac{\boldsymbol{k}^2 \sigma_x^2}{2}\right) \exp\left(-\frac{\omega^2 \sigma_t^2}{2}\right) \qquad (17.14)$$

with reciprocal standard deviations according to the *uncertainty relation*. In order to obtain the effective transfer function for the projection operator of a windowed image sequence, we need to convolve the transfer function of the projection operator (17.9) and obtain

$$\hat{h}'_{\boldsymbol{u}} = \hat{h}_{\boldsymbol{u}} * \hat{w}(\boldsymbol{k}, \omega) = \exp\left(-\frac{\boldsymbol{k}^2 \sigma_x^2}{2}\right) \exp\left(-\frac{(\omega - \boldsymbol{u}\boldsymbol{k})^2 \sigma_t^2}{2}\right). \qquad (17.15)$$

The δ plane is blurred in the $\boldsymbol{k}$ directions with a standard deviation of $1/\sigma_x$ and in the ω direction with $1/\sigma_t$. In effect, the velocity resolution is limited. The velocity resolution is inversely proportional to the wave number as indicated in figure 17.4. The velocity resolution becomes very poor for low frequencies and low wave numbers. A sufficient number of periods and wavelengths must be contained in the image sequence for projection operators to become velocity selective.

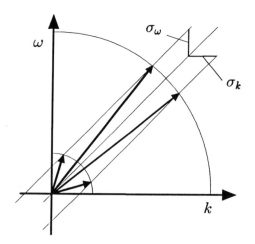

Figure 17.4: Illustration of the limited velocity resolution of a projection operator applied to a windowed image sequence.

17.3.2 Gabor Filters

The discussion about projection filters in the last section showed that they are not very appropriate filters for real-world image sequences since the velocity resolution is inversely proportional to the wave number. This means that we can only obtain a good velocity resolution for high wave numbers. In this section we discuss another class of velocity filters which selects a certain wave number and frequency range. This means that these filters respond to spatial structures in the chosen wave number range around k_0 moving with the *normal* velocity $u_\perp = \omega/|k|$. From such a filter operation, we cannot tell the true velocity of the object, since we select a spatial structure with a certain local orientation so that we cannot determine the complete velocity vector. Geometrically, we can illustrate this fact in the following way. We have obtained only two points on the plane that determine the velocity in the $k\omega$ space, the point (k_0, ω_0) and because of symmetry the point $(-k_0, \omega_0)$ (spectra from real-valued images are Hermitian). Through these points we can lay many planes which have in common the line connecting the two points.

Gabor filters belong to the class of *quadrature filters* which we discussed in section 7.2 and have the advantage that they can give a phase-independent "energy" estimate for the spatiotemporal gray value structure. Gabor filters are designed in the Fourier domain. Basically, they consist of a Gaussian function shifted to the point (k_0, ω_0). To construct a quadrature filter, we need an even real and odd imaginary transfer function of the following form

$$\hat{q}_+(\boldsymbol{k},\omega) = \frac{1}{2}\left[\exp\left(-\frac{(\boldsymbol{k}-\boldsymbol{k_0})^2\sigma_x^2}{2}\right)\exp\left(-\frac{(\omega+\omega_0)^2\sigma_t^2}{2}\right)\right.$$
$$\left.+\quad\exp\left(-\frac{(\boldsymbol{k}+\boldsymbol{k_0})^2\sigma_x^2}{2}\right)\exp\left(-\frac{(\omega-\omega_0)^2\sigma_t^2}{2}\right)\right],$$

$$\hat{q}_-(\boldsymbol{k},\omega) = \frac{i}{2}\left[\exp\left(-\frac{(\boldsymbol{k}-\boldsymbol{k_0})^2\sigma_x^2}{2}\right)\exp\left(-\frac{(\omega+\omega_0)^2\sigma_t^2}{2}\right)\right.$$
$$\left.-\quad\exp\left(-\frac{(\boldsymbol{k}+\boldsymbol{k_0})^2\sigma_x^2}{2}\right)\exp\left(-\frac{(\omega-\omega_0)^2\sigma_t^2}{2}\right)\right].$$

$$(17.16)$$

The convolution mask can easily be computed with the aid of the shift theorem (appendix A.2):

$$q_+(\boldsymbol{x},t) = \frac{1}{2\pi\sigma_x\sigma_t}\cos(\boldsymbol{k_0x}-\omega_0t)\exp\left(-\frac{\boldsymbol{x}^2}{2\sigma_x^2}\right)\exp\left(-\frac{t^2}{2\sigma_t^2}\right),$$

$$q_-(\boldsymbol{x},t) = \frac{1}{2\pi\sigma_x\sigma_t}\sin(\boldsymbol{k_0x}-\omega_0t)\exp\left(-\frac{\boldsymbol{x}^2}{2\sigma_x^2}\right)\exp\left(-\frac{t^2}{2\sigma_t^2}\right).$$

$$(17.17)$$

The convolution masks constitute plane waves limited by a Gaussian window function to a small number of periods and wavelengths, i. e., a *wave packet*. The frequency ω_0 and the wave number $\boldsymbol{k_0}$ of this wave packet correspond to the maximum of the transfer function, while the width of the mask is inversely proportional to the corresponding width of the transfer function

$$\sigma_x^2 = \frac{1}{\sigma_k^2}, \qquad \sigma_t^2 = \frac{1}{\sigma_\omega^2}. \qquad (17.18)$$

A narrow frequency and wave number response results in a coarse temporal and spatial resolution, and vice versa.

17.4 1-D Motion Determination

Since motion determination becomes more complex for higher dimensions, we take a stepwise approach. In this section we discuss motion analysis in a two-dimensional $\boldsymbol{x}t$ space with one space and one time coordinate. This allows us to work out the basic concepts. Then we can extend these to the two-dimensional motion problem.

17.4.1 Conversion of the Differential Method into a Filter Method

The continuity of the optical flux led to a simple solution for the velocity determination in the one-dimensional case. For further considerations in this section, we modify

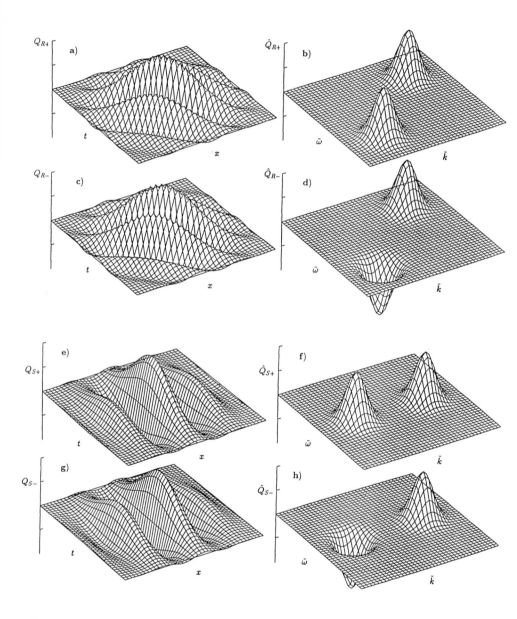

Figure 17.5: Transfer functions and convolution masks for the Gabor filter pairs in a two-dimensional xt and $k\omega$ space respectively: a) to d) selecting objects moving to the right; e) to h) objects at rest.

(15.32) for the one-dimensional case

$$u = - \sum g_x^2 \frac{g_t}{g_x} \bigg/ \sum g_x^2 = - \sum g_x g_t \bigg/ \sum g_x^2. \qquad (17.19)$$

This equation summarizes the essentials of the differential method well: At each pixel in the image, we compute the ratio of the temporal and spatial derivative and weigh the result with the factor $w(j) = g_x^2(j)$. We now want to convert this approach step by step into a filter method which can be applied in a two-dimensional space-time image.
1. Computation of the spatial and temporal derivatives using the operators

$$\mathcal{D}_t \text{ and } \mathcal{D}_x.$$

From an image pair, we have only one choice to compute the temporal derivative, namely to take the difference image. This corresponds to the asymmetric derivation operator $\boldsymbol{D} = [1 \; -1]$. In a space-time image we do not have this limitation. We can use the much more suitable symmetric operators as $\boldsymbol{D} = 1/2 \, [1 \; 0 \; -1]$ or a more precise higher-order approximation, as discussed in section 6.3.5.
2. Next we perform two point operations, the multiplications $g_x g_x$ and $g_x g_t$, which we can express in the operator notation as

$$\mathcal{D}_t \cdot \mathcal{D}_x \text{ and } \mathcal{D}_x \cdot \mathcal{D}_x.$$

Be aware that these operations are *nonlinear*.
3. The sums in (17.19) are necessary to average the results from different pixels in a small neighborhood. We can effectively perform this operation with a smoothing operator. The mask size gives the size of the window from which we take the pixels and also determines the spatial resolution of the computed velocity. In contrast to the simple differential method using only two images, we can now extend the smoothing along the time coordinate. In this way, the filter approach extends the differential method to a more robust velocity determination. In operator notation, we can write

$$\mathcal{B}_{xt}(\mathcal{D}_t \cdot \mathcal{D}_x) \text{ and } \mathcal{B}_{xt}(\mathcal{D}_x \cdot \mathcal{D}_x).$$

$\mathcal{B}_{xt}$ is a smoothing operator in both the x and t directions, e. g., a binomial filter.
4. Finally, we obtain the velocity by dividing the results of the two filter operations. This leads to the following velocity operator $\mathcal{U}$

$$^f\mathcal{U} = - \frac{\mathcal{B}_{xt}(\mathcal{D}_t \cdot \mathcal{D}_x)}{\mathcal{B}_{xt}(\mathcal{D}_x \cdot \mathcal{D}_x)}. \qquad (17.20)$$

The filter method is not only simple and effective but also very flexible. First, we can determine the spatial and temporal resolution by choosing an appropriate smoothing filter $\mathcal{B}_{xt}$. Second, we can apply any other filtering prior to the application of the velocity determination. This allows us to select from the image any other feature besides the original gray values. We may apply a high-pass filtering to make the velocity determination less dependent on illumination changes. With this prefiltering, we just choose the frequency and wave number range which should be used for the velocity

determination. We could, for example, first apply a spatial derivative. Then we obtain
a modified velocity operator

$$^{fd}\mathcal{U} = -\frac{\mathcal{B}_{xt}\left[(\mathcal{D}_t\mathcal{D}_x)\cdot\mathcal{D}_x^2\right]}{\mathcal{B}_{xt}(\mathcal{D}_x^2\cdot\mathcal{D}_x^2)}, \tag{17.21}$$

which is very similar to the differential geometric method discussed in section 15.2.3
(see (15.41)) if we include the weighting factors computed with the $\mathcal{D}_x^2$ operator.

17.4.2 The Tensor Method

As discussed at the beginning of this chapter, motion corresponds to orientation. Consequently, the orientation analysis in a two-dimensional image and the motion analysis
in the xt space are equivalent. We just need to exchange one of the space coordinates
by the time coordinate. Thus we can simply use all the concepts discussed in chapter 7 to determine one-dimensional velocity. In this section we use the tensor method
(section 7.3). From (7.27) and (17.2) we obtain the following velocity operator

$$\mathcal{U} = \tan\varphi = -\tan\left(\frac{1}{2}\arctan\frac{2\mathcal{B}_{xt}(\mathcal{D}_t\cdot\mathcal{D}_x)}{\mathcal{B}_{xt}(\mathcal{D}_x\cdot\mathcal{D}_x) - \mathcal{B}_{xt}(\mathcal{D}_t\cdot\mathcal{D}_t)}\right). \tag{17.22}$$

Surprisingly, this operator differs considerably from the filter approach derived from
the differential method (17.20). Is one of the two approaches wrong? We can first
investigate this question by analyzing how both operators respond on an image with a
constant velocity (17.3). The spatial and temporal derivatives are then given by

$$\frac{\partial g}{\partial x} = g'(x - u_0 t),$$

$$\frac{\partial g}{\partial t} = -u_0 g'(x - u_0 t). \tag{17.23}$$

With g' we denote the derivation of the gray value with respect to the one-dimensional
coordinate. Provided that

$$b(x, t) * g'^2(x - u_0 t) > 0$$

we obtain from (17.20):

$$u = \tan\phi = -\frac{-u_0 b(x, t) * g'^2(x - u_0 t)}{b(x, t) * g'^2(x - u_0 t)} = u_0 \tag{17.24}$$

and from (17.22):

$$u = \tan\phi$$

$$= -\tan\left(\frac{1}{2}\arctan\frac{2u_0 b(x, t) * g'^2(x - u_0 t)}{b(x, t) * g'^2(x - u_0 t) - u_0^2 b(x, t) * g'^2(x - u_0 t)}\right) \tag{17.25}$$

$$= \tan\left(\frac{1}{2}\arctan\frac{2u_0}{1 - u_0^2}\right) = u_0.$$

Despite the different operators, both give identical and *correct* results for an ideal local orientation. However, the operators differ in image regions which do not show a constant velocity. In this case, the simple filter approach offers no way to decide whether the estimated velocity is meaningful or not. In contrast, the tensor method gives useful criteria to detect such situations (see section 7.3.3).

17.4.3 The Quadrature Filter Set Method

In two-dimensional images, we can also determine the orientation with the quadrature filter set method as discussed in section 7.2. This method can be used for one-dimensional velocity determination as well. Such methods are also the basis of models used to describe motion vision in biological visual systems. Gabor-like quadrature filters are used for this purpose to determine the squared amplitude of the gray values in a certain frequency-wave number range, for which the terms space-time-energy and motion energy have been coined [*Adelson and Bergen*, 1985, 1986; *Heeger*, 1988]. These terms can easily be misunderstood. It is not the kinetic energy of the moving objects that is referred to but the energy (squared amplitude) of a signal at the sensor level in a certain $k\omega$ interval.

One of the simplest models for one-dimensional motion vision uses just three quadrature filters. In section 7.2.2 we proved that this is the minimum number necessary. This set of directional filters detects objects which are moving to the right, to the left, and those which are not moving. We denote these quadrature operators by $\mathcal{R}$, $\mathcal{L}$, and $\mathcal{S}$. Then we can obtain an estimate of the one-dimensional velocity using the operator [*Adelson and Bergen*, 1985; 1986]

$$^e\mathcal{U} = \frac{\mathcal{R} - \mathcal{L}}{\mathcal{S}}. \tag{17.26}$$

In order to connect this approach to our previous work, we show how to understand the simple filter or differential approach as an energy extraction method. First we rewrite the formula of the filter approach with a slight modification to smooth the images with the binomial mask $\mathcal{B}_{xt}$, before we apply the derivative operators

$$\mathcal{U} = -\frac{\mathcal{B}_{xt}\left[(\mathcal{D}_t\mathcal{B}_{xt}) \cdot (\mathcal{D}_x\mathcal{B}_{xt})\right]}{\mathcal{B}_{xt}\left[(\mathcal{D}_x\mathcal{B}_{xt}) \cdot (\mathcal{D}_x\mathcal{B}_{xt})\right]}. \tag{17.27}$$

Using the operator identity

$$\mathcal{AB} = \frac{1}{4}\left[(\mathcal{A} + \mathcal{B})^2 - (\mathcal{A} - \mathcal{B})^2\right] \tag{17.28}$$

we can rewrite (17.27):

$$\mathcal{U} = -\frac{\mathcal{B}_{xt}\left\{[(\mathcal{D}_x + \mathcal{D}_t)\mathcal{B}_{xt}] \cdot [(\mathcal{D}_x + \mathcal{D}_t)\mathcal{B}_{xt}] - [(\mathcal{D}_x - \mathcal{D}_t)\mathcal{B}_{xt}] \cdot [(\mathcal{D}_x - \mathcal{D}_t)\mathcal{B}_{xt}]\right\}}{\mathcal{B}_{xt}[(\mathcal{D}_x\mathcal{B}_{xt}) \cdot (\mathcal{D}_x\mathcal{B}_{xt})]}. \tag{17.29}$$

Thus we obtained a very similar expression as (17.26) with the filter operators

$$\begin{aligned} \mathcal{R}' &= (\mathcal{D}_x + \mathcal{D}_t)\mathcal{B}_{xt}, \\ \mathcal{L}' &= (\mathcal{D}_x - \mathcal{D}_t)\mathcal{B}_{xt}, \\ \mathcal{S}' &= \mathcal{D}_x\mathcal{B}_{xt}. \end{aligned} \tag{17.30}$$

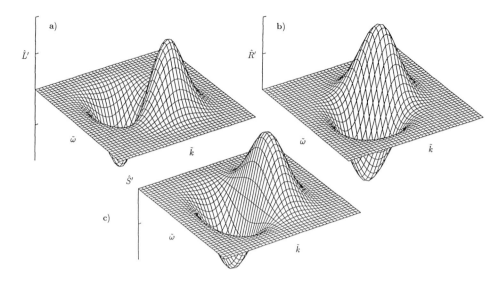

Figure 17.6: Transfer functions for the convolution operators (17.30) to detect objects moving to the right, left, or at rest: a) $\mathcal{L}'$, b) $\mathcal{R}'$, and c) $\mathcal{S}'$.

These filters are derivations of binomial filters. The transfer functions show that objects moving to the right, the left, and at rest are selected (figure 17.6). However, these filters are *not* quadrature filters. Squaring of the filter responses and further smoothing with $\mathcal{B}_{xt}$, however, approximately results in a phase-independent detection of the squared amplitude as with a quadrature filter. For a more detailed discussion of biological motion vision, the reader is referred to the collection of papers on "image motion" in *J. Opt. Soc. Am. A, Vol. 2*, February 1985.

17.4.4   The Phase Method

Principle
In section 17.2 we used periodic spatial structures to illustrate the sampling theorem for space-time images. The position and thus also the displacement of such structures is essentially given by the *phase*

$$g(x,t) = g_0 \exp[-i\phi(x,t))] = g_0 \exp[-i(kx - \omega t)]. \tag{17.31}$$

The phase depends both on the spatial and temporal coordinates. For a sinusoidal gray-value pattern, the phase varies linearly in time and space

$$\phi(x,t) = k_0 x - \omega t = k_0 x - u k_0 t, \tag{17.32}$$

where k_0 and ω_0 are the wave number and the frequency of the pattern, respectively. Computing the temporal and spatial derivatives of the phase, i. e., the gradient in the xt

space, yields both the wave number and the frequency of the moving periodic structure

$$\nabla_{xt}\phi = \begin{bmatrix} \dfrac{\partial\phi}{\partial x} \\[2mm] \dfrac{\partial\phi}{\partial t} \end{bmatrix} = \begin{bmatrix} k \\ -\omega \end{bmatrix}. \tag{17.33}$$

Then the velocity is given as the ratio of the frequency to the wave number

$$u = \frac{\omega}{k} = -\frac{\partial\phi}{\partial t}\bigg/\frac{\partial\phi}{\partial x}. \tag{17.34}$$

This formula is very similar to the estimate based on the optical flow (15.5). In both cases, the velocity is given as a ratio of temporal and spatial derivatives. Thus at first the phase method appears to offer nothing new. Replacing the gray value by the phase is, however, a significant improvement, since the phase is much less dependent on the illumination than the gray value itself. Using only the phase signal, the amplitude of the gray value variations may change without affecting the velocity estimates at all.

So far, our considerations have been restricted to an ideal periodic gray value structure. Generally, however, images are composed of gray value structures with different wave numbers. From such a structure we cannot obtain useful phase estimates. Consequently, we need to decompose the image into a set of wave number ranges. We may, for example, use a set of Gabor filters which have been introduced in section 17.3.2 and which select a certain wave number and frequency range from an image sequence. The even and odd filters, $+Q$ and $-Q$, result in filter responses which show either no phase shift or a $\pi/2$ phase shift. Consequently, we can use both filters to compute the phase as

$$\phi(x,t) = \arctan\frac{q_-(x,t)}{q_+(x,t)}. \tag{17.35}$$

From the partial derivatives, we obtain the velocity estimate according to (17.34).

Implementation
Direct computation of the partial derivatives from the phase signal is not advisable because of the discontinuities in the phase signal. From equation (17.35) we obtain phase values which are additively ambiguous by 2π and thus cause discontinuities in the phase signal if the values are restricted in the principal interval $[-\pi,\pi[$. As pointed out by *Fleet and Jepson* [1990] and *Fleet* [1990], this problem can be avoided by computing the phase gradient from gradients of $q_+(x,t)$ and $q_-(x,t)$. We begin with (17.35)

$$\begin{aligned}
\nabla_{xt}\phi(x,t) &= \frac{q_+^2(x,t)}{q_+^2(x,t)+q_-^2(x,t)}\left(\frac{\nabla_{xt}q_-(x,t)}{q_+(x,t)} - \frac{q_+(x,t)\nabla_{xt}q_-(x,t)}{q_+^2(x,t)}\right) \\[2mm]
&= \frac{q_+(x,t)\nabla_{xt}q_-(x,t)-q_-(x,t)\nabla_{xt}q_+(x,t)}{q_+^2(x,t)+q_-^2(x,t)}.
\end{aligned} \tag{17.36}$$

This formulation of the phase gradient also eliminates the need for using a trigonometric function to compute the phase signal. Using (17.34), the velocity estimate reduces to

$$u = \frac{q_+\dfrac{\partial q_-}{\partial t} - q_-\dfrac{\partial q_+}{\partial t}}{q_-\dfrac{\partial q_+}{\partial x} - q_+\dfrac{\partial q_-}{\partial x}}. \tag{17.37}$$

17.4.5   Accuracy of Motion Determination

Compared to other instruments, images only deliver rather low-resolution data. From our considerations on the sampling theorem in section 17.2, we know that the inter-image displacement must not be larger than half a wavelength of the smallest structures. Because of this restriction, displacement estimates would be worthless if they could not be performed with subpixel accuracy.

In order to test the accuracy of algorithms, computer-generated image sequences are more suitable. In this way, we know the true velocity exactly and can uncouple the algorithm-related errors from those related to the imaging sensor and the image formation. In an error analysis, *systematic* and *statistic* errors must be distinguished. Systematic errors in the velocity estimate are caused by deviations of the discrete derivative operators from the ideal derivative operator. This error is a function of the wave number. Statistical errors are introduced by noise in the signal which can be simulated by adding zero-mean Gaussian noise to the image sequence.

Figure 17.7 shows the result from an error analysis using the tensor method (section 17.4.2) and noisy sinusoidal waves with wavelengths between 2.4 and 20 pixels and an amplitude of 500 bits moving with 0.137 pixels/frame [*Jähne*, 1990]. Gaussian noise with a standard deviation of 50 bits was added to the image sequence. The computations were performed with 12-bit images. A $17 \times 17 \times 5$ binomial mask was used for spatiotemporal smoothing in (17.22).

Considerable deviations of the computed displacement from the correct solution occur when the wavelength comes close to the limiting value of two pixels (figure 17.7a). These systematic errors occur because the discrete spatial derivative operator becomes more and more erroneous for smaller wavelengths (see figure 6.24 in section 6.3.5). They reduce somewhat for higher-order approximations of the derivative operators but are still considerable. For large wavelengths, however, the systematic error is less than a $1/100$ pixel distance. Despite the low signal to noise ratio of 5, the statistical error generally is low (figure 17.7b). Since the response to the derivative operator is inversely proportional to the wavelength, the statistical error increases with the wavelength. The standard deviation is twice as large if the temporal smoothing is omitted (figure 17.7b). Unfortunately, the statistical and systematic errors show opposite trends: at low wavelengths, the statistical error is low, but significant systematic errors occur.

Systematic errors at low wavelengths can be reduced by a simple iterative approach. Using (17.22), the first estimate for the displacement is applied to transform the image sequence into a coordinate system moving with this estimated velocity and thus only a further correction term to the displacement has to be computed:

$$x' \quad = \quad x + u^{(k)}t$$

$$u^{(k+1)} \quad = \quad u^{(k)} - \tan\left(\frac{1}{2}\arctan\frac{2\mathcal{B}_{x't}(\mathcal{D}_t\boldsymbol{G}\cdot\mathcal{D}_{x'}\boldsymbol{G})}{\mathcal{B}_{x't}(\mathcal{D}_{x'}\boldsymbol{G}\cdot\mathcal{D}_{x'}\boldsymbol{G}) - \mathcal{B}_{x't}(\mathcal{D}_t\boldsymbol{G}\cdot\mathcal{D}_t\boldsymbol{G})}\right). \qquad (17.38)$$

Figure 17.8 shows that the iteration converges quickly to the correct displacement over nearly the full range of displacements allowed ($\pm\lambda/2$).

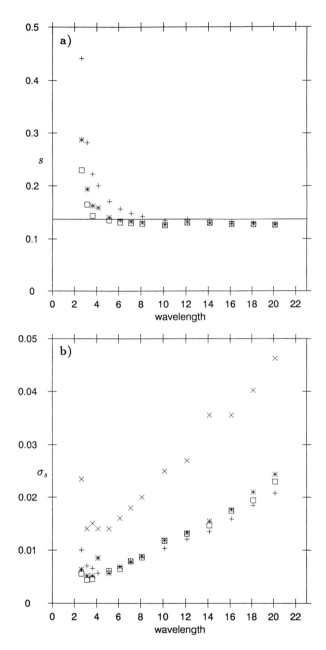

Figure 17.7: Application of the tensor method for 1-D velocity determination to computed image sequences, in which a noisy sinusoidal wave is moving with $s = 0.137$ pixels/frame. Different discrete approximations for the first-order derivative operators have been used: $+$ $^{(1)}D$, $*$ $^{(2)}D$, $\square$ $^{(1)}D$, $\times$ $^{(1)}D$ without temporal smoothing: a) computed displacement as a function of the wavelength; b) standard deviation of the displacement estimate as a function of the wavelength; from *Jähne* [1990].

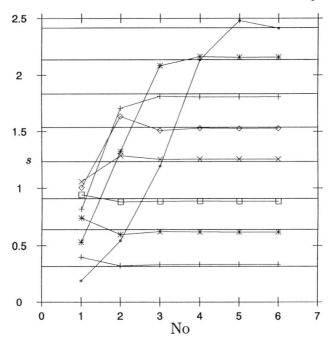

Figure 17.8: Test of the iterative refinement of the velocity estimate for a sinusoidal pattern with a wavelength of 5.13 pixels. The computed displacements are shown as a function of the number of iterations for displacements between 0.317 and 2.413 pixels/frame. The horizontal lines mark the correct values; from *Jähne* [1990].

17.5   2-D Motion Determination

In this last section we turn to the problem of estimating two-dimensional motion from space-time images. Here we discuss how to extend the approaches discussed previously in this chapter for 1-D motion determination to two dimensions. 2-D motion analysis has already been discussed in chapters 15 and 16 and we are aware of the complexity of the problem and the open questions. This final section of the book will also not provide final answers. It is rather an outlook onto the current research and should give an impression that the extension of image sequence analysis from two to many images of a sequence is a significant step ahead. We will briefly discuss all three major approaches, namely, the filter set, the tensor, and the phase method.

17.5.1   The Quadrature Filter Set Method

In three publications, *Heeger* [1987a,b; 1988] describes a method to estimate two-dimensional displacement vectors using a set of space-time quadrature filters. While it is easy to arrange the center frequencies and wave numbers in two-dimensional xt images (see section 7.), it is not trivial for 3-D xt images. Heeger, for example, uses a three sets of four space-time Gabor filters. Gabor filters have been discussed in section 17.3.2. Each filter set lies on a plane parallel to the $k_1 k_2$ plane. One is locatd at $\omega = 0$ to detect static patterns in different directions. The two other sets are located above and below the $k_1 k_2$ plane and filter structures which are moving in positive and negative axes directions, respectively. The centers of all the filters lie on a cylinder. The axis of this cylinder is the frequency axis. Therefore the all the sets select a certain spatial scale from the image sequence. Each set contains filters at angles of 0°, 45°, 90°, and 135°to the k_1 axis.

This filter arrangement combines spatial orientation and motion analysis. *Heeger's* approach contains the following steps:

- Computation of a Gauss pyramid for each image of the sequence. This step allows the same set of Gabor filters to be used for different spatial scales. *Heeger* keeps the temporal resolution the same for all levels of the Gauss pyramid. This means that the filters applied in higher levels of the pyramid extract higher velocities. The center velocities of the filters on the different levels of the pyramid are given by $\omega_0/k_0, \omega_0/2k_0, \omega_0/4k_0, \cdots$. Heeger does not combine the filter results from different levels of the pyramid but just selects the level which is best adapted for the displacements in the sequence. For displacements between 0 and 1.25 pixels/frame he takes the lowest level, for displacements between 1.25 and 2.5 the second lowest, and so on.
- Highpass filtering of all images on the selected plane in order to remove constant gray values and structures with low wave numbers.
- Convolution of the image sequence with the twelve quadrature filters. A fast algorithm using separable convolution masks is applied [*Heeger*, 1987b].
- Smoothing of the filter results with a Gaussian filter.
- Estimation of the two-dimensional velocity vectors from the 12 filter responses. Heeger uses a least-square method. A unique solution is gained only if the gray values are not spatially oriented.

Heeger was the first to report a filter-based approach to two-dimensional motion analysis. Generally, filter set methods are difficult to use in three dimensional spaces. The quadrature filter set that we used in section 7.2.1 for orientation analysis in two dimensions showed the important feature that the sum of all transfer functions resulted in an isotropic function. In section 7.2.2 we found that this was a requirement for a simple and accurate orientation estimate. Heeger's filter set does not fulfil this requirement.

17.5.2 The Tensor Method

In this section the tensor method is extended from two to three dimensions. Orientation analysis with the tensor method has been discussed in depth in section 7.3.

With the tensor method we think of the spectrum $|\hat{g}(\mathbf{k}, \omega)|$ of a neighborhood as the density function of a rotary body in $\mathbf{k}\omega$ space. The inertia for rotation around an axis in the $(\mathbf{k}_0, \omega_0)$ direction is given by:

$$J(\mathbf{x}_0, t_0) = \int\limits_{-\infty}^{\infty} \mathrm{d}k^2 \, \mathrm{d}\omega \, d^2[(\mathbf{k}, \omega), (\mathbf{k}_0, \omega_0)] \, |\hat{g}(\mathbf{k}, \omega)|^2, \qquad (17.39)$$

where the spectrum of the local neighborhood centered at $(\boldsymbol{x}_0, t_0)$ is

$$\hat{g}(\boldsymbol{k}, \omega, \boldsymbol{k}_0, \omega_0) = \int\limits_{-\infty}^{\infty} \mathrm{d}x^2\, \mathrm{d}t\; w(\boldsymbol{k}_0 - \boldsymbol{k}, \omega_0 - \omega)g(\boldsymbol{x}, \omega)\exp[-\mathrm{i}(\boldsymbol{k}\boldsymbol{x} - \omega t)] \qquad (17.40)$$

where $w(\boldsymbol{k}_0 - \boldsymbol{k}, \omega_0 - \omega)$ is a window function which determines the size of the neighborhood. In section 7.3 we discussed that the elements of the inertia tensor can be computed directly in the space domain using first-order partial derivative operators and smoothing operators. Using the abbreviations

$$\begin{aligned}
\mathcal{J}_{xx} &= \mathcal{B}_{xt}(\mathcal{D}_x \cdot \mathcal{D}_x) \\
\mathcal{J}_{yy} &= \mathcal{B}_{xt}(\mathcal{D}_y \cdot \mathcal{D}_y) \\
\mathcal{J}_{tt} &= \mathcal{B}_{xt}(\mathcal{D}_t \cdot \mathcal{D}_t) \\
\mathcal{J}_{xy} &= \mathcal{B}_{xt}(\mathcal{D}_x \cdot \mathcal{D}_y) \\
\mathcal{J}_{xt} &= \mathcal{B}_{xt}(\mathcal{D}_x \cdot \mathcal{D}_t) \\
\mathcal{J}_{yt} &= \mathcal{B}_{xt}(\mathcal{D}_y \cdot \mathcal{D}_t),
\end{aligned} \qquad (17.41)$$

the inertia tensor is given by

$$\mathcal{J} = \begin{bmatrix} \mathcal{J}_{yy} + \mathcal{J}_{tt} & -\mathcal{J}_{xy} & -\mathcal{J}_{xt} \\ -\mathcal{J}_{xy} & \mathcal{J}_{xx} + \mathcal{J}_{tt} & -\mathcal{J}_{yt} \\ -\mathcal{J}_{xt} & -\mathcal{J}_{yt} & \mathcal{J}_{xx} + \mathcal{J}_{yy} \end{bmatrix}. \qquad (17.42)$$

It has the following form in the principal-axes coordinate system (x', y', t'):

$$\begin{aligned}
\mathcal{J} &= \begin{bmatrix} J_1 & 0 & 0 \\ 0 & J_2 & 0 \\ 0 & 0 & J_3 \end{bmatrix} \\
&= \begin{bmatrix} \mathcal{J}_{y'y'} + \mathcal{J}_{t't'} & 0 & 0 \\ 0 & \mathcal{J}_{x'x'} + \mathcal{J}_{t't'} & 0 \\ 0 & 0 & \mathcal{J}_{x'x'} + \mathcal{J}_{y'y'} \end{bmatrix}.
\end{aligned} \qquad (17.43)$$

The inertia tensor contains the entire information on the first-order spatial structure of the gray value function in a local neighborhood. Without explicitly solving the eigenvalue problem, we can distinguish four different cases which can be characterized by conditions for the eigenvalues of the inertia tensor.

- *Constant gray value*
  The spectrum lies at the origin of the $\boldsymbol{k}\omega$ space. All elements and eigenvalues of the inertia tensor are zero. No velocity information can be gained:

$$J_1 = J_2 = J_3 = 0. \qquad (17.44)$$

- *Distributed spatial structure and constant motion*
  In this case, the spectrum lies on a plane intersecting the origin. The rotary body is a flat disk. The eigenvector to the *largest* eigenvalue is normal to this plane. Since the

motion is constant, the principal-axes coordinate system is moving with the scene. Consequently, $\mathcal{J}_{t't'}$ is equal to zero, and we obtain from (17.43) that the maximum eigenvalue is the sum of the two others:

$$J_3 = J_1 + J_2. \tag{17.45}$$

• *Spatial orientation and constant motion*
The spectrum is located on a line in $k\omega$ space. The gray value structure is said to show *linear symmetry*. One eigenvalue is zero. The corresponding eigenvector points in the direction of local orientation in the $k\omega$ space and thus gives both the spatial orientation and the velocity in this direction. The conditions for the eigenvectors are

$$J_3 = 0 \quad \text{and} \quad J_1 = J_2. \tag{17.46}$$

• *Otherwise*
If none of the above conditions is fulfilled, the spectrum is no longer planar, but three-dimensional. All three eigenvalues are larger than zero. The sum of two eigenvalues is larger than the third:

$$J_3 < J_1 + J_2. \tag{17.47}$$

The reasons for this condition are manifold. It occurs when
1. the velocity field shows a *spatial* discontinuity, for example, at the edge of a moving object;
2. the velocity field shows a *temporal* discontinuity, for example, when two moving objects are colliding;
3. the local neighborhood includes the superposition of the motion of two objects;
4. in any case, where the continuity of the optical flow is seriously distorted, for example at the edge of the shadow of a moving object or a specular reflex.

This detailed analysis shows that the tensor method does not only provide a velocity estimation but also a straightforward classification of the spatial structure of a small neighborhood with respect to motion analysis. The usage of the tensor method for motion analysis has first been proposed by *Jähne* [1989]. He also discusses a fast implementation of the eigenvalue analysis. A detailed study of the method is also given by *Bigün* [1991].

Generally, the methods discussed in this chapter to determine motion in space-time images question the classical approaches discussed in chapter 16. There we tried to infer the complete motion information from only two consecutive images of the sequence. Despite the fact that the locally estimated velocities from only two images are much more sensitive to noise and other distortions in the images (see also section 17.4.5), it now becomes clear that the determination of a continuous DVF was performed at a too early stage.

From the analysis of a image sequence containing many images we can extract much more information, before we need to put the locally gained velocity information together to a consistent picture of the motion in the scene. The tensor method provides a direct analysis of the discontinuities in the motion field from which we can draw conclusions about edges within moving.

The most radical departure from the classical concept has been formulated recently by *Fleet and Jepson* [1990] and *Fleet* [1990] with their suggestion to compute only *normal velocities* from directionally filtered images with the phase method (see section 17.4.4). The method to combine this normal velocities depends entirely on the nature of the scene. For a scene with transparent objects as water surface waves, where a local neighborhood can contain the motion of more than one object, we must use another method than for a scene with opaque rigid bodies.

A Mathematical Preliminaries

In this appendix, important mathematical preliminaries for digital image processing are summarized in tabular form. It is thought as a brief repetitorium and ready-to-use reference for this book. References to a detailed and adequate treatment are given for each subject.

A.1 Matrix Algebra

A.1.1 Definitions

An ordered set of M elements such as time series of some data is known as a *vector* and written as

$$
g = \begin{bmatrix} g_0 \\ g_1 \\ \vdots \\ g_{M-1} \end{bmatrix}.
$$

The nth element of the vector g is denoted by g_n. A *matrix* G of size $M \times N$ is a double-indexed ordered set with MN elements

$$
G = \begin{bmatrix} G_{0,0} & G_{0,1} & \cdots & G_{0,N-1} \\ G_{1,0} & G_{1,1} & \cdots & G_{1,N-1} \\ \vdots & \ddots & & \vdots \\ G_{M-1,0} & G_{M-1,1} & \cdots & G_{M-1,N-1} \end{bmatrix}.
$$

The matrix is said to consist of M *rows* and N *columns*. The first and second index of a matrix element denote the row and column numbers, i.e., the y and x coordinates, respectively. Thus the matrix notation differs from the standard Cartesian coordinate representation by a clockwise 90° rotation. Discrete images will be represented in this book by matrices with the starting indices 0 as shown above. All vectors and matrices which are related to coordinates in the two- and three-dimensional space will start with the index of 1. For a diagonal element of a matrix, the first and second index are equal.

An $M \times 1$ matrix is also denoted as a *column vector*, $\boldsymbol{g}$, and a $1 \times N$ matrix as a *row vector*, $\boldsymbol{g}^T$.

Some important operations with vectors and matrices are summarized in the following table:

Operation	Definition
Transposition	$G^T_{mn} = G_{nm}$
Matrix multiplication $\underbrace{\boldsymbol{G'}}_{M \times N} = \underbrace{\boldsymbol{G}}_{M \times K} \underbrace{\boldsymbol{H}}_{K \times N}$	$G'_{mn} = \sum_{k=0}^{K-1} G_{mk} H_{kn}$
Inner vector product $\langle \boldsymbol{g}, \boldsymbol{h} \rangle$, $\boldsymbol{g}^T \boldsymbol{h}$, or $\boldsymbol{g}\boldsymbol{h}$	$\sum_{m=0}^{M-1} g_m h_m$
Outer vector product $\boldsymbol{g}\boldsymbol{h}^T$	$G_{mn} = g_m h_n$
Determinant[1]	$\lvert \boldsymbol{G} \rvert$
Trace[1] $\mathrm{trace}(\boldsymbol{G})$	$\sum_{m=0}^{M-1} G_{mm}$
Inverse matrix[1] $\boldsymbol{G}^{-1}$	$\boldsymbol{G}^{-1}\boldsymbol{G} = \boldsymbol{I}$
Eigenvalues[1] λ	$\boldsymbol{G}\boldsymbol{x} = \lambda\boldsymbol{x}$
Eigenvectors[1] to eigenvalue λ	all $\boldsymbol{x} \neq \boldsymbol{0}$ with $(\boldsymbol{G} - \lambda\boldsymbol{I})\boldsymbol{x} = \boldsymbol{0}$

[1]Only defined for square matrices (see table below)

Special types of matrices follow. The superscript * denotes the complex conjugate for a scalar or matrix element and the transposed and complex conjugate for a matrix.

Name	Definition
Square matrix	$M = N$
Diagonal square matrix	$G_{mn} = 0 \ \forall \ m \neq n$
Identity matrix $\boldsymbol{I}$	$I_{m,n} = \delta_{m-n} = \begin{cases} 1 & m = n \\ 0 & \text{else} \end{cases}$
Symmetric matrix	$\boldsymbol{G} = \boldsymbol{G}^T$, $G_{mn} = G_{nm}$
Hermitian matrix	$\boldsymbol{G} = \boldsymbol{G}^*$, $G_{mn} = G^*_{nm}$
Orthogonal matrix	$\boldsymbol{G}^{-1} = \boldsymbol{G}^T$
Unitary matrix	$\boldsymbol{G}^{-1} = \boldsymbol{G}^*$

A.1.2 The Overdetermined Discrete Inverse Problem

The overdetermined discrete inverse problems occurred in sections 13.3.4 and 15.2.2. Here we derive the general solution. Given is a set of measurements collected in an N-dimensional *data vector* $\boldsymbol{d}$ and an $N \times M$ *model matrix* $\boldsymbol{G}$ which relates the measured data to the M unknown model parameters in the *model vector* $\boldsymbol{m}$:

$$\boldsymbol{d} = \boldsymbol{G}\boldsymbol{m}. \tag{A.1}$$

Generally for $N > M$, no exact solution is possible but only an estimated solution which minimizes the norm of the *error vector*, e, which is the difference between the measured data, d, and the data predicted by the model, d_{pre},

$$e = d - d_{pre} = d - Gm_{est},\qquad\text{(A.2)}$$

$$\|e\|_2^2 = \sum_{i=1}^{N}\left(d_i - \sum_{j=1}^{M}G_{ij}m_j\right)\left(d_i - \sum_{k=1}^{M}G_{ik}m_k\right).$$

Factorizing the sum and interchanging of the two summations yields

$$\|e\|_2^2 = \underbrace{\sum_{j=1}^{M}\sum_{k=1}^{M}m_j m_k \sum_{i=1}^{N}G_{ij}G_{ik}}_{A}$$
$$-\underbrace{2\sum_{j=1}^{M}m_j\sum_{i=1}^{N}G_{ij}d_i}_{B}$$
$$+\sum_{i=1}^{N}d_i d_i.$$

We find a minimum for this expression by computing the partial derivatives with respect to the parameters m_q to be optimized. Only the expressions A and B depend on m_q:

$$\frac{\partial A}{\partial m_q} = \sum_{j=1}^{M}\sum_{k=1}^{M}(\delta_{jq}m_k + \delta_{kq}m_j)\sum_{i=1}^{N}G_{ij}G_{ik}$$
$$= \sum_{j=1}^{M}m_j\sum_{i=1}^{N}G_{ij}G_{iq} + \sum_{k=1}^{M}m_k\sum_{i=1}^{N}G_{iq}G_{ik}$$
$$= 2\sum_{j=1}^{M}m_j\sum_{i=1}^{N}G_{ij}G_{iq}$$

$$\frac{\partial B}{\partial m_q} = 2\sum_{i=1}^{N}G_{iq}d_i.$$

We add both derivatives and set them equal to zero:

$$\frac{\partial\|e\|_2^2}{\partial m_q} = \sum_{k=1}^{M}m_k\sum_{i=1}^{N}G_{iq}G_{ik} - \sum_{i=1}^{N}G_{iq}d_i = 0.$$

In order to obtain matrix-matrix and matrix-vector multiplications, we substitute the matrix G at two places by its transpose G^T:

$$\sum_{k=1}^{M}m_k\sum_{i=1}^{N}G_{qi}^T G_{ik} - \sum_{i=1}^{N}G_{qi}^T d_i = 0$$

and finally obtain the matrix equation

$$\underbrace{\underset{M\times N}{G^T}\,\underset{N\times M}{G}\,\underset{M}{m_{est}}}_{\underbrace{M\times M}_{M}} = \underbrace{\underset{M\times N}{G^T}\,\underset{N}{d}}_{M}.\qquad\text{(A.3)}$$

This equation can be solved if the quadratic and symmetric $M \times M$ matrix $G^T G$ is invertible. Then

$$m_{\text{est}} = \left(G^T G\right)^{-1} G^T d. \tag{A.4}$$

The matrix $(G^T G)^{-1} G^T$ is known as the *pseudo inverse* of G.

A.1.3 Suggested Further Readings

Basic matrix algebra is the topic of the classical textbook by *Hoffmann and Kunze* [1971]. An intuitive introduction to discrete inverse problems is given by *Menke* [1984]. *Golub and van Loan* [1989] and *Press et al.* [1988] treat algorithms for matrix computations in detail.

A.2 Fourier Transformation

A.2.1 Definition

In one dimension, the *Fourier transform* of a complex-valued function $g(x)$ is defined as

$$\hat{g}(k) = \frac{1}{2\pi} \int\limits_{-\infty}^{\infty} \mathrm{d}x \ g(x) \exp\left(-ikx\right), \tag{A.5}$$

where $k = 2\pi/\lambda$ is the *wave number* of the complex exponential $\exp\left(-ikx\right)$ with the wavelength λ. The back transformation is given by

$$g(x) = \int\limits_{-\infty}^{\infty} \mathrm{d}k \ \hat{g}(k) \exp\left(ikx\right). \tag{A.6}$$

A function $g(x)$ and its Fourier transform $\hat{g}(k)$ form a Fourier transform pair denoted by

$$g(x) \ \circ\!\!-\!\!\bullet \ \hat{g}(k).$$

The complex exponentials, the *kernel* of the Fourier transform, constitute an orthonormal basis

$$\int\limits_{-\infty}^{\infty} \mathrm{d}x \ \exp\left(-ik'x\right) \exp\left(ikx\right) = 2\pi\delta(k' - k). \tag{A.7}$$

The n-dimensional Fourier transform is defined by

$$\hat{g}(\boldsymbol{k}) = \frac{1}{(2\pi)^n} \int\limits_{-\infty}^{\infty} \mathrm{d}^n x \ g(\boldsymbol{x}) \exp(-i\boldsymbol{k}\boldsymbol{x}). \tag{A.8}$$

The kernel of the multidimensional Fourier transform is separable:

$$\exp(-i\boldsymbol{k}\boldsymbol{x}) = \prod_{i=1}^{n} \exp(-ik_i x_i). \tag{A.9}$$

Therefore the n-dimensional Fourier transform can be separated in n one-dimensional Fourier transforms. For example, the two-dimensional Fourier transform can be written as

$$\hat{g}(\boldsymbol{k}) = \frac{1}{(2\pi)^2} \int\limits_{-\infty}^{\infty} \mathrm{d}x_2 \left[\frac{1}{2\pi} \int\limits_{-\infty}^{\infty} \mathrm{d}x_1 \, g(\boldsymbol{x}) \exp\left(-\mathrm{i}k_1 x_1\right) \right] \exp\left(-\mathrm{i}k_2 x_2\right). \tag{A.10}$$

The inverse Fourier transform is defined by

$$g(\boldsymbol{x}) = \int\limits_{-\infty}^{\infty} \mathrm{d}^n k \, \hat{g}(\boldsymbol{k}) \exp(\mathrm{i}\boldsymbol{k}\boldsymbol{x}). \tag{A.11}$$

A.2.2 Properties of the Fourier Transform

The theorems summarized here are valid for the Fourier transform in n dimensions. Let $g(\boldsymbol{x})$ and $h(\boldsymbol{x})$ be complex-valued functions, the Fourier transforms of which, $\hat{g}(\boldsymbol{k})$ and $\hat{h}(\boldsymbol{k})$, do exist. Let a and b be complex-valued constants and s a real-valued constant.

Property	Space domain	Fourier domain
Linearity	$ag(\boldsymbol{x}) + bh(\boldsymbol{x})$	$a\hat{g}(\boldsymbol{k}) + b\hat{h}(\boldsymbol{k})$
Scaling	$g(s\boldsymbol{x})$	$\hat{g}(\boldsymbol{k}/s)/|s|$
Separability	$\prod\limits_{i=1}^{n} g(x_i)$	$\prod\limits_{i=1}^{n} \hat{g}(k_i)$
Shifting	$g(\boldsymbol{x} - \boldsymbol{x}_0)$	$\exp(-\mathrm{i}\boldsymbol{k}\boldsymbol{x}_0)\hat{g}(\boldsymbol{k})$
Modulation	$\exp(\mathrm{i}\boldsymbol{k}_0\boldsymbol{x})g(\boldsymbol{x})$	$\hat{g}(\boldsymbol{k} - \boldsymbol{k}_0)$
Derivation	$\dfrac{\partial g(\boldsymbol{x})}{\partial x_i}$	$\mathrm{i}k_i\hat{g}(\boldsymbol{k})$
Derivation	$-\mathrm{i}x_i g(\boldsymbol{x})$	$\dfrac{\partial \hat{g}(\boldsymbol{k})}{\partial k_i}$
Convolution	$\int\limits_{-\infty}^{\infty} \mathrm{d}^n x' \, g(\boldsymbol{x}')h(\boldsymbol{x} - \boldsymbol{x}')$	$(2\pi)^n \, \hat{g}(\boldsymbol{k})\hat{h}(\boldsymbol{k})$
Multiplication	$g(\boldsymbol{x})h(\boldsymbol{x})$	$(2\pi)^n \int\limits_{-\infty}^{\infty} \mathrm{d}^n k' \, \hat{g}(\boldsymbol{k}')\hat{h}(\boldsymbol{k} - \boldsymbol{k}')$
Spatial Correlation	$\int\limits_{-\infty}^{\infty} \mathrm{d}^n x' \, g(\boldsymbol{x}')h(\boldsymbol{x}' + \boldsymbol{x})$	$(2\pi)^n \, \hat{g}(\boldsymbol{k})\hat{h}^*(\boldsymbol{k})$
Inner product	$\int\limits_{-\infty}^{\infty} \mathrm{d}^n x \, g(\boldsymbol{x})h^*(\boldsymbol{x})$	$(2\pi)^n \int\limits_{-\infty}^{\infty} \mathrm{d}^n k \, \hat{g}(\boldsymbol{k})\hat{h}^*(\boldsymbol{k})$

The following table lists important symmetry properties of the Fourier transform:

Space domain	Fourier domain
Even, odd $g(-\boldsymbol{x}) = \pm g(\boldsymbol{x})$	Even, odd $\hat{g}(-\boldsymbol{k}) = \pm\hat{g}(\boldsymbol{k})$
Real $g(\boldsymbol{x}) = g^*(\boldsymbol{x})$	Hermitian $\hat{g}(-\boldsymbol{k}) = \hat{g}^*(\boldsymbol{k})$
Imaginary $g(\boldsymbol{x}) = -g^*(\boldsymbol{x})$	Antihermitian $\hat{g}(-\boldsymbol{k}) = -\hat{g}^*(\boldsymbol{k})$
Rotational symmetric $g(|\boldsymbol{x}|)$	Rotational symmetric $\hat{g}(|\boldsymbol{k}|)$

A.2.3 Important Fourier Transform Pairs

Space domain	Fourier domain
δ function $\delta(x)$	$\dfrac{1}{2\pi}$
Box function $\Pi(x) = \begin{cases} a & \|x\| < x_0/2 \\ a/2 & \|x\| = x_0/2 \\ 0 & \|x\| > x_0/2 \end{cases}$	$ax_0\mathrm{sinc}(x_0k/2) = ax_0\dfrac{\sin(x_0k/2)}{x_0k/2}$
Cosine function $\cos(k_0x)$	$\dfrac{1}{2}\left(\delta(k-k_0) + \delta(k+k_0)\right)$
Sine function $\sin(k_0x)$	$\dfrac{i}{2}\left(\delta(k-k_0) - \delta(k+k_0)\right)$
δ comb $\displaystyle\sum_{n=-\infty}^{\infty} \delta(x-n\Delta x)$	$\displaystyle\sum_{u=-\infty}^{\infty} \delta(k-2\pi n/\Delta x)$
Gauss function $\dfrac{1}{\sigma\sqrt{2\pi}}\exp\left(-\dfrac{x^2}{2\sigma^2}\right)$	$\exp\left(-\dfrac{k^2}{2/\sigma^2}\right)$

A.2.4 Suggested Further Readings

A good introduction to the Fourier transform with respect to image processing can be found in *Gonzalez and Wintz* [1987]. *Bracewell* [1965] gives a more detailed discussion of the Fourier transform.

A.3 Discrete Fourier transform (DFT)

A.3.1 Definition

The one-dimensional DFT maps a *complex-valued vector* $\boldsymbol{g}$ onto another vector $\hat{\boldsymbol{g}}$ of a vector space with the same dimension M:

$$\hat{g}_u = \frac{1}{M}\sum_{m=0}^{M-1} g_m \exp\left(-\frac{2\pi i\,mu}{M}\right) = \frac{1}{M}\sum_{m=0}^{M-1} g_m\,W_M^{-mu}, \tag{A.12}$$

where

$$W_M = \exp\left(\frac{2\pi i}{M}\right). \tag{A.13}$$

The back transformation is given by

$$g_m = \sum_{u=0}^{M-1} \hat{g}_u W_M^{mu}. \tag{A.14}$$

In two dimensions, the DFT maps a complex-valued $M \times N$ matrix onto another matrix of the same size:

$$\begin{aligned}
\hat{G}_{uv} &= \frac{1}{MN} \sum_{m=0}^{M-1} \sum_{n=0}^{N-1} G_{mn} \exp\left(-\frac{2\pi i\, mu}{M}\right) \exp\left(-\frac{2\pi i\, nv}{N}\right) \\
&= \frac{1}{MN} \sum_{m=0}^{M-1} \left(\sum_{n=0}^{N-1} G_{mn} W_N^{-nv}\right) W_M^{-mu}.
\end{aligned} \tag{A.15}$$

The inverse 2-D DFT is given by

$$G_{mn} = \sum_{u=0}^{M-1} \sum_{v=0}^{N-1} \hat{G}_{uv} W_M^{mu} W_N^{nv}. \tag{A.16}$$

A.3.2　Important Properties

The following theorems apply to the 2-D DFT. Let $\boldsymbol{G}$ and $\boldsymbol{H}$ be complex-valued $M \times N$ matrices, $\hat{\boldsymbol{G}}$ and $\hat{\boldsymbol{H}}$ their Fourier transforms, and a and b complex-valued constants.

Property	Space domain	Wave number domain
Mean	$\dfrac{1}{MN} \sum\limits_{m=0}^{M-1}\sum\limits_{n=0}^{N-1} G_{mn}$	$\hat{G}_{0,0}$
Linearity	$a\boldsymbol{G} + b\boldsymbol{H}$	$a\hat{\boldsymbol{G}} + b\hat{\boldsymbol{H}}$
Shifting	$G_{m-k,n-l}$	$W_M^{-ku} W_N^{-lv} \hat{G}_{uv}$
Modulation	$W_M^{-kp} W_N^{-lq} G_{m-k,n-l}$	$\hat{G}_{u-p,v-q}$
Finite difference	$(G_{m+1,n} - G_{m-1,n})/2$	$i \sin(2\pi u/M) \hat{G}_{uv}$
Finite difference	$(G_{m,n+1} - G_{m,n-1})/2$	$i \sin(2\pi v/M) \hat{G}_{uv}$
Convolution	$(\boldsymbol{G} * \boldsymbol{H})_{mn} = \sum\limits_{k=0}^{M-1}\sum\limits_{l=0}^{N-1} G_{kl} H_{m-k,n-l}$	$MN \hat{G}_{uv} \hat{H}_{uv}$
Multiplication	$G_{mn} H_{mn}$	$(\hat{\boldsymbol{G}} * \hat{\boldsymbol{H}})_{uv} = \sum\limits_{p=0}^{M-1}\sum\limits_{q=0}^{N-1} \hat{G}_{pq} H_{u-p,v-q}$
Spatial Correlation	$(\boldsymbol{G} \star \boldsymbol{H})_{mn} = \sum\limits_{k=0}^{M-1}\sum\limits_{l=0}^{N-1} G_{kl} H_{m+k,n+l}$	$MN \hat{G}_{uv} \hat{H}_{uv}^*$
Inner product	$\dfrac{1}{MN} \sum\limits_{m=0}^{M-1}\sum\limits_{n=0}^{N-1} G_{mn} H_{mn}^*$	$\sum\limits_{u=0}^{M-1}\sum\limits_{v=0}^{N-1} \hat{G}_{uv} \hat{H}_{uv}^*$
Energy conservation	$\dfrac{1}{MN} \sum\limits_{m=0}^{M-1}\sum\limits_{n=0}^{N-1} |G_{mn}|^2$	$\sum\limits_{u=0}^{M-1}\sum\limits_{v=0}^{N-1} |\hat{G}_{uv}|^2$

A.3.3   Important Transform Pairs

Space domain	Fourier domain
δ function $\delta_{mn} = \begin{cases} 1 & m = 0, n = 0 \\ 0 & \text{else} \end{cases}$	$\dfrac{1}{MN}$
Constant function $c_{mn} = 1$	δ_{uv}
Cosine function $\cos\left(\dfrac{2\pi pm}{M} + \dfrac{2\pi qn}{N}\right)$	$\dfrac{1}{2}\left(\delta_{u-p,v-q} + \delta_{u+p,v+q}\right)$

A.3.4   Suggested Further Readings

The one-dimensional discrete Fourier transform is covered in detail by most textbooks on signal processing such as *Oppenheim and Schafer* [1989]. Special attention to the 2-D DFT is given by *Lim* [1990] and *Jaroslawskij* [1985]. Digital spectral analysis is discussed in detail by *Marple* [1987] and fast algorithms to compute the DFT by *Blahut* [1985].

B PC-Based Image Processing Systems

B.1 Overview

In this appendix we describe the architecture of modern PC-based image processing systems. It is not intended to give a survey of the market. Instead, we explain the basic components of image processing systems and thus provide some basic knowledge. It is important to be aware that different classes of image processing hardware are available in order to make an intelligent choice for a certain application. Generally, we can distinguish four classes of frame grabbers:

Hardwired frame grabbers. This type of image processing cards were the first to emerge on the micro computer market at the end of the 1970s and initiated the widespread use of digital image processing in scientific applications. The functions of these boards are hardwired and controlled via a set of registers in the input/output space of the host. Display of video images requires a separate RGB monitor. A typical example is the PCVISION*plus* board from Imaging Technology (figure B.2a).

Modular image processing systems with a pipelined video bus. A video bus system allows the integration of special purpose processing elements in a modular way to adapt the hardware to the processing needs. Certain types of image processing operations can then be performed much faster, most of them in real time. Examples for high-end modular image processing systems with a pipelined video bus include the Modular Vision Computers (MVC) from Imaging Technology (figure B.3), the IMAGE series from Matrox, and the MaxVideo 20 from Datacube. An external video bus system is also included in medium-cost image processing boards such as the VISION*plus*-AT series from Imaging Technology.

Frame grabber with programmable processor. This type of image processing boards include its own graphics, signal or general purpose processor to enhance image processing capabilities. Standard tools such as C-compilers and development tool kits are available to program the boards in a much more flexible and portable way than it would ever be possible with a hard-wired system. As an early example, we will consider the AT-Vista board from Truevision (figure B.2b).

Frame grabbers with fast bus to PC RAM. With the advent of fast bus systems for the PC such as the VESA local bus and the PCI bus, the way is paved for a new generation of frame buffers. These bus systems are fast enough that digitized image data can be transferred in real time to the DRAM of the PC. Since the bottleneck of slow transfer of image data is now removed, processing of image data on the PC CPU is now much more attractive. A frame buffer now needs to include only video input circuits and a DMA controller. Display of images can be performed by the PC graphics board. In this way, image processing hardware becomes much cheaper and a more integral part of PCs. Examples of frame grabbers of this kind include the Matrox Meteor, the Data Translation DT3155, and the PC_EYE1 from ELTEC (figure B.9).

We will discuss the major components of image processing boards, which are the *video input* (section B.2), the *frame buffer* (section B.3), the *video output* (section B.4), and the interface to the host processor. Pipelined video bus systems with dedicated image processing elements are described in section B.5 and are contrasted with programmable image processing systems in section B.6. Block diagrams of the boards discussed as typical examples can be found at the end of this appendix.

B.2   Video Input

The *video input* component is very similar in all frame grabbers (figures B.2a, B.8 and B.9b). First, the analog video signal is processed and the video source is synchronized with the frame buffer in a suitable way. Then the signals are digitized and stored after preprocessing with the input look-up table in the frame buffer.

Analog Video Signal Processing

All the systems which only process black-and-white video signals include a video multiplexor. This allows the frame buffer to be connected to a number of video signals. Via software, it is possible to switch between the different sources. Before the analog video signal is digitized, it passes through a video amplifier with a programmable gain and offset included in most boards. In this way, the incoming video signal can best be adapted to the input range of the analog-digital converter.

The MVC with the Color Acquisition Module and the Vista board, (figure B.4b and B.2) are examples for frame grabbers that can digitize color images from RGB video sources which provide a separate red, green, and blue signal. In order to capture composite color video signals in which the luminance and color information is composed in one video signal, a decoder is required which splits the composite signal into the RGB video signals. Such a decoder is already built into the Color Acquisition Module of the MVC (figure B.4b). These devices can also decode Y-C signals according to the S-VHS video standard. The Color Acquisition Module also features real time color space conversion (figure B.4b). Color video signals can be converted to and from various color coordinate systems. Of most importance for image processing is the HSI (hue, saturation, intensity) color space. In composite, Y-C, and YUV video signals, the resolution for the color signal is considerably lower than for the luminance signal. Consequently, only three-chip color cameras with RGB video output can be recommended for scientific applications. Color acquisition modules can also be used to capture video

Table B.1: Important parameters of the American (RS-170) and European (CCIR) video norms.

	RS-170	CCIR
Horizontal scan time	$63.5556\,\mu$s	$64.0\,\mu$s
Horizontal blank time	$10.7556\,\mu$s	$11.8414\,\mu$s
Horizontal scan frequency	$15.7343\,$kHz	$15.625\,$kHz
Vertical scan time	$16.6833\,$ms	$20.0\,$ms
Vertical blank time	$1.2711\,$ms	$1.5360\,$ms
Vertical scan frequency	$59.9401\,$Hz	$50.0\,$Hz
Number of rows	525	625
Active rows	485[1]	576[1]

[1]The first and last row are half rows.

signals from several synchronized black-and-white video cameras. In this way, *stereo images* or other types of *multichannel images* can be acquired and processed.

Synchronization

Besides the image contents, a video signal contains synchronization signals which mark the beginning of an image (vertical synchronization) and the image rows (horizontal synchronization). These signals are extracted in the video input by a synchronization stripper and used to synchronize the frame buffer (image display) with the video input via a *phase-locked loop* (PLL).

Some PLL circuits do not work properly with instable video sources such as video recorders. If digitization of recorded images is required, it should be tested whether the images are digitized without distortions. Digitization of still images is especially critical. It cannot be done without a time-base corrector. If a particular image from a videotape must be digitized, it is necessary that a time code is recorded together with the images either on the audio track or with the video signal itself. This time code is read by the computer and used to trigger the digitization of the image.

Nowadays, video signals can also be recorded in analog form on an optical disc which can be written to only once (WORM technology). Such systems, as for example, the Sony LVR-5000 and LVR-6000, allow for the recording of single video frames as well as continuous sequences. The images can be played back in forward and backward direction at variable speed. Furthermore, random access to any image on the disc is possible within 0.5 s. All functions of the recorder can be controlled via a serial interface. Because of the fast random access, the large numbers of frames and the weariless read back, this new medium is also eminently suitable for image data bases.

Most modern frame grabbers can process video signals according to both the American RS-170 and the European CCIR norms with 30 and 25 frames/s, respectively. The most important parameters of the two norms are summarized in table B.1. An image row according to the RS-170 standard is shown in figure B.1.

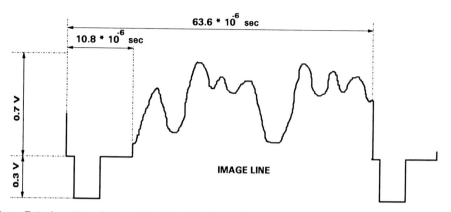

Figure B.1: A section of the analog video signal according to the American RS-170 norm showing one row of the image with the horizontal synchronization signals. The European CCIR is very similar. Only the timing is slightly different (see table B.1).

Table B.2: Typical resolutions of digitized video images.

	number of rows	number of columns	Pixel clock [MHz]	aspect ratio
RS 170, old standard	512	480	10.0699	1.10
RS 170	640	480	12.28	1.01
RS 170	740	480	14.3181	0.87
CCIR, old standard	512	512	10.00	1.48
CCIR, square pixels	768	572	15.00	1.00

Digitization

Generally, the video signal is digitized with a resolution of 8 bits, i. e., 256 gray value levels at a rate of 10 million pixels per second. The resulting digitized image contains 512×512 and 480×512 pixels in the European and American formats, respectively. For a long time, this has been a standard. Modern frame grabbers, however, are much more flexible. Thus the number of rows and columns and the pixel clock can be programmed in a wide range. Some typical resolutions are shown in table B.2. With the variable-scan acquisition modules (figures B.4a), it is also possible to digitize non-standard video signals, e. g., from electron microscopes, ultrasonic and thermal sensors, line scan cameras, and from high-resolution CCD-cameras such as the Kodak Videk Megaplus camera with more than 1000×1000 pixels. For practical applications, the following additional hints are important:

From the 576 visible rows of the European CCIR signal only 512 are digitized in the standard digital video resolution with 512×512 pixels. Unfortunately, there is no standard using rows. Consequently, every frame grabber may select a different sector. Generally, the pixels are not squares but rectangles (see table B.2). This fact is very important for videometry and filter operations. Isotropic filters become non-isotropic. In recognition of the importance of square pixels, most modern frame grabbers can operate in a square pixel mode.

The digitization rate generally does not coincide with the rate at which the collected charges are read out from CCD sensors. Consequently, sensor elements (*sels*) and pixels (*pels*) are not identical. This may lead to vertically oriented disturbance patterns in the digitized images. The Variable Scan Acquisition Module of the Modular Vision Computer (figure B.4a) includes a *pixel clock* input which allows the sel and pel clock rates to be synchronized to avoid such disturbances. Pixel-synchronous digitization is also important for sub-pixel accurate position, displacement, and size measurements (sections 2.2.4 and 17.4.5).

Standard video cameras work in the *interlaced* mode. This means that a frame is composed of two half frames which either contain the even or odd lines. These half frames or *fields* are scanned one after the other. Consequently, the two fields are illuminated one after the other with a time shift of half the time interval between two images. A single frame containing moving objects flickers because it is composed of the two half images illuminated at different times. For image sequence analysis this means that we must work with half images. In this way, the temporal resolution is doubled at the cost of the vertical resolution of the images.

Input LUT

The digitized image is read into the frame buffer via an *input look-up table* (LUT). Most boards incorporate 8 or 16 such tables, which can be selected by registers. LUTs allow a fast implementation of *homogeneous point operations* (sections 4.3.1–4.3.2) before the pixels are stored in the frame buffer. The LUTs can be accessed from the host either by hardware registers or by mapping the LUT memory into the address space of the PC. Writing to an LUT for 8-bit images which contains just 256 entrances is fast enough so that it can be performed interactively.

With the help of another register, single bit planes in the frame buffer can be protected against overwriting by the digitized video signal. With the input LUT a real-time segmentation can be performed and the segmented image can be stored in only one bit plane by protecting all other bit planes. Then we can store a whole binary image sequence in the individual bit planes of the frame buffer. In this way, the image sequence of the particle traces shown in plate 4 has been produced.

Digital Video Input

Since the beginning of image processing, imaging sensors were locked to the video standard of 30 (25) frames/s and a limited spatial resolution of 480 (580) lines/frame. Such a standard was required in order to be able to view images on monitors and to record them to video tape. For digital image processing, however, severe disadvantages are linked to this standard since it has been developed for television broadcasting. One of the most disturbing features is the interlacing of a frame into even and odd fields. Another severe limitation is, of course, that applications had to be adapted to the temporal and spatial resolution of video imagery.

For a long time, the only major deviation from the video standard were line sensors which found wide-spread usage in industrial applications. Today, we see the advent of

Table B.3: Specifications of various digital video cameras.

Camera	Sensor size (Pixels)	Frame rate (1/s)	Resolution (Bits)	Pixel clock (MHz)
DALSA CA-D1-128	128×128	900	8	16
DALSA CA-D1-256	256×256	200	8	16
Kodak Megaplus 1.4	1320×1035	6.9	8	10
Kodak Megaplus 4.2	2029×2044	2.1	8	10
Kodak XHF	1320×1035	30	10	2×20
DALSA CA-D9-2048	2048×2048	15	8, 10	4×15

cameras with digital output. Now there is no longer a restriction to frame rates and images sizes, as shown by the summary in table B.3. Of course, the rate at which pixels can be read out is still limited. Therefore, a tradeoff exists between spatial and temporal resolution. A similar tradeoff exists between the dynamics in brightness and pixel read-out frequency. Cameras are also available with resolutions of up to 16 bit. These cameras find applications in spectroscopy and photometrics. They can be used only with much lower pixel read-out frequencies. This limit will, however, be overcome in the future with multiple digital outputs.

The benefits of digital cameras are significant. First, a much higher signal quality can be achieved since it is no longer required to transmit analog video signals from the camera to the frame buffer. Second, a pixel in the digital image really corresponds to a sensor element in the camera. Thus the image preserves the exact geometry of the sensor allowing for precise geometrical measurements. This emerging field is called *videometry* in analogy to photometry. Third, sensors can be chosen that fit to the requirements of the application concerning spatial, temporal and irradiance resolution. Forth, digital cameras require a much simpler interface to computers. There is no restriction to the sensor size and frame rates within certain limits of transfer rates. Thus we should see an enormous diversification in imaging sensors in the near future.

B.3   Frame Buffer

The frame buffer is the central part of an image processing board. The digitized image is stored in the frame buffer. All image processing boards discussed here contain a frame buffer which can hold pixels with at least 8 bits (256 gray values). The frame buffer can hold 2 (PCVISION*plus*) to 16 (Vista) full resolution 512×512 images. This corresponds to 0.5 to 4 Mbytes of memory. Modular systems have the advantage that the frame buffer memory can be expanded to store long image sequences.

Frame buffers show a complex inner structure which allows digitized images to be written and read out simultaneously. While a new pixel is written into a memory cell, the old contents are simultaneously read out. In this way, the display of images is delayed by one frame interval. The frame buffer also contains a *dual-ported memory* architecture. Newer frame buffer architectures, as for example in the Modular Vision

Computer, feature independent timing for writing (image acquisition) and reading (display) of pixels in memory.

Besides the continuous and sequential access of the frame buffer for image display, the host can randomly access the frame buffer memory. Two concepts are used for host access. First, a selected part of the frame memory, generally 64 kbytes, is mapped into the address space of the PC. This part of the frame buffer can then be accessed by the host in the same way as any other PC memory. Second, the frame buffer can be accessed via hardware registers. Both methods allow a flexible addressing. After each read and write cycle, both row as well as column numbers can be in- or decremented automatically. In this way, rows and columns can be read or written without any additional addressing operations.

Frame buffers deeper than 8 bits are very helpful to overlay images with graphics, calibration grids, or segmentation and classification results. Furthermore, a 16-bit buffer can be used to store intermediate results or evaluated images. For many advanced filtering operations, such as the local orientation (chapter 7), an accuracy of 8 bits is insufficient. The images shown in plates 9, 12 and 13 have been computed with 12-bit deep images. More advanced image processing boards allow a flexible use of the frame buffers for 8-, 16-, 24-, or 32-bit images.

B.4 Video Output

The video output part generates an analog video signal from the contents in the frame-buffer so that the image can be viewed on a monitor or stored on a video recording device. All image processing systems discussed here contain a three-channel video output part, one channel for each of the colors red, green, and blue. In this way color images can be generated even from gray value imagery. In a gray value frame buffer, the digitized gray value is output to all the channels simultaneously. Before the gray values are converted to an analog signal, they pass by an *output LUT*. Each color channel contains its own LUT. If all three LUTs contain the same values, a gray value image is displayed. By programming the three color output LUTs with different tables, gray value images can be converted into pseudo color images (see also plate 7). In color image processing systems, each output channel can be connected to a different part of the frame buffer (see, for example, figure B.6a). In this way true color images, or more generally, multichannel images with 8 bits per channel, can be displayed. Like the input LUT, the output LUT can quickly be accessed by the host. This opens up the possibility of carrying out homogeneous point operations on the images *without* modifying the contents of the frame buffer (see sections 4.3.1 and 4.3.2).

The *pan-*, *scroll-* and *zoom* functions determine the part of the frame buffer which is accessed by the video in- and output part of the board. While the pan and scroll set the starting row and column, respectively, the zoom factor determines the size of the frame buffer. In the video output circuit, the image enlargement is performed by replication of pixels and scan lines. In the video input circuit, the zoom factor divides the digitization clock frequency and causes whole scan lines to be omitted in order to reduce the size and resolution of the image to be digitized. The possible zoom factors depend on the hardware of the frame grabber. While the PCVISION*plus* can zoom images only by a factor of two, other frame grabbers can zoom images by factors of 2, 4, and 8 or set the horizontal and vertical zoom factors independently.

Zoom, pan and scroll can also be used to digitize short image sequences and to play them back with adjustable speed. All image processing boards contain a register which allows the beginning of a new image (vertical blank signal) to be detected. The program waits for the next or several vertical blank signals and then sets the pan and scroll factors to the next free frame buffer area. On the Vista board with 4 Mbytes of frame buffer, a sequence of about 50 images with 256×256 pixels, or 200 images with 128×128 pixels and 8 bits depth can be digitized and interactively be played back.

B.5 Dedicated Image Processing Hardware

So far, we have only discussed dedicated hardware to capture and display images. Basically all image processing still has to be performed on the PC. This also includes the overhead to transfer the image data from the frame buffer to the PC and back again.

Dedicated processing hardware allows common image processing operations to be speeded up considerably. In this section, we will briefly describe the principle of parallel processing using a pipelined video bus and the concept of area-of-interest scanning to speed up processing. Then, the most important processing elements including arithmetic-logical units, filter processors, and histogram and feature extractors will be discussed.

B.5.1 Parallel Processing in the Video Pipeline

All computational modules described in this section are connected to each other by several *video busses*. As an example of an modular image processing system with a video pipeline bus, the Modular Vision Computer will be discussed (figure B.6a). Digitized image data (3×8 bits) from the acquisition modules can either be stored directly into the frame buffers A0, A1, and B1 or enter the video pipeline via the PBIN bus. Image data stored in the frame buffers can enter the pipeline via the video in bus (VB). Processed video data from the video pipeline can be stored in the frame buffers via the PBOUT bus. *Cross-port switches* (figure B.6) control in which order the video signals are piped through the video pipeline. Figure B.6b illustrates the various possibilities to connect the three computational modules on a CMC base board. Video data pathes can be splitted or merged again. Since several CMCs can be connected in series, this leads to a very flexible processing scheme.

All computational modules in the video pipeline operate in parallel. After a fixed delay, the data processed in one computational module is clocked to the next module in the pipeline. In this way, the delays in all processing modules add up. This means that

— except for a initial delay — there is no additional overhead for the parallel operation and that the computational power of all modules in the pipeline adds up linearly. If one or only a few runs through the video pipeline is sufficient, the corresponding operation is performed in real time. However, if an application requires an operation which cannot be performed by one of the processing elements in the video pipeline, it becomes the bottleneck and slows down the overall performance significantly.

B.5.2 Processing Windows: Area-of-Interest

For display, the frame buffer is continuously scanned row by row. In this way the pixels are put on a video bus with a rate of typically 10 MHz (see table B.2). Thus real-time image processing can be performed by clocking the pixels through additional processing elements at this rate and then writing the processed data back to the frame buffer again. In this way only full-resolution images can be processed. However, it is often necessary to process only a small part of the image. Operations on image pyramids (chapter 8) are typical and important examples. In such cases, the processing element would only be active when pixels of the window are put onto the video bus and thus would be idle most of the time.

In order to speed up operations on image sectors, some image processing systems can operate in a special mode called *area-of-interest* processing. In this mode, not the whole active frame buffer is scanned but only a small sector, the area-of-interest. Compared to the regular scanning mode, the processing time is reduced proportionally to the size of the window. Since also the clock rate during area-of-interest timing can be much faster than during the acquisition timing (for instance 40 MHz for the Modular Vision Computer (MVC) from Imaging Technology), processing faster than real time is possible. Therefore, even several processing steps can be performed by a computational module in series while still keeping up with the incoming video data.

B.5.3 Arithmetic Pipeline Processors

An *arithmetic-logical unit* (ALU), as it is integrated into the convolver logical unit (figure B.7a), is a basic computational module for image processing on the MVC. With this unit, logical and arithmetic operations can be performed with two images. This includes image addition, subtraction, and multiplication, computation of the minimum and maximum gray values, and operations between an image and a constant.

It is also possible to perform *convolution* operations by combining the ALU functions with the pan and scroll functions which determine the spatial offset of the image output onto the video bus. First, we need to reserve a part of the frame buffer to hold the result of the convolution operation. Initially, this *accumulation* buffer is set to zero. Then we multiply the image in the ALU by the first coefficient of the mask and add the result to the accumulator buffer. The pan and scroll function is used to apply a horizontal and vertical shift to the multiplied image which corresponds to the position of the filter coefficient relative to the central pixel of the mask. After performing this operation with all non-zero coefficients of the mask, the convolved image is divided by a corresponding factor. Division can be replaced by a shift operation, if the division factor is a power of two. This is, for example, the case with binomial smoothing filters (section 6.1.2). The ALU makes the computation of convolution operations much faster. Convolution of a 512×512 image with a 5×5 binomial mask takes only 8 iterations (section 6.1.2).

B.5.4 Filter processors

The computation time for convolution operations can further be reduced using special convolution processors which include parallel arithmetic units. The convolver chip L64240 from LSI Logic, for example, can compute a convolution of an 8-bit image with an 8×8 mask (8-bit coefficients) in real time. This corresponds to a computational power of 640 million multiplications and 630 million additions per second. A similar convolver chip is integrated into the Convolver Logical Unit of the MVC (figure B.7a). This chip performs a 4×4 convolution with 8-bit image data and 8-bit kernel coefficients with a clock rate of 40 MHz. With four iterations, 8×8 convolutions can be performed with an effective clock rate of 10 MHz.

The morphology computational module (figure B.7b) can perform rank value filter operations such as median, minimum and maximum filtering (section 5.1.3). The module contains four 3×3 rank value filter elements that can work in parallel or in series. Each of this rank value filters outputs either the minimum, median, or maximum value for grey value erosion, median, or dilation operation, respectively. After the rank-value filtering, two data streams can be fed into a arithmetic-logical unit and a 16×16-bit lookup table. In this way, advanced morphological operations such as the top-hat operator can be performed in one run through the module.

Furthermore, a binary correlator is available for the MVC (figure B.7d). This module allows binary morphological operations to be performed such as erosion and dilation (section 11.2) and binary cross-correlations (section 15.3.4) with mask sizes up to 32×32 in real time using the 1024-tap Binary Data FIR Filter chip from LSI Logic.

B.5.5 Histogram and Feature Extractors

Computation of histograms can be performed in real time with another computational module, the histogram/feature extractor (figure B.7c). The computed histogram is stored in a special buffer which can be accessed by the host. The module contains a second functional block that operates in parallel to the histogram extractor and that allows features to be extracted from an image in a flexible way.

B.6 Programmable Systems

Although dedicated image processing hardware such as the filter processors shows impressive performance figures, they seldom reach the peak performance, lack flexibility and are difficult to program. In the initial times of PC-based image processing, however, there was no alternative. The transfer of image data from the frame buffer to the PC memory and back again was slow and the general purpose computers were not powerful enough for the many operations required for image processing.

B.6.1 Frame Grabbers with Programmable Processors

Consequently, the integration of a programmable processor on the frame buffer seemed to be a valuable alternative. Since such a processor on the frame buffer can work in parallel to the PC, the overall performance is also enhanced considerably.

An early example of this concept was the Vista board from Truevision (figure B.2b). This board includes the *graphics processor* TMS 34010 from Texas Instruments. This processor is a general purpose 32-bit processor which provides a powerful instruction set for pixel processing. By these instructions, arithmetic and logical operations can be performed with pixels from two windows.

Equally important as the hardware are suitable software development tools. For the TMS 34010 based boards, extensive development tool kits are available. This includes an ANSI C cross-compiler, an assembler, a symbolic debugger, and utilities. Working with image data is much easier than on an IBM-compatible PC. In contrast to the maximum segment size of 64 kbytes, the TMS 34010 has a large linearly and bitwise addressable memory. The Vista board includes up to 4 Mbytes memory for image display, and additional 10 Mbytes for programs and image data with the VMX extension board. Image data for intermediate results can dynamically be allocated. In addition, image data may be used with all C data types. Another important aspect is the extensive graphics library available for the TMS 34010.

B.6.2 Frame Grabbers for Fast PC Bus Systems

The advent of fast bus systems on PCs such as the VESA local bus and the PCI bus will transform PC-based image processing again since a critical performance gain is achieved. These bus systems are fast enough to transfer digitized image data in real-time to PC memory. Sustained transfer rates up to 80 Mbytes/s have been reported for the PCI bus. The ELTEC PC_EYE1 frame grabber (figure B.9) is a typical example for the new concept of frame buffers with master DMA image transfer. The incoming analog video signal is digitized with a rate of up to 15 Msamples/s into 8-bit digital video samples. The samples are buffered in the direct memory access (DMA) controller and transferred via PCI burst transfers to any preselected PC memory address. Thus, the CPU is offloaded from transferring images into main memory and no extra, more expensive video random access memory (VRAM) is required for the intermediate storage of images as with conventional frame buffers. Assuming a typical sustained PCI bandwidth of 50 MB/s, the real-time image transfer still consumes only a fraction of the bandwidth and can be displayed in real time on fast graphics adaptors. Thus it is possible to process an image, while the next one is acquired simultaneously.

Table B.4: Benchmarks for typical image processing operations with the image processing software heurisko on the platforms as indicated. If not noted otherwise, 512×512 float images are used.

Computing time in seconds	i486DX2 66 MHz	Pentium 90 MHz	i860XP 50 MHz	PowerMac 8100/100
Fast Fourier transform	4.0	1.1	0.47	1.5
Horizontal derivation (edge detection)	0.28	0.09	0.10	0.08
same with 16-bit integers	0.16	0.08	0.09	0.07
Laplace operator	0.75	0.25	0.23	0.19
same with 16-bit integers	0.49	0.24	0.28	0.22
General 3×3 convolution	1.43	0.41	0.24	0.34
General 5×5 convolution	3.64	1.00	0.50	0.80
same with 16-bit integers	2.40	1.46	1.56	0.89
5×5 binomial mask	1.09	0.41	0.30	0.37
same with 16-bit integers	0.57	0.24	0.35	0.36
3×3 gray value erosion	0.95	0.48	0.47	0.40
same with 16-bit integers	0.64	0.32	0.51	0.31
binary 3×3 erosion	0.035	0.019	0.028	0.017
Gaussian pyramid	0.82	0.3	0.35	0.22
Laplacean pyramid	–	0.49	–	0.41
Histogram	0.67	0.26	0.21	0.16
same with 8-bit numbers	0.064	0.025	0.051	0.031

B.6.3   Portable Software Versus Dedicated Hardware

Modern PC architectures with fast PC bus systems as described in the previous section reduce the costs for image processing hardware considerably and thus will widen the usage of image processing for scientific and industrial applications. While the costs of even simple conventional frame grabbers often exceeded the price of a high-end PC, the prices of the first generation of fast bus frame grabbers have already dropped into the \$400 – \$1000 range in 1995. A frame grabber can now be reduced to a minimum of a video analog-digital converter and a DMA controller, as demonstrated with the ELTEC frame grabber (figure B.9). Image display can be handled with the largely expanded imaging abilities — including 24-bit true color display at high resolutions — built into standard graphics adaptors and is already supported by the operating system of modern personal computers and workstations.

This hardware development has another, equally important but often overlooked effect. It opens the way to portable image processing software. If all image processing and display is done on a general purpose hardware, then the only hardware dependent part is the handling of image input with the frame buffer. This task can be performed by a simple driver. All image processing software can then be written in a portable way, e. g., in ANSI C. Porting to a new platform then requires only a recompilation of the code. It is expected that this development will lead to an acceleration in the development and application of advanced image processing algorithms. Given the impressive performance of dedicated hardware as discussed in section B.5, the question remains how efficient and fast image processing can be performed on general purpose hardware.

First of all, it must be stressed that software development for dedicated hardware is much more difficult than for general purpose hardware. Dedicated hardware is in general also much less flexible. It is typically designed to run a specific type of algorithms. It might well happen that after the development cycle of the hardware more efficient algorithms are available but that they cannot be used because the hardware was not designed to run the modified algorithms.

Computation times for typical low-level image processing algorithms are summarized in table B.4 for different hardware platforms. The benchmarks have been computed with heurisko, a portable advanced tool kit and development platform for image processing (including image sequences and volumetric images) that has been developed by AEON Verlag & Studio in cooperation with the author[1].

From table B.4 it is obvious that in general, video-rate image processing is not yet possible with general purpose hardware. The performance figures are still impressive and show some interesting trends. First, integer arithmetics is no longer faster than floating-point arithmetics. For most of the operations shown in the table, floating-point arithmetics is even slightly faster than integer arithmetics. Second, the binary 3×3 erosion is performed faster than real time (19 ms for a 512×512 image). The more than 10-fold performance gain as compared to 16-bit gray value erosion is caused by the fact that with 32-bit words 32 binary pixels can be processed in parallel.

Third, it can be observed that the gain by efficient algorithms increases with the complexity of the operation. While a simple horizontal derivation (one subtraction) runs on a 90 Mhz Pentium processor only at about 2.8 million floating-point operations per second (MFLOPS), the general 5×5 convolution (25 multiplications, 24 additions) is much more efficient with 12.3 MFLOPS. Surprisingly, the computation of the Gaussian pyramid is even faster than the general 5×5 convolution. By the use of efficient algorithms, the 13×13 smoothing filter (169 multiplications and 168 additions for a direct computation) could be reduced to a few additions and multiplications. This means that the Gaussian pyramid is apparently computed with a rate of about 375 MFLOPS. This performance would be required by a "stupid" dedicated hardware that performs the 13×13 convolution directly in order to compute the Gaussian pyramid with the same speed.

This simple example illuminates that the focus for future progress in computational speed for image processing might very well be more on software than on hardware.

---

[1]For further information on heurisko contact AEON Verlag & Studio, Fraunhoferstr. 51B, D-63454 Hanau, Germany, Compuserve 100326,3156 (access from Internet: 100326.3156@compuserve.com).

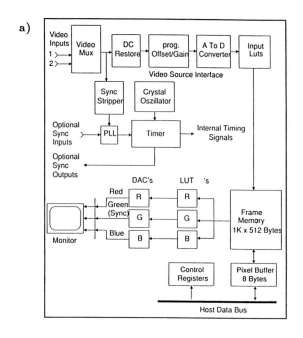

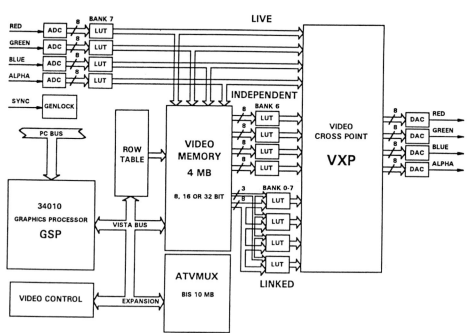

Figure B.2: a) Block diagram of the PCVISION*plus* frame grabber from Imaging Technology; b) block diagram of the ATVista board from Truevision.

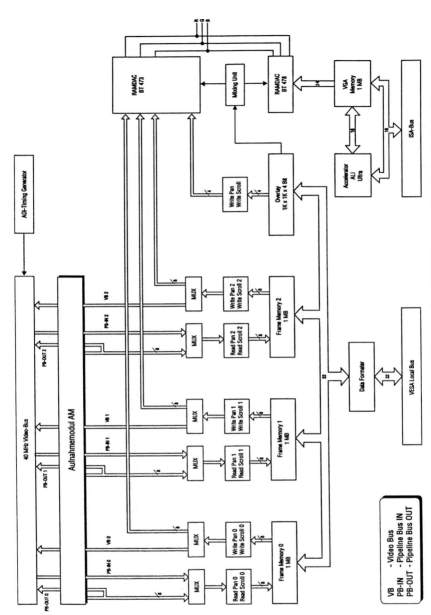

Figure B.3: Block diagram of the Image Manager Local (IML), a member of the Modular Vision Computer series from Imaging Technology.

a)

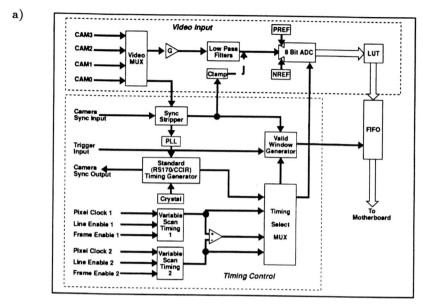

b)

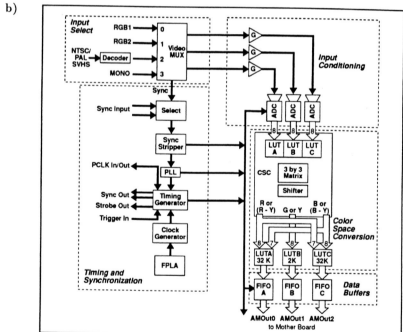

Figure B.4: Block diagrams of acquisition modules for the Modular Vision Computer (MVC) from Imaging Technology: a) the Variable Scan Acquisition Module (AM-VS); b) the Color Acquisition Module (AM-CLR).

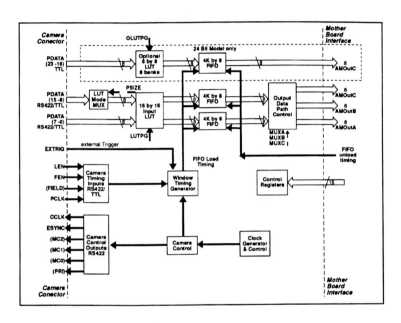

Figure B.5: Block diagram of acquision modules for the Modular Vision Computer (MVC) from Imaging Technology: the Digital Acquisition Module (AM-DIG).

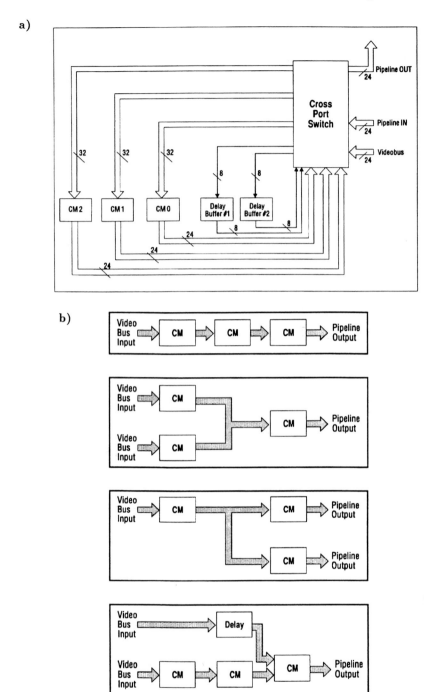

Figure B.6: a) Video pipeline as implemented in the Modular Vision Computer (MVC) from Imaging Technology; b) examples for the programmable configurations of the video pipeline of the MVC.

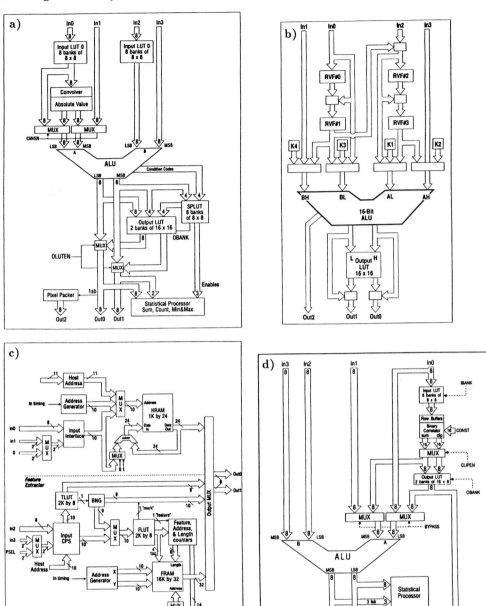

Figure B.7: Computational modules for the Modular Vision Computer (MVC) from Imaging Technology: a) Convolver Logical Unit (CM-CLU); b) Morphology Processor (CM-MMP); c) Histogram/Feature Extractor (CM-HF); d) Binary Correlator (CM-BC).

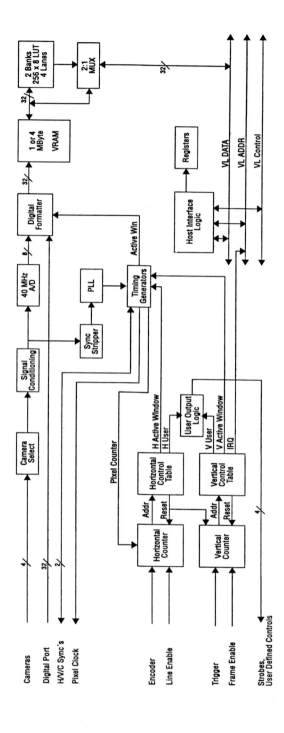

Figure B.8: Block diagram of the VESA local bus frame grabber from BitFlow Inc. with analog and digital video input.

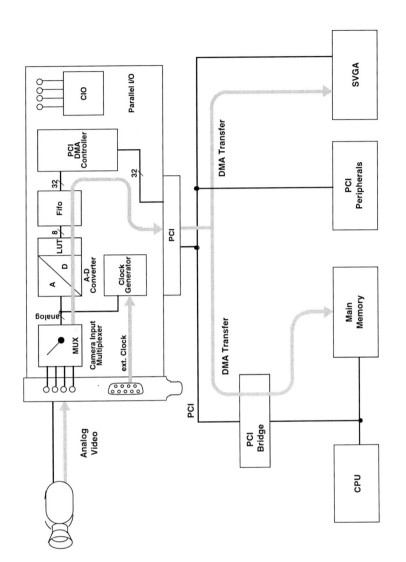

Figure B.9: Block diagram of the ELTEC PCI bus frame grabber with DMA transfer of image data to the PC DRAM.

Bibliography

Adelson, E. H., and J. R. Bergen, The extraction of spatio-temporal energy in human and machine vision, In *Proc. Workshop on Motion: Representation and Analysis*, Charleston, 1986, pp. 151–155, IEEE Computer Society Press, Washington, 1986.

Adelson, E. H., and J. R. Bergen, Spatio-temporal energy models for the perception of motion, *J. Opt. Soc. Am.*, A 2, 284–299, 1985.

Aggarwal, J. K., Motion and time-varying imagery - an overview, In *Proc. Workshop on Motion: Representation and Analysis*, Charleston, 1986, pp. 1–6, IEEE Computer Society Press, Washington, 1986.

Andersen, A. H., and A. C. Kak, Simultaneous algebraic reconstruction technique: a new implementation of the ART algorithm, *Ultrasonic imaging*, 6, 81–94, 1984.

Arce, G. R., N. C. Gallagher, and T. A. Nodes, Median filters: theory for one and two dimensional filters., Advances in computer vision and image processing, Vol. 2, edited by Huang, T. S., JAI Press, Greenwich, USA, 1986.

Barnsley, M., *Fractals everywhere*, Academic Press, London, 1988.

Barnsley, M. F., and A. D. Sloan, A better way to compress images, *Byte*, *13(1)*, 215–223, 1988.

Bigün, J., and G. H. Granlund, Optimal orientation detection of linear symmetry, In *Proc. 1st Int. Conf. Comp. Vis.*, London 1987, pp. 433–438, IEEE Computer Society Press, Washington, 1987.

Bigün, J., G. H. Granlund, and J. Wiklund, Multidimensional orientation estimation with application to texture analysis and optical flow, *IEEE Trans. PAMI*, 13(8), 775–790, 1991.

Blahut, R. E., *Fast algorithms for digital signal processing*, Addison-Wesley, Reading, Mass., 1985.

Bracewell, R., *The Fourier transform and its applications*, McGraw-Hill, New York, 1965.

Broit, C., *Optimal registrations of deformed images*, Diss., Univ. of Pennsylvania, USA, 1981.

Burt, P. J., The pyramid as a structure for efficient computation, In *Multiresolution image processing and analysis*, edited by Rosenfeld, A., pp. 6–35, Springer Series in Information Sciences, Vol. 12, Springer, New York, 1984.

Burt, P. J., T. H. Hong, and A. Rosenfeld, Segmentation and estimation of image region properties through cooperative hierarchical computation, *IEEE Trans. SMC*, 11, 802–809, 1981.

Burt, P. J., and E. H. Adelson, The Laplacian pyramid as a compact image code, *IEEE Trans. COMM*, 31, 532–540, 1983.

Carver, K. R., C. Elachi, and F. T. Ulaby, Microwave remote sensing from space, *Proceedings of the IEEE*, *73*, 970–996, 1985.

Chen, J. S., A. Huertas, and G. Medioni, Fast convolution with Laplacian-of-Gaussian masks, *IEEE Trans. PAMI*, *9*, 584–590, 1987.

Cox, C., and W. Munk, Statistics of the sea surface derived from sun glitter, *J. Marine Res.*, *13*, 198–227, 1954.

Crowley, J. L., and R. M. Stern, Fast computation of the difference of low-pass transform, *PAMI*, *6*, 212–222, 1984.

de Loor, G. P., and H. W. Brunsveld van Hulten, Microwave measurements over the North Sea, *Boundary Layer Meteorology*, *13*, 119–131, 1978.

Dengler, J., *Methoden und Algorithmen zur Analyse bewegter Realweltszenen im Hinblick auf ein Blindenhilfesystem*, Diss., Univ. Heidelberg, 1985.

Dickmanns, E. D., 4D-Szenenanalyse mit integralen Raum-/zeitlichen Modellen, In *Proc. 8. DAGM-Symp. Mustererkennung 1987*, Informatik-Fachberichte 149, edited by Paulus, E., pp. 257–271, Springer, Berlin, 1987.

Enkelmann, W., Investigations of multigrid algorithms for estimation of optical flow fields in image sequences, In *Proc. Workshop on Motion: Representation and Analysis*, Charleston, pp. 81–87, IEEE Computer Society Press, Washington, 1986.

Erhardt, A., G. Zinser, D. Komitowski, and J. Bille, Reconstructing 3D light microscopic images by digital image processing, *Applied Optics*, *24*, 194–200, 1985.

Feynman, R., *Lectures on physics, Vol. II*, Addison-Wesley, Reading, Mass., 1964.

Fischler, M. A., and O. Firschein (eds.), *Readings in computer vision: issues, problems, principles, and paradigms*, Morgan Kaufmann, Los Altos, California, 1987.

Fleet, D. J., *Measurement of image velocity*, Diss., University of Toronto, 1990.

Fleet, D. J., and A. D. Jepson, Computation of component image velocity from local phase information, *Int. J. Comp. Vision*, *5*, 77–104, 1990.

Goetz, A. F. H., J. B. Wellman, and W. L. Barnes, Optical remote sensing of the earth, *Proceedings IEEE*, *73*, 950–969, 1985.

Goldstein, H., *Classical mechanics*, Addison-Wesley, Reading, MA, 1980.

Golub, G. H., and C. F. van Loan, *Matrix Computations, 2nd ed.*, The Johns Hopkins University Press, Baltimore, London, 1989.

Gonzalez, R. C. and P. Wintz, *Digital image processing, 2nd ed.*, Addison-Wesley, Reading, Mass., 1987.

Granlund, G. H., In search of a general picture processing operator, *Comp. Graph. Imag. Process.*, *8*, 155–173, 1978.

Grawert, G., *Quantenmechanik, 2. Auflage*, Akademische Verlagsgesellschaft, Frankfurt am Main, 1973.

Harris, J. G., *The coupled depth/slope approach to surface reconstruction*, M.S. thesis, Dept. Elec. Eng. Comput. Sci., Cambridge, Mass., 1986.

Harris, J. G., A new approach to surface reconstruction: the coupled depth/slope model, In *1st Int. Conf. Comp. Vis. (ICCV)*, London, pp. 277–283, IEEE Computer Society Press, Washington, 1987.

Heeger, D. J., Model for the extraction of image flow, *J. Opt. Soc. Am.*, *A 4*, 1455–1471, 1987.

Heeger, D. J., Optical flow from spatiotemporal filters, In *Proc. 1st Int. Conf. Comp. Vis. (ICCV)*, London, pp. 181–190, IEEE Computer Society Press, Washington, 1987.

Heeger, D. J., Optical flow from spatiotemporal filters, *Int. J. Comp. Vis.*, *1*, 279–302, 1988.

Helmholz, H., Über die Integrale der hydrodynamischen Gleichungen, welche den Wirbelbewegungen entsprechen, *Crelles J.*, *55*, 25, 1858.

Hildreth, E. C., Computations underlying the measurement of visual motion, *Artificial Intelligence*, *23*, 309–354, 1984.

Hoffman, K., and R. Kunze, *Linear algebra, 2nd ed.*, Prentice-Hall, Englewood Cliffs, NJ, 1971.

Horn, B. K. P., and B. G. Schunk, Determining optical flow, *Artificial Intelligence*, *17*, 185–204, 1981.

Huang, T. S., *Two-dimensional digital signal processing I: linear filters. Topics in applied physics, 42*, Springer, New York, 1981.

Huang, T. S., *Two-dimensional digital signal processing II: transforms and median filters. Topics in applied physics, 43*, Springer, New York, 1981.

Jain, A. K., and T. Kailath, *Fundamentals of digital image processing. Prentice-Hall information and system sciences series*, Prentice-Hall, Englewood Cliffs, NJ, 1989.

Jaroslavskij, J. P., *Einführung in die digitale Bildverarbeitung*, VEB Deutscher Verlag der Wissenschaften, Berlin, 1985.

Jähne, B., Motion determination in space-time images, In *Image Processing III*, SPIE Proceeding 1135, International Congress on Optical Science and Engineering, Paris, 24-28 April 1989, pp. 147–152, 1989.

Jähne, B., From the measurement of mean fluxes to a detailed experimental investigation of the gas transfer process at a free wavy water surface, In *Proc. 2nd International Symposium on Gas Transfer at Water Surfaces*, Minneapolis, Minnesota, September 1990, in press, ASCE, 1990.

Jähne, B., Motion determination in space-time images, In *Proc. Computer Vision — ECCV 90, Lecture Notes in Computer Science 427*, edited by Faugeras, O., pp. 161–173, Springer, New York, 1990.

Jähne, B., and S. Waas, Optical measuring technique for small scale water surface waves, In *Advanced Optical Instrumentation for Remote Sensing of the Earth's Surface from Space*, SPIE Proceeding 1129, International Congress on Optical Science and Engineering, Paris, 24-28 April 1989, pp. 147–152, 1989.

Jähne, B., and K. Riemer, Two-dimensional wave number spectra of small-scale water surface waves, *J. Geophys. Res.*, *95*, 11,531–11,546, 1990.

Jost, W., *Diffusion in Solids, Liquids, Gases*, Academic Press, New York, 1960.

Kak, A. C., Image reconstruction from projections, In *Digital image processing technique, Vol. 2: Computational techniques*, edited by Ekstrom, M. P., Academic Press, Orlando, 1984.

Kass, M., and A. Witkin, Analyzing oriented patterns, In *9th Int. Joint Conf. on Artificial Intelligence*, pp. 18–23, Los Angeles, CA, 1985.

Kass, M., A. Witkin, and D. Terzopoulos, Snakes: active contour models, In *Proc. 1st Int. Conf. Comp. Vis. (ICCV)*, London, pp. 259–268, IEEE Computer Society Press, Washington, 1987.

Kittel, C., *Introduction to solid state physics*, Wiley, New York, 1971.

Knox, R. A., Ocean acoustic tomography: a primer, In *Oceanic Circulation Models: Combining Data and Dynamics*, edited by D. L. R. Anderson and J. Willebrand, pp. 141-188, Kluwer Academic Publishers, Boston, 1989.

Knutsson, H., *Filtering and reconstruction in image processing*, Diss., Linköping Univ., 1982.

Knutsson, H., and G. H. Granlund, Texture analysis using two-dimensional quadrature filters, In *IEEE Workshop Comp. Arch. Patt. Anal. Im. Dat. Base Man.*, Pasadena, CA, 1983.

Knutsson, H. E., R. Wilson, and G. H. Granlund, Anisotropic nonstationary image estimation and its applications: part I - restoration of noisy images, *IEEE Trans. COMM*, *31*, 388–397, 1983.

Kories, R., and G. Zimmermann, A versatile method for the estimation of displacement vector fields from image sequences, In *Proc. Workshop on Motion: Representation and Analysis*, Charleston, pp. 101–106, IEEE Computer Society Press, Washington, 1986.

Koschnitzke, C., R. Mehnert, and P. Quick, *Das KMQ-Verfahren: Medienkompatible Übertragung echter Stereofarbabbildungen*, Forschungsbericht Nr. 201, Universität Hohenheim, 1983.

Lenz, R., Linsenfehlerkorrigierte Eichung von Halbleiterkameras mit Standardobjektiven für hochgenaue 3D-Messungen in Echtzeit, In *Proc. 9. DAGM-Symp. Mustererkennung 1987*, edited by E. Paulus, Informatik Fachberichte 149, pp. 212–216, Springer, Berlin, 1987.

Lenz, R., Zur Genauigkeit der Videometrie mit CCD-Sensoren, In *Proc. 10. DAGM-Symp. Mustererkennung 1988*, edited by H. Bunke, O. Kübler, P. Stucki, Informatik Fachberichte 180, pp. 179–189, Springer, Berlin, 1988.

Levine, M. D., *Vision in man and machine*, McGraw-Hill, New York, 1985.

Lim, J. S., *Two-dimensional signal and image processing*, Prentice-Hall, Englewood Cliffs, NJ, 1990.

Lorenz, D., *Das Stereobild in Wissenschaft und Technik*, Deutsche Forschungs- und Versuchsanstalt für Luft- und Raumfahrt, Köln, Oberpfaffenhofen, 1985.

Mandelbrot, B., *The fractal geometry of nature*, Freeman, San Francisco, 1982.

Margulis, N., *i860 Microprocessor architecture*, McGraw-Hill, Berkeley, CA, USA, 1990.

Marple, S. L., Jr., *Digital spectral analysis with applications.*, Prentice-Hall, Englewood Cliffs, NJ, 1987.

Marr, D., *Vision*, Freeman, San Francisco, 1982.

Massen, R., U. Winkler, and A. Kolb, Contactless length measurement of non-woven webs, *Melliand Textilberichte*, *68*, 719–720, 1987.

Maxwell, E. A., *General homogeneous coordinates in pace of three dimensions*, Univ. Press, Cambridge, 1951.

Menke, W., *Geophysical data analysis: discrete inverse theory*, Academic Press, Orlando, 1984.

Nagel, H., Representation of moving objects based on visual observation, *IEEE Computer*, 14, 29–39, 1981.

Nagel, H., Displacement vectors derived from second-order intensity variations in image sequences, *Computer Vision, Graphics, and Image Processing (CVGIP)*, 21, 85–117, 1983.

Nagel, H., Image sequences - ten (octal) years - from phenomenology towards a theoretical foundation, In *Proc. Int. Conf. Patt. Recogn., Paris 1986*, pp. 1174–1185, IEEE Computer Society Press, Washington, 1986.

Niemann, H., *Pattern Analysis*, Springer, New York, 1981.

Oppenheim, A. V., A. S. Willsky, and I. T. Young, *Signals and Systems*, Prentice-Hall, Englewood Cliffs, NJ, 1983.

Oppenheim, A. V., and R. W. Schafer, *Discrete-time signal processing. Prentice-Hall signal processing series*, Prentice-Hall, Englewood Cliffs, NJ, 1989.

Peitgen, H., and P. H. Richter, *The beauty of fractals*, Springer, New York, 1986.

Pietikäinen, M., and D. Harwood, Depth from three camera stereo, In *Proc. Conf. Comp. Vis. Patt. Recogn., Miami Beach 1986*, pp. 2–8, IEEE Computer Society Press, Washington, 1986.

Pietikäinen, M. and A. Rosenfeld, Image segmentation by texture using pyramid node linking, *SMC*, *11*, 822–825, 1981.

Press, W. H., B. P. Flannery, S. A. Teukolsky, and W. T. Vetterling, *Numeral recipes in C: the art of scientific computing*, Cambridge University Press, New York, 1988.

Reif, F., *Fundamentals of statistical and thermal physics*, McGraw-Hill, Auckland, 1985.

Richards, J. A., *Remote sensing digital image analysis*, Springer, New York, 1986.

Riemer, K., *Analyse von Wasseroberflächenwellen im Orts-Wellenzahl-Raum*, Diss, Univ. Heidelberg, 1991.

Rosenfeld, A., *Multiresolution image processing and analysis*, Springer series in information sciences, 12, Springer, New York, 1984.

Rosenfeld, A., and A. C. Kak, *Digital picture processing, 2nd ed., Vol I and II*, Academic Press, Orlando, 1982.

Samet, H., *Applications of spatial data structures: computer graphics, image processing, and GIS*, Addison-Wesley, Reading, MA, 1990.

Samet, H., *The design and analysis of spatial data structures*, Addison-Wesley, Reading, MA, 1990.

Schalkoff, R. J., and J. Labuz, An integrated spatio-temporal model and recursive algorithm for image motion estimation, In *Proc. Int. Conf. Patt. Recogn.*, p. 530, Montreal, 1984.

Schalkoff, R. J., and E. S. McVey, A model and tracking algorithm for a class of video targets, *IEEE Trans. PAMI*, *4*, 2, 1982.

Schmidt, M., Mehrgitterverfahren zur 3D Rekonstruktion aus 2D Ansichten, Technical Report 17, Deutsches Krebsforschungszentrum Heidelberg, 1988.

Serra, J., *Image analysis and mathematical morphology*, Academic Press, London, 1982.

Shepp, L. A. and B. F. Logan, The Fourier reconstruction of a head section, *IEEE Trans. Nucl. Sci.*, *21*, 21–43, 1974.

Shirai, Y., *Three-dimensional computer vision*, Springer, New York, 1987.

Simonds, R. M., Reduction of large convolutional kernels into multipass applications of small generating kernels, *J. Opt. Soc. Am.*, A 5, 1023–1029, 1988.

Steurer, J., H. Giebel, and W. Altner, Ein lichtmikroskopisches Verfahren zur zweieinhalb-dimensionalen Auswertung von Oberflächen, In *Proc. 8. DAGM-Symp. Mustererkennung 1986*, Informatik-Fachberichte 125, edited by G. Hartmann, pp. 66–70, Springer, Berlin, 1986.

Stewart, R. H., *Methods of satellite oceanography*, University of California Press, Berkeley, 1985.

Strat, T. M., Recovering the camera parameters from a transformation matrix, In *Proc. DARPA Image Understanding Workshop*, pp. 264–271, 1984.

Suntz, R., H. Becker, P. Monkhouse, and J. Wolfrum, Two-dimensional visualization of the flame front in an internal combustion engine by laser-induced fluorescence of OH radicals, *Appl. Phys.*, *B 47*, in press, 1988.

Terzopoulos, D., Regularization of inverse visual problems involving discontinuities, *PAMI*, *8*, 413–424, 1986.

Terzopoulos, D., A. Witkin, and M. Kass, Symmetry-seeking models for 3-D object reconstruction, In *Proc. 1st Int. Conf. Comp. Vis. (ICCV)*, London, pp. 269–276, IEEE Computer Society Press, Washington, 1987.

Wahl, D., and J. Simpson, Physical processes affecting the objective determination of near-surface velocity from satellite data, *J. Geophys. Res.*, *95*, No. *C8*, 13,511–13,528, 1990.

Watt, A., *Three-Dimensional Computer Graphics*, Addison Wesley, Reading, MA, 1989.

Waxman, A. M., and J. H. Duncan, Binocular image flow, In *Proc. Workshop on Motion: Representation and Analysis*, Charleston, pp. 31–38, IEEE Computer Society Press, Washington, 1986.

Wierzimok, D., *Messung turbulenter Strömungen unterhalb der windwellenbewegten Wasseroberfläche mittels digitaler Bildverarbeitung*, Diss., Univ. Heidelberg, 1990.

Wierzimok, D., and B. Jähne, Measurement of wave-induced turbulent flow structures using digital image sequence analysis, *Proc. 2nd International Symposium on Gas Transfer at Water Surfaces*, Minneapolis, Minnesota, September 1990, ASCE, in press, 1990.

Zamperoni, P., *Methoden der digitalen Bildsignalverarbeitung*, Vieweg, Braunschweig, 1989.

Index

Color Plates

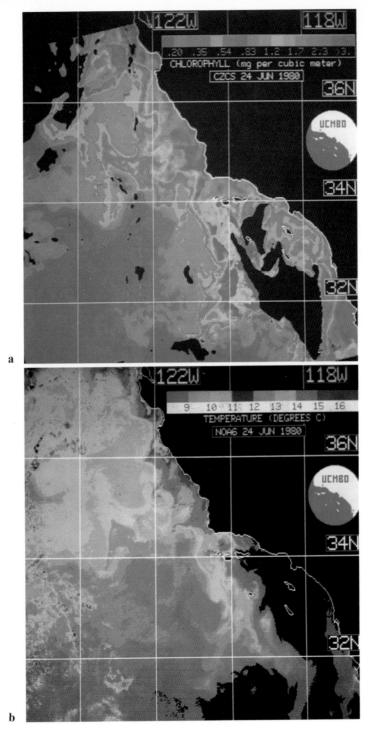

Color plate 1: Legend see following page

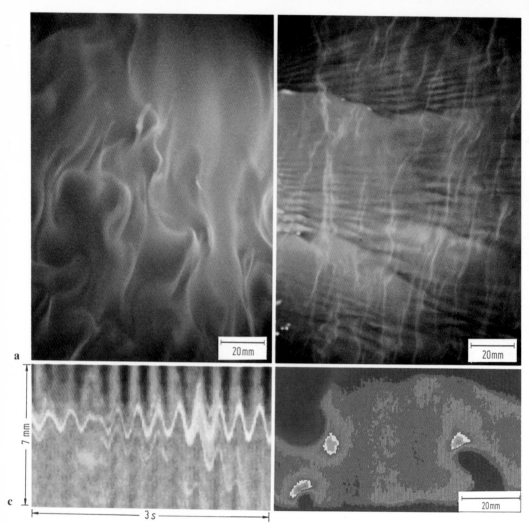

Color plate 2: (section 1.4) Examples for scientific applications of image processing: **a** and **b** Visualization of the penetration of a gas tracer into the water surface for studying the gas exchange between atmosphere and ocean. The images show a view onto the water surface from above. The greenish intensity corresponds to the momentary thickness of the mass boundary layer. **c** Time series of the vertical concentration profile of a dissolved trace gas in the vicinity of the water surface made visible by a fluorescent dye. **d** OH radical concentration in an experimental engine made visible by laser-induced fluorescence in a thin sheet

Color plate 1: (section 1.2.1) **a** Chlorophyll distribution in the surface water of the Pacific at the coast of Southern California as derived from a Coastal Zone Color Scanner image in the green-blue spectral range. **b** Temperature of the ocean surface water calculated from a NOA 6 satellite image taken in the far infrared from the same area at the same time

Color plate 3: (section 2.1.1) Demonstration of the complexity of illumination with computer generated images: **a** objects shown in the colors of their surfaces without any consideration of illumination; **b** shading of planar diffusively reflecting facets; **c** linear interpolation of the colors of the facets (Gouraud shading); **d** Phong shading; **e** texture mapping; **f** shadows and mirror images (environment mapping); images rendered with Caligari Broadcast from Octree Software, N. Y.

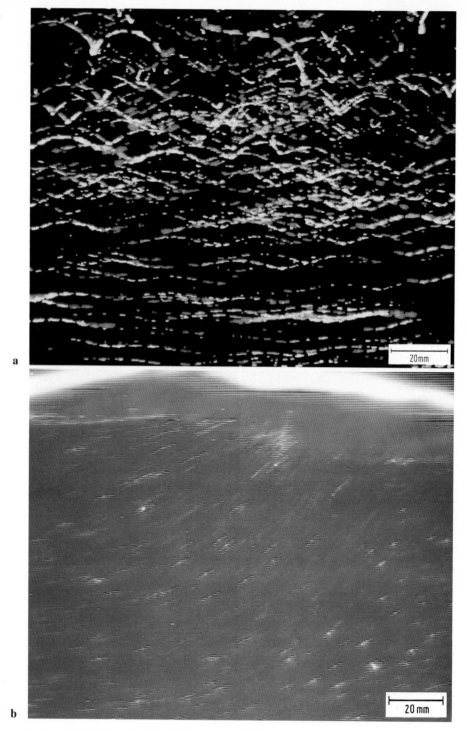

Color plate 4: (section 2.2.8) Image analysis of the turbulent flow directly below a wavy water surface. The flow is made visible by small particles: **a** superposition of 12 images; the traces from the different images of the sequence are coded in different colors; **b** single frame of the particle traces; from *Wierzimok* [1990]

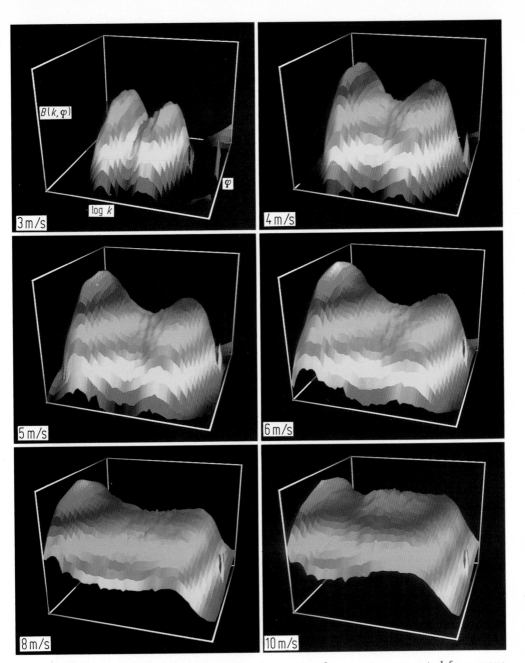

Color plate 5: (section 1.4) Two-dimensional wave number spectra computed from wave slope images (see figure 1.7 in section 1.4). Shown is the spectral density (coded in color for better recognition) as a function of the logarithm of the wave number and the propagation direction (log-polar coordinates). Each spectrum is averaged over 120 images. Unpublished data of the author from measurements in the wind/wave facility of the IMST, University of Marseille, at a fetch of 5 m and wind speeds as indicated

a

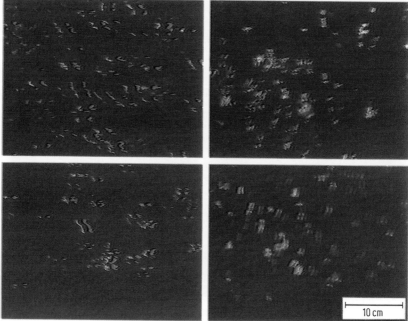

b

Color plate 6: (section 2.2.9 and 4.3.2) Stereo images: **a** computer generated stereo image; **b** use of stereo images to investigate the roughness (small-scale waves) on the ocean surface: the specular reflexes indicate zero-crossings of the slope of the surface while the height of the surface can be computed from displacement of the reflexes between the two images. The four images were taken within 2 s and show significant variation of the wave height. Measurements from S. Waas and the author at Scripps Pier, La Jolla, California

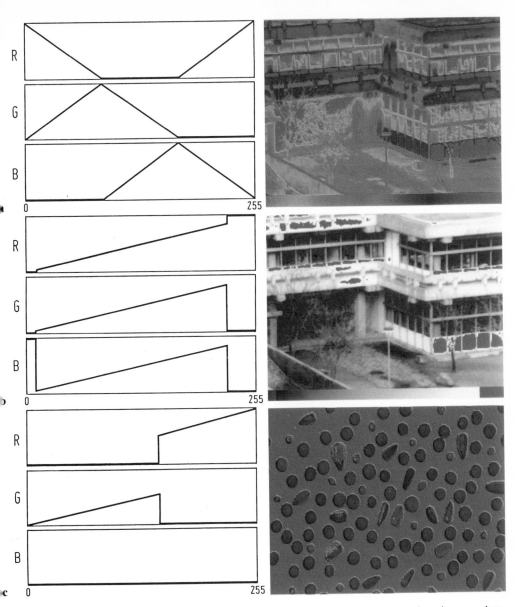

Color plate 7: (section 4.3.2) LUT operations to transform gray value images into pseudo-color images. The corresponding LUTs are shown at the left: **a** rainbow colors; **b** marking of too dark and bright gray values in blue and red, respectively; **c** color representation of image segmentation: the segmented objects are shown green, the background red

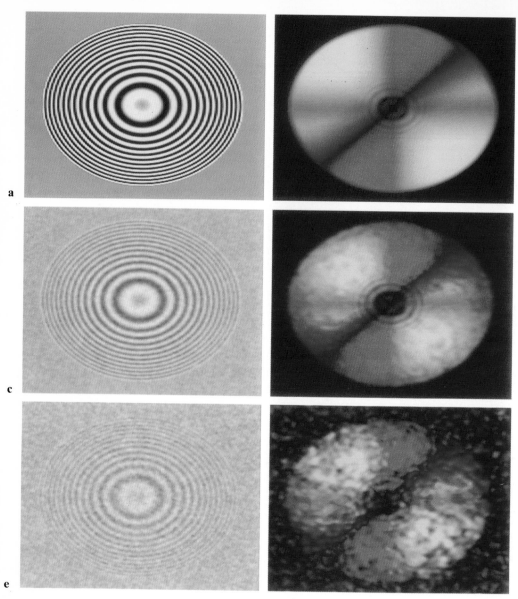

Color plate 8: (section 7.3.4) Tensor method to compute local orientation applied to a test image with concentric rings of a gray value amplitude a. The wave number increases with the distance from the center. Zero-mean normal noise with a variance of σ_n has been added. Left: original image; right: color coded orientation image as explained in section 7.1.2: **a, b** $a = 127$, $\sigma_n = 0$; **c, d** $a = 64$, $\sigma_n = 20$; **e, f** $a = 32$, $\sigma_n = 32$

Color plate 9: (section 7.3.4) Examples of orientation images: left original, right color-coded orientation image: **a, b** building of Heidelberg University; **c, d** tree rings; **e, f** two orientation images computed from images in which the wind-driven flow below a water surface is made visible by particle traces (see plate 4 and section 2.2.8)

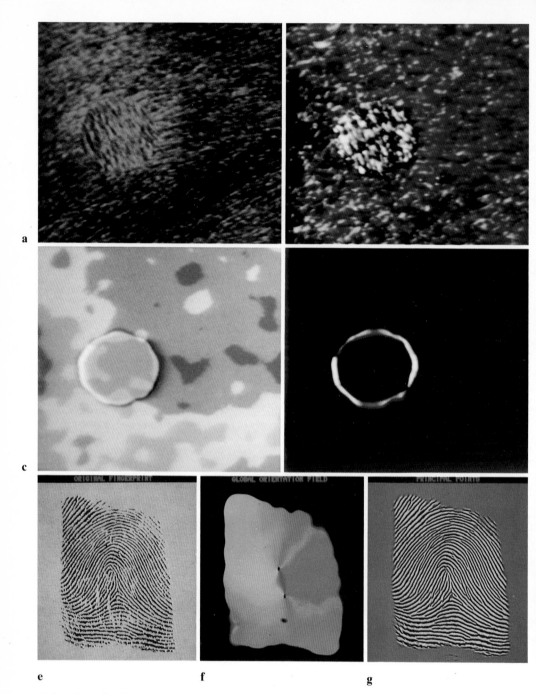

Color plate 10: (section 7.3.4) Examples for application of local orientation: **a–d** hierarchical image processing with vectorial orientation images: **a** a sector of a calfskin, in which a circular sector has been rotated; **b** orientation image; **c** averaged orientation image; **d** edges of the averaged orientation image; **e–g** adaptive image enhancement: **e** original fingerprint; **f** average orientation image; **g** enhanced image after two iterations; from Prof. Dr. Granlund, University of Linköping, Sweden

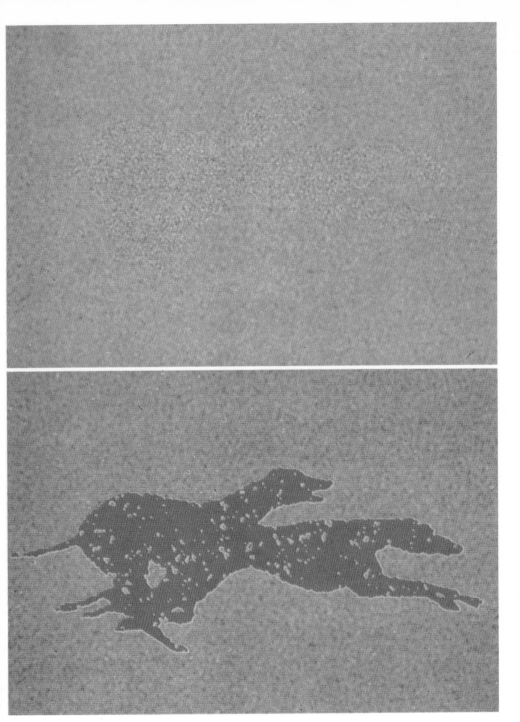

Color plate 11: (section 9.3.2) Detection of different scales by computing the local wave number: **a** original image; **b** all regions in which the local wave number lies above a certain threshold are marked red; from Prof. Dr. Granlund, University of Linköping, Sweden

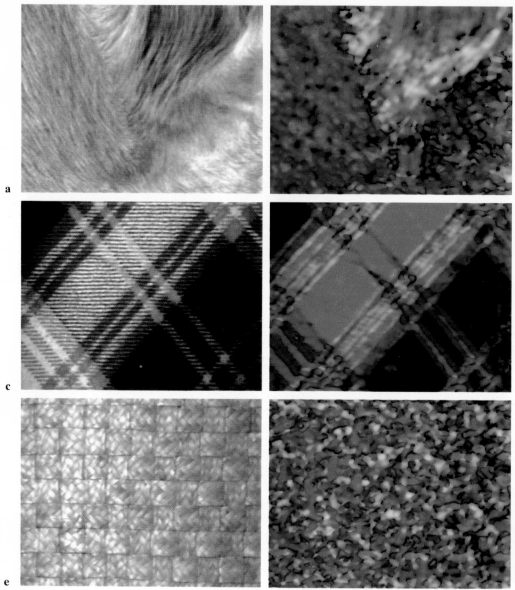

Color plate 12: (section 9.3.1) Usage of local orientation for texture analysis: left, original; right, orientation image: **a, b** dog fur; **c, d** cloth; **e, f** basketwork

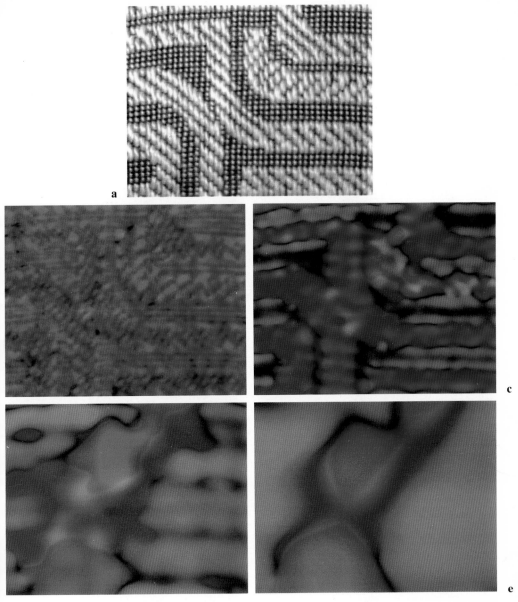

Color plate 13: (section 9.3.3) Combined scale and orientation analysis with the Laplace pyramid: **a** a sector from a cloth; **b**–**e** orientation images on the levels 0 to 3 of the Laplace pyramid

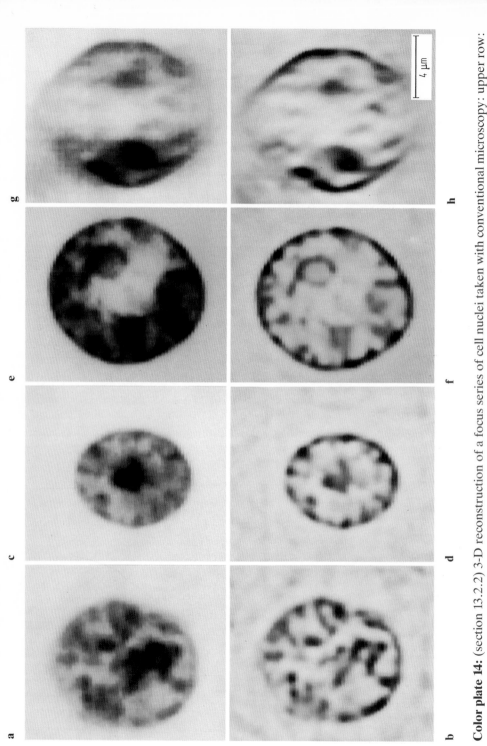

Color plate 14: (section 13.2.2) 3-D reconstruction of a focus series of cell nuclei taken with conventional microscopy: upper row: **a, c, e** selected original images; lower row: reconstructions of the images shown above; **g** *xz* cross section perpendicular to the image plane; from Dr. Schmitt and Prof. Dr. Komitowski, German Cancer Research Center, Heidelberg

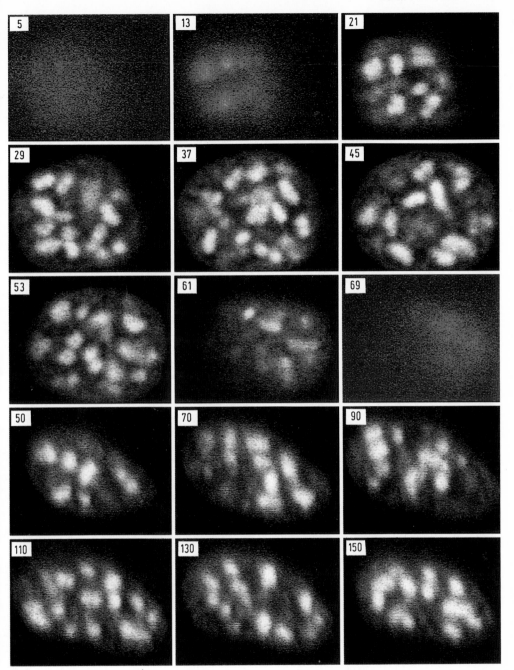

Color plate 15: (section 13.2.3) Focus series of cell nuclei images taken with confocal laser scanning microscopy. The upper 9 images are *xy* cross sections, the lower 6 *xz* cross sections. The numbers either indicate the depth *z* or the *y* position in pixels; from Dr. Kett and Prof. Dr. Komitowski, German Cancer Research Center, Heidelberg

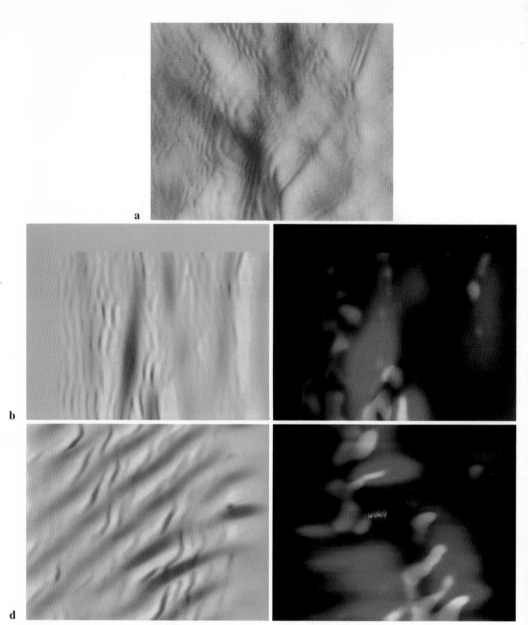

Color plate 16: (section 1.4 and 17.3.2) Analysis of an image sequence with water surface waves using Gabor filters: **a** single image of the sequence; superposition of two Gabor-filtered images with center wavelength of 4.7 and 1.2 cm in wind direction: **b** amplitude of the cosine filter; **c** energy; same but with an *xt* cross section: **d** amplitude of the cosine filter; **e** energy. The phase and group velocities of the waves can be inferred from the slope of the lines of constant gray values in the *xt* images. From *Riemer* [1991]